FOUR SPIRITUAL MASTERS

C000125766

Footsteps to Freedom tells of the astonishi
great spiritual master Lahiri Mahasaya.
in English the true stories of his son and grandson, Tinkari Lahiri
and Satya Charan Lahiri, who themselves became spiritual
masters. And it relates how Satya Charan Lahiri – the third and last
yogic master in Lahiri Mahasaya's lineage – passed the authority to
initiate Kriya Yoga outside the family to one of his most advanced
disciples, Prakash Shankar 'Guruji' Vyas.

AND A BEGINNER

Heidi Wyder was born in Sussex, England, in 1969. As a singer-
songwriter, she recorded two albums in the early 1990s. She was
awarded a degree in French and German at the University of
Exeter and subsequently trained and worked as a language teacher
in England. Today she lives in Switzerland with her husband and
children. She works as a teacher and writer, whilst trying her best
to practise the Kriya Yoga techniques given to her by "Guruji"
Vyas.

FOOTSTEPS TO FREEDOM

*Four Spiritual Masters
of Kriya Yoga*

And a Beginner

Heidi Wyder

---

*"He who knows others is wise;
he who knows himself is enlightened."* – LAO-TZU

kriya
SOURCE
PUBLISHING

First published in Great Britain in 2003 by
Kriya Source Publishing
Postfach 129
7214 Grüsch
Switzerland

www.kriyasource.com

British Library Cataloguing in Publication Data.
A catalogue record for this book is available from the British Library.

ISBN 3-9522761-0-3

Cover Illustration: "Let there be light" by John Reilly
Cover Design by Kathryn Honey

Printed and bound in Great Britain by
Apollo Press, Worthing, West Sussex

CONTENTS

Part One: Lahiri Mahasaya

Part Two: Tinkari Lahiri

Part Three: Satya Charan Lahiri

Part Four: Guruji (Prakash Shankar Vyas)

ACKNOWLEDGEMENTS

I could not have written *Footsteps to Freedom* without the blessing of my spiritual teacher, Yogi Prakash Shankar Vyas (Guruji). His collaboration in my research was invaluable. As spiritual master and authority on Kriya Yoga, Guruji has been there every step of the way to correct, clarify and answer my every query. It has been my privilege to share his wisdom in writing this book.

I would also like to thank:

Barbara and Paul Johnson, my mother and father, who gave so much time to proof-reading and editing. Their insight and constructive criticism have been a great strength. I am deeply grateful to them both for their support with every aspect of this work.

Angela Henderson, a special friend, who also worked as proof-reader and editor, for her understanding of the subject matter and her academic flair.

Andreas, my husband, for his encouragement and support, not to mention technical help.

Phyllis Gilbert, my grandmother, for her spiritual inspiration and understanding.

Finally, all the friends and relatives who have contributed specialist knowledge or simply acted as sounding boards for my thoughts and ideas.

HEIDI WYDER
August 2003

The publisher and author would like to thank the following for permission to quote copyright material:

Dr A. K. Chatterjee (author) and Mr A. Chatterjee (publisher and copyright holder) for extracts from the English translation of *Purana Purusha, Yogiraj Sri Shama Churn Lahiree* by Dr A. K. Chatterjee (Yogiraj Publication, 2000)

Swami Bodhasarananda for extracts from *Raja Yoga* by Swami Vivekananda (Advaita Ashrama Publication Department, 1998)

The Christian Science Publishing Society, for quotations from *Science and Health with Key to the Scriptures* by Mary Baker Eddy.

Although we have made every effort to contact copyright holders in order to obtain permission, this has not been possible in all cases. Should any omissions be brought to our attention, these will be amended in any future editions.

LAHIRI MAHASAYA

TINKARI LAHIRI

SATYA CHARAN LAHIRI

PRAKASH SHANKAR VYAS (GURUJI)

A SIMPLIFIED FAMILY TREE

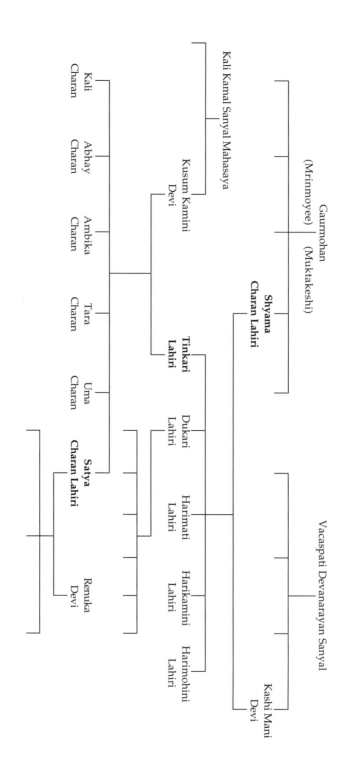

Gaurmohan
(Mrinmoyee) | (Muktakeshi)

Kali Kamal Sanyal Mahasaya

Shyama
Charan Lahiri

Vacaspati Devanarayan Sanyal

Kashi Mani
Devi

Kusum Kamini
Devi

Kali
Charan

Abhay
Charan

Ambika
Charan

Tara
Charan

Uma
Charan

Tinkari
Lahiri

Dukari
Lahiri

Harimati
Lahiri

Harikamini
Lahiri

Harimohini
Lahiri

Satya
Charan Lahiri

Renuka
Devi

CHRONOLOGY

1828   *SHYAMA CHARAN (LAHIRI MAHASAYA) born*
Tuesday 30th September 08.27[1]

1833   Muktakeshi Devi dies

1836   Kashi Mani Devi born

1846   Shyama Charan marries Kashi Mani Devi (aged 18)

1851   Shyama Charan posted to Gazipur

1852   Shyama Charan's office transferred to Varanasi; his father dies

1860   Shyama Charan offered job as house tutor for King of Nepal's son

1863   *TINKARI LAHIRI born*

1864   House "Garureswar" purchased

1866   Shyama Charan offered work as tutor for the Queen

1865   Dukari Lahiri born on Rath Yatra Festival

1868   Shyama Charan transferred to Ranikhet in November, receives Kriya initiation (aged 40) from **Babaji**

1868   First daughter, Harimati, born

1870   Second daughter, Harikamini, born

1873   Third daughter, Harimohini, born

1883   Sri Yukteswar receives Kriya initiation from Lahiri Mahasaya

---

[1] The exact date of Shyama Charan Lahiri's birth is somewhat uncertain, due to an inconsistency in his service records. However, in one of Shyama Charan's hand-written diaries, a horoscope written by the master himself gives precise details of the time and date of his birth, and is therefore generally accepted to be correct.

1895	*LAHIRI MAHASAYA mahasamadhi* 26th September (aged 66)
1905	**SATYA CHARAN LAHIRI born**
1922	Satya Charan receives Kriya from father Tinkari Lahiri (aged 17)
1930	Kashi Mani Devi leaves body on March 25th, in a fully conscious state (aged 94)
1931	Satya Charan Lahiri marries Nalini Devi
1932	Satya Charan Lahiri marries Renuka Devi
1934	*TINKARI LAHIRI mahasamadhi* (aged 71)
1931	Satya Charan Lahiri purchases house in Chausetti Ghat
1953	Renuka Devi dies
1956	*PRAKASH SHANKAR VYAS (GURUJI) born* 7th September
1978	Guruji graduates with Batchelor of Arts from Banaras Hindu University
1981	Guruji starts business in Patna Guruji's marries Vandana in February; returns to Varanasi; meets "Big Boss"
1985	Guruji receives Kriya Yoga initiation from Satya Charan Lahiri
1986	Babaji leaves his body Guruji authorised by Satya Charan Lahiri to initiate Kriya Yoga
1987	*SATYA CHARAN LAHIRI mahasamadhi* 22nd January (aged 82)

INTRODUCTION

"Science without religion is lame;
religion without science is blind." – ALBERT EINSTEIN

Though the major religions in the world may differ in their doctrines, they have been built on the monumental lives of masters who had something significant in common: they all tapped into an internal source whereby direct spiritual experience was possible. The words and deeds of Jesus Christ, the Buddha and Mohammed were kept alive by followers, through books and recitations passed from generation to generation. These spiritual masters predicted the future, perceived the immortality of the soul, and preached that man could find freedom from human suffering. Miracles gave authority to their words, for instead of nature controlling them, they controlled nature.

But the question of whether a spiritual seeker may emulate these great masters does not feature in most Western churches. There is no question of attaining such great wisdom and power through internal spiritual development. There is no method available enabling people to walk the same path as the spiritual masters, and the suggestion that such a method could even exist seems sacrilegious and frightening to some, whilst to others it simply contradicts what they have been taught to believe. For the Christian in particular, faith alone is deemed sufficient to attain salvation. We are not supposed to become masters ourselves.

In India, exactly the opposite has always been true. The Rishis, or sages who wrote the Hindu Scriptures over four thousand years ago, said that they saw God or the Absolute, and pointed to a method of inward concentration, or focusing the mind to the point of transcendental knowledge. Therein lay the key to religious experience through the universal science known as Raja Yoga.

Being a science, Raja Yoga involved a definite method which could be followed to its conclusion, where the very proof of the truths preached by the masters was to be found. The call was to practise; not to follow blindly or invest belief solely in the experiences of another. Though not a means to an end, no one owned the exclusive rights to perform miracles, for the ability was latent within each individual: what was possible for one, was possible for all. It was therefore considered ludicrous to talk about God and the soul without having personal experience.

In the West, the title "yogi" may be given to any individual who is proficient in yoga; in this book however, "Yogi" is used in its original sense, meaning an advanced practitioner of the science, or self-realised master. Raja Yoga is otherwise known as Kriya Yoga; a path leading to spiritual freedom and ultimate inner knowledge, which is "Yoga" in its truest sense, or "union with God".[1]

Although Raja Yoga was once widely practised in India, it unfortunately fell into the hands of people who misused it and wanted exclusive possession of its powers, until it virtually died out. That was, until Shyama Charan Lahiri of Banaras was initiated by his spiritual Guru[2] Babaji in 1868 and sent back to the sacred city to live as a householder and to revive the ancient spiritual technique by passing it on to anyone ready to receive it.

Despite Shyama Charan Lahiri's insistence on secrecy, word of his spiritual authority and miraculous works quickly spread across India. Kings, ascetics and householders of every caste, creed and religion sought out Lahiri Mahasaya, as he became known, all desiring to know the lost technique written about in the ancient Indian holy Scriptures. But only the disciples whom the master deemed fit to receive the method were initiated, as it required enormous effort and discipline on the part of the practitioner, and demanded love and dedication of the first degree. But to possess it was to own a priceless, timeless jewel of unspeakable power and rewards.

Kriya Yoga reached Western shores in the 1940s and is now practised worldwide; its name attracts thousands of new initiates each year.

However, according to a living spiritual master in India, who

---

[1] No parallel should be drawn here with the way man is sometimes perceived to be putting himself on a par with the Creator in the rapid advance of gene technology. Whereas a Yogi can see the future, ordinary man is ignorant of the long term consequences of his actions, including those of such scientific developments. Though a Yogi has power beyond imagination, he will never interfere with the course of nature without specific reason. And in sharp contrast to the way human science is often powered by greed and the desire for fame, the spiritual science of Kriya Yoga can only be said to be genuine if qualities such as universal love, compassion, truth, peace and non-violence develop in the practitioner as a natural side-effect.

[2] Since the word "guru" may be used to refer to a teacher of any discipline, for the sake of clarity, I shall make a distinction between "guru" and "Guru" throughout, using the capital letter when referring specifically to the self-realised spiritual master, or *Sadguru*. Please see the Glossary for a full definition.

will be introduced shortly and whose knowledge of the true path and authority as a Kriya Yogi stem from Lahiri Mahasaya's family lineage itself, the West has changed the original scientific method beyond recognition and discarded the principles exemplified by Lahiri Mahasaya as being inseparable from the practice. Nowadays, unsuspecting Western adherents and would-be practitioners are rarely, if ever, being given the original method. Instead they receive an incomplete technique: and so despite sincere efforts, they are trying to unlock a door without having the right key.

That Kriya Yoga should have been subjected to such changes and omissions since its arrival in the West is largely due, it seems, to a ubiquitous trend to unethically market much sought-after spiritual practices for financial profit. Many who claim to be authorities of Kriya Yoga teach an entirely different method to the one given by Lahiri Mahasaya, and are neither master nor practitioner. They exploit the Western tendency to want immediate results, with promises of a fast route to enlightenment.

Without doubt, today's abundance of false gurus will make it impossible to establish fact from fiction if knowledge of the actual source of Kriya is allowed to disappear without trace. In researching this book, it was found that even some of the best-known stories in the West about Lahiri Mahasaya have been in part exaggerated or sensationalised. Wherever these accounts have been published, the disciples or relatives connected to the master in question appear to be marketing and publicising Kriya for personal aggrandisement. The solution is to return to the original source, and in view of the ever-increasing numbers attracted to Kriya, it seems imperative to do so.

Furthermore, the West knows next to nothing of the extraordinary lives of the direct descendants of Lahiri Mahasaya, who followed in that great master's footsteps and were equally remarkable Yogis. For there were in fact three generations of spiritual masters who lived in Banaras, all of whom concealed their yogic powers from the eyes of the world. They lived as ordinary householders and passed on this scientific meditation technique of Kriya Yoga to sincere seekers of truth. They maintained secret lives, because it was the spiritual progression of each of their individual disciples which interested them rather than fame or money. First

Lahiri Mahasaya was succeeded by his son, Tinkari Lahiri; then the yogic heritage was passed further down the family tree by Tinkari Lahiri to his own son, Satya Charan Lahiri.

Footsteps to Freedom brings together the existing accounts of this unbroken lineage of spiritual masters for the first time, to provide a complete and faithful account of their spiritual tradition. Their lives are examples which speak for themselves in re-establishing Kriya Yoga as a method which cannot and should not be changed; likewise the principles which accompany it. Since the *Mahasamadhi*[3] of Satya Charan Lahiri in 1987, the original method and principles are now maintained by at least one spiritual master in India: Yogi Prakash Shankar Vyas, whom I call "Guruji". As Satya Charan Lahiri's most advanced disciple, he was authorised to pass on Lahiri Mahasaya's Kriya Yoga to others in 1986.

Guruji has helped me to collect together the stories of all three masters in Lahiri Mahasaya's lineage, and given his permission and blessing for these to appear in print, so that the original Kriya Yoga may be recognised in the West, as in the East. A substantial portion of the biographical material has been drawn from accounts authorised by these three masters and written by close disciples, which were previously available only in Hindi and Bengali. Although slight variations of a few of the stories can be found in other books – presumably because many of them were passed on by word of mouth – it is usually a matter of minor detail and the overall message has rarely been distorted. However, in such cases I have always drawn from the approved source closest to the master in question. Other accounts which appear in some well-known books, and which Satya Charan Lahiri told his disciples were fabrications or simply sensationalised, have been omitted entirely.

For the benefit of the Western reader, unfamiliar Indian words and yogic terms are printed in italics and explained in the Glossary, if not directly in the footnotes. Since the book spans over three generations of masters, I have included a simplified family tree and a chronology.

In most cases, I have used the traditional masculine gender in reference to God, Gurus and disciples, for ease of writing. Though

---

[3] A Yogi's final departure from earthly existence; the term is explained in more detail in Chapter Five: Kriya Yoga, Samadhi, and in the masters' stories themselves.

it may be partly justified since most Gurus are men, I should point out that from a yogic standpoint, as from most spiritual points of view, God or the Absolute is Omni-gender. It is a limitation of our human vocabulary that there is no adequate personal pronoun for the Creator of All, being neither He nor She. As a woman, I am also naturally convinced that men and women are equally capable of making spiritual progress as disciples, and of becoming spiritual masters.

I began collecting Guruji's inspiring stories and examples, and making notes of our discussions, soon after I first met him in 1995. These not only helped me to gain a basic knowledge and appreciation of Indian customs and culture, but were essential to my progress as a beginner in Kriya Yoga. Many of them have been included in *Footsteps to Freedom,* alongside the biographies of the three masters in Lahiri Mahasaya's lineage and limited details I have been permitted to share about Guruji himself.

My personal experiences in Kriya Yoga also form a part of the narrative, for although no two people have the same story to tell, perhaps it is nevertheless possible to offer a realistic view of what the beginner in this yoga field might expect. Not being one of the exceptional few to whom miraculous incidents occur at each practice session, I move towards the ultimate goal of yoga at snail's pace, understanding well that the most precious gift which the universe has to offer does not come without enormous effort and discipline, and is a challenge more wisely undertaken in footsteps than in strides.

Therefore the reader should not expect any promises about instant levitation, or lessons in how yoga can increase one's sexual prowess. These popular commercial gags have nothing to do with the deeper meaning of yoga and are of little significance next to the example left by the masters about whom I write.

However, the book tells of the peace to be found even on the first short stretch of this path, and of the awe-inspiring discovery that there is, in a very literal sense, an inner light within. There is no doubt in my mind that inner light and universal knowledge exist in everyone for the finding, provided the individual is willing to invest the time and effort required in order to discover it.

The value of this technique which Babaji left as a gift to mankind through Lahiri Mahasaya is inestimable. Soon after learning about

Kriya Yoga, I told Guruji how willingly I would exchange any amount of riches for initiation. Even if I were a billionaire. He only laughed.

'You don't understand,' he said. 'If I give you Kriya, I am giving you everything!'

Intriguing as it was at the time, five years later I was only just beginning to grasp his meaning.

Part One

Lahiri Mahasaya

Chapter One

MEETING THE MASTER

The Early Years

"No one ever travels so high as he who knows not where he is going." – CROMWELL

In a small Bengali village[1] a woman was paying her daily visit to the temple of *Siva*. She was sitting in meditation next to her two-year old son, who was mirroring her posture as usual, when she started at the sound of an unfamiliar voice:

'Mukta Keshi Devi - Mother!'

She opened her eyes and pulled her son onto her lap. Standing in front of her was a tall stranger in the orange robes of a renunciant. Her initial disquiet gave way to a sense of wonder at the depth of kindness in his sparkling eyes. Despite a long black and white beard, his smiling face radiated youthfulness.

'Don't be afraid,' he said. 'I have come to tell you that your son is no ordinary human child. In the future, Shyama Charan will help the sick and the suffering, and will give householders a secret yoga practice. I shall always be watching over him, so you need never fear for his safety.'

Having delivered his message, the man turned and quietly walked away, leaving Mukta Keshi Devi in a state of wonderment. Perhaps, she mused, it explained those visions whilst Shyama Charan was still in the womb. Picking up her son, she hurried home to relate the curious event to her husband.

IN 1833, a few years after the renunciant had prophesied a special future for Shyama Charan Lahiri, Mukta Keshi Devi passed away

---

[1] Ghurni, near the town of Krishnagar in Nadia District, West Bengal.

suddenly, leaving the welfare of the young family in the hands of her husband. She had been the second wife of the landlord Gaura Mohan, and a woman of the most compassionate, even-tempered and charitable nature. When the River Kharey flooded its banks in the same season, resulting in the loss of a substantial portion of the family estate, Gaura Mohan resolved to take the family away from Bengal. As a devoted father and a learned and religious man, he wanted to provide his children with an education which would assure them a more secure profession than his own.

They went to a place which he had visited several times as a pilgrim: India's holy city, *Kashi* or Banaras, and there Shyama Charan was sent to school. At the age of twelve, he attended the Government Sanskrit College. He kept himself physically fit and healthy though exercise and swimming, and he was also a conscientious student who excelled in languages, mastering English, Bengali, Urdu, Hindi, and Farsi. Another integral part of a good school education was Sanskrit and the religious texts from the Veda to the Upanishads, and Shyama Charan's teachers marvelled at his outstanding commentaries on these which displayed a rare maturity for such a young boy. But then his impeccable honesty and fairness, quiet, sensitive nature and exemplary patience were noticed by all who entered his sphere. There was no denying that the boy was special.

In India at that time, social custom obligated parents to arrange suitable marriages for their offspring as early as possible, preferably before the children reached adolescence. It was common to begin the search for prospective in-laws within the circle of family friends.

Gaura Mohan had a friend with a daughter and three sons, and the two families used to visit each other regularly. The daughter's name was Kashi Mani and on several occasions when she was playfully asked whom she would marry, the little girl would point to Shyama Charan without any hesitation.

'He will be my husband!' she would say.

As a result, their marriage was arranged at the earliest possible moment. Shyama Charan was eighteen years old and still studying at college when Kashi Mani Devi, nine years his junior, came to live in her husband's household and started to learn the duties expected of a wife.[2]

THE PATH which destiny was preparing for Shyama Charan Lahiri would not become clear until he reached the age of forty. Meanwhile, after completing his education, he became a government clerk in the Military Engineering Works Department. In 1851, he was transferred to Gazipur, where he was responsible for overseeing road construction and remunerating the soldiers. His salary was barely sufficient to support his family, so he also gave tuition in Urdu and Hindi to his superiors. A year later, at the age of twenty-four, Shyama Charan was relocated to Banaras. His father died soon after his return, and a quarrel flared up between the other brothers over rightful division of property. Peace being of the utmost importance to him, Shyama Charan and his wife moved out of the family home shortly afterwards and rented a few rooms in a two-storey house instead.

The following eighteen years saw him working for the government in several different locations. Financial pressures obliged him to continue giving private tuition, and gradually his reputation as an educator spread. Some of the more renowned people who employed him to teach their sons at this time were the *Maharajas* of Nepal and *Kashi*, and a wealthy businessman, Harashankar Prasad Singh.

He was also the home tutor of six children who were orphaned when they were still young, whereupon he continued to take responsibility for their education. He gave them the means to earn a living and a great deal of fatherly love and affection besides. One of the boys, Ram Mohan De, became a famous lawyer in Banaras, as did his son after him.

The welfare of others was always of prime importance to Shyama Charan, and in his eyes this was inseparable from education. With the help of some likeminded people, he opened the Bangalitola High School in Banaras and worked in its office each day. He was strict in enforcing the rules and principles of the

---

[2] Although Kashi Mani Devi and Shyama Charan Lahiri were married in 1846, Shyama Charan observed strict celibacy in the Vedic tradition as a *Brahmachari* until the age of thirty-five (even though the usual age for breaking celibacy was twenty-five): therefore the marriage was first consummated in 1862. (*Brahmacharya* is one of the four *ashrams* of life according to the ancient Scriptures; to be further explained in Chapter Four: Yogic Purification, Detachment.)

school, was always keen to see evidence of the students' progress, and insisted on the highest standards of integrity from all staff.

Later this group of philanthropists led by Shyama Charan Lahiri opened Banaras' first girls' school, although this, sadly, was doomed to early closure. There was a widely-held belief at the time, that an educated woman was destined to be a prostitute in the next life – a notion which finally began to lose its foothold in the 1950s. For this reason, Kashi Mani Devi was denied a formal education. However, Shyama Charan taught his wife to read and write, and thereafter, study of the Hindu Scriptures became a part of her daily routine.

Kashi Mani Devi was a devoted mother and wife. As Shyama Charan Lahiri was away for long periods in the early years of marriage, she learned to handle the household responsibilities. He would hand over all his earnings, for she was competent in managing the domestic finances. She was efficient, diligent and kind-hearted. No beggar who came calling left empty-handed and she was always prepared to cook and care for any guest who entered their home. In the meantime, she conscientiously put by whatever money she could. By 1864 she had saved enough to buy a house and the family moved to "Garureswar" a year after the birth of their first son, whom they named Tinkari Lahiri. A second son, Dukari, was born in 1865, followed by three daughters: Harimati in 1868, Harikamini in 1870, and Harimohini in 1873.

❖ ❖ ❖ ❖ ❖ ❖ ❖ ❖

My greatest desire was to travel the world, and the ambition was first voiced at the age of five. It never waned. My other aspiration was to become a teacher or an opera singer.

I had always loved singing and started having lessons at the age of seven. But the lessons stopped five years later, because my mother despaired at my aversion to singing in public. The memory is fresh even now – standing with shaking knees and cold sweat on my brow, frantically swallowing down the nervous saliva which rose in my mouth at regular intervals all through the piece and feeling ashamed at the self-consciousness. But afterwards there was a sense of triumph for having done it, so I took solos at school concerts whenever possible, and pushed myself through each ordeal. This determination to overcome the fear finally paid off, although I was almost twenty before my self-confidence had ripened enough to enable me to perform with pleasure.

My parents had always been regular churchgoers and as a child I was keen to go to Sunday school, to learn everything there was to know about God, listen to Bible stories and sing hymns. I was driven by a desire to be like my exemplary kind and patient grandmother, who helped those who wanted to rely on prayer rather than medicine for healing. Whenever I visited my grandparents during school holidays, she would reserve office-time so that we could talk God-related topics at length. These discussions were always a source of great spiritual inspiration.

All the way through school I was fortunate enough to have a close circle of friends, but many of my classmates doubtless considered me an oddball. For years, I was the subject of ruthless teasing, self-inflicted as a result of my intransigent religious convictions. There was a tendency to be far too outspoken at times when silence would have been the wiser option. But at the age of eleven, I did not have much of a grasp on wisdom. My mother tried to help by making a counter-effort to pull me back from spiritual space whenever she saw me losing grip on reality or practicality. She was justifiably concerned at the tunnel vision which had my route ahead so well mapped out that I was convinced nothing could possibly ever smudge the ink. The church was bound to play a significant role in my future, or vice versa.

Childhood was security and something I clung to for as long possible, reluctant right into my teens to see or hear anything which would disturb the peace of naivety. The rebellious phase of adolescence passed me by completely. It was more comfortable to watch my sister's fractions with our parents as she tussled her way through it, whilst learning on the sidelines to be the perfect diplomat.

My teenage years were somewhat burdened by a self-conscious paranoia that I was too fat and not pretty enough to be attractive to the opposite sex. Dreaming of having a boyfriend some day, there was half-way contentment in listening to friends who related everything from fresh infatuation to the pain of rejection. It seemed safer to observe this seeming battlefield at a distance for a while, and having committed myself to teetotalism at the age of fourteen after joining the church, the parties and night-clubs were not my

14 *Footsteps to Freedom*

scene anyway: a point of view not readily understood by my peers.

However, by the end of my school career I had earned exam results adequate for acceptance on a combined honours degree course in a respected university. My confidence had tripled and it was a relief to make a fresh start.

AT UNIVERSITY I studied French and German and worked enough to gain a decent pass. Student life with the opportunities it offered suited me well. My studies were complete in 1992 after a postgraduate secondary school teaching course. Having spent five years in further education, the urge to travel was stronger than ever, but I heeded advice to gain a few years' teaching experience before setting off around the world.

During my first year as a teacher I discovered a talent for song-writing. Motivated by the enthusiasm of those around me, I recorded two albums over the course of eighteen months. People were often moved to tears by some of the lyrics and came to tell me highly personal stories which the songs had stirred up within them.

The cathartic experience of writing came as something of a shock and opened up a catalogue of confusion. I had supposed myself to be a happy person, virtually immune from every kind of pain. Yet each time the guitar chords rearranged themselves into a melody inspiring fresh lyrics, my subconscious uncovered seemingly bottomless wells of sadness in my soul which had never been allowed freedom of expression before.

At the time it felt like a journey through an endless black tunnel. It would be easy to deal with, I thought, if only the problem could be located and analysed. Whilst on the surface my songs dealt with love-pain, there was obviously something else troubling me deeply. What that thing was exactly, I had no idea. Perhaps it was a new uncertainty about my own identity, or a fear that the inner face I perceived to be my own was nothing more than a thin mask which was starting to peel. Furthermore, possibility was mocking that perhaps I was not entirely content with some aspects of my chosen faith, despite always adamantly claiming to be.

As a result, I devoured several self-help books and began to keep a journal in the hope that doing so might reveal the hidden cause of my unrest. Whilst wandering in the old lanes of Brighton, I stopped at the window of a New Age shop and read about the camera which could photograph one's aura. I had passed the shop many times before and the only thought capable of crossing my mind up to that day was one of sheer dismissal. But after the fascinating photo was developed, my earlier scepticism for the shop and everything in it developed into a guilty interest, especially since the woman's analysis of my mental constitution turned out to be painfully accurate.

The wind was kicking up a storm. The more I looked for answers, the more questions came knocking at the door. The more I longed for a fulfilling relationship, the more elusive seemed love. The more I tried to regain a slim figure to be content with, the more the weight piled on. And as the songs of sorrow continued to pour from my soul, the more I despaired of ever finding my old jovial self again: or had it ever really existed? Even if writing was a means of purging the soul, the memoirs of a broken heart were nevertheless becoming a draining source of inspiration.

Towards the end of two years in teaching, I decided to travel in the hope of regaining mental balance. Yet suddenly the thought of replacing home comforts for a backpack was none too enticing. I cast about for an excuse not to go after all, but unsurprisingly a suitable one never materialised.

India was not a planned destination. Actually, my only motivation was that it looked conveniently on the way to Thailand on the travel agent's desk-top map. Apparently a stop-over there would not cost another penny. Having never been able to resist a bargain, let alone a spontaneous decision, a month in India sounded just fine.

I did feel a certain amount of trepidation about travelling alone though, especially the night before the big adventure was due to start. Sleep would not come due to an endless attack of butterflies in my stomach at the prospect of landing in Delhi at two o'clock in the morning. But there was no turning back and last-minute nerves were not about to undermine my longest held and most cherished ambition. Besides, there was hope of finding something new, or at the very least, a different source of inspiration to strum a tune to.

Looking for a Needle

"All men should strive to learn before they die
What they are running from, and to, and why." – JOHN THURBER

In November 1868 Shyama Charan Lahiri was transferred to Ranikhet, a Himalayan hill station at an altitude of 1829 meters. The only mode of transport to such remote locations was by horse and cart, so it was a long and arduous journey from Banaras. Having been promoted to Head Clerk, his duties once more included overseeing the construction of roads and barracks, and supplying provisions to the army.

There were no houses, so tents were erected as sleeping quarters and offices. The office work was minimal, allowing Shyama Charan plenty of time to explore the rugged landscape. Surrounded by the imposing beauty of soaring mountains, it was an idyllic setting. He would sit and gaze at the scenery and breathe in the pure, cool air. The atmosphere was as tranquil and lost in meditation as the native residents, who were *sadhus* living in simple huts.

Whilst walking along a lonely path soon after arrival, he was surprised by someone calling his name and looked up to see a renunciant walking at a brisk pace towards him. Quickly on the alert, Shyama Charan's first reaction was concern for the substantial amount of office money which he was carrying. It occurred to him that a gang might be in hiding, preparing for an ambush.

'Don't be afraid, Shyama Charan,' said the renunciant, smiling broadly, apparently reading his thoughts. 'I knew that you would come this way and have been expecting you. As soon as you have finished your office work today, come and see me. I will be waiting for you.' He was pointing to a cave entrance on a mountain some distance away. Shyama Charan noted a handsome face before the man turned and hurriedly departed, his long slender arms swinging by his sides.

As the day's work came to a close, a mystified Shyama Charan Lahiri was still undecided as to whether he should heed the renunciant's invitation. Since childhood, he had spent many an hour in the company of wise and learned *sadhus* in Banaras, sharpening his mind through spiritual talks. He had also heard numerous stories of good Himalayan saints and renunciants and could not dismiss the fact that this *sadhu* had known his name although they had never met. Curiosity tipped the balance, and he set off with long determined strides.

He walked until the sky turned to dusk and the narrow rocky trail became more difficult to negotiate. Feeling rather disquieted by the danger of wild animals and unsure of his orientation, Shyama Charan rested for a while. When he started up again it was almost dark and the path led through a thick forest, yet now it was as if he were being drawn by a magnet. And then he heard the voice again:

'Shyama Charan! Up here!'

The *sadhu* was smiling at him from the entrance of a cave and beckoning. Shyama Charan climbed the last stretch of mountainside.

'Can you not remember who I am yet?' asked the *sadhu*, taking him into the candle-lit cave after Shyama Charan had touched his feet in the customary gesture of respect. 'You have been here before. This was yours,' he said, placing a tiger skin water pot in Shyama Charan's hands. He pointed to various objects around the cave.

'Do you not recognise all these things?'

'How should I remember?' replied Shyama Charan, 'I've never been here before.'

'Your memory has been covered by the curtain of illusion,' said the *sadhu*, and very softly he touched Shyama Charan's head. It was as if a current of electricity passed right through his body, lighting up the memory of his past life in a single instant: Shyama Charan now recalled the time he had spent in the cave doing yoga *sadhana*, and he recognised the *sadhu* beside him as his spiritual Guru.

'All of these things belonged to you. I have kept them here carefully since your last life ended in this cave. For the past forty years I have been watching over you, waiting for the time to come again for your initiation.'

Shyama Charan had endless questions. They talked until his mind was calm and he was completely sure that after a long time he had again found the Guru he had dearly loved and known in his past life as "Babaji".

That night Babaji initiated Shyama Charan in Kriya Yoga in the cave on Drona Giri mountain. His disciple immediately attained the state of yogic ecstasy or super-consciousness known as *Samadhi*, and the sun had risen well over the mountains by the time he came out of his meditation.

Upon completion of his daily office work, Shyama Charan would hurry to see Babaji and to practise Kriya Yoga. Before long, he was so deeply rooted in his spiritual practice that he virtually forgot the existence of everything else around him, not to mention his family in Banaras. Life had begun anew and nothing could hold him back from meditation in every spare moment, experiencing freedom from earthly bondage in *Samadhi*. Having known the higher planes of yoga *sadhana* from his previous life, these were quickly and easily reattained. The spiritual connection, a bond of unconditional love between Guru and disciple had been rediscovered. So he was dismayed when Babaji told him how he had been brought to Ranikhet through the power of yoga and that now he could not stay.

'The superiors in your government office were going to post someone else as clerk to Ranikhet, but I made them change their minds and send you instead. But now your work here is finished. You have to return to Banaras soon.'

'Babaji, please,' Shyama Charan entreated, 'My only desire is to spend my life here close to you doing yoga *sadhana*.'

'No,' Babaji replied firmly. 'You must go home and live as a householder. You will practise *sadhana* and your life as a Yogi will be a great example for the many people who need you and are waiting for you. Show them the way of salvation. They have to face many difficulties in their lives and have little time, but you will give them the method for God-realisation which will enable them to remain with their families. This is the purpose of your life. Never forget it.'

'But how will I get time for practice, when I have to deal with worldly affairs and family life? How can I live in two worlds?'

'You must apply for a transfer and return to Banaras. Despite your responsibilities as a family man you will find time to practise and all kinds of yogic powers will come to you. In maintaining a domestic existence, householders will follow the ideal you stand for. Kriya Yoga is not exclusively for the renunciant, for not even they can find true freedom from this material world without practice. As a member of society, you are the only one whom I am authorising to initiate this Kriya path. There is nothing to be concerned about, and I will come to you whenever you desire to see me.

'You have to initiate those people over there,' he added, pointing to a couple of men who were resting nearby. 'They have been waiting for you for a long time.'

'Why should they receive Kriya from me when you are here?' asked Shyama Charan.

'Because just as you are my disciple and spiritually connected to me, they are spiritually connected to you and therefore your disciples, not mine!' laughed his Guru. Thus Shyama Charan received all the Kriya initiation procedures from Babaji, and initiated his first disciples.

Winter was well on its way, and as his Guru had instructed, Shyama Charan applied for a transfer on the grounds of his health being unsuited to the cold climate. A few days later the application had been authorised.

During the short seven weeks that he spent with Babaji in Ranikhet, Shyama Charan was prepared with many teachings, yogic secrets, and instructions for the task that lay ahead of him. He received permission to initiate all sincere spiritual seekers regardless of their faith or caste. Other *Siddhas* whom he met in the Himalayas wished him well before his departure. And it was with tears in his eyes that Shyama Charan bade his Guru farewell.

THE FIRST transfer order took Shyama Charan to Mirzapur in Uttar Pradesh. During a stop-over in Moradabad, he overheard a group of friends discussing religion. They were saying that no living saints possessed miraculous powers any more.

Having just rediscovered Kriya practice and his Guru, Shyama Charan could not resist contradicting them.

'We do still have great masters,' he said, 'and I can use my yogic power to bring such a master right here so that you can see for yourselves.'

Shyama Charan's words caused a stir of both disbelief and excitement, whereupon a separate room was prepared for him.

Once all the windows and doors had been closed, he laid a sitting mat opposite his own for Babaji, and began to meditate. His heart filled with love as he asked Babaji to come, and soon a bright circle of light appeared in the room. Within moments, Babaji was standing in front of him, but his countenance was stern.

'I have come because I gave you my word that I would come whenever you called me,' he said in a deep voice. 'But I am not for show; you had no real reason to call me.'

Shyama Charan was silent and full of remorse.

'In the future, I will only come when I feel that it is necessary for you to see me,' Babaji added.

'Please forgive me,' replied Shyama Charan, with his head bowed. 'I wanted those people to believe and have faith. But please, now that you are here, won't you show yourself to them?'

Babaji agreed and asked Shyama Charan to open the door. The appearance and blessing of a *Mahayogi* subsequently transformed the lives of the men waiting outside.

From that day on, Shyama Charan kept his experiences and practice secret. He rapidly attained new spiritual levels. His work colleagues had no idea that he was immersing himself in deep meditation every night, for he never showed any signs of fatigue in the execution of his daily tasks. However, since he always seemed mentally absorbed in his own world, he became fondly known as "Paglababu".[3]

One day he noticed that his superior, an English officer, was burdened by something and asked what was troubling him. Sounding desperate, the man explained that his wife in England was extremely ill. Not having heard any news for some time, he feared the worst. Shyama Charan's heart went out to him.

'I will get news of your wife,' he said, and went into another room to meditate. A short while later he came out, telling the officer that his wife's condition was improving, and that she had already sent news. He went on to detail the exact contents of her letter.

The officer was not entirely convinced. Although he had heard various stories concerning saints and spiritual phenomena in India, he was more than sceptical. So it was with astonishment that he

---

[3] "Pagla", or "Pagal", literally means "mad" or "crazy" (as in this instance usually used in the most affectionate sense of the word!).

opened a letter from his wife a few weeks later, containing the exact message that Shyama Charan had previously conveyed.

Even more extraordinary was her arrival in Danapur a couple of months later. When she came to see her husband at his office and saw Shyama Charan, she froze in astonishment.

'He is the saint,' she told her husband, 'whom I saw standing by my bed when I was sick in England. Through his divine grace I was healed.'

❖ ❖ ❖ ❖ ❖ ❖ ❖ ❖

My first month in India consisted of living on a houseboat in Srinagar, trekking in the Himalayas and seeing the sights of Agra. Every day was an adventure in itself. My fear of being alone proved to be unfounded, since there were many other Western travellers in exactly the same position as myself. We stuck together like glue, waiting for the initial waves of culture shock to subside.

By the time we got to Varanasi, or Banaras,[4] the sights and sounds of India were gradually becoming more familiar. The workings of the street commission business were also becoming clearer to me. Ignorance of this system had already proved expensive, and it seemed one could not be discerning enough. The streets were buzzing with the most winningly charming people promising to be your best friend for life after they had known you for just two minutes. They would spend days showing you every nook and cranny of the city at no charge, over-emphasising their complete indifference to the contents of your money-belt. In retrospect, however, it was clear that these were the people to avoid, because you would pay extortionate sums in every shop you entered with them. Your "best friend" would return to the shops later to pick up his percentage of your custom.

I was staying in the old city, in a maze of narrow cobbled lanes adjacent to the Ganges. My room on the top storey of the guest house overlooked the resplendent dome of the Golden Temple. Surrounding it, dozens of monkeys darted across the flat rooftops, shaking the branches and chattering in the sparse trees which fought for space amongst closely packed buildings. Often one

---

[4] During the British occupation of India, Banaras was renamed Varanasi. However, many people still refer to the holy city as Banaras.

would sit on the ledge right outside my door, eyeing the washing as it dried in the sun. The accommodation was cheap and simple, and all the guests in the area were other backpackers planning to stay for weeks or months.

The new freedom which accompanied living out of a rucksack was both refreshing and exciting. Mornings were spent either writing my diary or wandering through the crowded markets; admiring the shops displaying bronze statues, painted wooden toys and vivid arrays of hand-woven silken saris; passing temples on every corner and breathing in the soft fragrance of marigold garlands and butter candles, or an air laden with incense.

Some lazy afternoons drifted by in a boat on the Ganges, watching groups of buffalo being herded into the river for a dip; children playing cricket and flying paper kites; *dhobis* thrashing the washing clean on stone slabs and women laying out a rainbow of saris to dry in the sun. Or the time would pass drinking *chai* with friendly shopkeepers, and chatting to fellow travellers on the roof of the guest house.

A considerable number of the people I had met so far had told me that the reason they were travelling around India was to "find themselves". It was an intriguing concept. All of my first travel companions had been planning to do just that with the aid of readily available narcotics, whereas my new-found American friends were like-minded people whose motivations for travelling were not drug-orientated. Instead, they envisaged such a thing being possible through the medium of yoga meditation.

One of these American friends was a Reiki master. This laying-on-of-hands natural healing technique was unlikely to fit into my religious scheme of things, yet I decided to investigate it. After all, no one would ever know. In this place, no one who knew me for my high-minded principles could judge.

Learning Reiki opened my mind a crack: it triggered another mild streak of rebellion with the decision to visit an astrologer the following week, despite having previously sworn never to do such a thing in my life. Five hundred rupees was admittedly a ridiculously high sum to pay, but then he had predicted a great future for Goldie Hawn eight years before Hollywood lifted her to fame, and the letter she wrote him and signed photograph were framed on the wall of his cell-like room overlooking the Ganges as claim to his expertise. But in retrospect his words only made the future seem more inevitable and living in the present more imperative. My earlier philosophy to avoid fortune-tellers had no doubt been the wiser one.

Then there were those tantalising painted advertisements on walls throughout the lanes, with arrows pointing the way to yoga and meditation. Once again my curiosity was piqued, especially by the concept of meditation. Yoga was stretching and shoulder stands, because my mother used to go to a weekly class and we children would copy her postures whenever she practised. But meditation went into the realm of Eastern mysticism, whatever that was; the forbidden apple a good Christian should keep her hands off at any cost. Surely being tempted to look into such a thing would be tantamount to a lack of faith. It might threaten the theory that the heavily-relied-on religious books contained every single answer one could ever need in life.

Meanwhile my friends Cord and John were constantly enthusing about their yoga teacher and trying to persuade me to go for lessons too. They raved about the feeling of peace when they went for class and about how lucky they were to have met this teacher in particular, for he was indescribably special. Admittedly, it took weeks, but they finally managed to bulldoze my stereotyped view of meditation to some extent. Perhaps it really was time to dip a toe into the water. How could there be anything wrong with a spiritually-orientated discipline whose essence was silence and inner peace? Surely it could not damage the wall of beliefs guarding my inner security, which I was determined to keep intact in this city of Hindu deities!

Cord had recently been initiated into a meditation technique called Kriya Yoga. I asked him to tell me about it and what the practice involved, but apparently he was not allowed to reveal any exact details, which was disappointing. He simply said that he practised morning and evening and described Kriya as something amazing and powerful. His eyes shone as he spoke, convincing me to go and meet the man of wisdom whom they respectfully addressed as "Guruji". He was the authority and the one to ask about Kriya Yoga.

AT FIRST glance he looked ordinary and if anything rather stern. He invited me to sit, and listened whilst I informed him that my purpose in coming was to learn meditation, not yoga. It would be of special interest to hear about this Kriya Yoga which he had given Cord, too. But it was my last week in India, and there was no chance of prolonging the stay. My guitar had been shipped to Bangkok months before, since the original plan had been to find places to perform in Australia after travelling around Thailand.

Guruji did not answer at first. My eyes wandered to the portraits hanging on the wall behind where he sat. In the middle there was a striking large black and white photograph of a holy man. Having never seen anything quite like this picture before, I tried to identify what was so appealing about it. Perhaps it was the facial expression of authority and freedom. The gaze of pure tranquillity. Or perhaps it was the way the body seemed to radiate ethereal light.

'He is Lahiri Mahasaya.' Guruji's deep voice suddenly penetrated the silence, answering an unvoiced question. He paused before continuing.

'If you want to learn meditation, you will have to start at the beginning and practise Hatha Yoga.'

No doubt I must have looked somewhat disappointed, because yoga exercises did not particularly interest me.

'The Western world tends to think of Hatha Yoga as a method of exercising the body and relaxing the mind simultaneously – as something good for health only,' Guruji said. 'It is true that someone who practises daily will have less disease and may live a long life. But it is not an end in itself. Hatha Yoga was initially conceived by our ancient Yogis to prepare the body to sit for long periods of meditation. It is also for health, because it is hard to focus the mind if you are in pain and suffering. Only when the body is brought under control through *Asanas*, or postures, can we begin the difficult task of concentrating the mind in meditation.'

It hardly seemed fitting to argue. We began to practise Hatha Yoga. I was standing on the tips of my toes doing the first stretch, when Guruji suddenly remarked,

'Many people think that yoga is for a week. Yoga is for life.'[5]

This was news. Guruji was obviously serious. Suddenly I felt perplexed and half-ashamed at having come for lessons as a tourist

[5] It was years later when I realised that this early comment about yoga being for life was aimed very pointedly at me, and not something which Guruji said to everyone by any means.

with a week left in Varanasi.

'Well, it wouldn't hurt to be open-minded about it,' I thought to myself. 'Besides, I'm fairly supple already, and some regular exercise would do me good.' Since yoga did not involve running or anything too strenuous, it could even be quite an acceptable fitness option. Perhaps regular practice would help to shed a few excessive pounds as well.

I felt remarkably good walking back through the lanes from Man Mandir[6] to my guest house. Hatha Yoga had been better than expected, and the next hour was spent enthusiastically trying out the same exercises on the roof of the guest house, much to the amusement of the occasional passing monkey which stopped to watch.

Contrary to the time when I first arrived in India and could not wait to leave, by the end of that week I was regretting having sent my guitar to Thailand and asking myself why I had gone travelling in the first place. Virtually everyone else in the guest house regarded six months as an absolute minimum stay in India if you wanted to see something of the massive country and imbibe the cultural experience. And there I was, planning to skip from one continent to the other, hoping to take as many exotic snapshots as possible to prove that I had "been there". How woefully superficial that now seemed.

Life in India was far removed from the Western norm. The senses were bombarded with new, vivid impressions on a daily basis and there was a subtle indescribable something in the atmosphere which was missing back at home. New sources of inspiration were lurking around every corner, inviting you to discover who you really were or wanted to be. I found myself feeling more alive and awake than ever before, and more aware of how much reading, learning and searching there was to be done. The inner turmoil which had plagued me at home was becoming a thing of the past. Surely a light was beginning to shine at the end of the tunnel.

On my last day in Varanasi, I asked Guruji to explain the point of meditation. For the first time, we talked all through the lesson instead of practising Hatha Yoga as usual. He answered my question with a true story about a much respected *Sufi* saint.

---

[6] Man Mandir is an area in the old lanes of Varanasi on a river *ghat*.

Her name was Rabia, and one day she was seen searching for something in her garden. Some villagers saw her and tried to help. By midday, a dozen people had joined in the search. By the time the sun was beginning its descent, most of the village had heard that she had lost something in her garden, and had come to offer their assistance. But when it became almost too dark to see, someone ventured to ask what exactly it was that she had lost.

'I've lost my needle,' replied the old woman.

Everyone was confused and wondered if this could be the onset of madness, but continued to look out for a needle. A short while passed before someone else asked,

'Can you not remember where you lost it?'

Rabia straightened herself and looked around at the crowd that had gathered in her garden.

'Well now,' she said softly, 'I think I lost it inside the house.'

After a momentary silence, the villagers began to hoot with laughter.

'See how crazy the old woman has become!' they mocked. 'She lost her needle inside her house and is looking for it in the garden!'

Rabia was not moved in the slightest. As the hubbub abated, she spoke to them in a quiet voice.

'Who is crazy, you or I? I haven't lost my needle at all. I wanted to give you an example today in following your own principles! It is perfectly true that the thing which is lost inside cannot be found outside – so you have been laughing at your own stupidity. You work for nothing but materialistic pleasures and external gain, thinking that these can bring fulfilment. But happiness is internal. And when death comes knocking, you will wonder at how you wasted time in this world.'

THE STORY had me ponder even more what I was doing with my precious time travelling the world, let alone with the greater journey of life itself. What were the internal secrets of meditation? What was happiness according to Rabia? I had always appreciated the impermanence of our world, but that did not make this esoteric inner world of eternal joys any more visible. My friends seemed to derive something fantastic from meditation already, but when I closed my eyes, everything was dark. Unless it really was something which eventually came with practice.

Furthermore, the realisation was growing that India's beauty lay beyond the skin-deep. Though it would be a cliché to call India an atmosphere – it was indeed a tangible vibration which had me captured. It was hard to say goodbye to my friends now, and being in the presence of Guruji for a week of yoga had been a gift of peace which was equally difficult to leave behind. So I told Guruji of my resolve to continue practising Hatha Yoga in Thailand every day. My plan was to return in a couple of months, in the hope that he might declare me ready for meditation lessons by then.

Return to Banaras

"They change their clime, not their frame of mind,
who rush across the sea.
We work hard at doing nothing:
we look for happiness in boats and carriage rides.
What you are looking for is here, is at Ulubrae,
if only peace of mind doesn't desert you." – HORACE

A short while after leaving Ranikhet, Shyama Charan was transferred back to the office in Banaras. Kashi Mani Devi supported her husband as ever by working hard in the household so that he would be free to do *sadhana* after returning home from his worldly work.

Since it is disrespectful to address the Guru by his first name in India, Shyama Charan gradually became known as Lahiri Mahasaya.[7] Even Kashi Mani Devi's father Vacaspati Devanarayan Sanyal was quick to recognise the yogic powers of his son-in-law and requested Kriya initiation, thus becoming a disciple. Despite being an elder, he would address Shyama Charan as *Yogiraja* instead, which subsequently became the name most frequently used by other disciples.

The very first householder to receive Kriya Yoga from him in Banaras was a humble flower seller who sold garlands at the gate

---

[7] Lahiri (his surname) Mahasaya (*Maha* means "great" and *Saya* means "self-realised person"; *Mahasaya* is also a term which confers respect); Shyama Charan's chief disciple Panchanan Bhattacharya also addressed him as *Kashi Baba*. The most respectful term for a disciple in avoiding use of the Guru's name would be *Yogiraja* or "Barébaba"; however, in the interest of not confusing the reader and since Lahiri Mahasaya is the name by which Shyama Charan is best known in the West, this is the name I shall be using throughout.

of Kedareswar temple. And without the need for any publicity, disciples and devotees from all over India found their way to Lahiri Mahasaya.

HITLAL SARKAR was one such disciple – a family man of limited means who lived and worked in a Bengali village. He was well loved for his generosity as he never hesitated to share whatever he could with others who were worse off than himself. Whenever he was free, he would pass the time sitting by the River Ganges in absent thought. But a time came when he found himself becoming increasingly dissatisfied with life, as though something were missing. He had no idea what was causing the restlessness.

One day his mind was in such turmoil that he could not concentrate properly. He felt compelled to leave the factory where he worked and go somewhere, anywhere – and as he began to walk he became calmer. It seemed as if an invisible force were pushing him forwards, and finding himself at the station, he boarded the first train he saw. It took him to Howrah Station in Calcutta, and he made his way to the ticket offices.

'Please give me a ticket,' he said.

'Where do you want to go?' asked the ticket clerk.

Hitlal sighed. That was the problem. He had no idea where he should go, so he emptied all the money he was carrying in his pockets onto the counter.

'Give me a ticket according to the amount of money I have. Anywhere.'

The man at the counter saw that Hitlal was troubled, and thought to suggest the City of Shiva.

'Have you ever been to Banaras?' he asked Hitlal.

'No,' was the reply, and a ticket was promptly issued.

'By the grace of *Lord Siva*, may you find peace there.'

Thanking him, Hitlal caught the next train to Banaras. When it finally reached its destination he asked the rickshaw *wallah* to take him to the Bengali quarter. Hitlal was walking down a lane in this area of the city when a kind-looking man stepped out of a house and invited him to come in.

'You don't know me. Why are you asking me in?' Hitlal asked in surprise.

The man chuckled.

'Let me explain later. Now you are tired and hungry, so have a bath and something to eat, and rest for a while.'

Hitlal was indeed exhausted and his stomach was growling. Rather bemused, he accepted the kind offer of hospitality. The household servants took care of him and he learned that his host was a saint whose name he had heard in Bengal: *Yogiraja* Shyama Charan Lahiri. After he had rested, Lahiri Mahasaya called for Hitlal, who humbly prostrated himself at his feet.

'I brought you here because your time has come for initiation, Hitlal,' he said.

Hitlal became a great practitioner of Kriya Yoga in his lifetime.

ANOTHER to be touched by the yogic master's blessing was Jaipal Bhaghat. He sold milk and curd from a little shop near Lahiri Mahasaya's residence, from which he used to observe the comings and goings of disciples and devotees. Though he felt the deepest respect for Lahiri Mahasaya, Jaipal could never summon the courage to approach the great spiritual master to ask for a blessing, although it was his heart's desire to do so. He thought that he was too simple and ordinary.

One day, Jaipal saw Lahiri Mahasaya coming along the narrow lane in his direction, and he stood aside so that the master could pass by, making a bow.

'Come to me tomorrow, Jaipal, and I will initiate you,' said a smiling Lahiri Mahasaya, stopping right at the shop. The overjoyed milkman could hardly believe his ears.

After initiation, Jaipal's little shop always did extremely well and he was able to support his family for the first time without any financial worries. As soon as his sons were able to take over the business, he constructed a modest hut on the other side of the Ganges, and spent the rest of his life living alone and meditating, eventually becoming an advanced practitioner.

THE FAMILY of Chandra Mohan De lived next door to Lahiri Mahasaya. On completion of his medical studies in 1873, Chandra went to see the master to ask for a blessing. Lahiri Mahasaya questioned him thoroughly on several subjects, and the young graduate was thrilled to have the chance to show what he knew.

'And what is your medical definition of death?' he was asked.

Chandra answered the best he could whilst Lahiri Mahasaya listened; there was a twinkle in his eye.

'That is all very well, but perhaps you should examine me, and tell me if I am alive or dead.'

A straightforward examination rendered the young medical student speechless. He could not locate a single pulse or heartbeat, and there was absolutely no sign of any inhalation or exhalation.

'Should you not give me a death certificate now?' asked the Yogi.

Chandra was confused. Then a thought occurred:

'I could give you death certificate, but a dead man cannot talk – and you are talking!'

'That is quite true. But I wanted you to see that your modern medical science is limited. There is a higher knowledge which is out of reach except to the yogic practitioner.'

It was a day which Chandra Mohan De was never to forget. He became successful in his field as a doctor, but in addition he became a disciple of Lahiri Mahasaya and a Kriya Yogi.

A FAMOUS ayurvedic doctor from Calcutta named Paresh Nath Rai was a good friend of Lahiri Mahasaya's brother-in-law. One evening, in the company of Lahiri Mahasaya and a group of learned men, he was asked to talk on *Charaka*.[8] Being a rather arrogant man, he was proud to show off his expertise, and bathed in the appreciation of his listeners upon finishing the discourse. All except for one: the yogic master himself was not forthcoming with praise.

'What did you think about my explanation?' he boldly asked Lahiri Mahasaya.

'It was completely wrong,' came the unexpected reply.

Everyone was incredulous at the severity of the criticism, and Paresh's face twitched with anger.

'And what do you know about *Charaka*?' Paresh asked tautly.

'I know the truth about it,' the Yogi replied.

For several days Paresh nursed his hurt pride and pondered something his *ayurveda* teacher, Ganga Dhar Sen, had once said. Despite being an eminent authority on ayurvedic medicine, he had told Paresh that the knowledge he was giving him on *Charaka* was

---

[8] *Charaka* is an ancient Indian Scripture subtitled "The Book of Medicine" which was written by a group of great yogic masters.

from a human standpoint and therefore deficient. A Yogi was the only person who could really throw light on the subject, if Paresh were ever fortunate enough to meet one. So he humbly returned to Lahiri Mahasaya, and became his disciple.

Paresh advanced extremely quickly in Kriya practice and was so often in *Samadhi* that he frequently neglected his worldly responsibilities. Whenever this happened, Lahiri Mahasaya would come to his house and interrupt his practice. Paresh began to feel guilty at the trouble he was causing his Guru, since he lived quite a distance away, so he bought a house near to his Guru instead. He bequeathed a substantial portion of property to Lahiri Mahasaya's son, Tinkari Lahiri before he died.

HARI NARAYAN MUKHERJEE was a devotee of Lahiri Mahasaya and a post office worker. Although his colleague Kali had a beautiful wife, he was not faithful to her. A concerned Hari tried to steer Kali away from frequent infidelities, but his words fell on deaf ears. Nevertheless, Hari was convinced that if he could only get Kali to meet his Guru, his friend would change his ways. After several days of persuasion, during which his friend's disrespect towards Lahiri Mahasaya became almost intolerable, Hari finally managed to convince Kali to accompany him to the master's house. It was early evening when they arrived and Lahiri Mahasaya was preaching to a crowd of devotees. They sat down to listen. The following day, Kali wanted to go again. Soon he became a devotee himself and within a very short time he had completely lost his desire to be unfaithful.

❖ ❖ ❖ ❖ ❖ ❖ ❖ ❖

The decision had been made to return to Varanasi before the plane even touched down in Thailand. But it made sense to spend at least six weeks exploring the country a little, so I changed my ticket in Bangkok accordingly, collected my guitar and within a few days was headed for the north in an overnight bus to Chiang Mai.

It was something of a relief to see Thai supermarkets and shopping malls which resembled Western commercial life. Getting from one place to another was generally much easier and faster than it had been in India. The food also appealed more to my rather conservative taste-buds. Delicacies from the bakery restaurant such as wholemeal rolls, Danish pastries and fresh bowls of salad were savoured with new-found appreciation. Hot pancakes filled with chocolate and banana from the pavement stands were indulged in. Trips to the glass wagons packed with whole pineapples, watermelons and papayas, where the man cut the fruit into chunks and sold it in cellophane bags, were a daily treat. Life was still exciting and exotic, but it was plain sailing compared to India.

And yet each passing day was confirmation that my desire to learn yoga was greater than to continue globe-trotting. The thought of pursuing the tourist trail for even a month had lost much of its former appeal. There was plenty to see and do in Chiang Mai, but instead I spent the first fortnight in the room of my guest house reading second-hand books on Eastern philosophy, religion and quantum physics, only venturing out when hunger struck.

I liked the idea of a jungle trek with elephant riding and river rafting, but decided against it after learning how the tourist industry had uprooted the natural livelihoods of the hill tribes. So I left Chiang Mai having squandered every sight-seeing opportunity on offer, and took a bus to Mae Hong Son on the northern border. The night before leaving, I telephoned my parents and told them of my decision to return to India. My mother could not hide her concern.

'Are you sure that you haven't been hypnotised?' she asked.

She was such a trusting kind of mother, that it was a shock to hear such a thing could have occurred to her. A two-minute call was insufficient to reassure her that I was still in full possession of my senses, but calling home was too costly to allow a more detailed explanation. It was hard to know whether she had been convinced after hanging up. The weekly letters home always seemed equally inadequate to even begin to explain how the whole travel experience was changing me at a frantic pace, in ways I did not entirely understand myself. It would have to wait until I got home.

With regular daily practice, the Hatha Yoga exercises soon became much easier than they had been at the beginning. Curious to try sitting perfectly still in a meditation posture whilst gazing at the ticking hands of the alarm clock, I discovered that it was a very long way to spend five minutes. No doubt some instruction was needed, I thought to myself, and began to look forward to seeing

Guruji again.

In Mae Hong Son, quite by chance, I met an English couple who were going to a refugee camp in the jungle the following day, where they had volunteered to teach English. As soon as they heard that I was a teacher, they invited me to join them for whatever time I could spare. They had no teaching experience between them and apparently neither did any of the teachers in the camp, all of whom were parents trying to give the children the best education they could. Though conscious of my own limited experience, this couple were convinced of my qualification to organise some teacher-training.

The couple briefed me on the background of the refugees. They were the people of Karenni State, whose independence and autonomy dated back to 739 BC. However, there had been civil war since the 1948 Independence Bill when Britain relinquished its control and the Karenni, Karen and Shan states were passed into the hands of the Burmese military government, then known as the SLORC.[9] The SLORC took away their economic resources and submitted whole villages to a spectrum of atrocities from slave labour to torture, rape and murder. Ethnic cleansing was carried out to subdue the Karenni and other small states' fight for independence, democracy and human rights. As farming people, their only hope in resolving the chronic political dilemma was foreign assistance, but no help was forthcoming. Although Aung San Suu Kyi, leader of the NLD (National League for Democracy) had long since received recognition as a Nobel Peace Prize winner, she was fighting the cause of democracy from under house arrest whilst her supporters were subject to threats, imprisonment and torture.

We were drinking milkshakes in a peaceful restaurant as I listened, which only underlined the dichotomy: guerrilla warfare was an every-day occurrence three hours from where we were sitting. Chastened by my own ignorance of world affairs, I decided that if time was to be spent constructively in Thailand, here was the perfect opportunity.

When I was introduced to the Foreign Minister of the Karenni Embassy in exile, he assured me that my help would be welcomed

---

[9] State Law and Order Restoration Council. They have since changed their name to State Peace and Development Council, and the country's name from Burma to Myanmar.

in the camp, so we bought supplies of candles, chocolate and biscuits, and prepared for an exodus into the jungle.

It was a bumpy truck ride from Mae Hong Son. We arrived in the early evening to a cluster of bamboo and leaf-thatched houses built on the sandy curves of a shallow river, surrounded by thick jungle vegetation. One house had been constructed in the shape of a pyramid, which turned out to be the lodging of the maths teacher and his family. The school was situated right in the centre of the village, along with two churches, one Protestant and one Catholic. This in itself surprised us until we were told that most of the Karenni had been converted by Christian missionaries during the British occupation. We were to discover that the Karenni were a religious community and high moral standards an integral part of their culture.

It was scenic and peaceful – to our eyes almost idyllic, if it had not been for the harsh living conditions to which these people were accustomed. Even the most basic of amenities were lacking. Pigs, chickens and ducks wandered around the house enclosures of only the fortunate few.

We lived in a house reserved especially for guests, and a woman named Daisy had been allocated the job of cooking for us. There were two meals a day. Usually the accompaniment was rice, but as a treat there were sometimes Thai noodles instead. Meat was often served with the vegetables, but we felt guilty as our awareness grew that this was a luxury most refugees could not afford. On the other hand it seemed impolite to turn down the efforts made by the entire village to make us feel welcome and care for our well-being.

A few days after our arrival, I began teaching English after school to teachers and older pupils, rather apprehensive of their high expectations in my ability. But their reception was so warm that I soon came to enjoy the new challenge and started working to organise a couple of weekend teacher-training courses in language games and methodology.

On some evenings the roar of the generator drowned the hum of the jungle and frogs' chorus, as up to a hundred people gathered around the village television to watch a film. But the most common evening occupation was music: groups of men singing to the accompaniment of battered old guitars, whilst others tapped bamboo drumsticks against the table or tin teapots for a lively rhythm.

I began to write down the stories of various refugees, having resolved to do some fund-raising for the school when I got back home. Nothing could have prepared me for the tales of oppression and torture I would hear first-hand. Tears fell as they related their experiences and told of family members left behind or in captivity. The political complexities of the situation they faced began to unravel before my eyes. For the first time in my life I became painfully aware of the hypocrisy of Western governments and the effect of dictatorial regimes on ordinary people's lives.

Their courage was truly inspiring. They had nothing and yet were uncomplaining. Despite one tragic experience after another and no foreseeable hope for the future, they had not forgotten how to laugh, celebrate, sing and dance. They were a peace-loving people. Prayer was central in their lives and many refugees acknowledged that faith in God gave them the strength they needed to cope with the permanent instability of their situation. Upon questioning the headmaster of the school about how he managed to retain his joy and sense of humour in such testing circumstances, he answered that he had learned to be grateful for life itself; at the moment of waking each morning with the rising of the sun he would give thanks for being alive. His consciousness was permanently attuned to the fact that his survival was dependent on nature's gifts: the sun was the source of warmth and light; the plants and trees provided sustenance and shelter; water from the river quenched their thirst and was a place for bathing.

I wrote long letters home and asked my mother for advice in finding the best way to gather some publicity for their cause. They were trapped here as prisoners of the jungle whilst I was free to roam the world, and surely it was a moral responsibility to do something to help. Besides which, staying with the Karenni had been an unexpectedly enriching experience. Before leaving, I promised to do my best to come back later in the year with the basic materials they desperately needed for the school.

THE BIRD (A Song)

I am the bird
Trapped all my life
Dreaming a dream
And yet the small cage
Like heaven to me
You are the friend
Light of my eyes
You let me go
And I am afraid
For now I am free

So hold me a while
Can love's colours
Pierce my cold night?
Warmth in your hands
As softly you touch me
I want to trust
Day will break
This lonely inside
With or without you
I know I am free

Chapter Two

KNOWLEDGE MEETS WISDOM

Two Kinds of Charity

*"Charity is great, but the moment you say it is all,
you run the risk of running into materialism."* –
SWAMI VIVEKANANDA

Charity is the cornerstone of Christianity and to those of us
brought up in Western religious thinking, good works are essential
on the road to spiritual advancement.

Lahiri Mahasaya's life was characterised by his kindness to
others – and yet "kindness" is an impoverished description of his
actions. As an enlightened master with a panoramic viewpoint
over the whole universal order, he often stepped in to help others,
even to the point of altering life's natural course. This pure and
unconditional form of charity was always given in aid of a higher
purpose than the ordinary mortal could fathom.

Lahiri Mahasaya's closest disciple was Krishna Ram. He was a
Brahmin with two sons and a daughter, and he served his Guru
with unceasing devotion.

It is customary for Brahmin boys to receive the *sacred thread*,
worn by every male belonging to this caste, at a special ceremony.
One night, Krishna Ram's wife reminded her husband that the
time was approaching to arrange such a ceremony for their
younger son, and she was worried because they lacked the
necessary finances. Krishna Ram reassured her.

'The One whom it concerns will provide for this need,' he said.

The following day Krishna Ram went to Lahiri Mahasaya's
house as usual. When he opened his eyes after paying obeisance,
he saw the master taking some money from under his sitting mat.

'I am giving you thirty rupees for your son's *sacred thread* ceremony. Arrange it in accordance with the Scriptures so that it will be enough; it doesn't have to be a big affair.'

Krishna Ram was overwhelmed and at the same time discomfited by the offer. It was surely disrespectful to accept financial help from the master whose love and grace were beyond measure, when lowly human service was the most he could ever give in return.

'Why should you give me money?' he stammered.

'Listen, Krishna Ram. God blesses through the medium which He chooses. And this time he has chosen me, so why don't you take your money?'

Krishna Ram accepted with heartfelt gratitude and deep respect.

LAHIRI MAHASAYA'S help to others was always rooted in an advanced level of consciousness, as another disciple, Surendra Nath Bandopadhyaya, came to discover. He had just been given a holiday from his work in Rawalpindi and was taking the train home to Serampore. Banaras was on the way, so he decided to visit Lahiri Mahasaya. It was a long journey and he was tired when he arrived at the master's house. But upon seeing him, his Guru said,

'Surendra, what are you doing here? You must go home immediately!'

The devotee was confused and upset by the tone of voice, and thought he must have done something wrong.

'Listen, Surendra,' said Lahiri Mahasaya, gently this time. 'Take a bath and have something to eat, and then catch the first available train to your home.'

Surendra did not have the courage to ask why, so he did as he was told. Later when he stepped off the train in his home town, the first thing he saw was his brother running towards him.

'Why have you come so late?' he exclaimed. 'I sent a telegram two days ago telling you to come home immediately!'

'I didn't receive any telegram!' Surendra replied. 'Why, what's wrong?'

'Mother is dying. Come quickly.'

They hurried home to their mother who lay weak in bed, her arms open to greet Surendra.

'Here you are, Surendra! I have been waiting for you. My time has come.'

Having embraced her son, she passed away peacefully a moment later. Surendra now fully understood the reason behind his Guru's unusual behaviour.

A FURTHER example of the self-realised master intervening in the natural course of events is found in the following instance:

A family was travelling to visit Lahiri Mahasaya from a village some distance from Banaras. They were about four miles away when a cartwheel broke and the bullocks refused to move, not being able to pull properly any more. The cart-driver spent a long time trying to repair the wheel, without success. The father grew anxious, as it was already dusk and robbers were known to frequent that road after dark.

He prayed to his Guru, Lahiri Mahasaya, for protection. Then there was a jerk – the bullocks started moving and the cart was rolling along behind them. It was certainly extraordinary, but since all was well, no one thought any more of it until they reached their destination.

The sun had set by the time the family arrived at the master's house. They paid obeisance to their Guru, and told of the troubles they had experienced during the journey. But since it appeared that Lahiri Mahasaya was not listening, the father started repeating his story in a loud voice.

Meanwhile, sweat was pouring from the master's brow, and he suddenly interrupted the man.

'Do you not see how I am sweating? Somebody get me a fan!' he cried. 'Who do you think brought your bullock cart here?'

The devotees who were present were amazed to hear this, for it was a rare event for Lahiri Mahasaya to admit to having performed a miracle. Certainly he never did so without reason. It was further evidence that nothing was impossible for this *Mahayogi*, and a demonstration of the great love which compelled him to assist disciples in need. The man concerned wept tears of gratitude and humility.

ANOTHER initiate of Lahiri Mahasaya, Haripad Bandopadhyaya, worked in the district of Bankura and had to walk a few kilometres to the next village on business. He knew of a shortcut through a thick forest and decided to take it, although the path was narrow and deserted. However, his heart was light as he listened to the birdsong and admired the beauty of the forest along the way.

Suddenly he stopped in his tracks, having heard a loud rustling sound ahead. A moment later he was horrified to find himself face to face with a tiger. It was striding menacingly towards him. There was no escape, and Haripad was terrified. He prayed to his Guru for help,

'Please save me, *Gurudeva*, save me!'

The next moment he heard someone behind him, commanding the animal to go away. Haripad watched in amazement as the tiger turned and disappeared back into the forest. Weeping tears of relief and gratitude, Haripad completed his journey safely.

On his next visit to Banaras he prostrated himself at Lahiri Mahasaya's feet,

'You saved my life, Guruji!' he said.

Lahiri Mahasaya was smiling.

'And you were very scared,' he replied kindly.

MANY disciples wanted a photograph of their master, but Lahiri Mahasaya was against the idea at first.

'You will all forget to practise, and start to worship my picture instead,' he told them.

But his disciples would not give up pleading. They insisted that they wanted to be able to see him after he had taken *Mahasamadhi*, and finally he agreed.

The photographer and devotee of Lahiri Mahasaya, Ganga Dhar De, was commissioned for the task. When he arrived to take the photograph, Lahiri Mahasaya had a multitude of questions about the camera itself, and Ganga Dhar De explained the various mechanisms with great enthusiasm.

At last the time came to take the picture. But there was a problem. Ganga Dhar De could not see the Yogi through the viewfinder. At first he thought that the problem lay with his camera, but when he turned it to the other people in the room, they were clearly visible. He looked up perturbed, only to see Lahiri Mahasaya smiling softly, and he understood.[1]

---

[1] As if by putting a cloak around his body, a Yogi of Lahiri Mahasaya's stature has the power to make himself invisible. He can thereby prevent anyone from taking a photograph of him. Similarly, he may make his voice inaudible to others.

'Please have pity on me and let me take your picture, otherwise your disciples' request won't be fulfilled,' he said.

'Very well, go ahead and take it,' the master replied. And this time, when Ganga Dhar De looked through the viewfinder, he could see his Guru, and took the only existing picture of Lahiri Mahasaya.[2]

Some time later, a woman disciple came to Lahiri Mahasaya to ask for his photograph. As he gave her the picture, he said,

'If you think this is just a photograph, that is all it will be. But if you think of it as a girdle of protection, it can save you.'

She went home wondering what he could have meant, and hung the photograph on the wall of her house.

A few days later she was at home reading the *Bhagavad Gita* with a friend who was also a disciple of Lahiri Mahasaya. It started to rain heavily and thunder clapped directly overhead. The women were afraid and kneeled in front of the photograph.

'Lord, save us!' they prayed.

The next moment there was a tremendous crash as lightning struck the house. Inexplicably, however, no damage was done. The walls were as cold as ice. As the women explained later, it seemed as though the house had been covered by an invisible protective blanket which had saved them.

❖ ❖ ❖ ❖ ❖ ❖ ❖ ❖

It felt good to be back in India, for at least three months this time. Of course Guruji heard all about my adventures in the jungle with the refugees and of the plan to help them. I also explained that my desire to learn meditation had not waned in the slightest. Having read a little about Kriya Yoga since my last visit, I wanted to be initiated into this technique. But Guruji immediately became grave: one had to be ready to receive Kriya. The disciple had to promise to practise morning and evening for life. It was a very

---

[2] With the exception of one picture of Shyama Charan as a young boy. The photograph taken by Ganga Dhar De in the above story is the one shown in this book. It is a rare picture, for when Lahiri Mahasaya was ready for the picture to be taken, he entered the state of consciousness known as *Shambhavi mudra*: the position of perfection. First of all, he is sitting in the lotus position, and secondly, *Prana* is passing through the *Sushumna* channel in his spine. This is also known as *Kevala Kumbhaka*, or complete control on the breath which renders external breathing unnecessary. He is in *Khechari mudra*. Since the eyes are fixed internally in *Kutastha*, they are only half-opened and the eyelids are unblinking.

serious commitment.

Nevertheless, in my own mind there was no doubt that I had found a real purpose for travelling. A time was arranged for yoga lessons to recommence. My Hatha Yoga had improved tremendously in the past six weeks, and to my joy we soon began with a few meditation techniques.

My thoughts were still very much with the Karenni people in the jungle. When a letter arrived at the guest house from my mother, I opened it eagerly, knowing that it would contain news. She was aware that I wanted to do some fundraising for them on my return to England and was willing to help.

Her letter was phlegmatic and to the point. She was doing everything that she possibly could. She had written to the Karenni Foreign Minister and procured some documents which might help them. She had even found some interested work colleagues who had fundraising ideas themselves. And then she ended with a blunt admonition not to get too emotionally involved. It was impossible to solve the political and social troubles in one corner of the globe single-handedly.

'How on earth am I supposed to remain unemotional? How does she imagine I can be anything *but* emotional?' I felt hurt and angry, and the well-meaning comment prompted a flood of tears. These people were my friends. They were not some news item heard one day and forgotten the next.

I was still red-eyed walking down the lanes to my yoga lesson. Upon arrival, no time was wasted in telling Guruji how my mother expected me to remain dispassionate about the refugees' predicament. The memory of those people with their terrible stories and the notion that I was supposed to feel totally unaffected by it unleashed the next torrent of emotion. Hot tears streaked down my cheeks again.

There were many questions in my mind. Since the first time in Varanasi, I had been preoccupied with the question of human suffering, and the assumption that spiritual masters should alleviate it. If there were only a spiritual master like Jesus in Varanasi these days, I reasoned, he would go to the steps of Dasaswamedh Ghat where the lepers sat begging, and heal them all. And if the Yogis on the wall of Guruji's studio had possessed the same powers, surely they would have done the same. So would it not be possible for an enlightened spiritual master to solve the political crisis in Burma? After all, was it not the purpose of a spiritual master to help people?

But during the past week I had begun to sense that my theory on spiritual masters was flawed. Having read a few books on Eastern religion and meditation, a new picture was emerging of India as a land where innumerable saints and masters had performed miracles throughout the centuries through the power of yoga – miracles comparable to those of Jesus Christ in his lifetime; a disconcerting thought to my Christian-centred mind.

Now Guruji was saying that only few masters were destined to give monumental examples such as Jesus, the Buddha and Mohammed; for they came for a specific purpose in response to the needs of the society and time in which they lived. They were beacons whose light continued to transform millions of lives, even thousands of years after their physical departure from the world. The point of miracles was to teach and give people faith in particular circumstances of need. Only then could they bear fruit. A self-realised master would never misuse yogic power for the sake of ego, which explained why most spiritual masters of the past and present lived unknown to all but their close disciples. Mankind was sometimes propelled forward in its spiritual growth by those great masters, but at other times it had to learn at its own pace.

So perhaps a spiritual master would not heal Varanasi's lepers after all, because doing so would cause a stir throughout the country. It would hardly be a viable option if the master saw fit to lead a quiet existence. Apparently it would amount to a show of ego unless there was a special reason. But was there ego in my desire to help the Karenni? I still could not understand – or perhaps did not want to understand – why a self-realised person would withhold help from anyone who was suffering.

I learned over time how complex even the question was, let alone the answer. That day we just began to scratch the surface. Kriya Yoga, Guruji explained, was a practice of the masters, leading to self-realisation.[3] People would always be fascinated by miracles, but few were actually interested in finding God themselves. Everyone would gladly avail themselves of a master's yogic powers, wanting temporary relief from their suffering, but having received it, they soon forgot. Out of the ten lepers Jesus healed, only one returned to give thanks.[4] A master wanted to teach the few disciples who were ready to receive the key to salvation and prepared to make the effort to free themselves; not to create a stir in crowds moved by little more than curiosity. People loved to take pity on other people, but they would not take pity on themselves.

'There is a story about the Buddha,' Guruji said. 'A certain woman came to the Buddha carrying her young son who had just died. She begged the master to save him. He told her that he could do so, if she managed to bring him some mustard from any household in the village where nobody had died recently. Full of hope she took a pot and knocked on every door, asking if someone had died in the family recently. "But yes, of course," came the reply every time. With a heavy heart and empty pot she finally understood the Buddha's message and arranged for her son to be cremated.

'You see, it is extremely rare that a Yogi will interfere with the course of nature, although he has the power to do so. The person who is born in this world will certainly also die. It is natural. The master's aim is not just to heal sickness and raise people from the dead.

'There are two types of charity,' Guruji continued. 'The first serves the body. Ordinary people give food, money and clothes to the poor, for doing so eases the conscience. Whether they admit it or not, the ego feels satisfaction at having given this help. But how long does this kind of assistance last? The last bite of food is eaten and the clothes become worn, and the material want is never appeased. There is no doubt that helping others in this way is

---

[3] In the context of this book, self-realisation refers to the highest transcendental state of yoga or Absolute Union with God (Cosmic Energy), following which there is no rebirth. It is not to be confused with the prolific fads which teach that self-realisation can be attained in an instant. This book hopes to clarify from a scientific standpoint why such claims are false.

Lahiri Mahasaya's explanation of one of Patanjali's Yoga Sutras (no. 47) illustrates the idea of genuine self-realisation thus: "The inner Realisation of the Self is achieved only by the pure state of Samadhi, which is absolutely free from thoughts."

[4] St. Luke 17:12-19

good, but no self-realisation comes from such charity.

'An ordinary person uses his eyes to come to a judgement, but cannot see the complete picture. Many beggars are lazy and think that they can get more money from tourists than from working, whilst others are in genuine need. How will you recognise the person who really deserves your money for as long as it will last?

'The second kind of charity is the ability to give permanent help. Only a self-realised person can give this kind of charity, and we can only receive it when we understand the need to take pity on our own Self.[5] Its aim is to serve the soul rather than the body. Lahiri Mahasaya gave this example: we cannot give true service to God or worship Him in merely renovating a crumbling temple – we have to go inside to the deity.

'Hence there is no selfishness in working to know the meaning of Soul, or Self, because this knowledge enables us to give more than temporary help to others. This is the purpose of Kriya Yoga practice. A Yogi can give spiritual help as well as recognise the genuine physical need. His sight is not limited to the visual organs.'

It had often occurred to me that material help was not an ultimate solution. And never more so than in India. As a tourist, you soon became used to the automatic demand for "one rupee", "school pen", or "chocolate" which most children delivered whenever they passed. Guruji told me that someone who came to yoga lessons spent hundreds of rupees on pens and chocolate, and started distributing them amongst the children. But he soon regretted his charitable action, for wherever he went he was followed by an ever-increasing swarm of children with yet greater demands by the day. His money simply could not buy enough. Another time he gave two hundred rupees to a beggar and the following day was dismayed to see him in a virtual coma, surrounded by a ring of empty liquor bottles.

---

[5] "Self" used in this context refers to the higher spiritual Self or Soul in each individual which is immortal, and is not to be confused with the ego.

Swami Vivekananda says, "We are to take care of ourselves – that much we can do – and give up attending to others for a time. Let us perfect the means; the end will take care of itself. For the world can be good and pure, only if our lives are good and pure. It is an effect, and we are the means. Therefore, let us purify ourselves. Let us make ourselves perfect." (from *Living at the Source: Yoga teachings of Vivekananda*.)

But that could not change the plight of the refugee school. They badly needed some basic equipment and I was going home to raise the money to buy it for them. In my opinion, that had nothing to do with ego, nor was it purely about money. It was practical help in the name of education. I was still feeling quite emotional, and did not entirely want to accept the second concept of charity, although in Guruji's entirely balanced presence my mood was considerably improved.

'Do your fundraising,' said Guruji, smiling at me suddenly. 'It will be very nice.'

Medicine or Prayer?

"The prayer that reforms the sinner and heals the sick is an absolute faith that all things are possible to God, – a spiritual understanding of Him, an unselfed love." – MARY BAKER EDDY[6]

The disciple Jaipal once came in desperation to his Guru, for his son was dying of cholera. He prostrated himself at the master's feet for longer than usual. Lahiri Mahasaya was sitting in a meditative trance, with half-opened eyes. Jaipal waited patiently for him to give an indication that he was listening, whereupon he begged in a trembling voice,

'Please save my son!'

'Go to the market and buy some *Tikhur jilibi*,'[7] replied Lahiri Mahasaya. 'Let him eat until he is full.'

Jaipal obeyed and gave his son a large quantity of the sticky yellow sweet which his Guru had prescribed. Having eaten it, his son quickly recovered.

ON ANOTHER occasion, Kedar Nath Dey came to Lahiri Mahasaya for a similar reason. In this instance, however, it was his wife who lay on her death bed, and the couple had several young children. The man was at a loss to know how he would cope if she died. He struggled to hold back the tears as he explained to his Guru that it was cholera.

---

[6] Quotations by Mary Baker Eddy taken from *Science and Health with Key to the Scriptures*.

[7] *Tikhur jilibi* is a wheel-shaped sweetmeat made of an aquatic seed similar to the water chestnut.

'You had better find a good doctor to help her,' said Lahiri Mahasaya.

'But there is no point in calling a doctor!' he cried. 'If you have grace on her, she will live, and if not, she will die. It is in your hands alone, you will do as you wish. I am your humble servant.'

'Can you do whatever I ask of you?' Lahiri Mahasaya asked.

Hearing this, Kedar Nath Dey saw a glimmer of hope through the anguish.

'I will do anything you say,' he promised fervently.

'Very well. Go and buy a bottle of rose water and then come back.'

Kedar Nath Dey did as he was told, and returned with the rose water.

'Now you have to go to the toilet, and mix some of your stool with the rose water, and give it to your wife to drink immediately.'

Kedar Nath Dey was shocked; but as he sensed it was a test of his own faith, he thought better of it than to argue. It was his obedience which saved his wife, through Lahiri Mahasaya.

STILL a third account is told of how Lahiri Mahasaya healed a disciple of cholera. Prianath Karar[8] and his friend Rama were staying in Banaras to hear their Guru's teachings every day. Whilst they were there, Rama became extremely sick with Asiatic cholera, and Prianath asked Lahiri Mahasaya for advice about his friend's condition. First of all, Lahiri Mahasaya told Prianath to go to a doctor, reassuring him that Rama would get well. But no medicine was available which could cure the disease at that time, and the doctors soon pronounced the case hopeless: Rama could not survive.

Helpless and afraid, Prianath returned to his Guru and told him the situation in tears. He could not understand the master's apparent lack of concern. After a while, Lahiri Mahasaya got up and poured some castor oil from a nearby lamp into a bottle.

'Give him this to drink,' he instructed.

Prianath took it and quickly left. He feared that it was too late for any medicine and that his friend would surely be dead by the time he reached him. However, his trust in Lahiri Mahasaya was strong, for his Guru always knew everything.

---

[8] Later in life, Prianath Karar became famous as Swami Yukteswar Giri, the Guru of Paramahansa Yogananda.

Prianath returned to find a group of people gathered around the bed where Rama had just died. But full of faith, he poured a few drops between his friend's lips. Immediately, the body moved. Rama started to breathe again, and soon made a full recovery.

THERE was certainly no human logic in the medicines which Lahiri Mahasaya gave, except it seemed that the more doubt there was in a disciple's mind, the more bizarre were the medicines he prescribed. These unusual remedies generally served as tests in order to strengthen the faith of the disciple concerned. However, the healing itself was always the result of yogic power.

Lahiri Mahasaya also prescribed a self-prepared *neem oil* to many of his disciples, which cured the widest variety of ailments. It was a well-known fact that if anyone attempted to make the medicine without the master's blessing, the liquid would inexplicably be reduced to such an extent that it could not be used effectively. But for the most part, Lahiri Mahasaya would advise people to follow social convention and seek the help of a doctor whenever the need arose.

'A master will sometimes hide himself by playing games or causing confusion in the disciple's mind,' Guruji once told me. 'In India, we say that one sign of a self-realised person is when you cannot decide whether he is a wise man or a fool.'

❖ ❖ ❖ ❖ ❖ ❖ ❖ ❖

Having contracted malaria in the jungle in Thailand, my body was still fairly weak when I arrived back in Varanasi. A wretched cough started to tear at my lungs, which got steadily worse and was accompanied by regular vomiting. It made sleep at night virtually impossible, and a fellow traveller in the guest house offered me Valium. It was politely refused: not even the most innocuous of medicines ever passed my lips. Then Guruji asked if I had seen a doctor. No doubt he saw right through the brave face and attempts to play down how I really felt, but I was reluctant to explain my religious philosophy of relying exclusively on prayer for healing.

Yet the more I read about meditation, the more yoga lessons were spent in discussing my questions rather than practising Hatha. In the first place, I did not often feel fit enough to manage the physical exercises, and secondly, a battle was being waged in my mind. On the one hand there was a genuine interest in yogic masters and in the absolute religious experience to which their practice led – and on the other, a tendency to cling to a theoretical understanding which stemmed from the religious textbooks I had turned to for inspiration throughout my life. However much there was to learn, in principle I still believed that each and every answer was to be found between their covers.

At that point in time, I hardly knew anything about Guruji. He never talked about himself, he did not mention God, and yet his presence exuded authority and wisdom. With every passing day I spent with him, I became increasingly convinced that meditation could lead to spiritual planes known only to the masters: particularly after asking Guruji one morning to explain what Soul was. He had not answered directly, but the most wonderful knowing smile spread across his face and the light in his eyes shone. It was an unforgettable expression which spoke of direct personal experience.

'He can't tell me about Soul because he's *been* there!' was my immediate, stunned thought. I had never been at a loss for words when it came to describing God and his attributes, and yet now Guruji's face was enough to instil a desire in me to go one day to the place where he had been – however much practice it took. It had to be profoundly wonderful.

So if Guruji was as spiritually advanced as I imagined him to be, why did he set such store by medicine? Medicine was a human crutch, the use of which compromised God's great healing power as far as I was concerned. Prayer alone would heal my cough, if I could only have enough faith and trust. But the uncomfortable question was put to one side.

As the days went by, my health worsened. But a new journey had begun which could not end until every pressing question had been satisfactorily answered. These were now coming in thick and fast, which was a new experience in itself. So I had no intention of going home.

The current issue was why meditation involved concentrating the mind instead of thinking about God. This went against the grain. Where was the spirituality?

'If you think about it, the sum total of the world's knowledge has been won through concentration,' Guruji began. 'There is not one aspect of our lives in which concentration is not essential. The mind has to be focused when you are driving, otherwise you will crash. If you read a book without concentration, you have wasted your time. Sometimes my wife doesn't concentrate when she is cooking: just last week she put salt in the tea, and sugar in the rice!' said Guruji, making a face, and I laughed.

'You can imagine the result if a surgeon doesn't concentrate during an operation,' he continued, 'and think of a physicist who is discovering a new theory – how deep he has to go into himself! To achieve success in any field, the mind should be calm and quiet.

'So, we know the benefits which good concentration brings to any worldly work we do, and meditation develops this concentration also. But the real aim of meditation is spiritual. Meditation means concentration on Self, and the first step is to turn the mind upon itself. We have a highly developed sense of everything external, but we are blind to the internal world within ourselves. And yet everything is inside, true knowledge, eternal freedom, pure love. It takes a great deal of practice to find this inner world and the first task is to bring the mind under control.

'Where should we meditate? The best place to start is the breath, because this is where we can most easily see *Prana*, or cosmic energy, manifested in us. Close your eyes and let your mind watch the air as it naturally enters and leaves your body from the nose. See how long you can keep your mind there and don't be discouraged if your mind wanders. We have a saying here that the mind is like a monkey, always jumping,' said Guruji with a broad smile.[9]

I could relate to that. There was more than one jumping monkey in my mind. Before starting yoga classes, I had always imagined that my concentration was rather good. I had even had the

---

[9] "How hard it is to control the mind! Well has it been compared to the maddened monkey. There was a monkey, restless by his own nature, as all monkeys are. As if that were not enough, someone made him drink freely of wine, so that he became still more restless. Then a scorpion stung him. When a man is stung by a scorpion he jumps about for a whole day; so the poor monkey found his condition worse than ever. To complete his misery a demon entered into him. What language can describe the uncontrollable restlessness of that monkey? The human mind is like that monkey, incessantly active by its own nature; then it becomes drunk with the wine of desire, thus increasing its turbulence. After desire takes possession comes the sting of the scorpion of jealously at the success of others, and last of all the demon of pride enters the mind, making it think itself of all importance. How hard it is to control such a mind!" (from *Raja Yoga* by Swami Vivekananda.)

audacity to think myself quite well in control of my thoughts.

A few days previously, because I had been asking about Kriya Yoga so often, Guruji had given me various meditation exercises to practise on my own for at least twenty minutes a day. In addition to the *pranayama*, or breathing exercises of Hatha Yoga, I was now being asked to fix my concentration on points up and down the spine. It was excruciatingly difficult. The half-lotus position gave me pins and needles after five minutes. My hands were fidgety, and thwarted every attempt to focus the mind and stop it from darting off in every possible direction. The eyes were closed but the mind was busy chasing endless trivial thoughts about where to go for lunch; what I would order; the fact that the shampoo bottle was empty and I needed to buy some more, maybe some postcards too ... It was an endless mental cinema strip, interrupted only by a measure of aggression directed towards an irksome mosquito buzzing around my head.

Now beginning to despair of ever achieving any kind of mental calm, let alone the spectacular experiences that some meditators apparently had, I was more disillusioned than ever in my ability to concentrate. This was not amazing: it was frustrating.

'But I can't even concentrate for more than five seconds at a time during twenty minutes of meditation!' I lamented to Guruji, positive that he must consider me a hopeless case.

'This is very natural,' he said, not seeming surprised in the slightest. 'Next time, as you do your practice, be the observer and watch your mind. It is important to practise every day, because this is not so easy. But it is a preparation towards real concentration. You can already see that to harness and control the mind is not a question of intellect. It is a task which requires great devotion.'

So I was supposed to bring my mind under control. But as far as I was concerned, if you wanted to get in touch with God, you had to pray. And prayer involved thinking, not concentrating on the breath, on the spine, or on some point between the eyebrows. What did the breath really have to do with the God I had learned about in Sunday school and had called on in times of need?

On the other hand, my religion taught that prayer was not a question of petitioning, but more a letting go of ego, an acceptance of "Thy will be done",[10] and listening internally for a divine

---

10 From The Lord's Prayer, St. Matthew 6:9-13.

answer. And meditation aimed to conquer the ego and establish mental calm and peace where inner turmoil had been allowed to reign. So perhaps there was no contradiction after all. It was ironic to remember how my mind was prone to wander during a one-hour church service.

'What is prayer and how is meditation different?' I asked.

'Firstly, prayer is dualism,' said Guruji. 'There are two, you and God. But the aim of meditation is to unite. Then there is only One. This is the true meaning of yoga.' He paused slightly before continuing.

'You can also think of it like this. In the atmosphere surrounding the earth, there is a limit to the height that aeroplanes can reach. Man had to invent the rocket in order to enter space. When the rocket leaves the earth's atmosphere, the outer fuel tanks are dropped from the shuttle because they are no longer needed.

'The intellect or mind is like the aeroplane. The atmosphere in which it lives has certain limits. We can liken it to the plane of thought. But there is a space beyond that which is too subtle for the intellect to enter. The real Self lives in that place, but to break through the barrier, the ego, or mind, has to dissolve, being like the rocket's unwanted fuel tanks. Meditation goes entirely beyond words, thoughts and what is termed the intellect. It is the rocket which enables us to reach that space beyond.'

After another pause, Guruji added:

'When there is too much logic, the shuttle cannot even lift off the ground.'

I could follow the analogy. There was certainly no denying a tendency for me to analyse and intellectualise over spiritual matters, yet the more books I devoured on meditation, the clearer it became that one could never become an expert or taste the fruits of meditation through reading alone.

It was too bad that practice was such hard work. But I was having to admit that theory was one thing; knowledge quite another.

The Perfect Guru

*"At all times and in all places, people have been more
easily impressed by miracles, signs and magical spectacles
than by spiritual truths, especially when
the spiritual truths are difficult to take in."* – HOLGER KERSTEN

Lahiri Mahasaya was a healthy man, five feet and four inches tall with an attractive face. His skin was quite fair from the waist downwards, but his face and chest were rosy. He was always calm and talked little. But there was a presence so powerful about him that people, irrespective of whether they knew who he was or not, bowed their heads in respect and made way for him when they saw him in the street.

His lifestyle was as simple as his dress. He drank mostly milk and ate meagre amounts. He was fully vegetarian. In the evenings it was his custom to walk along the bank of the Ganges to his disciple Krishna Ram's house, and the two of them would discuss the *Bhagavad Gita*. Then he would return to his home where other devotees were waiting to ask his advice and hear him preach, which he did until nine o'clock. Most nights were spent in *Samadhi*, yet he was never affected by fatigue during the daytime.

Sometimes Lahiri Mahasaya would tell his disciples that they should not think of him as a Guru. In reality, he said, there was no difference between the Guru and disciple. He would describe himself as being very small and say how tiny man was next to God: he wanted his disciples to understand that the realm of Self, or the Kingdom of Heaven, could not be entered without humility. And yet he was fully emancipated as one having control over the elements, the power to change material substance, heal the sick and make the dead live once more. These miracles were pure tokens of love and never for show.

He would sit on a wooden bedstead in the lotus position, with his devotees on the floor in front of him. They did not need to speak if they wanted to ask him a question. He usually had his eyes closed and would open them as questions arose in his devotees' mind in order to reply. He would look at the devotee concerned and give a specific answer which was full of wisdom and formulated in such a way that the devotee could easily understand.

Having seen and heard the master, those who arrived with a burden of sorrow, loss or worry went home feeling at peace. His presence alone had the power to change lives drastically. Even people with highly materialistic aims who found their way to him departed as spiritual devotees.

In India, when people pay obeisance, it is called *Pranam.* This is a gesture of respect to an elder, or guru. Usually, the hands are brought together at the chest, symbolically close to the heart, or raised to the place of the spiritual eye at the eyebrow centre. The head is bowed, and it is usual to touch the feet of the person to whom respect is given. In the case of a spiritual Guru, disciples will usually prostrate themselves either by kneeling or lying before the Guru, with forehead to the ground. It is a sign of humility.

At the entrance to Lahiri Mahasaya's house, many disciples would touch the front doorstep with their forehead upon entering or leaving and pray for a few minutes – which was also *Pranam,* or a way of paying obeisance.

On countless occasions during the evening sessions with his disciples and devotees, Lahiri Mahasaya was observed raising his joined hands to his forehead, although it was not apparent to whom he was making or returning *Pranam.* The gesture was evidently not directed at anyone in the room where he was sitting, and it became a cause of wonder amongst the disciples. One evening when this happened, a disciple who hoped to solve the mystery got up from where he was sitting and went outside the house. There he observed a devotee making a long *Pranam* to Lahiri Mahasaya at the gate. Quite clearly, from inside the walls of his house, the master was returning the gesture of respect to this man outside.

AFTER retirement from his government position in 1880, Lahiri Mahasaya's pension was so meagre that he had to work as a tutor again. This time his employer was the *Kashi Maharaja,* Iswari Narayan Singh, and his pupil was the King's son. A boat would be sent to take him to Ram Nagar Palace on the other side of the Ganges, except during the rainy season when the river was too flooded and Lahiri Mahasaya resided at the palace.

The King was a learned and religious man who listened eagerly to his son's tutor's explanations of various Scriptures. But for a long time he had no idea that Lahiri Mahasaya was an advanced

Yogi. It was Girish Chandra De, a colleague in the royal service, who told the King one day,

'Shyama Charan Lahiri is no ordinary person. He is a perfect *Siddha Mahayogi*.'

The King was not particularly surprised, as the explanations of Scripture which he had heard from Lahiri Mahasaya were so deep that they were obviously drawn from personal experience rather than books. He resolved to accept him as his spiritual Guru, which he and his son, Prabhu, both did.

In India, the king was looked upon as a symbol of God, since his responsibility was to care for the well-being of all his subjects. Therefore anyone who desired an audience had to come to the palace, for there was no question of the king making any personal visit. Despite this, Iswari Narayan Singh very much wanted to come to Lahiri Mahasaya's house.

'You are my Guru,' he would say. 'Just once, I want to come and see you at your home and touch your feet there. When would be a good time for me to come?'

But Lahiri Mahasaya steadfastly refused. Firstly, he would not ignore the social customs of the day, and secondly, he knew that if the King came to his house, the entire city would soon be buzzing with the news. It would mean huge crowds at his door.

When word of Lahiri Mahasaya reached the ears of the Kashmir *Maharaja*, he sent one of his servants to seek out the great Yogi and enquire when a visit would be possible. Lahiri Mahasaya conceded, and instructed the man to tell the *Maharaja* to come at nine o'clock in the evening. It would be dark then and the streets would be empty. He was to dress in ordinary clothes rather than in the formal regalia usually worn by kings and could come with one other person if necessary. The final condition was that the visit should be kept secret.

The *Maharaja* arrived at the arranged time and first offered his deep respects. Then he asked why Lahiri Mahasaya had insisted on such secrecy. The master replied that if he had let the *Maharaja* come in the daytime, masses of people would have followed him to his house, and this was something he did not want.

The *Maharaja* received Kriya that night. News of the master reached several other ruling kings from Burdwan (West Bengal) and Nepal, who also came for initiation secretly in the night according to Lahiri Mahasaya's instruction.

When the time came for their eldest daughter's marriage, Kashi Mani Devi was worried. Although a date had been decided for the wedding, they had no money. Lahiri Mahasaya told his wife not to worry, that everything would be taken care of. Indeed, shortly afterwards, the *Kashi Maharaja* sent them a bag containing some gold coins intended to finance Harimati's wedding and the problem was thus solved.

BEING a perfect *Siddhayogi*, Lahiri Mahasaya was not limited to his physical body when he wanted to go somewhere, and he was seen by several disciples in his *astral body*.

As the *Kashi Maharaja*, Iswari Narayan Singh, grew old and death was imminent, he sent a message to his Guru asking him to come and give his blessing, or *Dharshan*. The answer which Lahiri Mahasaya gave to the King was, 'I hardly go anywhere these days, but we will see.'

He did not go; and the King died. Greatly disillusioned, one disciple[11] summoned the courage to ask Lahiri Mahasaya why he had not fulfilled the King's last heartfelt desire. To the surprise of everyone present, the master smiled and answered,

'I don't need my physical body to move from here. Don't worry, the King received my *Dharshan*.'

LAHIRI MAHASAYA usually spent the mornings in meditation, not receiving any visitors. Nevertheless, due to of a matter of some urgency, a disciple was hoping to visit him on the way to Dasaswamedh market one morning, but could see his Guru sitting in his room from the front gate, evidently absorbed in the higher planes. So he made *Pranam* and went on his way. A short while later at the market, he could not believe his eyes when he saw Lahiri Mahasaya shopping a little way off.

'It must be my imagination,' he thought to himself and stopped to look more closely.

There was no doubt that it was Lahiri Mahasaya, but surely that was impossible, so the disciple hurried back as fast as he could along the lanes, only to find his Guru in the lotus position, exactly

---

[11] The disciple in question was Tarak Nath Sanyal.

as he had seen him earlier. Again he made *Pranam* with deep humility.

'The mystery of your *lila*,[12] master, is beyond me,' he said quietly to himself.

It was clear that Lahiri Mahasaya had fulfilled his disciple's desire to see him that morning, but instead of letting the disciple see him at home, he had appeared to him in the market. There was no logical explanation, although it was known that whenever a disciple had a particularly strong desire, however deeply subconscious, he would often use his yogic power to fulfil it.

IT WAS a daily struggle for one particular disciple to practise Kriya. As a doctor who worked in the Navy, Govardhan Dutt persevered nonetheless, and whenever the ship docked in Calcutta, he would take the train to Banaras.

Lahiri Mahasaya asked Govardhan one day why he gave himself so much financial and physical trouble to come all the way to the holy city. Govardhan asked his Guru for a special blessing – the one thing he really desired was to see his master whenever he remembered him. Lahiri Mahasaya said nothing but gave a gesture of assent.

From that time on, whenever Govardhan prayed to his Guru aboard the ship, Lahiri Mahasaya would appear to him. When he retired, Govardhan settled in Banaras and reached a high level in Kriya practice.

BHAGABATI CHARAN GHOSH was a high-ranking officer in the Bengali South-Eastern Railway. When a worker named Abinash came to him one day requesting a week's leave to visit his Guru in Banaras, he replied that any spiritual quest was a waste of time which would only hinder his work and prospects in life.

Abinash was disheartened. But as he was walking home that evening, his superior passed him, being carried in a *palanquin*. Bhagabati Charan Ghosh alighted in order to accompany Abinash, whom he tried to convince further that there was no need for spiritual gurus and that he should concentrate on worldly success instead. Meanwhile, Abinash was praying to his Guru for help,

---

12 *Lila* means divine "play" or "sport". It also indicates the natural cyclic continuity of the cosmic force manifesting itself in creation.

neither agreeing nor disagreeing, but growing more desperate by the minute to find a way to visit Lahiri Mahasaya soon.

It was sunset and the two men were crossing a field when suddenly Lahiri Mahasaya appeared in front of them in his *astral body*.

'Bhagabati, you are too hard-hearted towards your subordinates!' he said in a resounding voice, and the next moment he was gone.

Abinash fell on his knees, his hands clasped together. Bhagabati stood speechless, shocked by what he had just seen and heard.

'You have leave to visit your Guru,' he said, finally. 'From tomorrow. And I think it will be best if you take me and my wife with you. I want to meet this *Mahayogi* too.'

Abinash travelled to Banaras the next day, accompanied by Bhagabati and his wife. They went straight to the home of Lahiri Mahasaya and humbly made *Pranam*.

Lahiri Mahasaya was sitting in the lotus position with closed eyes. When he opened them he gave a welcoming smile and said to Bhagabati,

'If someone is walking on this spiritual path, it is not right to stop them.'

Bhagabati Charan Ghosh and his wife asked to receive Kriya Yoga. Some years later after the birth of their second son Mukund Lal, the couple travelled to Banaras again to visit their Guru with the baby. Soon after their arrival at the house, Lahiri Mahasaya took Mukund Lal on his lap. Many disciples were present when he told the couple that their son would be a Yogi and show many people the path to self-realisation.

As the disciple of Sri Yukteswar Giri, Mukund Lal later became known as Paramahansa Yogananda and brought Kriya Yoga to the West in the 1940s.

❖ ❖ ❖ ❖ ❖ ❖ ❖ ❖

Whilst I had been away in Thailand, my American friends Cord and John had done what sounded like the Saints and Miracles Tour of India. There was a certain Sai Baba in the South who allegedly produced Rolex watches from the air, and a renowned woman saint who was currently touring the country with thousands of disciples in tow. Furthermore, they had witnessed strange, cult-like behaviour in the *ashram* of a world-famous guru, having stayed there a few days. I also gathered that groups of spiritual seekers regularly headed for the Himalayas in the hope of finding some elusive self-realised saint such as Lahiri Mahasaya's Guru, Babaji.

Before meeting Guruji I had never heard of self-realisation. Now it suddenly seemed to be the most common thing in the world, or rather, it had become a regular topic of conversation. Especially now that my friends Cord and John were back in Varanasi, also wanting to spend more time with Guruji. It provided plenty of food for thought. Miracles were immensely appealing, but some of the stories sounded surreal and almost too fantastic.

We talked over lunch one day about the pros and cons of having a guru who was famous. How much did you learn? With thousands of disciples in tow, did they ever have time for you? But there again, with so many followers, they had to be self-realised, didn't they?

Or was it preferable to have lessons with a yoga teacher who was not quite so eminent? At least what we were learning was personal and meaningful, and the wonderful stories which Guruji told were always incisively relevant to us as individuals. But was he self-realised? My friends thought so, though to my reasoning nothing obvious suggested that he was. He lived a perfectly ordinary life teaching yoga, as far as I could see. We all agreed that it would be interesting to find out if Guruji really was self-realised. But how were you supposed to know without seeing any miracles? In reply, Cord told me of a conversation he had overheard between Guruji and a Japanese man.

'It was whilst I was waiting for my yoga lesson,' Cord said. 'This Japanese man had heard that Guruji was a Yogi and was offering him a blank cheque, would you believe, in exchange for self-realisation. He wanted Guruji to touch him on the head!'

'What did Guruji say?' My curiosity was aroused.

'He told him that he had made a mistake and sent him away.'

The next day, as I waited for my lesson, my mind was formulating the best way to pose the big question. It seemed terribly disrespectful to ask Guruji outright if he possessed yogic powers. Besides which, he would almost certainly refuse to answer such a question anyway. It was better to forget it.

Then a man came out of the yoga studio looking annoyed, and I went in wondering what Guruji could have said to displease him.

'He came to ask where he can find a self-realised *sadhu*,' Guruji said.

Now I was on the alert. 'What did you tell him?'

'I said that if he had a pair of eyes he should be able to see for himself!'

There was no mistaking the irony in his tone of voice. 'This is Varanasi. The holy city,' Guruji sighed. 'Many foreigners come here and all they want to know is where they can find a real saint, *sadhu* or Yogi. Usually because they have read some sensational story and want to see miracles.'

It was the perfect cue.

'But Guruji, how is it possible to tell if someone is self-realised?'

'There is one example. Listen,' Guruji said, and he began to tell a story. It was about a man who went to his Guru asking where he could find a true master:

'There are many yogis around,' the man said, 'and although they seem to be good, I am by no means convinced that they are self-realised.'

'I see,' returned the Guru. 'I will help you, but first I need you to do something for me. I want you to go to the market and sell this stone for me, but on no account should you accept less than one hundred rupees for it.'

'With pleasure,' replied the man and took the ordinary-looking stone which his Guru had handed him.

The first shopkeeper in the jewellery market whom he approached turned it over in his hand with not so much as a spark of interest.

'This is a mere stone; why should I want to buy it?'

So the man left the shop and tried several more jewellers, but was offered ten or twenty rupees for it at the most.

'I'm sorry,' he told them all. 'But I have instructions not to sell it for less than one hundred rupees.'

Disillusioned, he began to walk back to his Guru's house. On the way he passed a gem shop and decided to give it one final try. The gem merchant took the stone and examined it through a magnifying glass.

'How much do you want for it?' he asked, trying to disguise his excitement.

'I won't sell it for less than one hundred rupees,' the man answered firmly.

'Very well, you shall have your one hundred rupees.'

The man was so shocked at this unexpected answer that he was speechless for a moment. Misreading the hesitation, the shopkeeper said, 'I'll give you two hundred!'

Now the man was really confused. The shopkeeper obviously wanted this stone quite badly.

'Let me go back to the owner and check with him first. It doesn't belong to me,' he said.

'Wait – name your price!' cried the shopkeeper. 'Five hundred – no, listen: I will give you one thousand rupees for it!'

'Really, I can't,' answered the man, feeling upset at the sudden turn of events. 'I must get permission first. Goodbye.' And he hurriedly left the shop.

A short while later he told his Guru what had happened.

'You had better return my stone to me.'

'Then why did you give it to me to sell?' asked the man.

'As a matter of fact, I don't want to sell it,' his Guru answered. 'I only wanted to answer your question. Look at what happened: the jewellery shops you went to specialise in gold and silver. So the gem merchant was the only person who realised that there was a precious diamond encased in this stone. If you learn to recognise a diamond when you see one you will treasure it, but if you are ignorant you will mistake it for a piece of glass and let it slip through your fingers.'

The Guru paused.

'Now perhaps you can answer for yourself why you have never seen a self-realised person,' he told his disciple. 'In order to see if someone is really self-realised, you will have to become self-realised yourself. Like understands like. This ability is not in our hands or in our eyes.'

Guruji had to elaborate further for me, because I was not sure if I had grasped the implication. Did a real saint or Yogi not emit a divine light or something?

Not quite, was the answer. A light or aura was something a Yogi could make visible to others completely at will. But recognition of a master's conscious level was a different matter. A radio had to be correctly tuned in order to receive certain frequencies, and an ordinary person's "radio" was plainly not tuned to the same frequency as that of an advanced spiritual Yogi.

Put another way, consciousness reaching up to the higher spiritual planes is like a very long ladder. From the ground, the person at the top cannot even be identified. You have to plant your own ladder and start climbing. The more you climb, the easier it becomes to make out various features of the person on the other ladder, and finally, when you reach a rung of equal height, there are no more hindrances to either recognition or communication. The prerequisite is the personal effort and lifelong practice it takes to climb up.

I asked Guruji if the famous saints in India which one heard so much about were self-realised, on the basis of their ability to perform miracles. He shook his head, probably at my slowness to grasp the real issue, and gave the question a more practical perspective rather than answering directly.

'There was a girl who came here for lessons. She told me that she had seen a famous saint and watched a miracle with her own eyes. Perhaps this was the reason she came to India. I said to her, "Very nice." And then I asked her if she got some practice from him. Perhaps a *Mantra* or a meditation? She was surprised at my question: "No, why should I?" she said. But I wanted to ask if there was any personal spiritual development. If there is no question of attaining the level of a master yourself, what is the point in seeing such things? Where is the benefit?'

Guruji fell silent and seemed absorbed somewhere for a while. I waited and then remembered something my brother had recently told me.

'Guruji,' I said, 'an Indian fakir who performs miracles was on television in England recently. Apparently he lay in the middle of a road and they drove a truck right over his chest. Then he got up, unhurt.'

'Yes, I know this man also,' Guruji replied. I seemed to have his full attention again. 'That man will point an iron rod at the eyebrow centre, the softest part of the body, and bend it. It is a yogic technique; a matter of concentration and years of practice. But what happens? Several thousand people may watch him one day, but the majority will have dismissed it as a show and forgotten all about it the next. A few might question what power enables him to do these things, but they will forget also. At the most, one person may want to become his disciple and learn the secrets behind the fakir's power. But what is the spiritual aim in doing these things? Actually, it is meaningless.

'There are many tricksters in India,' Guruji continued. 'Last week, there was a man on television who claimed that through the power of his eyes he could make some *paisa* coins turn to dust. The camera focused on his gazing eyes and very slowly the coins began to crumble. The people in the audience thought that it was a great miracle. It made me laugh actually, because I have a little knowledge of chemistry. *Paisa* coins are made of aluminium. When they are dipped into liquid mercury, there is no doubt that they will turn to ash in five to ten minutes.'

This was leading to the conclusion that miracles, or the number of disciples a master had in tow, were not necessarily linked to spirituality. It even seemed as though the pull of fame and riches could sometimes result in a misuse of yogic powers. I was still wondering if Guruji could perform real miracles, but one thing was becoming crystal clear – such wonders were evidently not the point of yoga.

My questions were exhausted for another day. Before leaving the yoga studio, I looked at the pictures on the wall behind Guruji. There was Lahiri Mahasaya, his son Tinkari Lahiri and his grandson, Satya Charan Lahiri, who had been Guruji's Guru. It struck me for the first time then that it would be interesting to research their stories. A lineage of hidden yogic lives that few people knew of. Perhaps through them it would be possible to find out a deeper truth about spiritual masters.

Certainly it was a fascinating prospect. The option of touring the nation in search of miracle workers had lost much of its glamour. Besides, doing so was not likely to satisfy in the long term. Maybe in Guruji's unobtrusiveness he was testing my desire for Kriya, to see if my motivation was genuine or borne of idle curiosity. The very thought made me all the more determined not to leave Varanasi until I had received Kriya Yoga.

THE OLD MAN'S ORDERS (A Song)

You told me stories
You became a friend
And the kids in the school were soldiers
'Cause they kicked you down and kicked you out
To a jungle life on the country's borders

Home you know is not a place
Anywhere will do, it's called survival
Hope and courage live a day, and die
When the guns hear the old man's orders

And all that I do, is shed a useless tear
All that I feel is lonely pain
In my mind's eye your smiling face
How did you learn to laugh again?
I want to be with you again

I watched the movie
I saw the scenes
Heard the screech of every bullet
You were every actor on the screen
Running for your life to the country's borders

Want to take you from that place
Where memories come back at night to haunt you
No one left to sympathize that you nearly died
Under the old man's orders

And all that I do is shed a useless tear
All that I feel is lonely pain
In my mind's eye your smiling face
How did you learn to laugh again?
I want to be with you again

Chapter Three

LEARNING TO BALANCE

Religious Tensions

"Religion is love; in no case is it logic." – BEATRICE WEBB

Lahiri Mahasaya was born to an upper class Brahmin family. Society was rigid in its insistence that a Brahmin could neither associate himself with those of a lower caste, nor with the Muslim or Christian. Every Hindu caste was expected to do the work designated by their ranking, and those who broke the rules of social convention were treated as outcasts.

And yet Lahiri Mahasaya insisted on giving his blessing to all who sought it. He taught that the same Soul was in everyone. He made no distinction between the highest caste Brahmin priest and the burning *ghat* owner who was classed as an "untouchable". He taught that the definition of a true Brahmin was a Yogi who had attained *Brahma* consciousness: therefore everyone had equal potential to reach the ultimate spiritual goal, whether born in a Brahmin family or not. Anyone who was ready for it could receive yoga *sadhana*, or Kriya practice, regardless of gender, social standing, religion or caste. He said that the main requisites were a human body and a genuine desire. As a result, men and women from every walk of life came to him for initiation.

Many people were angered by this and the Brahmin priests showered harsh criticism upon him for years. However, the practice which Lahiri Mahasaya taught was a provable science. His own purity and lack of hypocrisy ultimately won out, and social pressure was unable to prevent anyone who came to him from receiving his love and grace with complete equality.

Many of the devotees and disciples who came in the evening to hear Lahiri Mahasaya preach were Brahmins. But there was also a

man of lower caste amongst them: a lawyer named Ramprasad
Jaiswal. He liked to sit near the front in order to be close to his
beloved master, and this made the Brahmins indignant. One day, a
group of them told Jaiswal not to sit so close because his social
ranking did not allow it, but he refused to answer them.

A few days later, as the evening crowd gathered around to hear
him speak, Lahiri Mahasaya called Jaiswal to come and sit on his
mat with him. He made a point of moving over to make room for
the lawyer. Jaiswal did as the master bade him, feeling self-
conscious and inferior. At first the Brahmins were shocked and
angry, particularly one man called Rai Bahadur Girish Prasanna.
But the master's demonstrative action sent out a message which
could hardly be misinterpreted, and soon the Brahmins began to
feel ashamed of themselves. Rai Bahadur Girish begged his Guru's
forgiveness and pulled Jaiswal over to sit next to him.

Although with the passing of years Lahiri Mahasaya himself
became freer to bypass society's strict and discriminating laws
about the caste system, he remained practical about the issue.
There was a very clear division between Hindus and Muslims
which could not be ignored at the time. One story in particular
indicates that, whilst people from every walk of life entered and
left his house, the master knew that the reality in the rest of the city
was quite another matter:

Panchanan Bhattacharya was considered to be Lahiri
Mahasaya's chief disciple, for the master assigned responsibilities
to him as to no other, and he was also an advanced Kriya
practitioner. He often travelled from Calcutta to stay at the home of
his Guru in Banaras.

On returning to the house one morning after a bath in the
Ganges, Panchanan Bhattacharya saw a man in the lane a little
distance in front of him and could immediately sense that he was a
spiritual practitioner.[1] He increased his pace, wanting to catch up
with the man and converse with him. However, to his regret, the
man in front also sped up and soon disappeared from sight.
Panchanan Bhattacharya suddenly felt rather ashamed of himself
for being so drawn towards another yogi when his Guru was
Lahiri Mahasaya. When he got back he was met at the door by the

---

[1] A Kriya Yoga practitioner develops great sensitivity to the vibrations of others. This means that when
they meet or see someone, they can easily judge what kind of person they are.

great master.

'Could you not catch up with him?' Lahiri Mahasaya asked with a laugh, obviously joking with him.

Panchanan felt all the more guilty and began to cry loudly as he prostrated himself at the master's feet.

'Don't weep,' said Lahiri Mahasaya. 'That man was your brother-disciple. I have given him Kriya Yoga too. If you really want to see him, I can send for him.'

'No, I don't want to see him any more.'

'He is a Muslim,[2] and therefore did not want to meet you on the street,' the master explained with a kind smile.

THE HINDU Scriptures tell that there is no rebirth for the person who dies in *Kashi*. And this was the reason why a well-educated man of means came to Banaras in his old age because he wanted to die in the sacred city. He had been told about Lahiri Mahasaya and paid frequent visits to the house to hear the master's teachings. On one occasion, as the explanations of the *Bhagavad Gita* came to a close, he went to pay obeisance to Lahiri Mahasaya, saying that he had never heard anything like it, and had become a devotee. Despite being a self-realised master, Lahiri Mahasaya always showed respect towards elders in the way social custom demanded of the householder, and therefore told the man that it was not fitting for him to make *Pranam*.

One evening in the master's house, a disciple was explaining the spiritual meaning of the Scripture regarding death in *Kashi* according to Lahiri Mahasaya. He said that *Kashi* did not literally mean the city itself, but was a place in the body. It was a symbol of the third eye in the eyebrow centre, otherwise known as *Kutastha*. This was the place where spiritual vision was based. At the time of a Yogi's final death known as *Mahasamadhi*, all the *Pranas*, or airs in the body, having been controlled through yoga, were simultaneously drawn up to *Kutastha*, and the result was freedom from the cycle of birth and death, as the Scripture promised.

The old man was indignant and stood up. He found this particular teaching offensive, having always believed the literal meaning of the Scripture. Besides, he was so close to achieving his

---

2 His name was Abdul Gafoor Khan.

heart's desire to die in Banaras and thus end the cycle of birth and death.

'Please do not say this,' he implored, clasping his hands together. 'I am here to wait for my death, and with this opinion it seems you want to shatter the faith I have kept throughout my life.'

A few months later, the old man became very weak and asked Lahiri Mahasaya to visit him before death. When the time came, he had one request of the master.

'Please touch your feet on my head,' he said.

'What are you saying?' replied Lahiri Mahasaya, smiling. 'Before you die you must give me your blessing.'

The old man lifted up his hands in blessing, and passed away shortly afterwards.

❖ ❖ ❖ ❖ ❖ ❖ ❖ ❖

A tornado was ruthlessly tossing my long accepted and nurtured beliefs up into the air, returning them splayed and torn. It was shattering my faith and my vision of a future in the church; forcing me to step with trepidation on foreign ground and leaving me with the impossible task of picking up the incomplete remains of what seemed to be a puzzle. There was chaos where order had once been taken for granted.

Incessant coughing had just about sapped all of my energy. The most sensible thing would be to go home. But that was still out of the question. The mental struggle was causing more strife than my state of health, and could not be ignored. Going home would not resolve the question which had once more reared its ugly head regarding my stance on the healing of physical sickness through prayer alone.

Although Guruji understood that my reluctance to seek out a doctor stemmed from religious principle, he did not question it. This was no indifference though – I could feel his immeasurable care for my well-being. Somehow he understood the confusion which reigned in my mind concerning prayer and meditation; and it was clear that he also recognised my fear of the consequences of everything that I was learning.

My religion was based on the Bible and taught that Christ Jesus' words and deeds could be emulated even today. It claimed that its spiritual truths could be proved scientifically. Indeed, countless positive experiences resulting from prayer and trust since childhood meant that nothing could shake my firm belief in their validity. There were many people beside myself who had experienced wonderful healings throughout their lives without ever resorting to medicine. I viewed these healings as examples of God's love and care which increased the believer's faith and hope on the spiritual path.

Now I had established that the main aim of meditation was the destruction of ego, which coincided with my belief about the true function of prayer. But were my prayers for physical healing really free of ego? It was a painful question.

My prayers consisted of a mental affirmation of Oneness and spiritual perfection. Yet meditation was supposed to lead to *actual* Oneness. My linear thinking was being derailed.

Guruji's silence spoke volumes. I could not help noticing that there was no extreme in his behaviour or speech. No theory, nor religious doctrine, nor principle in the name of any cause. Just pure love, wisdom and balance.

So the day came when I finally talked to him about my dilemma. As I explained, my particular faith taught that physical problems could be healed through prayer and "spiritualisation of thought", and that every occurrence of illness was simply an opportunity to acknowledge and realise one's true spiritual being. Certainly medicine could cure too, but this dealt only with the symptoms rather than the underlying mental or emotional cause of the illness.

I asked whether or not yoga practitioners had any problem with the use of medicine. None whatsoever, was his answer. Prayer was good but there was no reason why it should necessarily exclude medicine. Taking medicine was not a denial of God's power. God was everywhere and in everything.

Guruji felt that a dogmatic abstinence of the use of medicine was a very hard path, and for the majority of people medicine was the most helpful method of curing physical problems. But the other extreme was not good either, if single-minded reliance on medicine excluded God and prayer altogether. There had to be a balance.

We had to find the humility to understand that we were tested in life, and the challenges which came our way were beyond our logic. Problems were not to be avoided and we had no choice but to face them square on. They provided the lessons we needed to propel us towards the reality of life. When we were in pain or trouble it should make us think of God. An Indian proverb said, "The body is a temple of disease." As soon as one form of suffering disappeared, the next was on its way. Guruji explained that the maxim was about looking beyond the human existence in order to question what is God, and whether there is a path to permanent peace; to make man seek the resting place of Soul and search for his real Being which is free from sorrow, disease and death.

It was therefore best to take whichever option enabled us to cope with life's difficulties, whether mental or physical, in a relaxed and confident way, which meant avoiding fanaticism and extremism.

I was beginning to see through the mist. Had I rather superficially believed that perfect health equalled spirituality? Had there sometimes been a reluctance on my part to admit when I was ill and needed help, because it seemed to pose a challenge to my faith?

The essence of yoga was balance, Guruji told me. Yoga was a provable science which had nothing to do with belief and everything to do with practice. Practice was the priority because it was a positive step forward on the path towards union with God. So if the yoga practitioner was sick, it was better to take medicine to alleviate the symptoms quickly and continue with practice, than to miss practice in the process of praying for healing. Taking medicine meant that the mind was not tied up in excessive thinking about a problem which could take time to heal. Prayer was helpful as a diversion for the mind, yet it was also a temporary solution. Permanent healing meant actually becoming one with God.

Though I felt torn at first, Guruji's idea and example of balance won me over and called for a descent from my high perch of principles. A doctor's appointment was made. To my surprise, I found that the acknowledgement of being an ordinary human being who needed and actually wanted a physical crutch eased a wearisome mental burden. After taking a medley of antibiotics for five days, my body began to mend. I could sleep normally again and the pain in my chest subsided.

Resorting to medical assistance previously would have made me feel uncomfortable and guilty at my own inadequacy in tackling the problem; a sobering indication that some measure of ego and pride had indeed developed in the subconscious, due to my long-held religious stance on healing solely through prayer. Conversely, my religion taught that ego, pride and guilt were the very obstacles to spiritual progress.

I could not help but remember the severe mental turmoil of some close relatives shortly before they died, because the fatal illnesses they faced refused to succumb to the prayerful approach to healing. Their lifetime history of complete reliance on God for physical aid had never let them down before. The awfulness of it had made me question not the religion itself, but how it was understood.

In theory, the spiritual truths of my religion were easy enough to read, affirm and "understand" on the plane of thought – but surely to attain the conscious level of Christ himself was another matter entirely. So if meditation claimed to hold the key to inner knowledge, the very least I could do was find out if such a thing was possible. There was nothing to lose and everything to gain. Keeping my thought positive and spiritually uplifted through prayer had always been helpful and still was; but doing so was clearly never going to make me a self-realised master. If practising meditation for a mere twenty minutes a day was the most effective spiritual path I had ever embarked upon – and it was certainly no easy discipline – what did I really know about God? What did I know about prayer and healing compared to a Yogi who had direct and profound experience of Him?

It took time before I realised what a positive and refreshing thing it was to have come face to face with my own ignorance. If it seemed as though some of my long-held views had come crashing down, then I should rebuild on the newly-laid foundations of personal experience gained through personal effort, rather than accepting borrowed knowledge and learned beliefs. Perhaps then there would be no contradictions.

From what I could gather from various books on spiritual masters of different traditions, it seemed that the truths of each religion would merge into one, if only they were properly understood. If the Buddha, Mohammed and Jesus had gathered in one room, would they have argued? I could not imagine so, since in one way or another they all said that they had *seen* God. They preached about the soul, about eternity and an ultimate truth; their common ground was direct experience. They told their disciples the same message in different ways through the limited medium of words, and religions were born as a result. But the intellect could never go deep enough; it was the barren rocky ground upon which the seed of differences and arguments grew, resulting in a harvest of religious wars, season after season. For words could be passed on from generation to generation, whilst true understanding evidently could not.

On the subject of religious differences, Guruji had an analogy:

Six blind men are washing an elephant. Each man is scrubbing a different part of the huge animal and is asked to describe what they think they are washing. The man washing the trunk says it is a pipe; the man occupied with the sides of the elephant says he is washing a wall; the man at the tail is convinced that there is a rope in his hands; the man washing one leg says he is standing by a pillar; the man at the ears thinks they are fans, and the man cleaning the broad back of the elephant says he is sitting on the floor.

The elephant represents God. The blind men are different schools of religious thought who believe they have the monopoly on God and a particular set of spiritual truths, yet venture no further than the limitations of human consciousness. Each man is correct, but their perspectives do not encompass the whole picture.

From a different angle, the men represent the human sciences which are seen as absolute. A medical practitioner knows from his own experience that, in most cases, five minutes after a man's heart stops, death is inevitable. Yet this law of nature is subordinate to the greater universal power which enables the Yogi to control his physical organs, stop his heart and circulatory system at will, and stay for anything from hours to weeks in the state of super-consciousness or *Samadhi*. Therefore, the cosmic power which belongs to God cannot be contained in religious theories any more than in things "scientifically proven" according to human reckoning.

There were many more questions which would have to be examined in due course: What was the cause of sickness? Was sickness illusion? Where did the power of spiritual healers come from? How did the Yogi heal? And so forth. But it was at least a start. My mind had been prised open a crack, but needed time and careful handling. A change was not going to occur overnight.

Why all the Secrecy?

"Give not that which is holy unto the dogs,
neither cast ye your pearls before swine,
lest they trample them under their feet
and turn again and rend you." – CHRIST JESUS[3]

Lahiri Mahasaya said that publicising Kriya Yoga was a fruitless exercise. He taught exclusively within the walls of his own house and always remained opposed to the idea of giving public lectures and speeches to the masses. There were several reasons for his insistence on secrecy and his wish to keep his yogic powers inconspicuous.

For one thing, some people were ready to receive Kriya Yoga whilst others were not. As it could only be given from authorised Guru to chosen disciple, the method itself was not to be shared with everyone. Initiates were instructed to keep quiet about Kriya practice, and to meditate in seclusion, since it was not a matter for idle curiosity.

Lahiri Mahasaya likened publicity in the name of Kriya to the way certain people of the city banged loudly on drums to inform people of the rising of the sun. It was unnecessary to announce something so obvious.

'Those who have eyes can see,' he would say. 'Those who are in need and are ready for this practice are bound to come.' Indeed, ever since Lahiri Mahasaya had started initiating Kriya Yoga, people had been drawn as if by a magnet to their Guru in Banaras through their own spiritual readiness, without any publicity whatsoever.

Many zealous disciples and devotees were in favour of forming *ashrams* and missions through a desire to see the fame of their master spread far and wide, but Lahiri Mahasaya chided them, saying that these were obstacles on the path to self-realisation and

---

[3] St. Matthew 7:6

nothing but the skeletons of true spirituality. He foretold that the practice of Kriya would be in danger of becoming obsolete through these in time. The objective would shift away from personal spiritual progress to organisational expansion. For a *sadhu* was not permitted to earn a living, and dependence on others could easily result in a preoccupation with money, fame and publicity.

The household *ashram* was the biggest *ashram*, he would say. There was no suggestion that supporting a family whilst practising yoga was an easy discipline, although it was easier to make progress if a disciple was free to practise in secret.

He insisted that no changing of one's own religion was to take place. The traditions of the various faiths were to be adhered to according to family background and environment. Lahiri Mahasaya taught that the Muslim should practise "namaz" (prayer) five times daily, the Hindu should sit in meditation four times a day, and it was the Christian's duty to kneel before God in prayer and read the Bible several times a day.

No new religion was to be formed, and certainly no proselytising in the name of Kriya Yoga. It was hardly appropriate to make a religion of something so far removed from conventional theory and doctrine as Kriya, since the method enabled seekers to find inner truth and liberation for themselves through practice.

MANY people in Lahiri Mahasaya's community, next-door neighbours included, were oblivious to the fact that they lived so close to a Yogi. Even some of his family members had no idea. It is told that two of his disciples regularly stayed in the same hotel in Banaras for seventeen years before discovering that they were brother-disciples, through a chance meeting one day at the entrance to the master's house.

Only the closest disciples were witness to his miracles to a greater or lesser extent; and there was always a deep purpose behind these. Although he could often have saved himself much physical trouble by using his yogic powers, he would instead go through the motions of a normal life. Such things were also highly effective in making people believe that he was a perfectly ordinary family man. The lesson to his disciples, however, was that whatever difficulties life presented, they were not to be avoided but dealt with; and despite any inconvenience, Kriya practice was not to be neglected.

An example of the extent to which Lahiri Mahasaya followed social convention was seen when his second son, Dukari Lahiri, became mentally ill in 1892. Several doctors pronounced Dukari's condition incurable. However, many people believed that a cure could be found in a village some distance away, where there was a certain *Kali* temple. So Lahiri Mahasaya made the necessary arrangements and set off on the long and arduous journey to the temple. Despite the considerable physical effort involved, when he returned to Banaras with the medicine, Dukari was not helped in the slightest by it. Finally, Kashi Mani Devi asked her husband why he had taken the trouble to get the medicine, when he could heal his son himself. In response, he gave Dukari a certain root, whereupon the young man made a full recovery.

ANOTHER time, Lahiri Mahasaya's nephew, Tarak Nath Sanyal, was suffering from a chronic stomach complaint. After an intensive course of medical treatment, he went to stay in Kanpur with his father's friend, in the hope that a change of location and climate would bring relief. However, during the visit, someone told him that there was no medical cure for his ailment: the only chance of recovery would be if a saint bestowed his grace on him, and there was one in Gorakhpur.

Upon hearing this, Tarak Nath started to pack his bag with hope in his heart once more. But his father's friend had overheard the whole conversation and asked him,

'Why are you going to a saint in Gorakhpur when there is a saint in your own family?'

'What do you mean?' asked a surprised Tarak Nath Sanyal. 'I am not aware of any saint in my family.'

'Don't you know about your uncle, Shyama Charan? He is a saint. And if you receive his blessing, there is no doubt that you will be cured.'

Tarak Nath recalled the numerous times that he had been to see his uncle and talked with him. No one ever had told him that he was a saint, and it had certainly never occurred to him either. As far as he was concerned, his uncle was an ordinary householder. However, the suggestion aroused his curiosity enough to make him set off immediately for Banaras.

Lahiri Mahasaya listened to his nephew's story and gave him some herbal medicine. Tarak Nath soon became well, and shortly afterwards received Kriya initiation. He became so engrossed in practice that his uncle had to remind him not to neglect his worldly duties. He told him that he had to work for a living and not become dependent on other people. Thereafter, Tarak Nath Sanyal became a successful English teacher, and in time also an advanced yoga practitioner.

LAHIRI MAHASAYA interpreted a total of twenty-six holy Scriptures[4] in the light of Kriya Yoga, and had his disciples Panchanan Bhattacharya, Prasaddas Goswami and Mahendranath Sanyal write these down and publish them for distribution. Not wanting to create any publicity for himself, he would not allow them to print his name on them; instead he instructed them to use their own names.

❖ ❖ ❖ ❖ ❖ ❖ ❖ ❖

'Do you believe in your grandfather?' Guruji was asking.
  'Of course I do.'
  'Do you doubt that your great-grandfather and your great-great grandfather existed?'
  'Not in the slightest,' I replied, wondering what this had to do with Kriya being a secret method.
  'But have you ever seen them?'
  'No ...'
  'That's exactly what I want to say. Many people deny the existence of God on the basis that they haven't seen Him. But using the same criteria, I could just as easily deny the existence of your great-grandfather. That's different, you may say, because he is dead. But usually our human tendency is to reject things that we haven't seen with our own eyes, is it not?'
  'I guess so.'
  'Tell me, who made all of this nature? You may not see any

---

4 These twenty-six Scriptures were: *Bhagavad Gita*; Guru Gita; Omkar Gita; Abadhuta Gita; Kabir Gita; Taitiriya Upanisad; Tejabindu Upanisad; Dhyanabindu Upanisad; Amritabindu Upanisad; Niralamba Upanisad; Manusanghita; Astabakrasanghita; Charakasanghita; Sri Sri Chandi; Yantrasar; Tantrasar; Linga Purana; Yogi Panini on Education; Kabir Doha; Japaji; Sankhya Darsan; Patanjali Yoga Sutras; Gautam Sutras; Vaisesika Darsan; Mimangsartha Sangraha and Vedanta Darsan.

Creator with your eyes, but there are signs everywhere in this world: if we see footprints on the ground leading up to a hut, we guess that someone is inside; a dog follows a new scent with excitement to find its source. Nature can teach many lessons, but it is up to us to decide if we wish to pay attention and discover the cause of everything.

'Many people believe in God, and plenty of others do not. But actually it is not a question of belief or disbelief. Suppose you are drinking a glass of water, and I tell you that there are particles of bacteria in it. You know that bacteria cannot be seen with the naked eye, so if you have a scientific mind, you will not take my word for it. You need an instrument, a microscope, and then you can discover for yourself whether or not I am telling the truth.

'It is not possible to see God with the naked eye either. If you want to see Him, you have to practise. The body is the instrument, and Kriya Yoga the method whereby we gain knowledge for ourselves. The place of inner vision is in the eyebrow centre. In India we call this spiritual eye *Kutastha*. Jesus was talking about this place when he said, "the light of the body is the eye: if therefore thine eye be single, thy whole body shall be full of light."[5] But practice is very subtle. It is easy to talk about God, but the experience one finds in practice is impossible to explain to others ...'

Guruji's voice trailed off and I waited for him to elaborate.

'So that is why Kriya Yoga is secret. There is nothing which you can achieve by talking about it. Personal experience is non-transferable. What is the use of passing on a method to someone who has no real inclination to practise? People tend to ridicule and dismiss things which they cannot and do not understand. Kriya Yoga is something precious: it is not a casual thing or a matter for curiosity.

'Lahiri Mahasaya did not initiate everyone who asked him for Kriya, because not everyone could receive it. A lifelong commitment is required. Only the Guru can know and judge who has the strength and readiness to practise. Secrecy protects the method from misuse. Another reason is that it cannot be passed on to many people at once. If someone changes the method or the tradition in which it is to be given, the disciple will gain nothing

[5] St. Matthew 6:22

compared to the benefits of the original Kriya Yoga. It is secret for these reasons only; there is nothing mysterious about it, actually.'

I contemplated what Guruji had said to me before about the Western idea of meditation being very "different". Self-realisation was occasionally the aim, but even then some believed it could be attained by meditating for five minutes a day, or in the presence of a group, or that it was something which could be passed on to others instantaneously. Yet apparently it was not as easy as people often imagined. Five minutes would never be enough. Not even a gathering of sages could become self-realised simultaneously. The individual's spiritual potential was reached according to *Karma* and the Guru's guidance. The *Bhagavad Gita* said that one amongst thousands truly sought to know God, and it was rare for even one of those seekers to attain the goal.[6] It was no common occurrence. And the master who had trodden the pathway to the Absolute would never say that such a journey could be undertaken in one lifetime. It was a matter of rebirth.

My mind had become considerably calmer. But although Guruji's words made perfect sense and had convinced me that there was indeed nothing mysterious or negative in the fact that the Kriya method was secret, it remained unclear what the implications would be as far as church membership was concerned if I became a practitioner of meditation.

'Don't change your T-shirt,' Guruji said to me that day as I tried to explain the latest dilemma. He wanted to make it clear that the Kriya disciple did not need to be obvious about practice. In the same way, Lahiri Mahasaya advised his disciples against becoming *sadhus* and abandoning their household responsibilities, because practice was about internal change and had nothing to do with an external change of dress.

Lahiri Mahasaya had said that anyone who was ready could practise. There was no requirement to give up or change one's religion. So in theory, there should not be a problem. As a scientific path of meditation, Kriya Yoga would deepen the way in which I understood my religion. It would involve hard discipline and personal effort and there would be no need to talk about it with other people.

---

[6] "Out of thousands one perhaps strives for perfection, and one perhaps out of those who strive actually finds me." *Bhagavad Gita* XII:3 (Lal)

Yet I was not entirely convinced that it was going to be so simple. For a start, although a number of Christian churches in the West had opened their doors to some types of meditation, mine was not one of them. Although the method itself was not to be shared, which made sense, people were bound to find out that I was meditating on a regular basis when I got home. My outlook had changed so drastically that church friends would probably think I had wandered off the spiritual course like a lost sheep. No doubt it would appear to them that the spiritual potential evident in previous years had gone to waste; an active future in church work squandered.

'It shouldn't matter what people think,' I tried to tell myself. And yet it mattered already. I could see a mighty blow to the ego heading in my direction.

'You have a saying in the West: "an empty mind is the devil's workshop" '

Guruji observed, interrupting my thoughts.

'Yes, we do,' I replied. Upon brief reflection, perhaps that was the reason I had been suspicious about learning meditation in the first place.

'The church had a reason for teaching this to the people. It is a misunderstanding and yet it served a useful purpose. Meditation is not something for everybody, and if the mind is not ready, nothing constructive or spiritual will be achieved. They didn't want people to sit around doing nothing and building castles in the air, wasting their time. But as an unfortunate result of this expression, many people who do not understand the goal of meditation tend to assume that it is a useless preoccupation in which nothing is achieved.'

Guruji paused for a moment.

'And yet meditation is the most worthwhile occupation of all. The Yogi who has control over his mind and can go into real "empty space" is the happiest person in the world. He has no cares and becomes the most useful person in society. Everyone seeks his help, because he alone stands above the laws of nature.'

AND WHAT of salvation? According to the orthodox Christian viewpoint, although admittedly not my own, everyone was a sinner. You had to believe in Jesus and accept Him into your heart.

'Which heart? This human one?' Guruji asked me, tapping his chest.

'Uh, no, not exactly.'

'Then how will I accept Jesus into my heart? What is this heart?'

It took me a minute to consider the question.

'I guess people mean consciousness, or soul.'

'Okay. Now, can anyone accept Jesus into their heart or soul? If I say I am accepting him right now, is that true?'

'Well, no, of course there has to be a feeling,' I answered. 'A surrendering of the ego. Faith and devotion. A sense that a higher force or guiding master alone can help and save the believer from hell.'

'Yes, it is a matter of the ego. But if I say I am surrendering, that my ego is dissolved, is that true? If I tell you that I have conquered my anger, will you believe it? My question is, can ego and anger disappear as a result of my affirmation that they have gone?'

I shook my head.

'So how will we conquer the ego to enable this surrender in the "heart"?'

This was getting tricky. I was not aware that people thought too much about how to conquer the ego. As far as I knew, the concept of salvation in most Christian denominations was essentially simple: believe and be saved. Know your place in the cosmic scheme of things as a sinner, which certainly ruled out getting above yourself by practising to become a master. Jesus died on the cross for the sins of the world. He did the work for us. Follow the precepts and love your neighbour. End of story.

'Few people are interested in finding the real meaning of salvation. Who is really prepared to follow Jesus Christ and know the cross he bore? They have a very superficial idea. Similarly, here in India people go to a guru and want to be saved and healed. They want to stay on the physical level and yet be freed of their pain and unhappiness.

'The cross is a symbol. It represents the "I" which is crossed; the destruction of ego.' Guruji was demonstrating what he meant with a gesture: holding up his right index finger and using two fingers of his left hand to cut it like scissors. 'This kind of salvation requires an effort to get up and walk with discipline. Then belief turns to faith. Faith turns into real devotion and finally there is understanding.

'Think of all the millions of living creatures in the world. My Guruji, Satya Charan Lahiri, used to say how strange it was that some animals had been given the instinctive knowledge to save themselves from drowning, whereas humans had to learn to swim. Man had to use his intellect rather than his instinct. Was there not a lesson to be learned from this difference in nature? Why was God kind to the animals and harder towards humans?

'It is obvious to us that a mother can provide food for her children, yet she cannot swallow for them. They have to eat for themselves. Likewise, we know that a student who learns diligently is rewarded by his own efforts. He cannot use his knowledge to help a fellow student during an exam.

'In India we have a parable about two farmers,' continued Guruji. 'One prays to the gods day and night to send some rain because there is a drought. He offers flowers and sweets to his deity, and when the rain does not come the first season or the next, he loses his crops and land. He thinks that the gods are angry with him and that he and his family are being punished. The second farmer is also in trouble because of the drought. However, he thinks carefully and it occurs to him to dig a well. Although the rains do not come, he is able to save his crops.

'The second man is like the Yogi. He knows that knowledge and power come from inside. He is the master of his destiny, because he seeks salvation through his own efforts.'

TO MY immense joy, Guruji told me a few days later that he was prepared to initiate me into Kriya Yoga the following week. By now there was no doubt in my mind that I wanted it more than anything else the world had to offer. As I told Guruji, if there was a choice between becoming a billionaire or receiving Kriya practice, I would choose the latter every time. That was when he laughed and told me that I did not understand.

'If I give you Kriya, I am giving you everything,' he said.

He was right. I did not understand.

Initiation

"We seek not to imitate the masters,
rather we seek what they sought." – FAR-EASTERN PHILOSOPHY

Married couples were usually initiated together. Lahiri Mahasaya said that when husband and wife both received Kriya, it was easier to make progress on the path of *sadhana*. The charge for initiation was five rupees and the master established this as a set amount. Babaji had instructed him that, with human nature as it was, Kriya Yoga should not be given for nothing. A closed fist symbolised the inability to share or receive anything, whereas the open hand could both give and accept. Therefore the physical contribution of giving money was a form of penance which reflected the inner desire and willingness to make a new start in life. The disciple had to see the inestimable value of Kriya and accept responsibility for hard practice from the moment of initiation.

Five rupees was a substantial amount in those days, and some poor people did not have the means to pay. Lahiri Mahasaya always knew when this was the case and would advance the money before the time of initiation. When a wealthy disciple heard about this, he gave one hundred rupees to be used to help poor devotees desiring initiation.

In India, the disciple fortunate enough to find shelter under the wings of a true spiritual Guru feels in his heart that whatever he owns belongs to the master, in return for having given him something priceless. And in this spirit, Lahiri Mahasaya reserved all the initiation money which he received for Babaji, his own Guru. Babaji did not come personally to Banaras but used to send a *sadhu* from his group of devotees to collect the money now and again.

Babaji talked frequently to these men about Shyama Charan Lahiri. One man in particular became quite jealous of Babaji's high praise for this disciple and questioned it, since Shyama Charan apparently lived the life of an average householder. Babaji said nothing at the time, but sent him to Banaras to collect the initiation money a few days later. The *sadhu* felt quite pleased about this, and imagined how he would put Shyama Charan to the test.

When he arrived in Banaras, however, Lahiri Mahasaya was

immediately aware of what was in the *sadhu's* mind. He sat up all night with the *sadhu*, discussing the deepest of spiritual topics until sunrise. By the time Lahiri Mahasaya suggested that they should go to the Ganges for a bath, the *sadhu* understood perfectly why Babaji so often talked about this great householder Yogi.

KAILASH CHANDRA BANDOPADHYAY was a Brahmin from Bishnupur in Bengal, who lived and taught in the home of a man named Shiv Das Bhattacharya. Being a devotee of Lahiri Mahasaya, Kailash's greatest desire was to receive Kriya Yoga from the master. However, he was poor and could not afford five rupees, so he asked Shiv Das to lend him the initiation money.

'I'll lend it to you if you give me Kriya Yoga after you have received it,' said a jovial Shiv Das.

Kailash agreed. But when he went to Garureswar on the day of his initiation, Lahiri Mahasaya's facial expression was serious.

'You have promised to pass Kriya Yoga on to someone, so I will not initiate you,' he said.

Kailash was dumbstruck. 'Really, I won't tell anyone,' he insisted, horrified at what he had done. But trying to change Lahiri Mahasaya's mind was useless and Kailash returned home feeling devastated.

A while later he summoned up the courage to tell Shiv Das what had happened. He told him that Lahiri Mahasaya knew everything and would not initiate him because of what he had promised.

'But I was only joking when I said you had to tell me about the initiation. Go and take Kriya,' answered Shiv Das.

Nevertheless, a lesson had been learned, and Kailash received initiation shortly afterwards. Later in life he became a renowned Yogi.

ANOTHER Brahmin who settled in Banaras after retirement used to spend most of his days doing *puja* and worship. He would visit Lahiri Mahasaya every morning after his bath in the Ganges in order to ask for Kriya Yoga initiation, and every day he would receive the same answer. Lahiri Mahasaya repeated that he would get initiation when his time came, but for now he should continue with his prayers and worship. The old man would go away feeling despondent.

Then an elderly woman arrived one day who likewise requested Kriya initiation. Lahiri Mahasaya told her to come the next morning after taking a bath. When she had gone, a disciple who had overheard decided to ask about this matter.

'Master,' he said, 'why is it that you continually refuse to initiate the religious-minded man who comes every day? And yet you immediately agree to initiate this woman who has come here for the first time today?'

'The Brahmin's inclination towards religion began only recently. His external worship is the best thing for him for the time being,' answered Lahiri Mahasaya. 'But the woman practised yoga meditation in her past life, and is ready for Kriya now. Therefore it is my duty to initiate her.'

Lahiri Mahasaya would say that for a starving person, food was the most important thing; and likewise those who were hungry for liberation from the bounds of the earth needed Kriya Yoga more than anything else.

❖ ❖ ❖ ❖ ❖ ❖ ❖ ❖

We were discussing the reason why not everybody could be given Kriya Yoga. That to be pious was one thing, but to develop an interest in meditation was quite another. Where did this "readiness" for Kriya come from?

It was a question of a person's state of mind, Guruji told me. Some people's minds were in a static state, influenced primarily by ignorant and injurious thoughts of darkness, or *Tamas*; others were ruled by a wild and active mind, whilst tending to seek enjoyment and power, known as *Rajas*; and finally, there was the dynamic mental state called *Sattva*, implying serenity and calmness, and a powerful intrinsic capacity to control the waves of the unruly mind.

All three of these mental states, known in India as the *gunas* of nature, were usually present in man to some extent, but for the person whose mind was ruled predominantly by the qualities of *Tamas* or *Rajas*, meditation was not usually possible. The *gunas* were the yardstick which determined an individual's potential for spiritual growth.

Before the yoga practitioner attained *Samadhi* and had risen above each of these states of mind, *Tamas* and *Rajas* could still influence the mind to a greater or lesser degree: explaining why, due to negativity or laziness, there was sometimes a reluctance to practise, whereas at other times there was no mental hindrance whatsoever; or even why some people could start Kriya practice and soon be distracted again by the pull of the material tide.

The ever-changing *gunas* were with us as ropes tied to our souls, said Guruji. The mind could be ruled by *Sattva* one day and by *Tamas* the next, and this was independent of our religious convictions. But it was true that the search often began with a belief in God and an openness to embark on a path which ultimately led to Him. Some day, due to the influence of the previous life, everyone was bound to ask questions about their true identity and the reason for our existence on earth. A burning desire to know what constituted real happiness and freedom, and to discover the "Cosmic Energy" which we call God, would inevitably be fulfilled.

'If you are very hungry,' Guruji continued, 'you will relish the food on your plate. But as soon as your stomach is full, the same food will begin to give you pain if you continue to eat. In this way, when we have enough of one worldly experience, we look for the next, until we learn that there is no lasting enjoyment in these things.'

He paused for a moment.

'Perhaps you have heard the story of Gautama Buddha.[7] Born a prince, his parents named him Siddhartha, and an astrologer predicted his future: either he would become an illustrious king or a renowned spiritual master. His parents were horrified by the second possibility. They were determined that their son should achieve fame as a noble king. So they shut him up in the palace in the hope of sheltering him from every unpleasant side of life which might lead him to question his perfect existence. He was given every kind of material comfort anyone could ever desire; riches, luxury, music and entertainment were all his.

'One day, Siddhartha was looking out of a window when he saw a body being carried on a stretcher and a mournful procession trailing behind it. He was perturbed by the sight and asked his servant what was happening.

---

[7] Gautama Siddhartha attained enlightenment in about 500 BC after which Buddhism was founded in northern India.

' "It is someone who has died, of course," replied the servant. "They are taking the body to the burning *ghat* for cremation."

'Now, death was an entirely foreign concept to Siddhartha and the event prompted his famous quest for the meaning of life. He ran away from the palace and went to the forest. He spent time with *sadhus* and in solitude, searching for the truth of existence. Many years later, he attained the state of enlightenment, or *Nirvana*, under the tree in Bodhgaya.

'So despite the fact that Siddhartha's parents made great efforts to prevent their son from becoming a spiritual master, they could not change what had to be. His time had come; he was driven by something inside him to find enlightenment, or *Nirvana*.'

It Was hard to establish how the authorised Guru decided whether or not a disciple was ready for initiation. The most elusive factor for me was that to some extent it depended on the "influence of the previous life". But clearly, the Guru alone was able to judge a person's true motivation, sincerity and desire. The aspiration to enter the spiritual field of Kriya had to have strong inner roots, and this was not necessarily something which devotees could know or see for themselves. Guruji had put me to the test and made me wait several months for initiation. Some people were given initiation within days, whilst others had to be patient for years. Many people came to the yoga studio asking for the method, but I knew that not everyone received it by any means.

Guruji said that certain basic qualities were necessary, such as love, honesty, non-violence, dedication and discipline. Being already present, these qualities could develop and grow through Kriya practice. If they were completely lacking, as in the person whose mind was mainly influenced by the *Tamas* state, they would not want to do practice anyway – it would be against their nature: and as he put it, "you can't change a stone into a diamond". Laziness, over-eating and having no control over sex made the body weak and were examples of obstacles to practice. There had to be an inner potential to balance: as *Krishna* tells Arjuna in the *Bhagavad Gita*,

"Arjuna, this yoga is neither for him who overeats, nor for him who observes a complete fast; it is neither for him who is given to too much sleep, nor even for him who is ceaselessly awake."[8]

Lahiri Mahasaya especially encouraged young people, saying that to receive Kriya Yoga in youth was a great advantage to success, because there was plenty of time to practise and develop. But Guruji also mentioned that he rarely initiated anyone of a young age who was not reasonably "settled". Because of the promise to do practice on a daily basis, it was best if the disciple had completed his education and was financially independent. We needed a roof over our head and an income, even if these things were secondary to our main purpose in life, he said.

When he saw that a person was ready for Kriya Yoga, Guruji said that it was his duty to initiate them. Readiness to receive the practice was essential to a disciple's success. Initiation was like a planted seed which would always remain with the individual, but its germination and growth was ultimately up to the disciple. Guruji emphasised that it was far easier to receive Kriya Yoga than to keep it up. Many people tended to think that it would be nice to do practice on a superficial level, but within a short time they were swept away by the attraction of material things once more and therefore unable to keep their promise.

'The majority of people,' Guruji added, 'are at the stage of using their intellect and of asking endless questions. They rather spend their time arguing over the "chicken and egg" question. Even if they are told that God is present in man and that the temple of worship is the human body, they will not grasp this truth and want to practise Kriya.[9] It will be of no interest to them that Kriya *pranayama* is essential to self-realisation and that God can only be realised through this *Prana*, or cosmic force in man. They will not understand that it is not possible to intellectualise about yoga. The only criteria is that one has to practise.'

JOHN and I were initiated together on the evening of 14th March, 1995. Since morning I had been apprehensive and excited, and finally it was time to make our way to Man Mandir Ghat. According to the Indian tradition for such ceremonious occasions, we went carrying our offerings of garlands for the seven portraits

---

[8] VI:16 (Gita Press)
[9] "These philosophers think it is awful if we go beyond thought; they find nothing beyond thought." – Swami Vivekananda

of the masters in Guruji's meditation room, fruit for the altar and a monetary contribution. Life was turning the page to a new chapter.

Before being given the method, we had to make our promises to Guruji. We were told not to reveal the method to anyone, and to practise twice daily for the rest of our lives. The minimum time would be fifty minutes. We should be conscious, Guruji told us, that life never gave enough time for practice next to work and family. In order to progress on the Kriya path, it was necessary to make time.

Then we were to read a chapter of the *Bhagavad Gita* daily. Doing so was important because this ancient Indian Scripture was specific to the holy science of Kriya Yoga and would give clarity to the journey, side-effects and goal of practice.

THE INITIATION took two hours. It became clear within the first five minutes why Kriya was not something in which anyone could take a casual interest and try out once or twice. No wonder it involved a commitment to practise. For one thing, the timing was absolutely essential. Like having to learn to walk a certain distance in a set amount of time without looking at your watch. This really was a scientific method.

My first attempt to practise that night was a disaster. What was supposed to take about fifty minutes took two hours. There and then I wondered if I would be able to keep it up, it was so difficult. A monstrous effort was needed to try again the next morning.

Progress comes with perseverance however, and in spite of my ever wandering concentration, within a few days I was starting to sit for the correct amount of time. Perhaps there was hope for me yet.

INSPIRATION (A Song)

Don't be concerned because I'm meditating
Making the journey to my heart
It is a secret lonely place
I go there to find my real face
It's time I found the courage
To make a new start

A storm is beating and rocking my boat
I'm struggling alone to keep it afloat
As long as I live day for day
In giving in to fear
The sky will never clear

I'm not concerned because you're hesitating
I'm watching as my horizons expand
When I find peace on the inside
I can see it on the outside
Feeling assured that life has the plan in her hand

The clouds are clearing, sky is turning blue
The love within is leading back to you
Guided across the sea
Until tranquillity
Is flowing out of me

Don't be concerned because I'm meditating
Follow me, listen to your heart
Close your eyes, see your secret place
Travel till we meet face to face
There is nothing to fear that can keep us apart

The storm is over, my boat is ashore
Never knew such inspiration before
Nothing ever has the power
However rough the sea
To take my peace from me

Chapter Four

YOGIC PURIFICATION

Love-Service

"I make firm the devotion of any worshipper,
no matter what his form of worship is.
And with that devotion he progresses in worship,
and obtains his desires, which I alone offer." – BHAGAVAD GITA[1]

Lahiri Mahasaya maintained that when Kriya Yoga was practised with true sincerity, internal character purification would result as a natural side-effect. The disciple would grow in sensitivity and loving-kindness, in wisdom, faith and devotion. Negative traits such as lust, violence and jealousy should diminish until they were erased completely. Such changes were genuine as they happened effortlessly through practice, and were not a matter of external sacrifice or renunciation. If such effects did not gradually become apparent, then the practice could not be called real yoga.[2]

The master did not equate devotion to a human feeling or emotion. Instead, he taught that devotion was first truly experienced at the time of self-realisation, when the practitioner became one with the Absolute in *Samadhi*.

Lahiri Mahasaya told his disciples, "[In the absence of] direct visualisation; love, devotion, affection are not born ... Again, does love and affection evolve from the very moment a child is born? Certainly not. The more one sees the child and rears him the more love and affection towards the child will develop gradually without the parent realising it. How is true love and devotion by

---

[1] VII:21,22 (Lal)
[2] The Indian Scripture Manu Smriti (a book related entirely to the practice of Kriya Yoga and giving guidance to the Kriya practitioner) names ten qualities of *Dharma*; these attributes should develop in an individual as a direct result of Kriya Yoga: fortitude, forgiveness, restraint of mind, non-stealing, purity, restraint of the senses, wisdom, knowledge, truthfulness and non-anger.

conjecture possible for the God you have not seen?"

He said that devotion was far more than a temporary focusing of thought on the divine, but rather a pure and constant state which occurred naturally as the mind ceased to look upon the external world. As internal vision developed, the individual experienced Self in *Kutastha*, or in the "spiritual eye" which existed in every human being. With steady practice, the practitioner's attraction for this inner world grew. He added,

"Thus [in the absence of] visualisation of the God-entity, actual love and devotion are not possible. It is exclusively dependent upon *Pranakarma*."[3]

Lahiri Mahasaya told his disciples that Kriya should always be practised with love and dedication, never mechanically. Quality was far superior to quantity; in other words, the spirit in which one did practice was more important than the time spent. And likewise, he always accepted the devotion shown to him by disciples in the spirit in which it was given.

One devotee who came to listen to his Guru preach every evening was a poor tailor named Matru. He wanted to serve Lahiri Mahasaya in some way, so he brought him two *betel* rolls. Lahiri Mahasaya happily chewed the *betel* after his lunch and dinner. Seeing this, Matru resolved to bring *betel* every day for the rest of his life. He continued to do this even after the master had left his body, bringing his offering to the house with a prayer and such sincere devotion that tears filled his eyes every time he did so.

Then there was a barber named Bhairav who was slightly mentally disturbed. Whilst others went to a different barber, Lahiri Mahasaya still had him come to his house every day to shave him, and to do some household chores. One day Bhairav was going up the stairs with a clay pot filled with water when he saw Lahiri Mahasaya approaching. As they passed each other, Bhairav tipped all of the water on the Yogi's head, chanting, "Hara Hara Mahadeva", which is a *Mantra* used to worship *Siva*. The master, understanding, smiled silently and carried on up the stairs to change out of his wet clothes.

Bhairav had been observed by a devotee who lived in the house, Amarananda Bramachari. He was angry that the barber had done

---

[3] Quotations on devotion from *Purana Purusha* by Dr A. K. Chatterjee.

such an apparently disrespectful thing, and when Lahiri Mahasaya was out for his walk by the Ganges, he tied Bhairav to a pillar and started to beat him. The poor man cried loudly at the top of his voice. Kashi Mani Devi heard the commotion and demanded to know the reason why he was beating Bhairav. After Amarananda had explained, she reprimanded him, since the master himself had not made an issue of it. It was clear that Bhairav was mentally ill and had not been knowingly disrespectful.

THERE was a woman disciple, Abhaya, who came from Calcutta to request her Guru's help. She had given birth several times, but none of her children had survived. She longed for just one child who would remain healthy. No answer was forthcoming as she sat before Lahiri Mahasaya and told him the cause of her unhappiness. It seemed that he was elsewhere, but finally he broke his meditation and again she repeated her heart's desire.

'You will get a daughter, Abhaya, but you must listen very carefully to my instructions and follow them without fail.'

'I will do anything you tell me,' said Abhaya, seeing a glimmer of hope.

'Your daughter will be born between twelve and four o'clock in the morning. You must light a lamp in the labour room before you give birth, and it must not be allowed to extinguish before the sun rises. Don't forget,' said the master.

As Lahiri Mahasaya had predicted, a daughter was born to Abhaya in the early hours, and she remembered to light the lamp before giving birth. But afterwards, she and the midwife both slept and did not see when the flame began to flicker. However, the door opened with a bang and Abhaya awoke with a start. She rubbed her eyes and was surprised to see Lahiri Mahasaya pointing at the lamp and saying,

'Look, Abhaya, the lamp is about to go out. Remember what I said. Fill it with oil.'

Abhaya got up sleepily and filled the lamp, by which time her Guru had disappeared. She cried in gratitude.

Soon afterwards when she talked about what had happened with Lahiri Mahasaya, he said to her, 'You disciples are in the habit of neglecting your responsibilities. Learn to be more watchful.'

Through the notes he made in his diaries, it is apparent that

Lahiri Mahasaya also gave help to many couples who were not able to have children.

❖ ❖ ❖ ❖ ❖ ❖ ❖ ❖

A simple man goes to see a Brahmin priest for advice. He asks to be taught how to pray so that he will see God.

'What an idiot he must be,' thinks the priest to himself, 'to imagine that he will ever see God! I shall play a trick on him.'

So the priest tells the man that the only way to see God is to hit a certain milepost with a bamboo stick without fail every day.

The man thanks the priest and goes home. Having taken the advice to heart, he does exactly as he has been told. He walks to the milepost day after day to administer it a hefty blow with the bamboo stick, his faith unwavering that one day he will see God.

One evening he is attending a feast, and in the middle of it he suddenly realises that he has forgotten to go to the milepost that day. Hurriedly excusing himself from the festivities, he goes to perform the usual ritual.

The next day he goes back to the priest and thanks him profusely.

'Why on earth are you thanking me?' asks the priest in surprise. 'Anyone would think that you had seen God!'

Tears of joy stream down the man's face.

'But I did see Him! It happened yesterday as I was hitting the post with my bamboo stick as usual.'

The priest realises that the man is telling the truth and is forced to face his own error and pride.

'How can it be?' he thinks to himself bitterly, weeping tears of self-pity. 'Though I have prayed to God all my life, I have never seen God, but this uneducated man hit a milepost and was blessed with a vision!'

RIDDING the mind of its desires is central to spiritual progress, and one of the most important things in Kriya Yoga is to practise without expectation. Even when we practise in pursuit of enlightenment, this represents a desire which must be erased. But doing so is no easy task. It is human nature to want everything in a hurry. Meditation is called on to bring visions, levitation and self-realisation, and fast.

Yet this does not happen, through Kriya Yoga or any other method of meditation. At least, not to a beginner like me. It was not long before I had grasped one of the reasons for the necessity of a solemn pre-initiation promise to practise daily for life.

There was no escaping the fact that progress was painfully slow in the beginning. For a start, I had to endure the discomfort of pins and needles until I became accustomed to sitting for a long time in the same position. Then it took months before I felt I could smoothly integrate all the limbs of the method into one whole and begin to cultivate the process. Much practice time was squandered in despairing over my inability to keep the mind where it was supposed to be, and in protesting over the huge mental effort required for such concentration.

As soon as the initial technical difficulties had been somewhat ironed out, I found that most of the time I was sitting down to practise without really knowing why I was doing it any more. I told myself endlessly that I really ought to sit down and get on with it because I had promised to do so. And yet I fought it. I failed to see the point. Nothing exciting ever happened during practice.

I knew that these internal fights were born of pure laziness. Occasionally though, when I acknowledged this and allowed myself to surrender my desire for results, the most unexpectedly satisfying practice sessions occurred.

If it had not been for the promise and the knowledge that Guruji expected it to be kept, I probably would have thrown in the towel within the very first month. It helped immensely to be with friends who could relate to these initial difficulties. Cord said he had also found Kriya tough at the beginning and was tempted to give up many times. What had kept him going was a promise to himself to give it one year's fair trial, and if there was no result or change to be seen by then, he would not continue. Now after just five months of practice, he assured me that he would not be giving up. There were ample rewards, so I should take heart.

However, I continued to compare my own modest results with Cord and John's greater-sounding achievements and often bemoaned my lack of progress to Guruji. Not only could they sit for much longer periods, but they could also concentrate better during practice. They already had some unbelievable experiences and visions to tell; why was I not getting any?

Sympathy was not forthcoming. 'Don't compare yourself to others,' he would say. 'Don't be distracted by expectations about what you think you should receive. Carry on, carry on. It isn't the quantity which matters, but the quality. Don't let practice become mechanical. Remember the parable about the simple man who hit a post with a stick and saw God. The key is to practise with love and devotion.'

THE FIRST effects of practice came in the form of visions. Though not heavenly ones, as I might have hoped. Instead, closing my eyes in meditation was like looking into a mirror which reflected back the most uncomfortable truths about my inner self.

One day during practice I had a flashback to the previous year. A telephone conversation with my sister replayed in my mind. I had tried to give her some well-meaning advice from my religious high horse at a time when she was very unwell. She had made it emphatically clear that she did not share my opinion, which had not particularly surprised or bothered me at the time.

Yet now suddenly it was obvious how much my words had hurt her feelings and how self-satisfied they must have sounded. I was certain that she had not forgiven me for such a show of insensitivity even now. Tears fell as I wrote her a letter of apology that same day, hoping to ease my conscience.

Meditation was about personal revelations. Far too many of them. It was about looking in that mirror which imaged the kind of person you were, as opposed to the kind of person you thought you were; actually feeling how people had hurt because of past things said and done; humble-pie on your plate twice a day with the bitter taste of honesty; having to swallow it and realising that you were nowhere near deep meditation yet. This was just the beginning.

NO WONDER that I was not a pleasant person to be around for quite a while. Hyper-sensitivity can result when you discover that you do not like yourself as much as you thought you did. In addition, practice was bringing a new issue to the boil concerning my church.

Perhaps it was during Kriya Yoga practice, or perhaps it was at other times, but the beliefs of other denominations, which had previously contradicted the doctrines of my own faith, were beginning to make perfect sense. The once clear lines between the various religions were fading so that the boundaries between them were barely distinguishable.

To someone who had always revelled in the challenge of intellectual religious debate and who had clutched with a steely grip to what she knew was right, the simple realisation that no one path was superior to another came as something of a shock.

Of course many different religious philosophies were necessary to cater for the huge range of individual needs and mental constitutions, although each led in the same direction and to the same goal. Each was rooted in Truth. It was natural to follow whichever route one found most helpful. The question was, which one could I best relate to now?

The answer was, none more or less than the other. I fought this unexpected broader perspective, unsure of what it meant. Kriya Yoga itself was not a religion, but had effectively transformed the analogy about the blind men washing the elephant into something more than mere theory.

My religion had been the right path for me up to now. It taught respect and tolerance towards every religion, love towards all mankind, and did not endorse proselytising. I was supposed to be a dedicated and active church member. But should a Christian be able to subscribe to the point of view of a Buddhist? Or that of a Hindu, or a Muslim? I kept thinking about what Guruji had said about not changing my T-shirt, and wondered how that was going to be possible. The *dedicated and active church member* part might cause a problem. It would take time to figure this one out.

FOR SOMEONE who had been so very much in possession of the answers upon first arriving in India, it was most unsettling to find these replaced by a never-ending stream of questions which I had never realised existed. It was a side-effect of being in Guruji's presence.

He had always been remarkably patient as I bombarded him with questions, but particularly since Kriya initiation he frequently declined to answer and would tell me instead to do practice, explaining that the answers would come automatically. 'This is what I want,' he would say, and remind me that true salvation was about inner learning.

Guruji's words soon began to ring true, and in the early stages it was certainly the most rewarding element of Kriya Yoga. My mind was beginning to find some peace. And as a result, when a question arose in my head, the answer often came as a reflex either immediately or a short while later. From the inside.

Detachment

*"The steadfast in wisdom, the steadfast of mind,
giving up the fruits of action, achieve the perfect state."* –
BHAGAVAD GITA[4]

At the end of the nineteenth century, there lived in Banaras a famous saint and renunciant named Trailanga Swami. Otherwise known as a "living *Siva*", he resided on a river *ghat* in the holy city for the last fifty years of his life, though it is claimed he was approximately 287 years old when he left his body. His disciples were few, but a swarm of devotees regularly flocked to the corpulent Yogi for a blessing, bringing him food and money.

He was an extraordinary character. Sometimes he would not eat anything for days, but when he did he could consume anything up to forty kilos of food in one sitting. When he was thirsty, he would drink from the river and as he did so, it was said that the water would change into milk. Furthermore, he used to walk to the other side of the Ganges on the water's surface, and had the ability to stay under water for hours on end.

Trailanga Swami refused to wear any clothes and he took no notice of repeated police warnings to cover his extremities. It was much to his amusement when the English police commissioner decided one day that he should be charged with indecency and put behind bars.

Trailanga Swami asked the commissioner,

'I am *Atman*.[5] How do you intend to lock me up?'

It was a good question. To the fury of the police commissioner,

---

4 II:51 (Lal)
5 lit. Soul.

the Yogi was observed walking around on the roof of the jail, moments after having been incarcerated in a cell.

'Lock him up again!' the commissioner ordered his men. 'And this time use more locks!'

But there was no preventing a second escape, and this time the cell in which Trailanga Swami had been imprisoned was flooded.

'Why is your cell flooded?' asked the police commissioner, joining the saint on the jailhouse roof.

'Why did you lock me in?' retorted the Yogi. 'I needed to urinate. That is the reason for the flood.'

'And how did you escape this time?'

'Soul cannot be put behind bars,' came the reply.

The commissioner made a note in his book that the Swami was not to be locked up again, as it was evident that he was not subject to any kind of worldly constraints, least of all bars and padlocks. The event appeared in the local newspaper, which was how many people learned about Trailanga Swami.

A DOCTOR named Gopal Chandra Bandopadhyaya was a disciple of Lahiri Mahasaya. Together with a friend he often went to visit Trailanga Swami, and one day they decided to ask their Guru to come and see the famous "living *Siva*". Lahiri Mahasaya agreed and the three of them went to Panchaganga Ghat where the Swami was sitting in silence as usual, surrounded by his devotees.

Upon seeing Lahiri Mahasaya approach, Trailanga Swami got up and walked quickly to meet him. The two *Mahayogis* embraced each other. They spent a few moments together without exchanging a single word. Then the Swami went back to where he had been sitting and Lahiri Mahasaya returned to his home.

There was huge curiosity amongst Trailanga Swami's following. They had never seen him embracing anybody before, nor had they ever laid eyes on Lahiri Mahasaya. As the Swami rarely spoke, he used to answer questions by writing on a slate. To the amazement of his devotees, since he had never been known to praise anyone before, he now wrote that Lahiri Mahasaya was a greater Yogi than he. For whilst he had renounced worldly possessions including his undergarments in the quest for Truth, Lahiri Mahasaya had attained self-realisation whilst living as a family man. This was the more remarkable achievement.

Soon after this meeting with Trailanga Swami, Lahiri Mahasaya's fame as a householder Yogi began to spread to the far corners of India.

DURING his lifetime, the King of Banaras, or *Kashi Maharaja*, sometimes paid visits to both Trailanga Swami and another famous renunciant in the city whose name was Bhaskarananda. The King would talk about his Guru Lahiri Mahasaya with so much love and devotion that Bhaskarananda wanted to meet the great householder Yogi for himself. However, since society forbade a renunciant from entering any household, he begged the King to convey his deepest respects to Lahiri Mahasaya and to pass on a request for the Yogi to come and see him. The King did so, and although Lahiri Mahasaya was reluctant at first, after numerous requests he finally agreed. Later, having learned the principles of Kriya Yoga, Bhaskarananda received initiation.

PANCH KORI BANDOPADHYAYA was a devoted disciple who wanted to become a *sadhu*. The atmosphere in his home was not particularly conducive to Kriya practice and he thought that it would be better to become a renunciant. So he visited his Guru one day to ask for permission.

'Which will weigh more on your body, the *sacred thread* you wear over your shoulder as a Brahmin now or the long matted hair you will grow as a *sadhu*?'[6] Lahiri Mahasaya asked his disciple. 'Do you want to be a *sadhu* for the sake of publicity, so that people will recognise and respect you? Is this the way you want to earn a living? Don't start depending on charity. Forget this foolishness. Live in a household, earn your own money, and do Kriya practice. A person who thinks that they have become detached simply by donning the ochre robes is no more a *sadhu* than the donkey whose hide is the same colour.'

Panch Kori went away hanging his head. However, later in life he became an advanced practitioner and well known as Kesha Bananda Brahmachari.

THERE were several reasons why Lahiri Mahasaya would not

---

[6] A *sadhu* does not have his hair cut as a sign of bodily detachment.

advocate the path of renunciation, despite the traditional link with spiritual life:

Firstly, the principle of doing *sadhana* for God-realisation whilst living as a householder in society was the way of life of Indian saints in the Pauranic age, over five thousand years ago. In accordance with the ancient Vedic culture he emphasised that man's social and family duties were not to be neglected or ignored. The disciple was required to practise twice daily in order to steadily develop his spiritual potential whilst earning his living so he could meet his worldly responsibilities.

Yet for centuries, saints and yogis had retreated to the mountain caves and forests to practise yoga, and as a result the practice of self-realisation had become exclusive and lost to the layman and society at large. This was the reason Babaji had given him Kriya Yoga with the strict instruction to maintain his domestic existence. Yoga was to be re-established in society now that the mental climate was favourable.

Lahiri Mahasaya lived up to this ideal by supporting his family through teaching, and never making any attempt to pass on his responsibilities to anyone else. He expected other practitioners of Kriya Yoga to follow suit. Having sufficient income of his own, he had no expectations of his disciples as far as money was concerned. Gifts from the heart were the only ones he accepted.

He was aware that many gurus had no source of income other than through donations from disciples and were therefore preoccupied with the amount of money their disciples would bring. This kind of dependence on others only caused unnecessary worry, he said, and was an additional reason why many *ashrams* and missions were often engrossed in creating publicity for themselves.

Secondly, Lahiri Mahasaya knew that the old ideology practised by the yogis was a hard and unrealistic option for the majority of people. The luxuries of society had weakened man's constitution to the extent of making him unlikely to seek God through renunciation. By having to suppress his desires, the *sadhu* had to shun all but the most basic of material possessions. Yet the master said that physical hardship of this nature was likely to disturb the mind and therefore be a hindrance to effective meditation. It was important to take care of the physical body properly, since it was the instrument through which self-realisation was possible. He would ask, 'Where is the necessity of renouncing the world in the search for God, when He can only be found in the body?'

Furthermore, the renunciant could not afford to put a foot wrong, for fear of being ostracised, whereas the householder enjoyed more freedom. The many *sadhus* who came to Lahiri Mahasaya had to make secret nightly visits for teachings and initiation, since Indian culture did not allow a renunciant to enter anyone's home; something which has not changed to this day. However, the master would tell these *sadhus* who had already taken their vows of renunciation to stay in their *ashrams*, just as he would tell the householders to stay in their homes.

'We need physical support on our journey through life,' he would say, 'but our real aim is to realise God. So do practice with heartfelt determination and make it your priority, but do not cease to live as a member of society.'

IN INDIA there is a widespread belief that to eat the left-over food from your Guru's plate is to receive his benediction. This was the reason why a disciple who invited Lahiri Mahasaya for lunch cooked huge quantities of rice, vegetables and fish, and purposely piled the dishes high on his Guru's plate throughout the meal. He had planned that he and his family would partake of the remaining food and be blessed accordingly.

Knowing the man's thoughts, Lahiri Mahasaya threw away his leftovers. After washing his mouth and hands he said,

'I am not going to give you what is left on my plate. Krishna says in the *Gita* that real benediction for the soul is when all your pain and suffering comes to an end. Unstable *Prana* is the cause of every pain, and through *Pranakarma*[7] you will get stability and freedom from the cycle of birth and death. You should work for this kind of benediction instead.'

Another disciple present at this meal resolved to invite Lahiri Mahasaya for lunch at his own home. He prepared a number of tasty dishes, including several fish curries. During the meal he pressed his Guru several times to take some. At first Lahiri Mahasaya did not respond, but then it seemed as if he had

---

7 *Pranakarma* is another term for Kriya Yoga practice. Lahiri Mahasaya never let anyone eat left-over food from his plate.

suddenly heard what was said, whereupon he got up from the table. The disciple was alarmed and asked his Guru why he had left his food.

'Since when do I eat fish?' Lahiri Mahasaya said. 'Why are you giving me fish to eat?'

The disciple humbly made *Pranam*. He told his Guru that he had been present at the other disciple's house who had served fish for lunch, and on that occasion he had observed the master partaking of it with apparently no qualms whatsoever.

Lahiri Mahasaya was surprised. 'I ate fish? But I am fully vegetarian!' he said.

Indeed, Lahiri Mahasaya was a strict vegetarian and always had been. To the disciples, the event was further confirmation of just how genuinely detached their Guru was from the world.

AFTER spending each night in *Samadhi*, it was Lahiri Mahasaya's habit to walk to the Ganges for a bath at Ranamahal Ghat with his closest disciple Krishna Ram, before returning to his room for more meditation. The intensity and effect of *Samadhi* on the human body is something quite incomprehensible to the non-practitioner, and Lahiri Mahasaya tended to stagger somewhat on those early morning walks to the river. This curious sight caused a *betel* seller whom they always passed to frequently joke about how drunk this Bengali *baboo* was so early in the morning. His amusement was replaced with profound respect, however, when the man later came to understand who Lahiri Mahasaya was, and discovered the cause of his apparent intoxication. He subsequently became a disciple.

Lahiri Mahasaya was returning to the house after a morning bath one day when a man stopped him in the lane and pointed out that his foot was bleeding profusely. The master tore a piece of cloth from his *lunghi* and bandaged his foot before continuing to walk home.

Once back in his room, he sat and entered the state of *Samadhi* again. A while later, someone passing the room observed a thin rivulet of blood running from the master's room through a hole in the wall. In alarm, they entered the room and after calling many times the master finally came out of *Samadhi*. Upon being asked if he was hurt, Lahiri Mahasaya's expression was blank; he could not remember. The disciple pointed to the blood on the floor.

'Ah, yes,' replied the master, suddenly remembering. 'I was coming back from the river and my foot was cut, so I tied a cloth around it.'

Indeed, his foot was badly cut, and still bleeding. He had tied the bandage around the wrong foot.

THERE was a *Siva* temple in the grounds of the house which Kashi Mani Devi visited daily. She performed the rituals of *puja* in the way she had learned from childhood. Lahiri Mahasaya had always encouraged her to worship as she desired, although since Kriya Yoga was an internal practice, he did not pray to the deities as she did.

Kashi Mani Devi's father Vacaspati Devanarayan Sanyal was a disciple of Lahiri Mahasaya. At the age of a hundred, when he was on his deathbed, Kashi Mani Devi insisted that her husband go and offer the last *Pranam*, customary as a gesture of respect to elders. But Lahiri Mahasaya only chuckled in response. When the time came for the final visit, the master did not make *Pranam* as his wife had demanded. Kashi Mani Devi was dismayed at the apparent lack of respect, oblivious to the fact that her husband was actually respecting her father's wishes. The old man had long since ceased to allow his son-in-law and Guru to give him *Pranam*.

During a visit to her parents in Banaras, the married daughter Harikamini Lahiri developed Asiatic cholera, much to the fear and consternation of her mother. In those days many people died of this disease, so Kashi Mani Devi asked her husband if Harikamini would survive. Lahiri Mahasaya did not answer, nor did he seem particularly affected by the news of his daughter's ill health. However, as a result of Kashi Mani Devi's incessant demands that he save their daughter, he instructed his wife to grind a certain root with three black peppercorns and give it to Harikamini to drink.

But Kashi Mani Devi's mind filled with doubts about the nature of her husband's prescription. If their daughter died, she considered, she would have to admit to her daughter's in-laws the strange concoction which she had administered as medicine, whereupon they would surely be blamed for the death. So she finally decided to ignore Lahiri Mahasaya's instructions and gave Harikamini the medicine prescribed by the doctor instead. The following day, Harikamini died.

At the time of her death in the evening, Lahiri Mahasaya was with his disciples as usual, throwing light on the *Bhagavad Gita*. The chief disciple, Panchanan Bhattacharya was reading. Suddenly a great crying and commotion was heard coming from the room above, interrupting the proceedings. Someone asked what had happened.

'They are crying because my middle daughter is dead,' said Lahiri Mahasaya.

'That will be enough for today,' said Panchanan Bhattacharya, closing the *Bhagavad Gita*.

'They are doing their work: you do yours,' said Lahiri Mahasaya. It appeared to everyone present that he was completely unaffected by his daughter's death. He was prepared to continue elucidating the Scriptures as if nothing had happened. But the devotees and disciples present did not demonstrate the same calm. They could not concentrate under the circumstances, so Lahiri Mahasaya softly told his disciple to close the book.

The following day, Lahiri Mahasaya's brother-in-law Raj Chandra Sanyal came to visit the house.

'Ordinary people feel grief at the passing of someone close – do you not feel the same way?' he asked.

Lahiri Mahasaya smiled at the question.

'Everyone feels sorrow but it is different for the Yogi,' he answered. 'A marble which hits a hard surface is deflected, whereas it can easily sink into soft ground. Certainly, a Yogi has to face many kinds of adversity, but grief and other woes do not have any impact on him. He is not affected in the same way as the ordinary person.'

THERE was no questioning Lahiri Mahasaya's detachment from the physical plane of existence. He explained to his disciples that such mental remoteness from earthly circumstances was a natural occurrence in Kriya Yoga, when the principal air in the body, known as *Prana-vayu*[8] eventually becomes permanently established

---

[8] There are 49 airs in the body, all of which stem from *Prana-vayu*. Five of these airs are major and five are auxiliary to them. *Prana-vayu* is the principal one of these 10 airs, as it permeates the thoracic region and head including the sensory functions of eyes, ears, nose and mouth. When the Yogi leaves his body in the final departure or *Mahasamadhi*, it is this air which he raises to the point of *Kutastha* in order to cease the function of the body. He is subsequently free from the cycle of birth and death.

in the head through long practice of *pranayama*. The Yogi becomes settled in *Kutastha* or in a state of union with God, and his concentration is always at the point between the eyebrows. The result is genuine detachment from the material world.

'Think of the Rajasthani women who carry pitchers on their head,' the master would say. 'They converse and joke with each other whilst walking and yet keep their concentration on the water vessel to keep it from falling. Similarly, you should keep your mind fixed in *Kutastha* whilst going about your worldly duties. But remember that the women would not be able to carry the pitchers on their heads without practice, just as you cannot keep your mind in *Kutastha* and perform other tasks without yoga *sadhana*. It depends upon your practice of Kriya.'

❖ ❖ ❖ ❖ ❖ ❖ ❖ ❖ ❖

There was certainly no shortage of *sadhus* in Varanasi. They were usually clothed in saffron robes and wore simple wooden sandals. Some clutched the trident of *Siva* in one hand as a support; most had long matted hair twisted up on top of their heads into something resembling a bird's nest. Their faces were often smeared with sandalwood paste, and fat worship beads, or *Rudraksa mala* hung from their necks.

Some were to be seen worshipping at the shrines, or engrossed in reading the Scriptures, oblivious to the world passing by; they gave the impression of being genuine in their spiritual search. Others, on the other hand, were to be found resting on stone slabs in the old lanes offering to pose for the camera at the cheap price of two rupees, or were down on the *ghats* drinking *chai* with Western travellers.

Without doubt, renunciation was still an integral part of Indian culture. I learned that it had its roots in the ancient Vedic philosophy of spiritual education which divided a Hindu's life into four *ashrams* or stages, each having a duration of twenty-five years. This system suffered a decline during the British occupation of India.

The first was *Bramacharya ashram*. After receiving the *sacred thread* at the age of eight, boys were sent to live with a guru where they were taught grammar, Sanskrit and the Scriptures. At the end of this stage, the young man was expected to have completed his studies. Meditation was also important, for during this period the student was to become firmly established in spiritual consciousness.

The second was *Grihastha ashram*, when worldly duties had to be fulfilled as a spiritual householder. The stability of the other *ashrams* depended upon it. It was the time for marriage and family. You had to earn a living and take care of your social responsibilities, whilst remaining detached from the fruits of work and free from expectations and desires. Life's joys and sorrows had to be faced without being thrown off balance.

Then came *Banaprastha ashram*. From the age of fifty to seventy-five, a person was to begin to mentally prepare for the coming exodus into the "forest". This meant that it was time to begin disconnecting oneself from family and society, in readiness for the fourth and final stage of life or *Sanyas ashram*. For the final years of a human life were to be spent in complete dedication to the spiritual life as a *sadhu* or *sannyasi*, having broken family ties and become detached from the material world.

Thus, when the time came to leave kith and kin, your worldly responsibilities towards the parents who raised and saw to your education had been fulfilled. Of course, if a young individual had no desire to get married and the parents had died early in life, there was nothing to stand in the way of a life of seclusion.

Lahiri Mahasaya further elucidated this system of dividing a human's life into four stages. He explained that its significance was universal when interpreted spiritually, for the *ashrams* were actually about states of consciousness attained in Kriya Yoga:

At the beginning, the focus was in *Brahmacharya ashram*, where the true master was the inner Self, and the master's hermitage the place between the eyebrows or *Kutastha*. In *Grihastha ashram*, the family house represented that state of balance or tranquillity, where the practitioner perceived everything within and without as being equal. *Banaprastha ashram*, or retirement to the solitary forest, was indicative of the state of *Samadhi*, when the breath was raised upwards to the forehead through the spinal cord. At this stage, the mind "dissolved" and Oneness was attained. Finally, *Sanyas ashram* symbolised the mind which was completely free of ego and desire. This was genuine renunciation – a state of consciousness which occurred naturally through Kriya Yoga, stemming from neither reason nor intellect.

Furthermore, the master showed through his own example that renunciation was but a symbol of detachment from the material world. The mere act of leaving family and possessions was an easy and meaningless step as far as the true sense was concerned. The orange robes of a *sadhu* were conspicuous but not necessarily indicative of a person's level of consciousness. True spirituality and detachment were inner states attainable though Kriya *pranayama* and no self-realised householder would have the need or desire to show off.

'BUT WHY,' I asked Guruji rather indignantly one day, 'did Lahiri Mahasaya appear to be drunk after meditation?'

'During Kriya Yoga practice, a fluid called *Amrit* or "holy nectar" is secreted from the brain which the yogi catches on the tip of his tongue,' Guruji replied. 'It is absorbed by the whole body and has an intoxicating effect. The practitioner feels ecstasy. The secretion gives the body nourishment, so it is possible to control hunger, thirst and the five senses. It is also very good for health.

'We have stories in our Indian Scriptures about how *Lord Siva* became "drunk". Most people don't know in which way he was drunk and so they take the superficial meaning. During the Hindu festivals of *Sivaratri* and *Holi*, many people drink *bhang lassi* to get high. It is a nice excuse to consume alcohol and *bhang*. Yet *Siva's* condition is actually a representation of the yogi who drinks this water from the brain in Kriya Yoga *sadhana* and becomes spiritually intoxicated as a result.'

So that was what Cord and John referred to as "brain juice". Cord had already caught a drop or two, and of course the effects had been spectacular. Perhaps it would happen to me too some day, I thought wistfully.

Nevertheless, some of those other stories had not seemed fitting of a perfect spiritual master either.

'How come Lahiri Mahasaya saw one foot bleeding profusely and then tied a bandage around the other?' I wanted to know. 'And what kind of a vegetarian eats fish by mistake?'

'Listen,' said Guruji. 'When the mind of an ordinary person registers pain, concentration automatically focuses on the wound.

Therefore it seems inconceivable that someone could tie a bandage in any place other than where the injury actually occurred. However, the fact that Lahiri Mahasaya did this shows complete detachment from his body. It is very rare. His concentration was so completely with the Absolute in *Kutastha*, that there was no feeling of pain in his foot.

'The state of concentration which results when a Yogi attains super-consciousness is beyond the imagination of the ordinary person. Food is essential for the physical body, and even a Yogi has to eat. But whilst eating, the Yogi's concentration may be elsewhere.

'We project our own level of consciousness onto others. It is virtually impossible to recognise a genuine master who has chosen to live discreetly as an ordinary member of society. Our expectations correspond to our own understanding, so we tend to presume or simply misunderstand.'

There did not seem to be much point in asking, 'Why was Lahiri Mahasaya so indifferent to his own daughter's death?'

Presumably, if a master has overcome life and death in this world and reached a state of omniscience whereby his daughter's given life span is known to him, then it is no wonder that he can remain unmoved by her death. As far as he is concerned, it is no more than a transition to her next life. For a Yogi, the cycle of birth and rebirth is only broken through *Mahasamadhi*, or final exodus from human existence.

So PICTURE a man who frequently sits with closed eyes and appears to be asleep. Imagine him at lunch-time with his family, when he misses huge chunks of the conversation and cannot always follow the chatter and laughter. He often appears to be tired and "spaced out". Physically present, but most definitely mentally absent.

'He is so forgetful, it drives me crazy!' exclaims Guruji's wife. They have argued because when she sent him to the market for the vegetables, he returned with three heavy bags. An enormous quantity which will never keep. Particular distress is caused by the cucumber. What is she supposed to do with five kilos of cucumber, for heaven's sake?

His own mother told me one day about the time he ate at least sixteen *chapatis* for lunch. She could hardly believe how hungry he seemed, but she went on cooking, thinking that he would tell her to stop when he was full, as he usually did. When he finally got up he was oblivious to the enormous quantity he had eaten.

Such apparently negative idiosyncrasies were confusing and seemed unfitting companions of wisdom and spiritual authority at first glance. But the time was not far distant when such things would begin to make me wonder about Guruji.

The Mahasamadhi of Lahiri Mahasaya

"So when this corruptible shall have put on incorruption,
and this mortal shall have put on immortality,
then shall be brought to pass the saying that is written,
Death is swallowed up in victory. O death, where is thy sting?
O grave, where is thy victory?" – ST. PAUL[9]

'What is death?' a devotee asked Lahiri Mahasaya.

'Death is when the dynamic *Prana* becomes still, yet the consequences of past actions remain. *Samadhi* is also a kind of death, but in that state the consequences of past actions are no longer existent.

'We inhale and exhale continually. Each inhalation is a symbol of life, just as each exhalation is a symbol of death, since a person has to die when he is no longer able to draw breath. Thus life and death exist at every moment for the living being, caught in the continual cycle of birth and rebirth. Yet nobody realises that such death is not real, for it is inevitably succeeded by rebirth. Actual death is to return to the source and merge with *Brahma*, the Creator. Only when *Prana* is completely and permanently stilled, is there no rebirth.'

IT WAS fairly late in their marriage when Kashi Mani Devi began to realise the magnitude of her husband's spiritual realisation. She awoke one night and could not see him anywhere in the room. Wondering where he was, she lit a lamp and saw him levitating in *Padmasana*[10] in a corner of the room. Immediately, her eyes filled

---

[9] 1 Corinthians 15:54-55
[10] Otherwise known as the lotus position.

with tears of humility and shame, for not having recognised his spiritual standing as a *Mahayogi* before. She considered how she had treated her husband as an equal through scolding and contradicting him, and arguing with him: all past behaviour towards him which may have been disrespectful now flooded into her mind and caused her great worry. As soon as she could speak to him again she begged his forgiveness and asked for Kriya initiation. The next day Kashi Mani Devi became her husband's disciple.

KASHI MANI DEVI was doing *puja* in the *Siva* temple one day when she heard someone behind her. When she turned around, she was surprised to see her husband, as it was unusual for him to come to the temple at that time. He was smiling softly.

'My work is done and the time is coming for me to leave this world,' he told her gently. 'I am going to leave my body in six months. You are the only person I am telling now, but do not grieve for me. After I have left my body, do not let them move me from the room. I will come back. If you cannot see to this, then I want to be buried in my house.'

Kashi Mani Devi did not attribute much importance to his words. It was certainly not the first time he had mentioned that he would leave his body and return to it again. She thought that he was probably in a spiritual trance, and therefore not fully conscious of what he was saying.

However, the closest disciples were also informed three months before Lahiri Mahasaya planned to leave his body in *Mahasamadhi*. As the days went by and only one month was left, a carbuncle appeared on the master's back. Kashi Mani Devi sent a message to Tinkari Lahiri, who was working in Delhi, to come quickly. The family doctor Purna Chandra Bandopadhyaya was called, but his medicinal treatment proved to be ineffective. A second doctor arrived from Calcutta, Lahiri Mahasaya's disciple Hem Chandera Sen. He wanted to operate but the master smiled and said that it would be better to let nature take its course. The disciples applied Lahiri Mahasaya's own *neem oil* to the growth. In the past this antiseptic lotion had cured everyone who had been given it without exception, but on the master himself there was absolutely no improvement. Everyone began to feel that the situation was hopeless.

The disease was unrelenting and the *Mahayogi's* health steadily declined. A constant stream of anxious devotees and disciples came bringing gifts and offering their services. Lahiri Mahasaya continued as ever to give them his time and to answer their questions. Krishna Ram remained at his master's side almost continually.

It was recorded by Panchanan Bhattacharya, chief disciple of Lahiri Mahasaya, that before the great master took *Mahasamadhi* and was lying sick in bed, there was no smell whatsoever from his urine or stool discharge. Even the pus from the growth on his back was completely odourless. He understood that it was one sign of the Yogi's perfection in all the *Siddhis*; contrary to appearances, he was no ordinary person. The master would leave his body to be present everywhere.

Nonetheless it was incomprehensible to those around him that the *Mahayogi* should now be suffering from a fatal disease and lying in bed, considering the many occasions when he had helped and healed others and shown himself to be free of physical bonds. However, one day Tinkari Lahiri came to discover that appearances were deceptive regarding his father's illness.

It happened the day before *Mahasamadhi* in the afternoon. He had recently arrived from Delhi and was taking care of his father. Lahiri Mahasaya was lying on the bed and seemed to be in great discomfort. Tinkari was in the next room but could see his father due to a mirror on the wall. He was astonished to observe him suddenly get up from the bed as if he were not sick, walk over to the bookshelves, pick out a few books and look through them before climbing back into bed.

Tinkari marched indignantly into the next room.

'If you are healthy enough to walk, why are you lying in bed using a bedpan?' he scolded. 'You could at least go as far as the drain!'

'Where were you?'

'I was watching you from the other room.'

Lahiri Mahasaya smiled. 'Everyone has a desire to serve me, therefore I am lying in bed. Otherwise their desires will not be fulfilled,' he said.

BHUPENDRA NATH SANYAL once told his fellow disciples the story of how Krishna Ram was asked of Lahiri Mahasaya what he desired:

Krishna Ram had served his master faithfully and almost continually for the last months prior to the *Mahasamadhi*. He had felt that Lahiri Mahasaya would not receive proper service if he was not there to give it personally. The master told Krishna Ram that he was very pleased with him and that he would get whatever he asked for. Krishna Ram's eyes filled with tears and his body began to shake. Choked by emotion, he could not get the words out at first. But when Lahiri Mahasaya pressed him again to name his heart's desire, he humbly answered that he wanted nothing more than a place at his Guru's feet.

'You will get it,' answered Lahiri Mahasaya with a smile. Krishna Ram prostrated himself, holding his master's feet with his hands.

Krishna Ram lived in solitude on the bank of the Ganges at Ranamahal Ghat following his Guru's passing. Tinkari Lahiri used to pay him the occasional visit and observed the yogic *Mahasamadhi* of Krishna Ram many years later.

A CLOSE disciple of Lahiri Mahasaya, Swami Pranabanada of Udaipur, heard that his Guru was preparing to leave his body and wanted to leave for Banaras immediately. He was packing his bag hastily when Lahiri Mahasaya appeared in the room.

'Pranabanada, don't hurry; it is no use. I will have left my body before you get to me,' he said.

The man could not hold back the tears.

'Why are you weeping?' asked the master. 'I am only leaving my physical body. The *Sadguru* exists forever.'

BEFORE taking *Mahasamadhi*, Lahiri Mahasaya also appeared to Panch Kori Bandopadhyay in Haridwar. The master was surrounded by light and told his disciple to come to Banaras quickly. Panch Kori obeyed and arrived shortly before his Guru was about to leave his body.

In this way, Lahiri Mahasaya made many of his disciples not only aware of his imminent physical departure, but also conscious of the level of yoga *sadhana* he had reached as a final example. They could thus better understand that he was truly free of all human ties and would continue to exist even after his earthly form was no longer visible.

Nevertheless, there was a great deal of distress amongst many disciples and devotees who felt that their only real support would be taken from under them if he were no longer there.

'This yoga *sadhana* is immortal. It has always existed in the past and it will continue to exist in the future,' Lahiri Mahasaya told them with half-closed eyes, the day of *Mahashtami*.[11] Many people had gathered at the house because this was the day he had chosen to leave his body.

'Kriya Yoga will never disappear, and when you are walking on this path you will always be protected and supported. The more man progresses on the spiritual path, the more he will be interested in *Pranakarma*: for Kriya is a scientific practice.

'From time immemorial people have been striving to free themselves from this world. In the future, this great immortal yoga which my *Gurudeva* gave to me will be practised in every household. Man will begin to work for his liberation and the path of salvation will become broad once more.'

He was sitting in the lotus position on his wooden bedstead. He gazed at his disciples in front of him and saw them weeping inconsolably.

'Do not lament for me,' were his last words to the disciples. 'My time has come. It is only my physical form which will be gone. I am always with you.'

It was September 26th 1895, at twenty-five minutes past five in the evening.

ACCORDING to Indian culture, when a *sadhu* dies he can be buried, but the married householder must be cremated. So although there was some discussion whether or not to bury the master in his house as would be fitting for a *Mahayogi*, the final consensus was to take him for cremation. For Lahiri Mahasaya had lived as a family man and used to place the greatest emphasis on following the social customs and responsibilities required of a householder.

When the time came and last respects had been paid according to Hindu custom, a long funeral procession made its way to

---

[11] *Mahashtami* is the eighth day of the *Durga puja* festival.

Manikarnika Ghat on the bank of the Ganges. The stretcher was laid on the funeral pyre ready for cremation. The body of the *Mahayogi* was not stiff. Tinkari placed the fire torch in his father's mouth, as tradition still demands of the eldest son.

The grieving women stayed at home with Kashi Mani Devi, who suddenly remembered her husband's words to her in the temple six months previously. The funeral procession had left some time ago, so she begged her brother to run to the *ghat* and stop the cremation. But he arrived too late; the body was already burning.

Some time later, the disciples did find mention in Lahiri Mahasaya's diaries of a desire to re-enter his body if he left it before taking *Mahasamadhi*. One such entry written years before he actually left his body read, "If my body dies today, bury it underground, I may rise again." It suggested that the master had not yet reached the point of ultimate realisation needed to take *Mahasamadhi*, and was planning to complete the journey by returning to the same physical body if he died beforehand.

Despite this, *Mahasamadhi* was the Yogi's final departure, and Lahiri Mahasaya had never wavered from his principle to follow the social conventions demanded of the householder. A burial would have been inconsistent with the way he had lived his life, and realising this, Kashi Mani Devi's brother Bhagwan Sanyal was able to comfort her. She felt as though she had made a dreadful mistake.

'Don't feel sorry,' he told her. 'He must have said this thing whilst in a state of Soul-absorption. It is another sign of his detachment from this world. There would have been no difficulty had he been a renunciant. But our culture says that a married person has to be cremated. It could not have happened this way if it had been not his final will. He must have changed his mind and placed a curtain over your memory.'

MANY of Lahiri Mahasaya's disciples became famous throughout India. One of these, Nilmadhab Mukhopadhya, became known during his lifetime as Swami Pranabananda. As a disciple he attained such a high level of yoga *sadhana* that it became difficult for him to do his job. He wanted more time to do practice, so he asked his Guru for advice. Lahiri Mahasaya told him to apply for early retirement, giving any reason he wished, although this seemed an impossible proposal as no one qualified for retirement without having worked the required number of years. Mukhopadhya did so, giving ill health as his reason. The next day the doctor and higher authorities accepted the application without question. He was then able to practise freely until he finally became a famous Yogi.[12]

There was also Sai Baba of Shirdi, Maharashtra, who always kept his master's name secret. He was a follower of Guru Nanak. In his lifetime many people knew him as Saidasbaba and went to him to receive his blessing, but very few knew that he had obtained Kriya Yoga from Lahiri Mahasaya – a fact which has been gleaned from the great master's handwritten diaries.

By now it was mid-March and the temperature in Varanasi was rising steadily by the day. We were looking forward to the cool mountain air and tranquillity of Nepal. A group of us, all Guruji's disciples, had decided to travel together. The Himalayas sounded like the ideal place to regain my physical strength and mentally prepare for the journey home. It was just a question of getting there, because although the medicine had improved my condition considerably, it was still virtually impossible for me to step outside the guest house without my stomach turning at the slightest unpalatable odour, and this was difficult to avoid in the narrow lanes of the old city.

We were due to leave at midnight. Seven hours by train to Gorakhpur, then a five-hour wait, and finally a bumpy thirty hours by bus to Pokhara. Hardly an appealing thought, even in a state of fitness. But Guruji had assured me that I could make it and there was nothing to do but trust.

A few hours prior to our departure I lay in bed in the guest house dormitory, barely able to move and wondering why Guruji

---

12 This was a most exceptional case. It should in no way be concluded that Lahiri Mahasaya frequently helped disciples to leave their jobs, for he did not. Pranabananda was extremely advanced in Kriya Yoga, and with his Guru's blessing he was able to devote his time fully to practice, thus enabling him to develop further maturity in *Samadhi*. For although many people may practise Kriya, few people ever attain such a high state.

Therefore the principal message to be drawn from this story is that the words of a *Mahayogi* always come true: despite the apparent impossibility that Pranabananda would be granted early retirement, his request was accepted just as Lahiri Mahasaya had predicted.

had said the journey would be no problem when I still felt so weak, sick and dizzy. It took a supreme effort to muster enough energy to get up and pack my rucksack. Self-pity made me all the more conscious of being nothing but a burden on my friends, Cord and John. If it had not been for their patience and constant loving care, I would never have managed to stay in Varanasi for so long. It would be impossible to ever repay the moral support which they had given me, but they were always telling me not to worry about it.

I could not stop fretting. In an attempt to calm down, I tried to concentrate on the breath, watching it pass through my nostrils, in and out, with closed eyes. Very slowly. In and out. More deeply. In and out. And then I saw the most vivid shade of purple that I have ever seen in my entire life. It grew from a miniscule point until it filled the space inside my head. 'No colour like that exists on earth,' I remember thinking. It was indescribably beautiful. The sight of it amounted to a small miracle which made me glow inside through sheer happiness. And then, for the few remaining hours in Varanasi, I was able to sleep more peacefully than for a long time and awoke feeling rested.

THE FIRST stretch of the journey ended with our arrival at Gorakhpur to an early morning haze. As we were walking through the station, we saw a dead body lying on the concrete floor covered up to the neck with a blanket. Someone who had spent the night waiting for their train had not woken up. We were numbed by the sight but also conscious that we would have been far more shocked six months previously. Cord commented that it would be an interesting topic to write a song about, but this woman's lonely death did not exactly catch my imagination as being particularly inspiring.

My thoughts were still with the woman as we got on our bus and began the long journey to Pokhara. Everything I had seen and experienced in India had undoubtedly left its mark on my consciousness and would never be forgotten. However, much had changed over the past months: my eyes now looked at India in a very different way. Maybe it was because the culture-shocked tourist mentality had long since been dealt with, and comparisons with Western life had ceased to be important. Now scenes which had seemed bizarre or abhorrent before had become a part of real life. The unexpected belonged to the norm in India.

Life did not come gift-wrapped over here, I thought to myself. It was transparent and tangible. But we all agreed: India was the most wonderful and fascinating place to be. The colours were more vivid, the festivals more jubilant. People laughed more, shouted more and cried more. There was beauty whichever way you turned. Thinking about it made me feel extremely reluctant to go home the following month, but as my funds were running low there was no choice.

Upon closer analysis, I decided that the India experience had given me a new perspective on life which made me think and want to live differently. Home seemed like a world wrapped up in cotton wool by comparison. A cosy existence, where it was easy to turn on the television to prevent the brain from pondering the deeper meaning of life. Life revolved around family, work and money. Thoughts about God were mostly reserved for church on Sundays and for times of need.

A smooth ride was guaranteed on a Western bus, and the doors and windows had to close properly if the company wanted to hold onto its licence to carry passengers. The simplest hostels usually had hygienic kitchens, clean flushing toilets, central heating and comfortable beds. There was a luxurious abundance of scrumptious food: salads and breads; cereals and cheeses; chocolates and cakes. It made my mouth water to think about it.

Being here certainly served as a powerful reminder of global economic imbalance. The lion's share of the world's resources and riches belonged to the West, and we were guilty of taking it for granted, giving little or nothing in return. But politics aside, it now seemed to me that the spirituality I had found on this side of the globe was far more valuable than all the luxuries which the West had to offer – genuine spirituality, which was hidden and perhaps could only be stumbled upon. I would not exchange this entire experience for anything in the world. My heart had been searching for something without knowing what it was, and had found it in India. Now I had made a promise to Guruji, a commitment to Kriya Yoga, and must never give up practising, however hard it became.

One day we had to die. That was the reality. We would have to leave our loved ones and all accumulated possessions behind and go as empty-handed as the new-born baby enters the world. Guruji had said that the moment of death was the most significant event in a person's life. For at that instant, we see what we have done with our life. We realise how we have spent or wasted our time, and receive a glimpse of the actual spiritual purpose of life. Whereupon the soul takes its direction according to the further lessons which have to be learned the next time around.

By now my mind was more open to the idea of rebirth. In the context of what I had learned so far about spiritual masters, it sounded a more plausible theory than having only one life. Besides, there seemed to be little sense in judging either one way or the other when I did not know. It was exactly the kind of thing which Guruji said had nothing to do with belief but could be found out through experience. A Yogi who had the ability to see the past and the future was more likely to be an authority on the matter.

Guruji had said that the ordinary person did not really die but passed from one life to the next. The only person who could die was the Yogi. Actual death occurred only when external breathing ceased naturally through practice. At this point of complete absorption in the Absolute, the restless mind and senses "died". These being vanquished, inner realisation was attained, together with the key to eternal life.[13] A spiritual master was eternal and everywhere.

That was one huge, incomprehensible thought which gave my intellect indigestion; although perhaps it was conceivable to have had enough of going around in circles and want to leave the human arena altogether. I could not help thinking that it did seem rather pointless to die and be reborn time after time. If that truly was the case, it was all the more reason to start hacking at the chains which bound the soul to the material world.

THIS reminded me of one of Guruji's true stories. It was about a wealthy man named Doonichand who lived in Lahore. As a

---

[13] Below are a few of the Biblical references to this yogic state:
"Be still and know that I am God." Psalms 46:10
"I die daily." 1 Corinthians 15:31
"He that overcometh shall not be hurt of the second death." Revelation 2:11
"Blessed are the dead which die in the Lord from henceforth." Revelation 14:13

devotee of Guru Nanak[14] he decided to invite the master to his house one day. The roof of his home was adorned with a number of flags, and when Guru Nanak enquired their significance, the rich man told him that he installed a new one every time he earned one *lakh*[15] rupees. The Guru smiled but said nothing.

As Guru Nanak was taking his leave, Doonichand asked for guidance in which way he could serve him.

The Guru handed him a needle. 'Take this and keep it for me,' he said. 'I want you to return it to me in your next birth.'

'Very well,' replied the man, and as soon as the Guru had left he gave the needle to his wife to keep safely for him, explaining what Guru Nanak had said.

His wife was shocked at her husband's simplicity. 'But you cannot take anything with you into your next life!' she exclaimed.

So Doonichand ran after Guru Nanak with the needle, and when he caught up with him, he said that he could not take it with him into the next life.

'If you can take so much money with you, surely you can take a needle!' replied the Guru.

'No one can take anything with them when they die.'

'If it is not even possible to take a tiny needle into the next life,' said Guru Nanak, 'then what is the point in accumulating such enormous wealth?'

Doonichand realised the truth of the Guru's words and changed his lifestyle from that day onwards.

Guru Nanak had not implied that earning money was unimportant, since doing so was necessary for survival. However, to be engrossed in material living was a waste of time, as we could not hold onto either wealth or possessions.

NEPAL was absolutely beautiful. We stayed in a place called Banana Lodge which commanded a panoramic view of the surrounding mountains and overlooked a cobalt lake. Quiet and stunningly picturesque, it was like having arrived on holiday at last.

---

14 Guru Nanak (1469-1539) founded the Sikh religion. Lahiri Mahasaya gave an explanation of Guru Nanak's *Japuji*, which is to the Sikh what the *Bhagavad Gita* is to the Hindu. It is evident from his life and works that Guru Nanak was a self-realised master who also practised Kriya Yoga in some form or other. Similarly to Lahiri Mahasaya, he did not endorse asceticism, but taught that union with God had to be attained through *sadhana* under the guidance of the *Sadguru* whilst living in society.

15 One *lakh* is equivalent to one hundred thousand rupees.

Refreshingly cool nights and warm balmy days.

Fortunately, the journey had not been as difficult as anticipated and my health was steadily improving. There was time to sleep, read and attempt to increase the length of my meditation practice. The struggle to concentrate continued, but during one particular session during those weeks I heard the vibration *Aum* resonating loudly in my head, which was cause for encouragement.

Guruji had told us before we left Varanasi that we had to be as strong as soldiers if we wanted to stay in this field of yoga and absolutely determined not to give in to laziness and discouragement. 'Carry on, carry on', as he would frequently say.

So another month of wholehearted concentration on Kriya Yoga in an atmosphere of peace was invaluable. There was plenty of time to assimilate the lessons learned over the past months before the return to a very different social climate. I was somewhat apprehensive about returning home, conscious that everything would be the same as ever, and I might feel like the stranger who no longer fitted in, changed beyond recognition by six months in India. It was hard to envisage how it would be, but I was almost ready.

After Pokhara we spent a few days in Chittwan National Park and went elephant trekking. This was an old ambition of mine and had it not been fulfilled, the time in Asia would have seemed somehow incomplete.

The final destination was Kathmandu. By the time we arrived in the bustling capital, sight-seeing did not appeal. I wandered aimlessly up and down the streets near our guest house browsing in shops for last-minute gifts for my family until the realisation dawned that I wanted to go home. Wasting no time, I sought out the nearest travel agent and booked a ticket for the first possible flight to Delhi. Another forty hours on a Nepalese bus was too much to contemplate. The following day my rucksack was packed once more, and it was time to bid Cord and John a sad farewell. During the intense time spent with them, they had become true friends.

I HAD been practising Kriya Yoga for a couple of months when things started to happen. Always when I least expected them to. In the aeroplane on the way home, I had my eyes closed and was vaguely contemplating having a doze. Yet when it started happening, I was conscious of being quite awake.

It did not fit into the category of a dream. There was no comparing it to night dreams or those one had in the early morning on the verge of waking. It was more akin to a beautiful and peculiar vision. There I was, floating as if bodiless, whilst still having a body of sorts. Other people were around me and we communicated with the utmost clarity without the need for any words – through some kind of telepathy. Striking was the realisation that misunderstandings of the human kind did not exist here. I felt free and life was wonderful because I was known.

Then it was gone and I opened my eyes.

Whatever it was, it gave me a certainty that a higher and better level of evolution than the human plane existed, although perhaps it was no more than another step on the ladder leading to knowledge of an Absolute Reality.

BETWEEN WORLDS (A Song)

Strange, how things happen like a pattern
Unexpectedly, the colours change with time
Aching feet that followed lines, and worldly signs
Drifting far behind, the mind would understand
The way things seem to be

Eyes that flicker, come and go, and through the blindness
Whisper who are you, who knew so much before?
Numb and cold, the feeling lingers
Stretched black fingers reach to touch a sleeping soul
Caught in the web of time

It's not the easy way – but home is far from here
Painful game to climb from the stage
Illumine star and storm-filled scenes
Daggers drawn chase elusive dreams
No time exists, no way to find out what it means

Words lose the battle, blood of purple hue
Sifted salty waters turn to dew
The pain will clear, and heaven will not hear
The explosion of silence
I will disappear

Chapter Five

KRIYA YOGA

What is Kriya Yoga?

"Raja Yoga is the science of religion,
the rationale of all worship,
all prayers, forms, ceremonies, and miracles." –
SWAMI VIVEKANANDA

Kriya Yoga is a scientific meditation technique which ultimately leads to what is termed "self-realisation". In the Hindu Scriptures, self-realisation is also referred to as spiritual knowledge, Soul-knowledge, or *Brahma* knowledge. "Kriya" means "action" and "Yoga" is "to unite", or "receive union".

Raja Yoga and Karma Yoga are basically other names for Kriya Yoga. Lahiri Mahasaya made it clear that the immortal Karma Yoga of the *Bhagavad Gita* was also the Kriya Yoga he revived; that it was the method known and passed down throughout the ages and written about in the Indian Scriptures from the Upanishads to the Maharabhata. Thousands of years ago, the ancient sages of India realised that everyone came from one source and must again return to where they came from through complete absorption into the Divine. They said that to work for our own salvation by walking the path to God was the ultimate purpose of human life.

Patanjali practised something akin to the Kriya Yoga passed on by Lahiri Mahasaya: his *Yoga Sutras* are known as the book of Raja Yoga. Many other spiritual masters in the past have had knowledge of a similar kind of self-realisation technique including King Janaka, Socrates, Jesus Christ, Saint Paul, Saint John, *Kabir Das* and Guru Nanak, to name but a few.

Whenever Kriya Yoga has suffered a decline to virtual extinction in certain ages, a spiritual master has always been sent to re-establish the technique amongst mankind. Lahiri Mahasaya's grandson Satya Charan Lahiri writes in the introduction of *Purana Purusha* that the method of practice became lost over the course of time until nothing remained but the mystic syllables. Knowledge of these were enough for generation after generation of gurus to continue initiating in their role as spiritual preceptor to the people. However, whispered syllables in the ears of disciples alone were of no benefit to anyone without the accompanying technique.

Lahiri Mahasaya said that it was impossible to become self-realised without any yoga *sadhana*. Unstable mind or *Prana* was the cause of pain and discord and had to be brought under control through Kriya Yoga. The mind produced an effect which could be likened to waves on the ocean preventing man from glimpsing the seabed, or vision of his spiritual heritage. These waves could not be controlled through will-power alone. In Kriya Yoga, external respiration was turned inward, which gradually and automatically stilled all the waves, making the mind controlled and constant. This in turn resulted in freedom from negative traits including anger, hatred, jealousy and ego.

OVER the past half century yoga has taken an increasing hold in the Western world. To some extent it has even been turned into a fad, seeking to appeal to a consumer market. New methods of yoga and meditation are constantly being propagated around the world, many of them attracting followers through the promise that five to ten minutes a day will lead to self-realisation and ultimate freedom, or that a few months will suffice to steady the vibrations in the *Chakras* and raise the *Kundalini*.

To avoid disappointment, it is best to be wary of such claims. If someone has achieved a particularly advanced level of consciousness in the previous life, they may quickly and effortlessly reattain it in the subsequent incarnation, as was the case when Shyama Charan Lahiri met his Guru, Babaji. However, such events are rare and exceptional. Unfortunately, the reason why false gurus enjoy such a booming trade is reflected in the Western tendency to sensationalise and to want and expect everything in a hurry.

The most commonly known form of yoga in the West is Hatha Yoga, which is the physical form of yoga involving postures or

Asanas. Other lesser known fields of yoga include Karma Yoga (the yoga of action); Bhakti Yoga (the yoga of devotion); Jnana Yoga (the yoga of Soul-knowledge) and Laya Yoga (the yoga of salvation). Although it is frequently believed that these forms of yoga exist independently of each other, they are inseparable as linked steps on the path of Raja Yoga, or Kriya Yoga. For example, Hatha is needed to enable the body to sit perfectly still in the same posture for long periods of time; Raja Yoga stills and controls the mind and, in Laya Yoga, union with the Absolute is achieved.

However, freedom from earthly bondage requires effort and dedication of the first degree. The original Kriya Yoga is no "quick fix", and Patanjali's eight steps of yoga, briefly explained, should lend the concept "yoga meditation" a realistic perspective once more. Each of these eight steps have to be mastered in turn, and as the practitioner who has been given the original method of Kriya Yoga will appreciate, none may be omitted.

The first step is *Yama*, which leads to the cultivation of qualities such as truth, non-violence, non-stealing, restraint of the senses, forgiveness and so on. The second is *Niyama*, known as "rule", and is composed of the following: internal and external purity; knowledge which can only be personally received from the Guru; listening to the sound of *Aum* and holding onto the Self.[1] The third step is *Asana*, which implies that a firm seat is required in practise so that the body cannot disturb the necessary pointed concentration of the mind. The fourth is *Pranayama*, which far from simply meaning breathing exercises, implies a practice culminating in the actual cessation of breath. The mind is purified and separated from the five senses. The fifth step is *Pratyahara* or "inwardness", in which the mind is drawn inward to *Kutastha*, having been freed from the senses. The sixth step is *Dharana*, known as the "glimpse of tranquillity". This means that although the practitioner is accustomed to seeing *Kutastha*, the mind is still inclined to wander and has to be brought back to that point. The penultimate step of yoga known as *Dhyana* literally means "meditation": the practitioner can remain in *Kutastha* without breaking consciousness for a minimum of three minutes; there is full Soul-absorption in that transcendental state of no-breath

---

[1] The five Sanskrit terms composing *Niyama* are: *Socha, Santosa, Tapa, Swadhyaya* and *Pranidhana*.

tranquillity, and in this state, the mind is static, thought non-existent and the senses have been conquered.

The reader may now appreciate to what extent the word "meditation" is misunderstood in the West. For when an ordinary person (including myself) says that they are meditating, they are actually only attempting to concentrate their mind or thoughts inwards, or on a fixed object. This is not meditation or *Dhyana* in its true sense. Therefore, when the great spiritual masters are referred to in this book as sitting in "meditation", the implication is that after seating themselves, they in fact entered the breathless state of *Samadhi*.

Samadhi is the eighth and final step of yoga. When *Dhyana*, or true meditation, is perfected – in other words, the practitioner can stay in unbroken concentration in *Kutastha* for at least three consecutive hours – the practitioner attains the level of consciousness known as *Samadhi*. Every branch of yoga leads to this end, in order to complete the circle of human existence and gain freedom from karmic bondage. In explanation of one of Patanjali's Yoga Sutras, Lahiri Mahasaya says of this step,

"When the seeker gets beyond the awareness of meditation and is attuned in the ultimate state of Consciousness, which is similar to Voidness, but full of Bliss, he has reached the true state of Samadhi, or Attunement in Oneness." [2]

The Benefits of Kriya Yoga

When learned and practised under supervised guidance by a qualified yoga teacher, even Hatha Yoga *Asanas* bring the mind to a more peaceful state. Sickness and psychosomatic problems are healed through regular practice. Concentration on the breath in Hatha *pranayama* keeps the body's cholesterol level under control, as well as being a cure for high and low blood pressure, and many allergies, anxieties and other problems. However, Hatha Yoga is a branch of yoga which primarily aims to strengthen the human body. Every muscle and organ of the body including the heart may be brought under perfect control, yet the spiritual progress may not be compared to that attainable through Kriya Yoga. In the introduction of *Purana Purusha*, Satya Charan Lahiri writes,

[2] From *Lahiri Mahasaya's Commentaries on the Yoga Sutras of Patanjali*. For a more detailed explanation of these eight stages of yoga, the reader should refer to this book, in particular Chapters 2 and 3.

"The practice of Hatha Yoga imparts physical benefits no doubt, but it does not provide any lead in the finding of the soul within the body nor does it make the mind still. Again, one cannot enter the spiritual realm if the mind is not made still. For this the practice of Raja Yoga is essential. Until self-realisation, permanent settlement or visualisation of *Kutastha*-consciousness occurs, till then human life cannot be complete."

In Kriya Yoga, the physical body undergoes an even more intensive process of purification. The mind begins to find peace and the body becomes healthier, even after a short time of practice.

The brain and memory capacities of the Kriya practitioner develop at a rapid rate so that it is possible to gain extensive internal knowledge about the mechanisms of the body. Consciousness evolves to the extent where Kriya reveals the secrets of man's true identity, birthright and relationship to God.

The sexual potential increases through Kriya Yoga, as does life expectancy, since the slowing down of the heartbeat stems the natural processes of decay in the body's tissue and cells. However, it should be remembered that these are side-effects of practice and not the aim of Kriya Yoga, which is to unite with God. Also, real perception and wisdom are not to be confused with intellectual knowledge, logic, or any kind of emotional feeling.

Similarly, any desire to levitate, materialise and dematerialise the body at will or gain other powers would not be a valid reason to take up the practice. Although it must be acknowledged that these are possibilities of practice, they bring bondage rather than freedom as long as their attraction is connected with the material world of enjoyment and power. Therefore, when developments or special powers known as *Siddhis* appear, it is vital for the practitioner not to focus on them for they are obstacles on the path towards self-realisation. In his writings, Patanjali frequently warns against them.[3] Whatever a yogi may gain on the worldly scale having succumbed to the temptation of misusing the *Siddhis*, is lost to him on the spiritual scale.

Attempts to "market" yoga and meditation in the name of good

---

[3] In *Raja Yoga*, Vivekananda writes the following in explanation of Patanjali's 51st Yoga Sutra: "When the Yogi has seen all these wonderful powers, and rejected them, he reaches the goal. What are all these powers? Simply manifestations. They are no better than dreams. Even omnipotence is a dream. It depends upon the mind. So long as there is a mind it can be understood, but the goal is beyond even the mind."

health or sexual prowess alone are frequently successful, but the reality is that the spectrum of spiritual benefits which accompany the regular and sincere practice of Kriya Yoga cannot even be put into words, let alone be marketed as a product. Although this book details various events pertaining to the lives of the spiritual masters in Lahiri Mahasaya's lineage, these in themselves are in no way sufficient to paint a full picture of their spiritual realisation. What they experienced was of an entirely internal and mystical nature, not to be seen or shared by anyone else. And although a true master may give a sign of his inner realisation through his miracles, these are without exception manifested exclusively as a spiritual lesson for the disciple or devotee and are never for show.

The Human Body as the Vehicle to Self-Realisation

"Knowledge is experience;
anything else is information." – EINSTEIN

Respiration and Pranayama
The ancient Yogis of India who used to live in the forest made the observation that the life-span of every living creature is determined according to their respiration. Cats, dogs and rabbits breathe in and out some forty times per minute, and live for between ten to twenty years. Animals with slower respiration such as the snake, elephant and tortoise have a far greater longevity. The giant tortoise, for example, takes approximately four breaths per minute and lives for up to three hundred years.

The Yogis realised that the same principle applies to the human being. Man normally breathes fifteen to eighteen times per minute, or 21,600 times in a twenty-four-hour period. At this speed of respiration, the mind is influenced by the senses and thoughts revolve around worldly matters. In times of stress, anger or mental anxiety, the rate of breaths generally increases to twenty times per minute.

Conversely, in slowing down the breath by taking long and deep respiration, the heart pumps purified blood to the organs which is charged with oxygen, thereby bringing the carbonised system of the blood under control. The mind and body are cleansed and become more healthy. Under normal circumstances nature dictates that the cells in the body must gradually die, but the advanced Yogi who does a great deal of *pranayama* is able to halt this process and actively recharge those cells with energy.

Even the Kriya practitioner who learns to take just one or two breaths per minute in *pranayama* recharges and magnetises the cells which would otherwise rapidly decay: the long breath increases the ability to concentrate, whilst simultaneously being one of the first steps to conquer death since the natural life-span is automatically extended as a side-effect of practice.

Due to the amount of times man normally takes respiration, he has to take birth and rebirth millions of times. His brain and conscious level develop very slowly. Through natural breath, it is never possible to reach *Samadhi*, but the advanced Kriya Yogi can achieve self-realisation through personal effort in twelve, twenty-four, or forty years, or a couple of lifetimes at the most. Kriya *pranayama* practised in one life is always transferred to the next and is never lost. The chain of *Karma* resulting from all those lives is gradually broken as the Yogi frees himself of ego and desire.

It is possible for the ordinary person to develop the conscious level greatly even in one lifetime. Hence Kriya is often referred to as "the aeroplane route to God". Kriya Yoga practised over the course of one year for some eight hours daily would give man the equivalent of 365,000 years of natural development in body, mind and intellect. For the Kriya practitioner, the same amount of practice therefore reduces one million years of natural evolution to three years. Although the effect of Kriya is truly astonishing, great concentration and discipline are required.

MAN IS usually unaware of the connection between respiration and mind. But whilst the mind is unstable, we are subject to health and sickness, joy and sorrow, strength and weakness, and so on. Mind is *Prana* in its unsteady stage, and causes us to breathe through the nostrils. We are able to hold our breath for a short while, but to control the mind is far more difficult since *Prana* is more gross than mind.

The rising and falling of the lungs, which in turn produces breath, is the most tangible evidence of *Prana* which ordinary man knows. The most straightforward way to gain control of *Prana* is therefore though respiration, and in Kriya Yoga, this is done through what is called *pranayama*. When *Prana* is stilled, the mind, not to mention every muscle, nerve and organ in the body, becomes subservient to the will of the yogic practitioner.

ACCORDING to the Indian system of yoga, there are 72,000 fine nerves which carry messages around the body. Air flows through subtle channels inside these nerves, some of which are particularly important in meditation.

Although we breathe subconsciously through two nostrils, the cosmic force known as *Prana* controls each inhalation and exhalation. The left channel or nerve is known in Sanskrit as *Ida nadi* and the right channel as *Pingala nadi*. These run through the spinal cord and work alternately in our bodies. When one is open, the other is closed, and the change occurs automatically at regular hourly intervals.

There are eight types of *pranayama* in Hatha Yoga, where concentration is focused on *Ida* and *Pingala*, the external channels. These types of *pranayama* include alternate breathing, and *Ujjayi* which involves inhaling for ten seconds and exhaling for twenty. Every type of *pranayama* has several limbs, including inhalation (*puraka*), exhalation (*rechaka*), and retention (*Kumbhaka*).

In between these external channels known as *Ida* and *Pingala*, is another more subtle nerve, *Sushumna*. It is a hollow canal, and at the moment that the external channels change, a little air is sent through *Sushumna*.

In Kriya Yoga *pranayama*, concentration is focused directly on *Sushumna*, rather than on *Ida* and *Pingala*, for this is the most superior of all *pranayamas*. In order to go deep in meditation we have to find this nerve which runs through the *Chakras*, or the body's energy centres, from the bottom of the spine to the top of the head.

ALTHOUGH it is widely believed that *pranayama* means breathing exercises alone, the word in fact implies the end goal of these exercises. *Prana* can be translated as "life force", and *Ayam* means "expansion" – the two words combined refer to the "expansion of the life force" in *Kevala Kumbhaka*, which is a stage of *Samadhi* when external breathing is rendered unnecessary since *Prana* has been brought under control. This state is attained through a great deal of *pranayama*, whereby the external *Ida* and *Pingala* channels are balanced. Thereafter, respiration becomes deep and internal in *Sushumna*. There is no will-power involved in this whatsoever. A Yogi who takes respiration from this central channel is still able to talk and his voice will sound the same. In this state of "tranquil breath", the mind is still. The sound "Sohum" is heard by the practitioner, meaning, "That I Am".[4] Deprived of oxygen, the organs and cells in the body cease to function whilst remaining preserved until the Yogi chooses to reactivate them upon returning to what is referred to as the "dynamic state of *Prana*".

Prana may therefore be explained in simple terms as the cosmic energy in every living thing. Acting in the external world of science it is also the power behind steam, electricity and other forms of energy. Swami Vivekananda says,

"That part of *Pranayama* which attempts to control the physical manifestations of the *Prana* by physical means is called physical science, and that part which tries to control the manifestations of the *Prana* as mental force, by mental means, is called Raja Yoga."

The Chakras and Kundalini
There are seven *Chakras*, or energy centres, in the human body situated at different positions on the spine as if strung upon an invisible thread.[5] Although the literal meaning of *Chakra* is wheel, a better translation is "vortex" or "whirlpool", for they regulate the circulation of *Prana* in particular areas of the human body. The *Chakras* have been likened to lotus flowers because of their shape, being characterised by varying colours and numbers of petals. The lotus is also a spiritual symbol in India, since it is something of great beauty which grows in murky waters.

Coiled up at the root *Chakra* (*Muladhara*) is a power called the *Kundalini*. The aim of every type of yoga and meditation practice is to awaken this latent power. After much Kriya *pranayama* the layers of the mind unfold as it makes its passage through the hollow *Sushumna* canal striking each nerve centre as it goes. Upon reaching the brain, highest consciousness or the perception of the

---

4 These words also appear in the Bible: "And God said unto Moses, I AM THAT I AM". (Exodus 3:14)
5 The names of the *Chakras* are as follows: root (*Muladhara*), sacral (*Svadhishthana*), solar plexus (*Manipura*), heart (*Anahata*), throat (*Visuddha*), brow / third eye (*Ajna*), and crown (*Sahasrara*) *Chakras*.

Self is experienced in a blaze. The soul finds freedom at last. A stanza from the *Bhagavad Gita* refers to this state: "Were a thousand suns to explode suddenly in the sky, their brilliance would approximate the glory of the sight."[6]

The *Chakras* in an ordinary person are in a state of constant vibration. However, a false perception often reigns in the West about the *Chakras* themselves, not to mention about the awakening of the *Kundalini*. People frequently come to Guruji saying that they have come for help because they feel that their *Kundalini* has awakened. He asks them why they have come to him, for if their *Kundalini* has awakened, they are already a highly advanced Yogi and will never need help from any other person for as long as they live.

Swami Vivekananda says in *Raja Yoga* that this ultimate limb of yoga is the end of all worship. He adds that wherever supernatural power or wisdom is to be seen, some small current of *Kundalini* power will have entered the *Sushumna* channel, whether the person is aware of this or not:

"The man who thinks that he is receiving response to his prayers does not know that the fulfilment comes from his own nature, that he has succeeded by the mental attitude of prayer in waking up a bit of this infinite power which is coiled up within himself."

Although the rousing of the *Kundalini* may partially occur through some other kind of worship as Vivekananda suggests, in Kriya Yoga the vibrations in the *Chakras* are sequentially steadied through a scientific method. In order to give a more realistic idea of what is involved in awakening the *Kundalini*, Lahiri Mahasaya calculated that it takes approximately 200,000 Kriya *pranayama* to stabilize one *Chakra*. And only when the first six have been brought under control, can the *Kundalini* awaken.[7]

Guruji explains further that when the *Kundalini* awakens, super-consciousness and the higher planes of yoga are experienced. The Yogi who has awakened *Kundalini* becomes omniscient. He no longer needs to sit in practice for so long and remains effortlessly in spiritual consciousness, even whilst going about worldly chores.

The yogi passes through seven stages or dimensions of consciousness on the way to attaining self-realisation. Symbolism

---

[6] XI:12 (Lal)

[7] In addition, the practitioner must have untied the three "knots" in the body; these will be explained in the following section: The Stages of Kriya Yoga.

relating to this fact may be found in the holy books of every religion. In this context, the Christian may be interested to re-examine St. John's Revelation in the Bible, a chapter teeming with yogic symbolism. The most obvious are the allusions to the number seven:

"And he had in his right hand seven stars." – Rev. 1:16

"The seven stars are the angels of the seven churches: and the seven candlesticks which thou sawest are the seven churches." – Rev. 1:20

"And I saw in the right hand of him that sat on the throne a book written within and on the backside, sealed with seven seals." – Rev. 5:1

The churches refer to the seven energy centres in the spine, which seal these states of consciousness, and must be opened through practice in the quest for eternal Realisation. The otherwise incomprehensible super-sensory experiences described in the Book of Revelation may therefore be fully understood by the advanced yogic practitioner.

Apart from the visual experiences, the airs in the body produce certain internal noises – hence the yogi also hears sounds and may smell particular fragrances during practice. In Hindu *puja*, there is extensive use of various instruments such as bells and conches, since these are external representations of those sounds heard internally by the advanced practitioner. In one particular diary entry, Lahiri Mahasaya writes (date unknown):

"When *Apana* air enters the *Anahata Chakra*, then ten types of *Anahata* sound can be heard – chirr, continuous chirr, small bell, conch, lute, rhythm, snake-charmer's flute, wooden tom-tom, concerted drum music, prolonged bell."[8]

The Stages of Kriya Yoga

Kriya Yoga is divided into three steps or stages. The aim of these stages is to release the *Granthis*, or psychic knots in the body. These so-called knots prevent the steadying of the *Chakras* and rising of

---

[8] From *Purana Purusha*.

the *Kundalini*, since they prevent *Prana* from flowing along the *Sushumna* channel. They are known in ascending order as *Brahma Granthi, Vishnu Granthi* and *Rudra Granthi*. *Brahma Granthi* is associated with the throat *Chakra*. The second knot, *Vishnu Granthi* is associated with the heart *Chakra*, and *Rudra Granthi* with the root *Chakra*. As each of these knots is released, *Kundalini* is able to rise through the *Sushumna* channel to the next respective *Chakra*. Each stage in Kriya whereby the *Granthis* are released also has sub-steps, and again, none of these steps or stages can be omitted. It should not be forgotten that they can only be learned directly from the self-realised Guru.

The First Step involves untying the knot of the tongue (practising *Khechari mudra* and achieving it), and releasing the knot of the navel (untying the silver chord which binds the astral body to the physical body through the navel):

In the process of opening the tongue knot, and in order to achieve *Khechari mudra*, seven special techniques are taught which are practised in proportion to each other. Furthermore, some special *pranayamas* are taught in this first stage of Kriya Yoga. After long and dedicated practice, the Kriya practitioner achieves *Khechari mudra*, and, by mastering the mystic *pranayama*, his consciousness expands beyond the physical limits. For the first time he is able to establish some control over inhalation and exhalation.

Next, the practitioner qualifies to untie the navel knot, which allows him to achieve a certain degree of control over the silver chord which binds the astral body to the physical body. With the help of the second *pranayama* he is able to relocate this silver chord from the navel to between the eyebrows.

The Second Step involves opening the knot of the heart (going higher and gaining control over the life force; in the language of the mystics, seeing Lord Krishna (*Kutastha*) face to face):

There are three major sub-steps of this practice, each more advanced than the previous one. By the power of the first *pranayama* in this practice, the practitioner is able to concentrate and bring his life force from the forehead to the heart, and subsequently becomes qualified to receive the second *pranayama*.

Here, he can maintain and concentrate his life force inside the heart, and enjoy periods of the yogic breathless state. When he becomes adept at this, he receives the third and last sub-step, at which point the pulse and heartbeat begin to cease, although there is no physical death.

By the end of the second step, the practitioner may behold the four-armed Lord Vishnu face to face – as a mystic symbol of increased energy and development of certain *Siddhis* – for with two arms man is limited, whereas with four arms, there is greater power. The forces of *Prana* and *Apana* which were separated previously are joined.

The Third Step involves untying the knot in *Muladhara* (root) *Chakra* (realising the force behind the life force and, again in the language of the mystics, seeing *Lord Siva* face to face):

The Yogi who has succeeded in opening the heart knot now receives the final teaching from his Guru, enabling him to know the essential universal form, the essence of time and the light of all lights referred to in the *Bhagavad Gita*. There are two sub-steps in this last technique. By the practice of the last *pranayama*, the Yogi becomes liberated and at one with time. Few practitioners ever attain to this state. *Lord Siva* in this ultimate stage of yoga is a symbolic representation of controlled energy – time becomes non-existent for the Yogi and his body does not decay in this state of consciousness.

The Hindu deities and what they symbolise for the Kriya Yogi will be examined in greater detail in Chapter Ten: Tantra Mantra and the Gods, Mysterious Encounters.

Samadhi

It has already been mentioned that *Samadhi* is the final step in the eight-fold path of yoga. Ordinary people are only familiar with the lower and middle states of consciousness: unconsciousness, sub-consciousness, and consciousness. Few are aware that the mind can rise to the state of super-consciousness known as *Samadhi*.

Sitting down at a table to eat, man is conscious of consuming the meal before him. He is equally conscious when he takes exercise. However, he remains totally unconscious of how his body reacts internally in assimilating the food or the way it burns energy through sport. The mind is active and accompanied by ego during all waking activities executed consciously, whereas there is no ego present when actions are done unconsciously. For example, in the state of sleep or unconsciousness, man breathes, dreams and even changes positions; the mind is still at work though ego is not present.

Since the ego is also non-existent in *Samadhi*, or super-consciousness, it may be asked how it is possible to prove that a man in *Samadhi* has not descended to one of the lower planes of consciousness. Swami Vivekananda points out that when man awakens from sleep, he is no more spiritually advanced than he was when he lay down, and answers the question thus: "... by the results of the work, we know that which is below, and that which is above ... when a man goes into Samadhi, if he goes into it a fool, he comes out a sage."[9]

Samadhi is beyond reason, beyond the intellect and beyond the workings of mind. It is a question of practice, not theory, and therefore it is impossible to philosophise on the subject. However, the reality and existence of this state, which is scientifically attainable through Kriya Yoga, has produced spiritual masters, saints and prophets throughout every age: and their experiences of super-consciousness are the foundations upon which the major religions of the world are built.

The great spiritual masters taught that we should love our neighbour as a result of their insight gained through *Samadhi*. They understood the law of cause and effect and recognised all of creation as being linked; that everything is One. They knew that the answer to mankind's most fundamental questions was to be found in this actual state of Oneness: What is man? Is the soul immortal? Is there an omnipotent God in control of the universe? And so on.

Once the yogic practitioner has attained *Samadhi*, the mind remains fully awake though untouched by the mental tiredness which afflicts the ordinary person. Although the body is a physical tool which requires a certain amount of rest, when the Yogi sleeps there is no descent into the unconscious state. Instead, the human

---

[9] From *Raja Yoga*.

body is forgotten and he enters his *astral body*.

In *Samadhi*, the Yogi feels an ecstasy incomparable to any worldly joy, free from body-consciousness, the mind and senses. However, the attainment of this level is not the end of yoga: even though respiration is controlled, practice does not cease.[10] To be able to stay in *Samadhi* for increasingly longer periods is equally a matter of practice, for there is more than one stage of *Samadhi*.

First, there is *Sahaja Samadhi*, followed by the deeper *Savikalpa Samadhi*. This state of deep meditation can be called "conscious death" or the "deathless state", because the heartbeat stops completely and the body's cells neither increase nor decay. The need to breathe externally ceases spontaneously in the state of *Nirvikalpa Samadhi* (also known as *Kevala Kumbhaka* in Kriya Yoga).

The Yogi who has overcome death itself in *Samadhi* can consciously determine the day when he will leave his body. After taking final *Mahasamadhi* he will not come back to earth, for the specific purpose for which he came to the world will have been fulfilled. He is no longer tied to the chain of rebirth, having attained the highest level of consciousness possible, leading to the merging with the Absolute, and perfection in all of the eight *Siddhis*.

Kutastha

Kutastha is the place of spiritual perception located between the eyebrows of every human being, directly opposite the sixth *Chakra* (*Ajna Chakra*). It is also referred to as the Third Eye, the Eye of Wisdom, and the Transcendental Eye. As a symbolic reminder of this place it is customary for Indian women to wear a *bindi* on the forehead. When a Brahmin priest performs *puja*, he strokes red powder onto the eyebrow centre of the person he is blessing.

The word *kut* is derived from Sanskrit meaning "anvil". It is that which remains unchanged and unchangeable, though the goldsmith creates numerous objects by using it to mould and shape. In the same way, although the universe is in a state of constant change, *Kutastha*, being triangular in shape, is immutable and eternal.

Throughout the ages, many saints and masters have referred to

---

[10] Lahiri Mahasaya often referred to this state as "the pause of Kriya".

this centre of inner perception in the body, for it is where they realised the Absolute. Lahiri Mahasaya said that *Kutastha* was where heaven, or Soul-perception was manifested, and from where *Prana* and all of creation originated.

Speaking of *Kutastha*, Jesus said, "the Kingdom of God is within you"[11] and, "The light of the body is the eye: if therefore thine eye be single, thy whole body shall be full of light."[12] God is realised when breath ceases at *Kutastha*, for the Absolute can be experienced there in unchanging form, being the one Reality, true substance and Soul. Sin is non-existent in the Yogi who realises *Kutastha* and has overcome the mind and senses.

Kutastha is within the grasp of every human being, but for the ordinary person who is unaware of its existence, reality is entirely external. There is only darkness behind closed eyes. At the time of initiation, *Kutastha* is revealed to the initiate by the self-realised Guru, and this "awakening" remains with the initiate permanently. However, without practice, *Kutastha* is like a sun covered by dark clouds which can only be cleared through personal effort. The inner light to be seen in *Kutastha* is also the destroyer of death, and Kriya practice erases the fear of death day by day even for the beginner.

Transcendental perception is within reach in *Kutastha*; there are no impediments to vision, which becomes telescopic, so that things thousands, or even millions of miles away may easily be seen. Knowledge regarding the past, present and future is unfolded in *Kutastha*. There is neither light nor darkness in what Lahiri Mahasaya describes in his diary as the "infinite void"; it is entirely different from the sky since *Kutastha* is beyond the five elements. In the Kriya practice of *Yoni mudra*, even the beginner finds the spiritual enchantment of experiencing in *Kutastha* what is referred to as the Soul-moon or the Soul-sun.

However, tremendous commitment, devotion, patience and time are required in order to reach the point of stilling the *Prana* to achieve full realisation in *Kutastha* through *pranayama*, in other words to find God and knowledge of the entire cosmos in the human body rather than in the church, temple or mosque.

---

[11] St. Luke 17:21
[12] St. Matthew 6:22

"THE EXISTENCE of the present void depends upon the existence of the infinite void. That crystalline void is evergreen and infinite, that is *Brahma*. *Atmasurya* also merges in that infinite void, because the sources of origin and merging for everything is that infinite, amorphous, ageless, immortal, infinite void. Now I am feeling extremely ecstatic and this ecstasy is arising and travelling within. I have reached that inaccessible place where none else than a yogi can reach i.e. I have arrived at the sublime still state. Now I have to travel a long distance in the path of that infinite void meaning I have to attain that state of merging."[13]

How to Recognise the Original Method of Kriya Yoga

"Behold, thou desirest truth in the inward parts:
and in the hidden part thou shalt make me to know wisdom." –
PSALMS [14]

The Guru

In its original Hindu sense, the word "guru" means "spiritual teacher", although it has now come to mean teacher, mentor or expert in any field. Since there are so many so-called gurus, the real meaning of *Sadguru*, or genuine spiritual master who is able to guide each of his disciples to self-realisation, has been lost to some extent. The commitment between *Sadguru* and disciple transcends space and time, and no true Guru takes on the responsibility of a disciple's spiritual advancement lightly. On the part of the disciple, there must be surrender to the Guru in order for any progress to be possible on this spiritual path. Further explanation of this is given in Chapter Ten.

Kriya Yoga is uniquely a Guru-disciple path. In the Vedic age, the words *Guru-param-para* meant being personally initiated by the Guru and was known as "the righteous way". Throughout history the greatest spiritual masters were initiated by a teacher, from *Rama* and *Krishna* to Lahiri Mahasaya. Likewise, Jesus went to John the Baptist to be initiated, or "baptised", saying, "Suffer it to be so now: for thus it becometh us to fulfil all

---

[13] From one of Lahiri Mahasaya's confidential diaries (from *Purana Purusha* by Dr A. K. Chatterjee).
[14] Psalms 51:6

righteousness."[15] Despite being on a conscious level beyond the need for ritual, these true spiritual masters have always received initiation themselves in acknowledgement of the righteous way of *Guru-param-para*.

This point is further emphasised by Swami Satyeswarananda, who says, "... the relationship between the *Guru* and the disciple develops only when both of them meet physically and have accepted each other ... (In the absence of a physical meeting and acceptance on the part of the *Guru*, the person's attempt to treat a Yogi as his or her *Guru* is a mere subjective fantasy and there is no *Guru*-disciple relationship which has taken place.)"[16]

Various persons claiming to be authorities in the Kriya field nevertheless tell of having received initiation or even authorisation to teach Kriya Yoga from Lahiri Mahasaya or his Guru, Babaji, in a dream. Although people making such claims may be telling the truth as it appears to them, their so-called initiations are not genuine.

Furthermore, in the Kriya Yoga tradition a disciple can have only one specific and personal Guru, just as a person has only one father or mother. If the Guru takes *Mahasamadhi* and instructs his disciples as to whom they can go to for advice after he has gone, then they can do so, but there is no question of the practitioner having a number of gurus at one time.

The Guru of Kriya Yoga knows when a disciple's time has come for initiation and will never initiate anyone on a casual basis. The potential for inner concentration plus a favourable influence of the previous life to enable a disciple to succeed are prerequisites. Some people are attracted by the idea of trying out one meditation technique after the other, but for Kriya Yoga there must be the dedication to last a lifetime. It is important to concentrate fully on one practice, otherwise perfection or freedom will never be reached. The original Kriya is a complete technique, so the practitioner does not require any other *Mantra* or practice for God-realisation. Likewise, in the subsequent stages of Kriya, it is the Guru who determines when the disciple is ready for further initiation. Through the spiritual link he is always aware of how much his disciple is practising and whether or not Kriya is being done correctly.

---

[15] St. Matthew 3:15
[16] From *Babaji*.

Lahiri Mahasaya advised against the establishment of *ashrams* and institutions in the name of Kriya Yoga. Perhaps one of his concerns was that Kriya Yoga would become something akin to a religion dependent on a supreme Guru's teachings, and that these would be used to compensate for the fact that the initiating swami was not self-realised himself. All of the masters in Lahiri Mahasaya's lineage made it clear that for success on this path, nothing could replace the self-realised personal Guru, independently authorised to teach through having reached the highest planes of yoga himself.

Addiction to intoxicating substances is undesirable in the Kriya Yoga field. However, in particular circumstances the Guru may initiate a person who is ready for Kriya despite an addiction, for given time the habit will automatically be controlled through practice.

"A MAN may be wicked, and yet make an astronomical discovery, but in religion it is different, because no impure man will ever have the power to reach the truths of religion. Therefore we have first of all to see that the man who declares himself to be an *Apta*[17] is a perfectly unselfish and holy person; secondly, that he has reached beyond the senses; and thirdly, that what he says does not contradict the past knowledge of humanity. Any new discovery of truth does not contradict the past truth, but fits into it. And fourthly, that truth must have a possibility of verification. If a man says, "I have seen a vision", and tells me that I have no right to see it, I believe him not. Everyone must have the power to see it for himself."[18]

Why Kriya Yoga is a Scientific Technique
There can be no question of making changes and adjustments to a scientific technique, as Lahiri Mahasaya's grandson Satya Charan Lahiri once told a disciple[19] who asked if there was some easier way to practise Kriya. Satya Charan Lahiri told him that no section of Kriya practice may be omitted.

---

17 *Apta* is used here in the sense of self-realised master or Guru; the literal meaning of the word is "attained".
18 From *Raja Yoga* by Swami Vivekananda.
19 The disciple in question was Shamboo Nath Kavayateertha.

When asked by the same disciple if it would suffice to practise once a day, Satya Charan answered with an allegory: though the body will not die if it is given food only once a day, it does need adequate sustenance for good health. The same applies to the mind and soul which are nourished through Kriya practice. When Kriya is done twice daily, the practitioner gains an unspeakably profound inner peace and the benefits of practice become all the more quickly noticeable.

Satya Charan Lahiri added that the reason why there were so few perfect Kriya Yogis left was because the original method as given to his grandfather by Babaji barely seventy-five years previously had been subjected to enormous change, and particularly since it had reached Western shores in the 1940s.

Many simplified and shortened versions of Kriya Yoga are indeed on offer today, particularly in the West, but there is no benefit in practising a mutilated version of Lahiri Mahasaya's technique. Some gurus teach fourteen Kriya *pranayamas* as being one limb of the method, though this is a blatant adaptation of the original. Perhaps they reason that the beginner is not likely to do practice correctly and therefore increase on the number given by Lahiri Mahasaya. They are correct in realising that it will take time until the beginner can achieve what is termed "excellent" *pranayama*, but perfection must come with daily practice, and correct numbers are essential for results.

Since Kriya Yoga is a scientific technique, each part of the practice is to be completed within a certain amount of time. The minutes and seconds are precisely defined for a reason. Though practice should be executed with devotion, Lahiri Mahasaya would say that Kriya is also "as accurate as mathematics" and placed great emphasis on the importance of numbers and timing as being the key to success. It should be obvious that in respect of these calculations, no exceptions or differences can be made to simplify matters for Westerners. Only the original method can take the practitioner to the goal. The minimum time which Kriya Yoga can take is fifty minutes in the morning, and one hour in the evening. The disciple receives a table from the Guru with the numbers he requires for each extra set which is practised.

Numbers have an importance beyond human imagination for the role they play in the make-up and function of the universe and in maintaining creation. The numbers three and seven carry particular significance, as does twelve. The number twelve and its multiples are especially important for inner consciousness, for control on the breath and *Samadhi*.

As already mentioned, in Kriya the vibrations in the *Chakras* are successively brought under control, through *pranayama*, whereby no individual can expect to stabilize even one *Chakra* without having practised a minimum of the calculated 200,000 *pranayamas*. One Kriya *pranayama* takes 44 seconds, hence the yogi practising for twenty-four hours will only take 2000 breaths as opposed to the ordinary person's 21,600 breaths.

Lahiri Mahasaya made further calculations; for example, that man can distance himself from the senses through just twelve excellent *pranayamas*; that he may acquire a basic realisation of the soul's existence through 144 excellent *pranayamas*; that 1728 excellent *pranayamas* lead to the state of *Dhyana*, as will 20,736 excellent *pranayamas* result in *Samadhi* for a short while. The breathless position called *Kevala Kumbhaka* may be attained following 1,061,000 *pranayamas*.[20]

WHEN spiritual masters such as Jesus Christ and Trailanga Swami were witnessed walking upon water in the past, observers hailed it as a miracle. Lahiri Mahasaya did not openly demonstrate that he too possessed this ability, but his confidential diaries reveal his knowledge of the scientific rationale behind this extraordinary control over the elements:

"… walking across water is not a difficult task. While practising *Pranakarma* when the *Prana-air* ceases or the breathing motion ceases for at least an hour, then no matter how deep the water is or how distant it is, it becomes possible to walk across it because then the essences of water, void and that of the Soul-Sun are the same and then the Self also attains the same form. When *Prana-air* is stopped easily from the external motion, then it is possible to make this body light and walk across the reverse water-

---

[20] Each of the first five *Chakras* are unlocked following at least 200,000 pranayama per *Chakra*; subsequently when the heart *Chakra* is opened, the practitioner will be in the breathless state of *Samadhi*. When all three knots (*Granthis*) have been untied and the practitioner has completed a further 61,000 pranayama, the practitioner reaches *Kevala Kumbhaka*, and as a result, *Kundalini* can pass freely through Sushumna and is awakened. This is known as *Kundalini Bhedan*.

current also. This state arrives when *Kevala-Kumbhaka* occurs."

There are many other extracts from his diary written in 1873 where he talks even more directly about his personal experiences of this state:[21]

"Today while walking, my feet lifted from the earth."

"When *Kumbhaka* occurred automatically while practising *Pranakarma*, I realised that the body attained buoyancy and lost weight ... Achieving this type of *Kevala Kumbhaka* state the body is being pulled upwards."

"Today I have severed all connections with superficial nature and am travelling exclusively within, immense bliss is ensuing from this. I could further comprehend that now I was levitating with my *Asana* posture intact ..."

REFERENCE to this yogic ability may also be found in *Patanjali's Yoga Sutras*:

"By conquering the current called *Udana*,[22] the Yogi does not sink in water or in swamps, he can walk on thorns etc., and can die at will."[23]

Initiation Procedure

Some so-called gurus "initiate" groups of twenty to five hundred people in one session. They do not turn anybody down, which would suggest more interest in fame and money than in the progress of their disciples.

However, Kriya Yoga comes from India and the Indian tradition should be followed. Therefore, if a guru initiates more than a couple of people at a time, it is another sign that he has veered away from the original method and principles of Kriya Yoga.

---

[21] From *Purana Purusha* by Dr A. K. Chatterjee.

[22] *Udana* is one of the five principal airs of the body which circulates and regulates the upper portion of the body including the throat and lungs. When conquered, and the air which normally circulates between the root and throat *Chakra* ceases, the gravitational pull of the lower airs in the body cease resulting in the Yogi's body becoming as light as air. He can also walk in mud or sand without leaving any trace of his footprints.

[23] *Patanjali's Yoga Sutras*, number 40.

Lahiri Mahasaya's Kriya Yoga will only ever be initiated to an individual or a married couple at a time, or in special circumstances to a maximum of three people. A specific date which is astrologically favourable will be chosen by the Guru.

Once initiated, the disciple should be prepared to return to the Guru in order to have Kriya checked on a regular basis – according to Lahiri Mahasaya, every six months. Since I do not manage to travel to India biannually, I questioned Guruji on this point. He said that although Lahiri Mahasaya stipulated this, it is understandably difficult for his Western disciples to have their Kriya checked so often. Therefore they must come whenever it is possible and practical for them to do so. The principle stands, and periodic check-ups of practice are necessary to enable the disciple to make proper progress.

Personal experience tells me that the disciple who is practising seriously will want and need these check-ups, since questions relating to practice arise frequently.

The Promises
Firstly, the disciple has to promise sincerely to practise Kriya Yoga morning and evening for life. Lahiri Mahasaya said that if there is adequate dedication, there should never be any need to miss a practice. Although the person living a domestic existence has responsibilities to meet and challenges to face, great blessings are guaranteed particularly if practice is not neglected even in times of trouble. If the practitioner is able to harness the mind in times of sickness and practise despite physical weakness, the problem will disappear all the more quickly. Naturally, formidable discipline is required if this first promise is to be kept, and there should be no complacency on the part of the disciple.

Secondly, the disciple is expected to maintain the principle of secrecy: he must promise not to reveal the actual method of practice to anyone else.

Thirdly, the disciple promises to read a portion of the *Bhagavad Gita* every day. According to Satya Charan Lahiri, preferably at least one chapter. Doing so helps the practitioner to understand the nature of the Kriya Yoga path and experiences along the way, though reading alone does not replace the need for actual self-realisation practice.

Fourthly, the male disciple promises to treat all women as his mother, excepting the wife, just as the female disciple promises to treat all men as her father excepting the husband.

The disciple may also be expected to promise to refrain from consumption of intoxicating substances including alcohol and tobacco.

An Outline of the Original Method

Lahiri Mahasaya gave five practices in the first initiation of Kriya. Through these, the five main airs in the body called *Prana, Apana, Samana, Vyana and Udana* are brought under control. The master said that when these airs had been steadied, all the other airs in the body were automatically and effortlessly controlled.

Exact specifics of time or numbers relating to the actual method of practice cannot be included here for reasons pertaining to the principle of secrecy. There should be no misunderstanding of the fact that without direct and personal initiation from the authorised Guru, Kriya Yoga cannot be practised.

However, it may be re-emphasised that although the need for correct timing is inseparable from the original practice, this remains the most commonly overlooked factor by those who are teaching Kriya Yoga in an altered form.

1. *Talavya* is the key to Kriya Yoga and the method is incomplete without it. In this practice, the obstruction of the tongue is removed by stretching it up into the nasal cavity so that the lower surface lies upward against the upper palate. Pressure points at the back of the mouth and in the palatal cavity are thereby stimulated, affecting the whole body and promoting internal healing. A foetus in the mother's womb has its tongue in this position until the moment of its exit into the world. This position is known in yoga as *Khechari mudra*.[24]

For the Kriya practitioner, the method of *Khechari* can only be taught by the authorised Guru. No surgery is involved.

Some gurus teaching Kriya these days seem to be ignorant of the

---

[24] In Sanskrit, *Khe* means "sky" and *charya* means "one who moves". This explains why the practice of *Khechari mudra* is also referred to as "Inner-Outer-Space Kriya", whereby the advanced Yogi ceases to be limited by the bounds of the physical body, and having attuned its vibration to an ethereal state, may travel both inside and outside of it.

natural steps taken in order for the practitioner to attain the position of *Khechari mudra*. They tell their disciples to fold the tongue back and imagine that it is reaching to the brain. However, doing so is ineffective and not to be compared to the method taught by Lahiri Mahasaya.

At intervals, the brain secretes a fluid known in Sanskrit as *Amrit*, meaning "nectar" or "elixir of life", from the posterior fontanel. This secretion is extremely valuable for the body's health and rejuvenation when caught on the tip of the tongue. It also has the effect of making the practitioner feel intoxicated, and bestows the energy to stay for long periods in meditation. Even the beginner notices less laziness. The body becomes light. Lahiri Mahasaya also said that this practice was the key to gaining victory over the senses, since other benefits of *Khechari* are control over hunger, thirst, sleep and the need to urinate and defecate.

As long as the practitioner is not required to speak, it is possible to go through daily life in *Khechari mudra,* and be benefited by the state of inner peace and stillness which this practice affords. *Khechari mudra* ultimately leads to the state of purity requisite to attaining perfect tranquillity through which the Self may be realised.

Many references may be found in the ancient Hindu Scriptures pertaining to the consumption of meat, beef or veal, whilst in the same vein the principle of non-violence is being taught. The seeming contradiction is solved and real meaning revealed with knowledge of *Khechari mudra*. In the Bible Jesus says, "I have meat (tongue) to eat that ye know not of."[25]

2. *Pranayama* is for the control of *Prana* and *Apana*: the upward force of the breath is known as *Prana*, and the downward force is *Apana*. Though they function in opposite directions, through practice they naturally become controlled and unite. Once this occurs, the practitioner is able to take internal respiration through *Sushumna*.

3. *Nabhi Kriya* (also known in the West as Navi- or Navel Kriya) is for the control of the *Samana* air. In the navel there is also a light,

---

[25] St. John 4:32

or a second "sun" in the body. This essential practice is often omitted entirely by various so-called teachers of Kriya Yoga.

4. *Yoni Mudra* is a practice for Soul-realisation, whereby the Kriya practitioner may experience the inner light which exists in *Kutastha*, even on the first attempt during initiation. The doors of the senses are forcefully closed and the mind is fixed at the point between the eyebrows according to the method personally imparted by the Guru.

5. *Maha Mudra* controls the airs *Vyana* and *Udana*. During practice, the body may feel very light.

Other Technicalities
After eating a full meal, there should be a gap of three to four hours before starting Kriya practice.

During Kriya practice, there should be no interruptions: the practitioner should neither talk, nor open his eyes. He should only get up if the call of nature deems a break necessary, and then recommence where he left off.

SECRETS OF LOVE (A Song)

Three empty days
Two far apart
And One is all I want
And One is all I need

The sunset, perfectly calm tonight
Cool moon
Dressed in a ghostly white
Costume,
Making a show, and you know
It can tell all the wonderful secrets of love

Three empty days
Two far apart
And One is all I want
And One is all I need

At sunrise, seven new colours rise
Whose eyes dare to look at the sky's
Blue dance
Making a show, and you know
It can tell all the wonderful secrets of love

Secret, this destination
A burning fire

The ocean fills all the empty space
Rainbows line up to take their place
Inside
Making a show, and you know
They can tell all the wonderful secrets of love

Three empty days
Two far apart
And One is all I want
And One is all I need

Part Two

Tinkari Lahiri

Chapter Six

SPIRITUAL AID

Love for Creatures Great and Small

"I do feel that spiritual progress does demand at some stage that we should cease to kill our fellow creatures for the satisfaction of our bodily wants." – MAHATMA GANDHI

Tinkari Lahiri was born to Kashi Mani Devi and Shyama Charan Lahiri in 1863, during a phase of the full moon. It was evident early on that the first son would also become a spiritual master, and so Tinkari received initiation in Kriya Yoga whilst he was still at school. He attended the Bangalitola High School and then spent two years completing his formal education at the London Missionary College in Banaras.

In 1880, a marriage was arranged with the parents of Kusum Kamini Devi from Shivpur village in Pavana district. As the eldest of Kali Kamal Sanyal Mahashaya's twelve children, the girl was just twelve years old at the time of the marriage.

Soon afterwards, Tinkari Lahiri's working life began. Initially he took a teaching position in a school in Bihar, but he resigned after some time because he missed his home city Banaras and wanted to return. He then lived at home for a while, immersing himself in long daily practice of Kriya. When the next job presented itself, it took him to another state once more, but when he returned to Banaras after that job ended, he again spent as much time as possible practising Kriya Yoga, with the support of his father.

Tinkari used to spend much time alone even as a child and needed an atmosphere of peace and quiet. He would often leave the house at night in order to meditate on the banks of the Ganges. This upset Kusum Kamini Devi, who thought that perhaps her husband did not like her. But Lahiri Mahasaya was quick to notice his daughter-in-law's anxiety, and told Tinkari that he was to stay with his wife during the nights.

The couple had six children during the course of their marriage: Kali Charan, Abhay Charan, Ambika Charan, Tara Charan, Uma Charan, and lastly, Satya Charan.

TINKARI LAHIRI had been sitting in meditation for fourteen hours on one occasion, and Babaji appeared in the house. Lahiri Mahasaya was shocked to see his Guru, and asked,

'Now, suddenly? – Why are you here?'

Babaji replied, 'Tinkari was remembering me.'

Lahiri Mahasaya chided his son and told him not to give Babaji any trouble.[1]

A CHARACTERISTIC which showed itself from an early age was Tinkari Lahiri's rare love for plants and animals. It shone in his eyes. And it was both surprising and incomprehensible for many others to observe this great sensitivity towards every living creature, large or small.

He would visit a boatman on the river called Ganesh, who kept a menagerie of pigeons and dogs. There he would spend many hours petting the animals. He used to take pity on the hungry dogs in the lanes and sometimes cooked rice to feed them. Fishing was strictly forbidden by Tinkari Lahiri on the lake of the family property near the house. But perhaps the most surprising thing was his refusal to kill a single mosquito, despite being bitten when they came out in number at dusk.

He once had a pet dog at home which doted on its master. Tinkari found it as a forlorn puppy on the street, took it home and washed it carefully. The first night the puppy slept on the bed and by morning it was sleeping peacefully on Tinkari's chest. Kusum Kamini Devi was worried about what she should do, because her husband's long beard evidently needed washing. The dog had relieved itself before settling down again, with rather undesirable

---

[1] This event was told to Lahiri Mahasaya's grandson Satya Charan Lahiri many years later by Ram Padarath, one of Tinkari's most advanced disciples. Upon hearing the story, Satya Charan went to his father to ask if it was true.

'Who told you this?' Tinkari had asked.

'Ram Padarath.'

And Tinkari Lahiri had seemed somehow disappointed and refused to reply.

consequences. However, her husband did not seem to be in the slightest concerned. He just laughed and remarked how comfortable the puppy had made itself.

Tinkari was also observed taking extraordinary care of a sick bull in Delhi during an unusually cold winter. With a heart full of compassion that keenly felt the animal's pain, and realising it was near death, he went home to fetch a blanket. He knew that the bull was cold and covered it up to the head. But that was not sufficient to warm it, so he made a log fire, and sat with the creature until morning. The bull did not die that night, but slowly began to recover instead.

THEN there was the property in the district of Jaunpur, which Lahiri Mahasaya's disciple Paresh Nath Rai had given to Tinkari since he had no children of his own. The ayurvedic doctor had hesitated in offering this land to his Guru's son at first, since Tinkari usually refused all gifts. He was relieved and pleased when Tinkari accepted.

Although it was an additional responsibility, the land was potentially very profitable due to a large forest rich in palas trees.

In those days, sealing wax was a valuable commodity made from the saliva of a tiny insect which lived in the palas tree. However, in the process of taking the silk cocoons for manufacture into wax, these insects died. Furthermore, palas leaves have always been multi-functional in India for packaging pan, *betel*, and flower garlands; plates are still made by pressing the leaves. So it was not long before the Yogi was approached by a businessman.

Tinkari Lahiri was informed that he could become rich without any effort whatsoever. The contract was ready and waiting for a signature.

The Yogi, fully aware of the consequence for the insects of the forest which were to be annihilated in the process of this profit-making, and seeing the greed in the man's mind, listened with extraordinary patience. But finally he spoke up.

'If you have finished talking, you may go,' he said. 'I do not wish to sign any contract for this forest.'

❖ ❖ ❖ ❖ ❖ ❖ ❖ ❖

Having been vegetarian in India, one of the first things I did upon landing on Western soil again was to go into a fast-food chain, licking my lips at the thought of some fried chicken with chips.

It was not as if vegetarianism had been such a terrible hardship. It was rare for me to buy meat for myself anyway. As a student I had been vegetarian for a couple of years until I decided to relax my principles somewhat by eating meat at least when invited for a meal in someone else's house. It had simplified life at such times and I did enjoy it on occasion.

There were no special restrictions in Kriya Yoga about being vegetarian as such. But I knew that the yogis in Lahiri Mahasaya's lineage had been strictly vegetarian, and Guruji was too. Apparently, a person in the higher stages of yoga had no desire for meat. Kriya practice somehow purified the cells of the body until it neither wanted nor needed it.

However, I had also gathered that suppressing desires was not required of me, nor was it a good idea to do so, and therefore saw no problem in getting my teeth into a juicy breadcrumb-coated piece of chicken as soon as possible.

But it was a sad disappointment. I tried hard to enjoy my meal, but the chicken tasted strange. Meat did not taste good any more. It failed to satisfy. Was this because of Kriya, I wondered.

Sitting on my stool watching London go by outside the window, I finished the remainder of my French fries and pondered some of Guruji's stories on the subject of yogis and animals:

THE BUDDHA'S cousin once shot down a bird in flight with his arrow. The young master, Gautama Siddhartha, rushed to where it had fallen wanting to administer first aid. His cousin followed and wanted to claim the wounded bird. But Siddhartha refused to give it to him. He said,

'One who can save life is greater than the one who would take it.'

An argument ensued, and the boys told Siddhartha's father why they were fighting. The father gave the bird to the Buddha who healed it and set it free.

THERE was a self-realised saint named Vijay Krishna Goswami from Vrindavan who refused to kill mosquitoes. Every day he was badly bitten and once he became very sick and feverish with malaria.

His good friend Kutu Bubi was also frequently bitten and Vijay could not bear the thought that she might contract the disease too. Because of the severe pain it had caused him, he decided to communicate with the mosquitoes on her behalf.

The insects responded to the vibrations sent out by the Yogi, and Kutu Bubi was never bitten by a single mosquito again.

IN THE mid-nineteenth century, Trailanga Swami used to meditate in the forest where the *Maharaja* of Nepal hunted tigers for sport. As the *Maharaja* was chasing a tiger one day with his javelin poised in the air, his prey came to a sudden halt. It lay down next to a saint who was sitting under a tree. The King was forced to stop.

'Please sir, is this tiger your pet?' said he, addressing the Swami respectfully.

'No it isn't. Why do you want to kill this tiger?'

'Because I am the King!' came the indignant reply. 'This is my forest and hunting is my favourite sport.'

'I see,' the holy man said. 'Tell me something: it seems that you are able to kill a tiger, but are you also able to give it life?'

The King was taken aback by the question and answered that he could not.

'In that case,' continued the Swami, 'if you do not have the power to give a creature life, what gives you the right to take it away?'

With these words, Trailanga Swami turned and walked away. The tiger stayed close to the Yogi's heels for protection. And from that day forward, the King never killed another animal.

ON ANOTHER occasion, Trailanga Swami was invited by the owner of a burning *ghat* to come to a feast. In an attempt to put the vegetarian Yogi to the test, his host prepared cooked meats of every kind, and pressed the Swami to eat.

'I cannot eat meat,' the holy man replied.

'Why not? Of course you can. I eat meat.'

'Very well,' said the Yogi to his host. 'If you can eat anything, so can I.'

Then Trailanga Swami passed a stool into his own hand.

'Here. Eat this,' he said, holding it out to his host with a smile.

'How can I eat that?' the man exclaimed in horror.

'This is exactly my feeling about eating meat,' replied Trailanga Swami. Then he was silent for a moment before looking down at his hand again.

'Don't worry, it is a *gulab jamun* now. Take it – it's good!'

Indeed, the excrement in his hand had turned into a sweet. He took a bite before handing it to the doubting man to taste.

'Never test a Yogi,' said Trailanga Swami, who was known for his ability to transform material substances.

The owner of the burning *ghat* apologised humbly and admitted that he had always wanted to see such a miracle.

WHEN Sri Shankaracharya[2] was invited to a feast by the owner of a burning *ghat* in Banaras, his host was disappointed that the self-realised saint did not turn up, despite having promised to do so. He spent the evening looking out for him as he served the meal and was irritated all the while by an annoying dog. It pestered him constantly and tried to steal food from the plates. Eventually, he beat the dog so hard that it left howling miserably, its tail hanging between its legs.

Since Sri Sankaracharya had not kept his word, the burning *ghat* owner went to look for the saint the next day in order to demand an explanation.

'I was at your feast!' replied Sri Sankaracharya. 'But you were serving meat, and you know very well that I'm vegetarian. That is to say, I can't eat meat in this body which is why I entered the body of a dog. It was the only way to enjoy your food, but you beat me and sent me away.'

---

[2] Sri Shankaracharya was born around 788 AD. He lived in a small village named Kaladi, in Kerala, South India.

Helping the Needy

"He who sees me (the Universal Self) present in all beings,
and all beings existing within Me, never loses sight of Me,
and I never lose sight of him." – BHAGAVAD GITA[3]

Tinkari Lahiri was thirty-two years old when his father took *Mahasamadhi.* As the eldest son, responsibility for the welfare of the family fell to him. He had hoped to find work in Banaras at last, but despite his education, no suitable posts were available. After a long period of waiting and searching there was no alternative but to look elsewhere.

He went to Calcutta and found a clerical position in a post office. As his father had done before him, he succeeded in balancing his worldly responsibilities with his spiritual practice.

For a while he lived with his *Guru-brother* Panchanan Bhattacharya, and later rented a place of his own in the Howrah area. But it was not to be for long. The activities of the Bengal Independent Revolutionaries forced the British to move the capital from Calcutta to Delhi in 1911, and many government offices were relocated in the process. Thus in the same year, Tinkari was also transferred with his department to Delhi.

Due to the great influx of new offices and businesses in Delhi, colonies were built to provide enough accommodation for the workers who had come in droves from other areas of India. Shortly after Tinkari Lahiri was transferred and began to live in one such colony, there was a widespread outbreak of smallpox which soon had the entire city in the grip of panic.

Although everyone was living in such close proximity to each other, Tinkari soon observed that wide cultural diversity in both language and lifestyle was causing so much social division that no one was taking any interest in the plight of their neighbours. He was distressed to see people abandoning each other, leaving even family members to die alone in order to save themselves. Weeping was to be heard everywhere, the sick suffered helplessly, and death was so rampant that the business of cremation was becoming problematic.

---

[3] VI:30 (Gita Press)

One Bengali family came to Delhi with their faithful servant, who had been with them for several decades. But the moment he contracted smallpox, they wasted no time in deserting him. Tinkari Lahiri heard about this man and went to see him. His glands were swollen and he was lying in bed in severe pain. He listened to the disillusioned servant's pitiful story, as he related how over the years he had been treated as one of the family; trust in their genuine love for him was the only reason he had left his own family to accompany them to Delhi. And yet in his hour of need they had left him to die alone. Worst of all, he had no means of getting word to his own family.

Tinkari was shocked. His eyes filled with tears of compassion. He wondered at the depths to which man with his superior intellect could stoop, and considered how even animals gave love in return for kindness, neither forgetting nor being capable of such duplicity and hypocrisy.

The dying man gave Tinkari *Pranam* in thanks for his care. Tinkari responded by tenderly lifting the man's head into his lap. The old servant seemed to find some peace at last and passed away. So it was the Yogi who covered the body with a blanket and carried it over his shoulder to be cremated. He paid for the wood and stood making *Pranam.*

Although Tinkari was also new to the city and its inhabitants, he soon observed that such situations were not unusual, and began to act. Whenever he was not in the office, he went out to meet people and to speak with them. He would say that if everyone only cared for his own individual needs, society as a whole would remain helpless. Strength could only be achieved if they pulled together and helped each other. He encouraged people to forget their own selfish fears and to be of service to their fellow man. They were effectively standing on a battlefield, and the imperative was to fight rather than run away. We can help and save each other, he insisted.

People began to listen and see the logic in what Tinkari was saying. It was more than rhetoric for they saw him live every word. He was always ready to give practical help. He was centred, had a powerful aura, and gave the people with whom he came into contact fresh hope and a sense of direction in the face of a frightening situation. And this spurred others into action. Soon,

Tinkari had formed a group dedicated to passing on the message to others and helping the needy.

YATINDRA NATH BANDHOPADHYAYE was born and brought up in Calcutta. When he was young, jobs in the city were scarce and it was not without great effort that he finally found one. But no sooner had he started work, when the office informed him of an imminent transfer to Delhi. The news came as a shock, because his family was dependent on him. There was his mother to consider, and an aunt whose husband had passed away whilst Yatindra was still a child. This aunt had always given her sister and nephew a great deal of loving support. But at the time when they were forced to make the long journey, she was weak and unwell. Although it was a critical situation, a delay was not possible.

Yatindra Nath managed to find a place to live when they arrived in the new capital of India, but the family had not foreseen the severe change of climate. In Calcutta, they had only ever needed thin clothing and perhaps one shawl for the wintertime. Now they were faced with one of Delhi's coldest winters and could hardly bear to go outside. Their skin cracked and their bodies fought to resist the harsh conditions.

It was too much for Yatindra Nath's aunt. Her condition rapidly deteriorated until on the fourth day after their arrival, she suddenly died in the evening. Yatindra and his mother were devastated.

As if grief and shock were not enough to bear, they were now faced with a dilemma. There was a cremation to be organised and it should be done properly. But having just arrived they knew nobody at all, besides being unfamiliar with the new surroundings. Yatindra felt disorientated, yet the burden of responsibility lay on his shoulders.

His mother was weeping with her head on her sister's chest. Not knowing which way to turn or what to do with himself, Yatindra lit a lantern and went to sit outside the front door.

Hardly a moment later, a young man appeared out of the darkness.

'Has someone from Bengal died here recently?' he asked Yatindra Nath.

'Well, yes – my aunt died this evening.' The question came as a shock.

'Did anyone else die here?' the stranger questioned further.

'That I don't know.'

'In that case, I have come to the right place. Do you have any bamboo to make the stretcher?'

'We arrived in Delhi only four days ago. We don't have anything.'

'Very well, I will see to it.' And with that, the young man turned on his heels and disappeared into the black night, leaving Yatindra Nath to sit wondering who the man was, where he had come from and who could have sent him. There was no logical explanation.

A short while later, the stranger returned carrying a couple of bamboo poles.

'Come on,' he told Yatindra, 'this is no time for sitting around. We have to get to work.'

The stranger handled the initial preparations with both skill and speed. He wrapped the body in cloth and had Yatindra help him lift it onto the stretcher he had made. Then, taking the head of the stretcher and instructing Yatindra Nath to take the other end, he led the way to the burning *ghat*, taking short cuts whenever possible.

When they arrived he called someone over to help, and issued instructions as to what was to be done. His organisation was impeccable, and he handled everything with such perfect assurance that Yatindra could not help wondering whether he was a priest.

When the cremation ceremonials were over, the mysterious helper accompanied Yatindra back to the house and wanted to take his leave.

'*Baba*, what is your name?' asked Yatindra's mother. 'Are you a god? Please introduce yourself to us before you go.'

'Mother, there is no point in telling you my name.'

'Oh, but you have to say!' she insisted. 'At least, *Baba*, you must come to the feast in thirteen days. If you do not come, her soul will not get peace.'

'Don't worry,' replied the stranger. 'I will be there.'

And on the day of the feast, the stranger returned as promised and introduced himself as Tinkari Lahiri, the son of Shyama Charan Lahiri Mahasaya.

YATINDRA NATH and his mother had not heard of Lahiri Mahasaya. But they swore to themselves after this miracle that it was a name they would never forget. Some time after Tinkari helped them in their hour of need, Yatindra came to be introduced to Lahiri Mahasaya's disciple Sri Keshwananda Brahmachari. And it was from him that he received Kriya Yoga initiation.

WHEN Tinkari Lahiri returned to Banaras after finishing his work in Delhi, it was to be a permanent move back home. The land which Paresh Nath Rai had given to the family provided sufficient income and at least released them from financial worry. Tinkari was thus once again able to devote himself to Kriya Yoga for long stretches each day whilst taking care of the family and household duties.

The amount of time which Tinkari spent in internal practice by no means blunted his awareness of what was going on around him. He once more showed his fearlessness in the face of death when there was a case of smallpox near his home. The disease had struck a priest living in an *ashram* and all the other inhabitants of the hermitage had made a hasty departure, leaving the man helpless and completely alone. To get a doctor to come was a virtual impossibility because the patient's chances of recovery were so slight, and the fear of infection too great.

Tinkari Lahiri wasted no time in hurrying to the *ashram* as soon as he heard about the dying priest. He reassured him that there was no need to worry, and spent day and night nursing him. To the astonishment of many, the priest made a full recovery.

❖ ❖ ❖ ❖ ❖ ❖ ❖ ❖ ❖

My parents were relieved to find that their daughter had not been hypnotised after all. They had endless questions about Guruji and even expressed an interest in finding out about meditation for themselves. My fears of a negative reaction on their part towards my commitment to a lifelong meditation practice, the specifics of which could not be shared, turned out to be completely unfounded.

Perhaps their interest was sparked by intrigue in the changes which had obviously occurred in me. Besides, my mother had always worried that my religious standpoint verged on fanaticism. Now it was clear, even to myself, how much broader my view had become. Some of Guruji's balance and practicality had definitely rubbed off. Since nothing negative could be said about that, I was free to do my daily Kriya practice without any interference or objection from the family.

Fortunately, a whole month of much needed relaxation and recuperation at home lay ahead before a couple of prearranged summer jobs were due to start. But some work had to be done for the Karenni refugees straight away.

The bulk of the fund-raising work was done through successfully enlisting the help of sixth-formers in two secondary schools. They managed to raise a substantial sum between them. In addition, a couple of my mother's work colleagues organised a sponsored walk in aid of the Karenni, and other donations came in as a result of articles in local newspapers which reported my experiences in the jungle. Within a relatively short time, it was clear that the refugee camp was going to get the equipment it so desperately needed.

Normally, I considered, one should feel excused in thinking one had done something good. A pat on the back was well-deserved for making such an admirable effort to help. There was no doubt that the refugees would be exceedingly grateful. Even as a gesture it would give them hope that they were not entirely forgotten in their plight.

Guruji had said something about how very subtly the ego can play its part in this kind of charity. At the time I had not wanted to listen. But now practice was again having the effect of mirroring the size of my ego back to me. It was clear that Guruji had wanted me to see for myself and it was somewhat discomfiting as usual to do so.

There was nothing particularly glamorous about talking to school pupils at assembly or the appearance of my picture in local newspapers, but these things, together with praise heaped on from all sides, were elements which contributed to the swelling of some inner pride. It was another lesson in the obscure workings of the human mind and how cunningly the ego could disguise itself.

Only the Yogi could give permanent help, Guruji had said. To get to that stage would certainly require a lot more effort than it had taken to be interviewed by local journalists and enthusing others to help fund-raise for a humanitarian project, I considered. But then one could only help according to one's present ability, surely. And I was not a Yogi yet.

THE SUMMER was spent teaching English as a foreign language to teenagers in the two schools I had worked for the previous year.

The second appointment meant teaching on a residential course, and was particularly strenuous this time around. Three long weeks of late nights made Kriya Yoga a struggle to manage each morning. Practice was also difficult to fit in later in the day when I was off-duty, either afternoon or evening. The problem was the stipulation that there had to be a minimum of a three-hour gap after a meal before starting to meditate. And afterwards one had to wait half an hour before eating.

Guruji had impressed upon us the importance of this rule. *Pranayama* could not be done properly unless the body had finished digestion so that the air was free to flow. Just as it was unwise to eat directly before doing sport, the same principle applied here. It caused unnecessary pressure on the stomach and made the body weak. It could also cause vomiting and pain.

In my free afternoons I often needed to catch up on lost sleep. After lunch one day, something strange occurred. Sleep had not yet come and I was resting in bed. Then suddenly some extremely loud voices began to shout right into my ears from either side. They were so close that it was frightening. In desperation for them to go away I tried to open my eyes but could not. My mind fought to fend off the voices. When the phenomenon finally stopped, the memory of exactly what they had said quickly faded and all I could remember was that there had been some connection with Kriya.

The experience rather shook me up. It had not borne the slightest resemblance to any kind of dream. It was upsetting and the memory stayed with me for weeks. An explanation was needed, but that would unfortunately have to wait until the next meeting with Guruji.

SEPTEMBER came at last and the money earned over the summer was once more exchanged for a bundle of traveller's cheques. The rucksack was packed. My original ticket with an unused sector from Thailand to Australia was still valid and I had decided to use it. Then the plan was to return to Varanasi for five months and perhaps rent a small flat this time.

My main aim was to become stronger and more disciplined in Kriya Yoga because it still felt so hard. To return immediately to a normal working routine might mean forgetting everything and giving in to the temptation to stop practising. Then there was a vague notion of writing a book: I already had quite a collection of Guruji's stories in my diary and had been curious to learn more about the yogis in Lahiri Mahasaya's lineage. For these masters had maintained their path of self-realisation away from publicity and fame in what seemed to be the true essence of yoga.

And Guruji was at the end of that lineage. Guruji, who never talked about his own experiences, but instead always gave examples from the life of his own Guru, Satya Charan Lahiri. Surely the surface of what there was to know about Guruji had not even been scratched.

THE FIRST task was to stop off in Thailand and spend the raised money on school equipment. The school's headmaster travelled down to Bangkok to meet me and help with the shopping. I saw everything delivered safely to the Karenni embassy in Mae Hong Son and then spent a week in the refugee camp. It was wonderful to see everyone again and they could hardly believe that they now had an impressive supply of long-awaited books and equipment.

Right then, I was the guest of honour. But being there made me truly grasp for the first time what Guruji had tried to explain about charity a year previously. The reality was that this kind of help was sadly impermanent and insufficient. In a few years the books would become outdated and the mountain of paper and pens used up. These things could not solve the refugees' long-term problems. Food supplies had been depleted since my last visit. The guerrilla warfare was moving nearer to the camp and shots could often be heard at night. Things were steadily getting worse. It was an altogether tragic situation.

When Lahiri Mahasaya spoke to his disciples on the subject of charity, he said that social convention demanded that we be charitable to those less fortunate than ourselves, and that such external service was a good thing. However, one had to be aware that giving to the poor did not lead to self-realisation, nor was it a lasting help. To truly serve God meant to serve one's own soul. Unstable *Prana* was the cause of suffering and pain and it was man's highest duty to make it constant. Through Kriya *pranayama*.

Or as Guruji put it: 'We are prepared to do everything for others and nothing for ourselves.' Yet the best way to help the world was actually to take pity on our own soul. To have mercy on Self.

Everything always seemed to boil down to the one word: practice. A consideration of the kind of charity a spiritual master could give as opposed to what I had just given to the Karenni ensured that any remaining feelings of personal pride were swiftly blown away.

THE TIME in Australia was highly memorable, particularly Cairns. I stayed in the popular backpackers' lodges and went on as many trips as my budget allowed to the sun-drenched beaches, remote islands and virgin rainforests of the North.

For a short while I went on an "adrenaline trip" which began with a bungy jump. This was easily the most petrifying self-induced experience of my life. In retrospect though, a fantastic one. It was followed by a tandem skydive a few days later, and within the same week I went on a trial scuba-diving experience on the Great Barrier Reef.

Perhaps it was Kriya Yoga which had the effect of making me look at things differently, forcing me to analyse more and ask where the attraction for this kind of extreme sport came from. Was the free fall purely undertaken for fun or for the challenge it posed? Or was the rush which sent every nerve in the body quaking an attempt to find a new external satisfaction? If that were the case, how fulfilling was the experience really?

Without a doubt, these were adventures never to be forgotten. Powerful and positive experiences as far as overcoming fear was concerned. A sense of achievement was partly justified. No doubt, it was a part of my character to relish such challenges.

But admittedly another more negative character trait was to enjoy showing-off at times. Once the display of courage had been immortalised on video, I became aware that watching it subconsciously charged the ego.

Such considerations were further evidence that it would be a long time before my ego was overcome. They made me realise that

Guruji's example and the practice of Kriya Yoga had made a substantial difference in my life after just six months. Such things simply would never have occurred before.

Regular Kriya practice satisfied in a way which nothing else could. It was food for the soul. Bungy jumping could not match it. Even as a beginner with hopeless concentration it was evidently possible to discover in some limited way that satisfaction and happiness really did come from inside. Throwing oneself off a forty-meter tower took guts, but admittedly not half the effort required for a single session of meditation.

Life's real challenge consisted in taking up the sword in the destruction of ego. In *Krishna's* motivating words to Arjuna in the *Bhagavad Gita*, "Slice with the sword of knowledge this disbelief in the *Atman*! Disbelief is the product of ignorance. Find strength in discipline, and rise, Arjuna!"[4] This was undoubtedly one of my favourite stanzas to date, and one which needed repeating when laziness struck. It told about the inner fight which required the discipline of regular practice, not to mention the love and dedication to last a lifetime. In order to succeed you had to have the humility to work in silence in the inner chambers of being. A place where there was no cheering from the sidelines and no video to capture the moments of glory.

It was the essence of travel. Walking through life and encountering good experiences and bad. Making mistakes and trying to learn from them. Going places and doing things and occasionally glimpsing the *why*. Understanding that there was a purpose in everything.

The soul's silent voice directs the events of each individual life towards its own end. Carving out a path, regardless of whether its existence is acknowledged or denied. The soul holds the key to the heart's secret desires and waits with endless patience for as long as the search for gold at the end of the rainbow continues to satisfy. It knows that it can provide the circumstances to redirect our gaze as soon as the illusory nature of external glitter becomes apparent to us. It stands in readiness for the moment we ourselves choose to seek and unlock the secret of True Love in our inner being.

---

[4] IV:42 (Lal)

Integrity and Relationships

"This above all: to thine own self be true,
And it must follow, as the night the day,
Thou canst not then be false to any man." – WILLIAM SHAKESPEARE

The Rani Bhawani estate was run by a board of three trustees who looked after the concerns of a temple, a guest house and a scholarship for students. When a position on the board became vacant, the remaining members voted that Tinkari Lahiri should join them. Neel Ratan Bandhopadhyaye was sent to fetch him, and found the Yogi sitting on the balcony of his home, far away in deep concentration.

When the proposal was first put to him, Tinkari said that he did not have time. But Neel Ratan refused to go away. He told Tinkari how much he was needed on the board, and emphasised that as the estate was a charitable organisation, he would be doing work for the welfare of the less fortunate. Finally, Tinkari agreed to come along.

However, before long Tinkari Lahiri realised that there were certain irregularities in the day-to-day running of the estate and he resolved to see these corrected. One example was the frequent misuse of charity funds by those in responsible positions.

He discovered that Neel Ratan Bandhopadhyaye was taking money for his *palanquin* to the office every morning from the estate. Tinkari knew that Neel Ratan was actually quite rich aside from receiving a designated salary for his work and opposed the use of office funds for travel expenses.

'I'm old now, I can't walk to the office any more,' was Neel Ratan's excuse.

'I'm not saying that you should walk,' answered Tinkari matter-of-factly. 'I'm just saying that you shouldn't be taking money for your *palanquin* from the estate.'

Neel Ratan took offence at Tinkari's words, especially since he had been working as a trustee for so many years. He considered such gratuities his right. But Tinkari would not be moved and established a rule so that it would no longer be possible to extract travelling expenses from the office funds.

It Was not the only thing that Tinkari Lahiri objected to. The temple had to provide a benediction once a day for the people who came to eat, and for that purpose there was a kitchen which made *puris*, vegetable and *halwa* at the expense of the estate. When Tinkari was brought some food one morning, he asked what it was for and gathered that it had been sent from the temple.

The next day when he asked Neel Ratan why the trustees were receiving temple food, he was informed that this was the way things had always been done.

'But it isn't fair!' exclaimed Tinkari. 'Why are we taking this food which is meant for the poor people? We are paid employees!'

Realising that the temple was making almost double the amount of food necessary in order to feed the employees, Tinkari insisted that the temple should make food for the benediction twice a day instead. That way, the poor could be given a meal morning and evening. And remunerated workers were to look after their own needs.

When he passed the temple kitchen one day, Tinkari observed a boy standing outside the window holding up a cloth into which the cook was piling various foods. He did not say anything at the time, so the thieves were not aware that they had been caught in the act.

However, Tinkari paid a visit to the cook at his home that evening. When he explained why he had come, the cook attempted to deny everything. Tinkari silenced him.

'I'm telling you, because I saw you. You are poor and need to work for a living. But I'm warning you. You will be dismissed if it happens again.'

One Day, Tinkari asked his youngest son to take a letter to the post office. It was a personal letter which he had written in the estate office.

'And take this one *paisa* for the *Krishna* temple,' he said.

Satya Charan did as he was asked, and wondered about the one *paisa*. So in the evening when they sat down for a meal, he asked his father why he had been given money for the temple.

'I wrote a personal letter with the ink belonging to the trust,' Tinkari answered. 'That was not right, but in giving money to the temple my sin will be forgiven.'

TINKARI LAHIRI taught his disciples the greater importance of Kriya over study of the Scriptures. He was always ready to help disciples further with the method of practice and several of them reached the higher planes of Kriya Yoga.[5] However, he became increasingly taciturn after his father's *Mahasamadhi*. He often appeared to be in a trance.

Beni Prasad Khatri was Tinkari Lahiri's closest disciple. Over a period of many years the two of them would go to the river every evening for a few hours and talk. But many other disciples were too much in awe of their Guru to disturb him with their problems, so when they needed advice on any matter of importance they often went to Beni Prasad and asked him to approach Tinkari on their behalf.

At one time Pri Rampadarath came to his friend Beni Prasad in a quandary. His wife had died, leaving him to care for a young daughter alone. Despite a great deal of pressure from friends and family to remarry, he did not really want to. On the other hand, he said, it was hardly possible for him to take care of his daughter properly on his own and there were other reasons besides, compelling him to take a second wife.

Pri Rampardarth was an advanced practitioner, and Beni Prasad understood that from the point of view of practice, he must be reluctant to remarry. He advised his friend not to feel coerced, but Pri Rampardath became all the more adamant that he had no choice.

Beni Prasad decided to talk the situation over with his Guru. He told Tinkari that he and his *Guru-brothers* were advising Pri Rampardath against marrying a second time, but that their friend would not listen. However, he would surely be convinced if his Guru intervened.

Tinkari did not reply. The next day Beni Prasad tried again.

'Won't you please tell Pri Rampardath that he should not remarry, before it's too late?'

'You are wrong to think of stopping this marriage,' said Tinkari abruptly. Then raising his voice, 'There will be three more marriages.'

Beni Prasad was astonished at the vehemence of his Guru's

---

[5] Maheshwar Dutt from Bankura in Bengal; Beni Prasad Khatri; *Pandit* Kashi Hari Charan Bandhopadyaye; Kali Sharma; Sachindra Bhushan Chattopadhyaye; Pramath Nath Nandi.

words but heeded them. He took back the advice he had given to his friend.

The Yogi's prediction came true. Pri Rampardath's second and third wives both died early on in life. Due to family pressure, Pri Rampardath thus married a total of four times.

❖ ❖ ❖ ❖ ❖ ❖ ❖ ❖ ❖

I met someone in Thailand and delayed my flight to India for a further two weeks. It was a dreamy short-lived friendship but from the outset, I did my utmost to convince myself that there could be a future in it, for the sake of self-justification. The young man was extremely sincere.

Before long, however, I found myself seriously wondering to what extent it was self-delusion. Relationships had never been my strong point, whereas getting carried away in an emotional whirlwind was my speciality. One night following a heated argument, I went down to the deserted beach alone and cried hot tears for thinking that transitory physical closeness was remotely worth the emotional hurt which always ensued. I prayed with my whole heart for some guidance.

A few days went by before the prayer was answered in a most unexpected way. It was late at night whilst I was lying on my back with closed eyes, though not yet contemplating sleep. I had pushed the recent upset to the back of my mind.

There was a bright picture in my head. The clear vision of a face, accompanied with the simultaneous thought-flash, 'my husband'. It was not anyone I knew. And it came and went so fast, that holding on to the details of the face was impossible for long, though not for want of trying. Warming, reassuring, intriguing. Had I really seen my future husband?

My wonder soon slipped into feelings of guilt. The face had borne no resemblance whatsoever to the man lying next to me. All my heart had ever really wanted was to find the right man: to be happily married was my most cherished dream. If only the roller-coaster of attraction, romances, disappointment and heartache would stop. The same mistakes were repeated over and over, and perhaps being a slow learner I still had not grasped how to get off the ride.

As a result, the relationship had to come to a rather abrupt end, though we parted on very amicable terms. Only the future could tell whether or not I would meet "the face" some day. For the present it felt imperative to return to India and focus on my primary motivation for the second year of travel.

And once again I sat in a departure lounge, waiting and thinking. The one who so wanted to follow in the footsteps of the great masters. A little more humbled and feeling very human indeed.

BACK in Varanasi, the rucksack was safely deposited in my guest house and I hurried down the familiar cobbled lanes to Man Mandir Ghat. I could hardly wait to see Guruji, and to tell him about the face. To talk about relationships and pour out some kind of confession. To ask, why did I always make the same mistakes? Sexual attraction was a minefield – was I not eligible for some guidance? How would I ever make any significant spiritual progress at this rate?

Guruji asked plenty of questions about my trip. Whenever there was a short pause, I tried to tell him what was really pressing on my mind. But as soon as I opened my mouth, we were interrupted. The telephone rang, his wife brought in the tea, his son came home from school and disciples dropped by with gifts of fruit. It was impossible.

'I just need the reassurance that there is some hope for me yet,' I was thinking to myself, but before I could make a last attempt to get the words out, an Indian disciple knocked on the door. He had some important matter to discuss with Guruji, so I was told to go and rest. I got up extremely reluctantly, and made *Pranam* by touching Guruji's feet.

'Guruji, there was something I wanted to tell you.'

'I know,' he replied. His eyes said enough to lift the burden. It was okay.

DURING the first week back in Varanasi, I told Guruji about the unpleasant experience of the voices in my ears which had occurred on the language course in summer, and asked what it meant. To my great surprise a broad smile spread across his face as if something wonderful had happened.

'It means your fight has properly begun,' he told me. Which sounded reassuring, although I was none the wiser.

THE THEME of relationships came to a head again about a month later. Yet another ill-destined attraction from which Guruji saved me before I plunged headlong once again. Guruji had warned me in advance that something would happen and to be careful. He said that I would understand when it happened, and was free to take his advice or not, just as I pleased.

At the time I had no idea what he was talking about. Then a week later an incident occurred involving a man, and Guruji's words came back at a crucial time to save me from making what would have been a huge mistake. The reason why became clear almost immediately following the incident.

Having told Guruji the next day of the unexpected and sudden turn of events, he smiled. I was still somewhat shaken and asked him how he had known, but he only said that it was his duty as a Guru to protect and look after his disciples. If a disciple was practising Kriya conscientiously, and some occurrence was likely to make her go astray or falter from the path, he could sometimes give help. For example, in the form of a warning. That was, unless a lesson really had to be learned the hard way.

ALL OF THIS happened in November 1995, and it depressed me again. Before my yoga lesson one morning, I decided that we had to discuss my disastrous relationships and resolve the matter for good. Perhaps Guruji would advise me to forget about the opposite sex, in which case I would become an ascetic and avoid contact with men altogether. Perhaps it would be quite a good idea.

It was no wonder that Indian *sadhus* headed for the caves of the Himalayas to avoid such worldly distractions. If sex was supposed to be the most powerful energy in man, how were you supposed to concentrate on meditation and make any progress on an intense spiritual path? The most incredible spiritual insights were probably within easy reach if only recurring sensual desires could be banished from one's brain.

It transpired that Guruji was not in favour of my idea to forget about men altogether. He said it was true enough that sexual energy could distract and disturb the mind. Because of this, as far as the spiritual practitioner of Kriya Yoga was concerned, a healthy marriage was an especially positive and important social institution. In the stability of wedlock the mind was able to settle. Where mutual love and trust entwined in a happy relationship, sexual energy was directed according to need rather than pure physical attraction or lust. It kept the flame under control and thus facilitated progress on the spiritual path.

This flame could not be ignored or extinguished. Guruji explained that the Hindu goddess *Durga* was pictured seated on a tiger, as a symbol of complete yogic control over sexual energy, for an ordinary person could not stand up to a tiger's extraordinary strength and power. He added that since sex was such a dominant force in man, it could easily take control of the mind. Some people amputated their sexual organs thinking that that it was the best way to suppress the energy. But such drastic measures did not alter or bring the consciousness to a higher level.

As Guruji said: 'Sex has to be controlled naturally through practice. Have it and control it but don't destroy it. We have to live in this world and follow the spiritual path. In marriage these things can be brought into balance.'

Furthermore, the Indian Scriptures made it perfectly clear that marriage was a natural way for two people to join and journey towards their upward goal together, since it was man's birthright to find the sacred world within. Respect and love were nurtured in the relationship. Thus yogis and saints of the past were always married householders, and like Lahiri Mahasaya, Tinkari Lahiri and Satya Charan Lahiri, they did not interfere with nature without exceptional reason, nor did they endorse opposing the natural course of evolution. Even the deities which were worshipped by Hindus led married lives.

Sexual energy was life-energy. It was needed for work, the development of the brain, strong will-power, a good memory and for yoga practice. It was not something to be wasted. Therefore, the person who could control their desire achieved results in Kriya far more rapidly than one to whom intercourse was a form of entertainment. It was a question of energy storage, for the path of self-realisation required great spiritual strength. Whereas the ordinary person lacked the power in his eyes to stare at a naked light-bulb for a long time without damaging them, in time the

Kriya Yogi automatically developed the internal power to withstand the intensity of the equivalent of thousands of light-bulbs as a prerequisite to making safe progress on the spiritual path. But this was not possible without sexual control.

The sexual freedom permitted in the West was not altogether a positive thing, Guruji said. At least, he had seen many broken hearts coming into his yoga studio because of it. Sex outside of marriage was a flame which could easily turn into a fire.

Sex was viewed differently in India, due to the culture of arranged marriages. I had to admit arriving in India with shallow, preconceived ideas on this custom, mostly due to articles in the Western press which frequently honed in on sensational horror cases for the sake of "human interest", and conveyed an overall negative picture of the system. However, having since discussed the subject with people of every generation in Varanasi, it now appeared to me that the percentage of arranged marriage successes was probably equal if not higher than the so-called "love-marriages" of the West. Of course not every arranged marriage continued happily ever after, but the high success rate was nevertheless keeping the age-old system prevalent.

Besides, now I had learned something about the spiritual reasoning behind this system of marriage. The emphasis was on family, not on worldly enjoyment. Procreation was nature's law, and marriage the stable institution allowing man to progress more rapidly on his spiritual quest.

GURUJI often said things to me which I did not understand at the time. It appeared that he knew my heart and mind better than I did myself. So if only he could arrange a marriage for me, that would be more than acceptable to my way of thinking, and I suggested the idea half-jokingly. He smiled. No doubt he sensed my anxiety about whether a husband was "out there" for me or not.

He told me to wait, to be patient. Which is the worst thing you can tell an impatient person like myself.

'How long do I have to wait?' I ventured to ask. Guruji looked at me sternly as if I were pushing it. There was a long silence and Guruji sat there with his eyes closed. It was almost time for his next class.

Then he looked at me and said,

'For family side, you have to wait four years.'

NOW THERE was a juicy tip, I thought to myself as my rickshaw began to roll bumpily along Dasaswamedh road. I was going to meet my husband in four years. Somewhere around November 1999. Rather a long time away, but I had asked for it. Now the resolution was to concentrate on Kriya Yoga and keep clear of any romance that came my way until then.

MY ANGEL (A Song)

Because I can't see you
Because I can't feel you
Because I keep missing you each night
Because I would hold you
Because I would reach you
My angel will be with you tonight

Over the mist to clear blue skies
Nothing clouds her laughing eyes
She loves you
Till your spirit's high
Over the mountains, shores and seas
Finding heaven's here with me
She says, I'll show you
You can learn to fly

With silvery wings that shine like stars
You'll hear a message with your heart
She loves you
Exactly as you are
I dream away
She finds a way
To keep you safe through night and day
She says, I love you
No matter where you are

Haunted by questions
Followed by questions
Answers which find several ways to go
When will I see you?
I feel that I need you
Oh my angel
Show me where to go

Chapter Seven

PERSONAL EFFORT IS REQUIRED

The Effects of Longer Practice

"That thine alms may be in secret:
and thy Father which seeing in secret himself
shall reward thee openly." – CHRIST JESUS[1]

It became apparent during his childhood that the youngest son, Satya Charan, was destined for the Kriya Yoga path. A disciple asked Tinkari Lahiri one day,

'Will one of your sons follow you, from whom we can ask for help in the future?'

Tinkari pointed to Satya Charan, who was eight years old and playing nearby. 'The boy was born for this purpose,' he replied. 'He will take care of the welfare of you people.'

Satya Charan gained good marks at school and studied hard, but before he had finished school he asked his father to initiate him in Kriya Yoga. Since the elder brothers were all graduates and postgraduates, Tinkari encouraged his youngest to finish his education first. He told him that he would receive initiation when the time came. However, Satya Charan entreated his father day after day until Tinkari gave in and consented to initiate him at the age of seventeen, which was a year before he finished his schooling.

Kusum Kamini Devi and her husband loved Satya Charan dearly. They were proud of the way he managed his responsibilities, household tasks included. His father was well aware that Satya Charan slept on average just two and a half hours a night since having received Kriya Yoga. Yet the boy lovingly

---

[1] St. Matthew 6:4

looked after his parents' needs, and gradually began to take over responsibility of the family property outside of Banaras from his father, as his elder brothers were living and working in other cities. This work gave him the means to live. He insisted that further education in addition would be too much, and to the surprise of the rest of the family, Tinkari accepted his son's decision not to go to university.

However, Kusum Kamini Devi was anxious about Satya Charan and asked her husband if he was sure about letting their son discontinue his studies. She was worried that when they were no longer there and the property was divided amongst the sons, Satya Charan would be stranded with an inadequate income.

Tinkari listened to his wife and was silent for a while.

'I will give him something more,' he said finally.

The close family circle became aware of these words and knew of Satya Charan's early success in yoga. No one had any doubt that he would attain to the highest spiritual levels. He was well loved in the family for he was dependable, conscientious and had a wonderful sense of humour. But it remained unclear what Satya Charan would receive to help him through life, and whether Tinkari's words referred to material or spiritual gain, or both. However, it was well known that anything which Tinkari predicted always came true.

Owing to the influence of his previous life, and through Kriya Yoga which he practised twelve to eighteen hours each day, by the time Satya Charan was about twenty-five he had experienced *Samadhi* and was an advanced Yogi. The disciple Beni Prasad Khatri overheard an interesting exchange between father and son one morning.

'Somebody was awakening *Kundalini* today. Was it you?'

'How did you know?' Satya Charan asked his father.

ANOTHER time, when Satya Charan was in his mid-twenties, he went to the cupboard where his grandfather's Kriya diaries were kept, and started to read them.

'What are you doing? Close it!' a loud voice boomed at him.

Shocked, he turned around to see his father's angry face.

'There is no need to read this,' said Tinkari Lahiri. 'Do your yoga *sadhana* and then you will know everything.'

UPON retirement, Yatindra Nath settled in Banaras. One evening as he was taking a stroll along the river bank, he stopped at Chausatti Yogini Ghat in astonishment to see a face which he recognised. A saint with a long beard was sitting on a wooden bench and appeared to be in *Samadhi*. Although his face had changed a little, Yatindra Nath immediately saw that it was the same man who had helped with the cremation of his aunt all those years ago in Delhi. He stood transfixed, gazing at the Yogi in wonder. Tinkari Lahiri was sitting as still as a statue, completely oblivious to the activity on the *ghat*. Children were laughing and playing; people were shouting and bathing in the river, and the Yogi's eyes remained fixed and unblinking in *Shambhavi mudra*.

How many times Yatindra had thought about him over the years and wondered where he lived! He was so happy to see him again that he finally walked over to touch the master's feet.

'Who are you, and why are you giving me *Pranam*?' asked the Yogi in a deep voice.

Yatindra reminded him of the invaluable help he had given his family a long time ago.

'I don't know, I don't remember,' replied the Yogi, and sank once more into deep meditation.[2]

IN 1926, Tinkari Lahiri's eldest son Kali Charan died suddenly at the age of forty, just a few days after the death of his own wife for whom he had been grieving. It was a double shock for the whole family, including Kashi Mani Devi who was by then ninety.

A priest was called to discuss the rituals for cremation. It would have been usual for the father to take charge of the arrangements, but instead Satya Charan was appointed. From taking the body to the burning *ghat*, to the subsequent thirteen days of mourning, *puja*

---

[2] Yatindra Nath Banhopadhyaye told his story to Satya Charan Lahiri and a group of others years after Tinkari took *Mahasamadhi*, when he came to the house in order to pay his respects to his *Paramguru* (meaning "Greater Guru", or "Guru of one's own Guru") Lahiri Mahasaya. He was on the way to meet his own Guru, Sri Keshwananda Brahmachari from Vrindavan who was staying in Banaras for a few days. Yatindra made *Pranam* to the photograph of Lahiri Mahasaya and his eyes fell on the photograph just below of the great master's son Tinkari Lahiri. The picture stirred up memories and he began to weep. Everyone present begged to know the reason for his tears. When his story came to an end, nobody spoke a word for a while. Then a discussion erupted on why Tinkari had not been able recall the event when he saw Yatindra again on the *ghat*. It was finally concluded that the Yogi only had one motive, and that was to help others at a time of great need. But he remained detached from the action, and therefore such things did not stay in his memory.

ceremonials and the traditional feast at the end, it was the youngest son who organised everything.

On the day of Kali Charan's death, Tinkari Lahiri broke with custom and went to work in the afternoon at Rani Bhawani estate as usual. Upon returning home, he walked down to the River Ganges and sat on the *ghat*. His expression was peaceful and he seemed to be in a trance. There were no tears, nor any sign of anger or suffering. He was as detached from happiness as he was from pain. His children found him resting there and asked him to come home with them. Speaking softly, he told them to go along without him, that he would follow shortly.

The other members of staff at the estate could not understand it. They had never known anyone quite like Tinkari Lahiri before. It was shock enough when one's parents died, but to witness the death of one's own offspring was unbearable. It was the worst possible scenario one could imagine as a parent. The son embodied the future. Who could comfort and ease the pain of someone who experienced such tragedy? Yet this man had come to work on the day of his son's death, and naturally they had told him to go home.

'Why?' he had asked. He told them that he was there to do his daily work. And everyone had noted his ability to execute that work with the usual perfect concentration.

Tinkari Lahiri saw himself as the provider. It was his duty to go to work and earn money. He could see no point in sitting around the house and weeping with everyone else for thirteen days. He felt that he could leave those things to the other family members.

Of course he was questioned by many about his apparent calm whilst everyone around him was in mourning. And he replied that through Kriya practice it was possible to face even the worst challenges which life presented with ease. Yes, the death of a son was particularly painful. Yet the parent could never be more than a human guardian. A perception of Truth afforded the insight that one's children belonged in reality only to God and eliminated any sense of personal loss. What came from God had to return to Him when the time came.

Tinkari Lahiri's other sons were nonetheless unsettled in the face of their brother's death and Satya Charan asked his father one day how they would cope when he was not there to take care of them any more. Tinkari said that whatever happened in life, one's personal responsibilities were never to be neglected. Then he added,

'And in the desert, even in the desert, God is very near.'

❖ ❖ ❖ ❖ ❖ ❖ ❖ ❖

Christmas was coming. I had not spent a Christmas at home with the whole family for years and the intense longing to do so now gave me no peace. Finally, I called my parents to tell them of my decision to come home for a fortnight over the holiday period.

I had only been home for a few days when my parents said that they would like to invite Guruji and his family to stay the following summer. For months I had been sending my mother books to feed her new-found appetite on the subject of yoga meditation. Apparently she was coming to the same conclusion as I had earlier, that meditation in theory soon ceases to be satisfactory. Now they wanted to learn more for themselves but were not particularly keen on the idea of travelling to India. Did I think they would like to come?

The suggestion came out of the blue and was a wonderful plan as far as I was concerned. Numerous discussions with my parents on the subject of yoga had made me very much wish that they could meet Guruji themselves.

TEN DAYS later saw me climbing the steep stone steps up to Guruji's apartment, happily carrying the letter of invitation and some Christmas biscuits which my mother had sent.

Guruji smiled a warm welcome. It struck me right then that he already knew the contents of my letter. So I handed it to his wife, Vandana, who had become a special friend over the past months. She read it and squealed in delight.

'We're going to England! I didn't believe you! We're really going to England!'

Once she had calmed down, Vandana told me that a few days after I had left for the Christmas break, Guruji had told her that her wish was soon going to come true. They would all be going to England next year. And she had told him not to say such things. She would only believe something like that when she saw the proof. Like a letter of invitation.

DURING that second year I lived in three different places. For the first few months I stayed with Guruji's parents-in-law, who treated me as a daughter of their own. Ganga Dhar Mishra spoke good English, but his lively wife did not. This provided an incentive to take some Hindi lessons. After a few weeks even the rickshaw drivers and market sellers began to smile and reward my efforts to speak their language with enthusiasm and some respect, and it was pleasing to see the prices descend from the tourist to the Indian rate.

Then I moved to a little flat in Assi Ghat which turned out to be less than ideal. The place was overrun with monkeys and the landlord was rather too nosy for my liking. However, being independent was good, especially having purchased a gas cooker and water filter. I bought fresh vegetables from the market and enjoyed a break from *masala*, by spicing my food conservatively with salt and pepper.

When Cord and John arrived in Varanasi for a couple of months, it was a good excuse to leave the flat and move to a new place they had found, a small lodge with only six rooms in the narrow lanes of the old city.

THE GOOD thing about being with friends who were also Guruji's disciples was not just the exchange of positive experiences in Kriya Yoga, but the reassuring knowledge that we often had the same difficulties.

Laziness had always been a standing joke amongst us. Cord and John were envious of the seven-day break I got every month, since practice was not allowed during menstruation. The body was weak at that time in terms of being able to do Kriya and also had to be "clean" for practice. It was true that I relished being able to sleep for longer on those days. The only other "official" times when one could skip practice were during a thunderstorm, since the electrical current produced in Kriya Yoga could attract lightning to where one was sitting; also during sickness when the body was too weak to sit, and directly after eating.

It is inevitable that if you are an ordinary person trying to keep up a discipline, whether it be in sport, music or Kriya Yoga, there are times when you feel a reluctance to practise. It is a part of the package that tests the disciple's steel and determination to become a master.

All of us had bouts of severe lethargy quite frequently.

'I think I just heard thunder. Didn't you guys?' John would say, failing to suppress a grin. Cord would hold his head and pretend that he had a temperature.

'Maybe. But I think I'm coming down with something anyway.'

'And I'm starving,' I would add. 'Anyone coming for supper?'

We could produce endless amounts of excuses between us and original ones added to the list were always the cause of great hilarity. Sometimes we made a pact between us to miss practice because the guilt was less when we were being as lazy as each other.

After a while, what we did not find quite so amusing was the fact that when we went for our lesson together on any given morning after one of these delinquent evenings, the first question Guruji would pose was always the same:

'So? How was practice?'

Which had us hanging our beetroot faces and mumbling something unintelligible.

FEBRUARY arrived and the festival of *Sivaratri* was approaching. Guruji told us that on certain auspicious days such as *Sivaratri* we should attempt to spend a whole day doing Kriya *pranayama* if we could.

We had learned that after Kriya Yoga practice, it was best to take a silent rest for about half an hour to enable the body to readjust. Now Guruji said that on *Sivaratri* we should stay in our rooms and avoid talking or going outside. He explained that *pranayama* caused the airs in the body to become lighter and move up to the head. This made the mind very relaxed and quiet. Any sudden or loud noises could easily shock and as a result weaken the body's nervous system. Especially if the practitioner was not yet used to practising for lengthy periods.

Guruji hinted at the end of one lesson that something rather extraordinary had happened to him during meditation on a certain *Sivaratri* some years ago. His eyes sparkled, but he was revealing no details. Cord was certain that he must have met Lahiri Mahasaya's Guru Babaji, but we could do no more than speculate.

I hoped that we would find out one day what his secret was.

Unfortunately I was not feeling well on the day of *Sivaratri*. My best effort was unimpressive. Three hours was the upper limit for my first attempt to meditate for hours on end. It was a huge strain on the concentration and I kept having to stretch my legs because of pins and needles.

The others had a fantastic day and managed far more than me. Which was typical. So I resolved to make a second attempt the following Saturday. This time it was not a frustrating struggle, and several hours of *pranayama* took me deeper than ever before. In the early evening I fell asleep completely exhausted, but totally peaceful. It was almost as if my mind had been through the wash. There was nothing to think, nothing to worry about and it was still. Pure bliss.

The next day our yoga lesson was at eleven o'clock, by which time the effect of the previous day still had not worn off. It was hard to speak. There was no desire to speak. It seemed as if doing so would shatter the beautiful silence inside. When we arrived at the studio I wanted to convey to Guruji what I had experienced. But what exactly was it? No idea. The expression on Guruji's face told me that he understood perfectly. If anyone knew that words could never describe that thing, it was Guruji, I thought to myself.

In the months which followed, prolonged meditation was attempted several times more whenever I could muster the mental strength needed to make the effort. After each time I determined that it should be done every week, because the after-effects were so stunning. However, it did not quite work out as I had planned, due to sheer laziness. The reason why this was such an obstacle was clear: Kriya Yoga wielded a powerful sabre, and the ego feared decapitation. But recognition of this fact did not always provide the courage required to force the ego to face its most dreaded enemy either.

However, it was noticeable that all rewards were proportionate to the amount of effort put in. Those days of long practice were life-changing experiences. The sweet after-taste never went away. It was not about seeing visions of angels or experiencing sensational miracles. This was very different indeed; everything was so silent.

It should not be forgotten that I had only been meditating for a year, and these extended periods of practice were both imperfect and fidgety. But the "high" afterwards was a taste of paradise. It was like treading on Holy Ground and leaving an imprint of gratitude on your soul, the memory of which would remain forever.

I began to understand why Guruji never talked about God. And why he frequently declined to talk at all. There were no words for it. It was strange to think back to how my spiritual food in the past had been listening to inspiring church services and lectures. The positive vibration generated on such occasions had the power to uplift as much as the sermons themselves, but words alone could no longer compete with experiencing the indescribable in Kriya Yoga.

At the time of initiation, I had wondered why a disciple had to swear to practise for life. The only answer I had found before was that the promise had kept me going thus far: because it was so often a question of forcing yourself to practise when you felt lethargic, and of shutting your ears to the voices inside which cried that there was no point in making the effort.

Now a different answer had been unearthed. As a result of longer practices that went deeper for the first time, the *have to* of practice began to give way to the *want to. Need to.* Kriya Yoga, whether one realised it at the beginning or not, was perfect soul nourishment. Depriving the soul by discontinuing practice would more than likely result in general dissatisfaction with life itself. I recognised that having tasted spiritual food of this nature for myself, my inner being would never be content without it again.

It was the fight described in the *Bhagavad Gita*. Initially, Arjuna wants to put down his arrow. He cannot bear the prospect of fighting his relatives: the senses, the ego. But when the soul is ready for freedom and the heart desires to break the chain of birth and rebirth, there is actually no turning back. It has to keep fighting and learning and will suffer if it opts for cowardice. Running away has its price, but freedom of choice still remains. In one life or another, the lesson that there is no lasting happiness in this transitory world has to be learned.

The Eye of a Yogi

"What a pair of eyes beholds is not radiant because the eyes have their limitations. It is not possible to behold the radiant Self with the physical eyes. The radiant Self can only be realised by the grace of the Guru, or the Master, that is, through the blessing of Kriya practice." –
LAHIRI MAHASAYA[3]

It was a particularly rare event for disciples to openly witness the yogic power of Tinkari Lahiri, because he went to such lengths to keep this aspect of himself hidden.[4] However, due to his great love for a disciple, there was at least one occasion when he was forced to make an exception.

When Sachindra Mohan Chattopadhyaye's wife Mrinalini Devi contracted tetanus, the doctors did their best to treat her, but to no avail. Soon every muscle was affected, and her body twisted through the convulsions. Her eyesight had deteriorated and she was in severe pain.

Seeing his wife on the threshold of death, Sachindra Mohan rushed to tell his Guru about his wife's illness and that there was no hope for her life. Tinkari Lahiri came out of his deep meditation to listen, and then hurried with his disciple back to where Mrinalini Devi lay.

When they arrived, there were several people surrounding the bed. Tension and gloom hung in the air as they waited for the inevitable. Upon seeing Tinkari in the room, the sick woman asked him as a last favour to sit with his feet touching her head. Her eyes were flooded with tears.

It seemed for a moment as if Tinkari was at a loss to know what to do. For one thing, it was not usual for a *Sadguru* to interfere with the course of nature. When a circumstance was to be changed, there was a definite reason for it and everything was to be done secretly. Nothing was impossible though, and all of nature stood at the Yogi's command if he willed something.

At last, Tinkari Lahiri did as Mrinalini Devi had asked. Not only did he sit at her head, but the witnesses present observed how the

---

[3] From *Lahiri Mahasaya's Commentaries on the Yoga Sutras of Patanjali.* (Explanation of Sutra no.18)
[4] Satya Charan Lahiri says of his father in the introduction of *Purana Purusha*, "Father was very grave and reserved by nature and used to incomparably conceal himself."

colour slowly returned to her cheeks. The spasms ceased and her previously contorted face began to look normal again. Incredibly, she got up from her bed a while later to touch the master's feet in *Pranam*. All signs of the illness were completely gone. And Tinkari Lahiri was smiling.

TINKARI LAHIRI and Beni Prasad Khatri were purchasing a few goods at a shop when a gentleman approached them.

'Excuse me,' he said, addressing Tinkari Lahiri, 'I am searching for the house of the great master Lahiri Mahasaya. Do you know him?'

Tinkari shook his head. 'No, I don't know Lahiri Mahasaya,' he replied.

The man went on his way. Beni Prasad shook his head in disbelief that he could have heard a lie pass the lips of such an advanced Yogi as he knew Tinkari Lahiri to be. He summoned up all his courage to ask,

'Why did you tell him that you don't know Lahiri Mahasaya? You are his son!'

'It wasn't a lie,' he answered. 'I do not know the higher planes where he lives – who can know Lahiri Mahasaya!'

Now Beni Prasad understood. He knew that a Yogi always told the truth, but sometimes used words to purposely confuse. If Tinkari responded in this way, he must have known that the man was merely curious and not seriously interested in seeking initiation. For a Yogi could instantly recognise a person's inner feeling and devotion for God. And Beni Prasad was quite aware that no one received initiation from Lahiri Mahasaya without the requisite devotion for God and readiness to take practice seriously. He would always pour holy Ganges water into the hands of his initiates, and make them swear a solemn oath on it to practise for life, not to disclose the method to anyone and to remain "hidden".

ONE OF Tinkari Lahiri's most advanced disciples, having attained *Samadhi*, was Sri Maheshwar Dutt. He became authorised to initiate Kriya Yoga and frequently wrote to his Guru to inform him about new disciples, and tell of his own progress in the higher stages of Kriya. Sometimes he asked questions, and the answers which Tinkari returned in a few short sentences were carefully copied into a notebook. This record of a twenty-five year long correspondence is still in existence and contains insights and diagrams on a very advanced level of Kriya Yoga.

One of Sri Maheshwar Dutt's disciples was the renowned Dr P. Nandi from Calcutta. A learned and wealthy man, Dr Nandi was exceedingly kind and gentle by nature, according to his Guru's correspondence to Tinkari Lahiri. Even at the time of initiation and first attempt at Kriya *pranayama*, tears came to his eyes because he was so moved. He had an immediate experience of the "light of Soul" at the point between the eyebrows in *Kutastha*, and thereafter made rapid progress in Kriya.

Later on, Dr Nandi also developed the ability to see the light in *Sushumna*. It excited him so much that he wanted others to be able to see it. As a result he invested substantial time trying to develop a scientific piece of equipment which might make it detectable to the human eye. His efforts were in vain, however, and he decided to consult Tinkari Lahiri on the matter.

Tinkari told him that *Sushumna* was an extremely fine nerve. It was a red-coloured ray of light made up of many minuscule particles which passed through a tiny hole and ran from *Muladhara Chakra* to *Sahasrara Chakra*.[5] He said that the light of *Atman* did not have a gross existence, therefore it would never be possible to detect it with scientific equipment. Nor could it ever be seen with the human eye. Tinkari also reminded Dr Nandi of the self-realised poet *Kabir Das* who writes in one of his couplets that this soul-light of *Sushumna* is only seen through the grace of the Guru.

TINKARI always disliked the idea of having his photograph taken. However, Sri Maheshwar Dutt wanted one very much and persuaded Satya Charan to organise it. He gave his Guru's son ten rupees and asked for a print of the master sitting in the lotus position to be sent to him in Bengal when it was done. Naturally, Satya Charan wanted to know why he would not ask Tinkari himself, and Maheshwar Dutt answered that he lacked the courage to do so.

A famous photographer named Sri Umanath Chakravorty lived locally, and Satya Charan arranged for him to come to the house.

---

[5] From the root to the crown *Chakra*.

When he informed his father that he should prepare to have his photograph taken, Tinkari seemed shocked. A moment later an expression of anger crossed his face.

'Why have you arranged for a photograph? What is the purpose?' he demanded to know.

Satya Charan was taken aback by his father's reaction and replied timidly,

'There is a reason. How will people see you in the future without one?'

Tinkari was not convinced and declared that he would make himself unrecognisable by painting his face black and white before the picture was taken. Satya Charan saw no choice but to confess that it had been Maheshwar Dutt's idea, and that he had already accepted ten rupees to pay for it.

'And you didn't ask for my consent first?' Tinkari answered. However, he finally agreed.

The photographer arrived and set everything up for the picture. He laid a large tiger skin on the floor, which was intended to give his subject a demeanour of importance. The *Lord Siva* was always pictured sitting on a tiger skin. But as soon as Tinkari Lahiri saw it he shouted,

'Take that tiger skin away!'

There were plenty of attempts to persuade him otherwise, but Tinkari, who did not want to advertise his spiritual standing as a *Mahayogi*, adamantly refused to have his photograph taken on anything other than an ordinary cushion.

A DEDICATED devotee from Rishikesh who was an ayurvedic doctor often came to see his Guru and every time he asked for Kriya initiation.

'You will get it when your time comes,' Tinkari told him.

He was finally initiated some six years after he first asked to receive Kriya. The reason why he had to wait so long was evident only to the master.

BANSIDHAR KHANNA was initiated into Kriya Yoga by Lahiri Mahasaya when he was young and remained devoted to the Lahiri family until he died. Being well aware of this particular disciple's sincerity and dedication, one day Tinkari decided to put him in charge of all matters pertaining to the family property in the village itself. Bansidhar was reluctant to take the position at first, feeling overawed by the responsibility. However, Tinkari Lahiri finally persuaded him, knowing what an excellent job he would do.

Lahiri Mahasaya's disciple performed his duties with humility and in the spirit that he was working for God. An intelligent man, he kept the accounts impeccably. He was also popular amongst the tenants in the village who appreciated his honesty. Tinkari Lahiri always accorded him the freedom to do as he saw fit regarding the property, never giving him any kind of order. But this worried Bansidhar somewhat, especially since Tinkari never asked to see the accounts. He knew that he would feel happier if his master would assure himself that everything was correct.

So he wrote a letter asking Tinkari to check the accounts. The Yogi replied that there was no need, and that Bansidhar should continue the good work. However, Bansidhar persisted with his request until Tinkari finally agreed that he might bring the books to Banaras. He then went through them one by one, writing on each page "checked and found correct" and adding his signature. When he finished, he told Bansidhar to go home, leaving the disciple astonished at the Yogi's trust in him.

On another occasion, all the account books were once more transported to Banaras by camel for checking on Bansidhar's request. Tinkari piled the books in a small room, and told Bansidhar to go, assuring him that he would take a look.

When he had gone, Tinkari poured kerosene over the books and lit a match. His son Satya Charan saw what he was doing and ran outside.

'Don't you want to see the accounts?' he asked.

'I have seen them and everything is in order,' replied Tinkari as he set light to the books.

❖ ❖ ❖ ❖ ❖ ❖ ❖ ❖

The year 1996 turned out to be quite eventful. In the late spring Guruji and his family came to visit us in England. Both of my parents had yoga lessons after work each day and soon received Kriya Yoga initiation themselves, as did a long-time friend of mine who had been going to yoga classes for years.

Apart from the teaching, there was plenty of time for the family to go for walks and see something of the area. Their camera accompanied every outing and worked overtime. Personally, I always felt rather nervous about taking pictures of Guruji with my own camera, and this was not without reason. In Varanasi, we had heard numerous stories about people who came to the yoga studio for lessons and tried to take a picture of Guruji before they left. For no apparent reason, whenever a viewfinder was aimed at him, the camera either failed to perform or completely broke down. Guruji maintained his ignorance about the cause, but it was certainly something of a phenomenon.

During that first visit, two separate groups came to our house to meet and hear Guruji speak: a local yoga group and some people from my church youth group. Sitting in on both of these sessions proved to be an eye-opener.

When the yoga group came, Guruji answered questions and told stories as usual. The reactions showed how one answer after another corresponded exactly with the enquirer's experience. Guruji would show his surprise every time as if it were mere coincidence and smile innocently. I had experienced it so often myself, but here I could observe quite clearly that he automatically knew what people needed to hear and therefore said the right things. Everyone present went away with something they had been able to relate to and understand. My intuition told me that this ability was something much higher than mind-reading.

Then the church group came. I was especially excited for this group of friends to meet my spiritual Guru, because I wanted them to understand my reason for taking up the practice of meditation. When Guruji began to say all the wrong things, I could hardly believe my ears. They had no questions of their own and as soon as he began to talk about astrology, I squirmed, and wondered why he did not seem to notice that he was putting them off completely.

This particular subject was guaranteed to shut down the brain cells of anyone from my church, to whom astrology was the science of superstition: no one who believed in it could possibly know anything about God and spirituality. Stone walls were being mounted all around the room. I watched the closed faces and saw it happening. He gave them plenty of opportunities to rise to the challenge, but no one seemed capable or willing to muster a single question about what he was saying. Some of them had come from quite a distance and he was sending them away with less than nothing. No hint of who he really was. As if he actually wanted them to think that he was completely ignorant.

When the hour came to a close, I wondered if the main lesson had been for me. It had been a most humbling demonstration of Guruji's lack of human ego. He had hidden himself totally, having absolutely nothing to prove to anybody, unlike myself. But then the spiritual master was not supposed to exercise yogic power for show. And as he had said many times, Kriya Yoga was no matter for idle curiosity.

'Only one has the possibility,' he told me after the meeting. Which confirmed my suspicion that he had been playing a game. Indeed, the group had heard enough and were ready to move out to the garden for tea, with the exception of one woman who stayed to talk with Guruji on her own. Something had drawn her to Guruji and aroused her interest, and she went home with a pile of books on meditation from my bookshelf.

DURING my time back at home, it became evident that not every churchgoer had the inclination to find the Absolute through meditation. I tried to share the idea with several church friends that God could be perceived and experienced through meditation; I tried to tell them that Guruji could explain all the passages which described the steadying of the *Chakras* and stages of super-consciousness in St. John's Revelation, and that Jesus' walking on the water was not a question of having enough faith as implied by the church, but of turning the breath inward to the *Sushumna* channel – no impossible feat for a Kriya Yogi such as Lahiri Mahasaya in the higher stages of practice. But my enthusiastic chatter was most frequently met by an indignant response. No doubt the whole thing sounded rather unorthodox and unchristian.

Guruji tried to explain to me once more why not everyone could practise Kriya. He likened it to the way a child had to go through one class after another and could not jump from the first to the fourth year. We learned the alphabet and then how to spell, until eventually we took reading and writing for granted.

Another analogy was that not even the tadpole could turn into a frog until the first part of its metamorphosis was complete. Readiness for Kriya Yoga was a question of what conscious level a person had already attained, whereby no stage of development could be omitted.

It took a long while for this to really sink in.

LAHIRI MAHASAYA told his disciples not to leave their religion or become a *sadhu* once they received Kriya Yoga. I could appreciate that from a social and cultural point of view, for a Hindu to become a Muslim, or for a Muslim to become a Buddhist would hardly be acceptable even in modern India. His primary message on the subject had been for the disciple to remain inconspicuous about Kriya practice.

If you told someone in India that you had learned some new meditation technique, they would not bat an eyelid. Meditation was the heart and soul of Eastern religions. Their philosophies had been shaped by the experiences of numerous yogis, swamis and *Sufi* saints, who perceived the spiritual world through practice.

However, for the people in my church, it soon became apparent that my changed view on the subject of medicine was rather too controversial. This was only partly due to Kriya Yoga. I had also recently learned about, and become interested in, so-called "Vibrational Medicine",[6] or energy-healing – a scientifically based return to the ancient Eastern knowledge of the body's energy centres, or *Chakras*, and the meridians. Systems of healing from acupuncture to homeopathy to Reiki took into account the "whole man" made up not only of a biochemical structure but of other invisible bodies: mental, *astral* and causal. They looked to find the deeper causes of sickness from the standpoint that man has an immortal soul which journeys through many lives on the physical plane.

It could not be denied that many of my ideas had changed. I no longer understood in the way I had been taught as a child in Sunday school. And since I did not want to confuse, create any upset or make anyone angry, it seemed as though the wisest course of action would be resignation from church membership which demanded an active commitment I no longer felt able to fulfil. This

---

[6] A most comprehensive book on the subject is Richard Gerber's *Vibrational Medicine for the 21st Century* (Piatkus).

did not mean that I wanted to stop going to church altogether, and it did seem rather ironic, since my faith was stronger than ever. Yet it was the only way to remain "inconspicuous".

My decision was misunderstood by some parties. Somebody mentioned to my parents that perhaps one day I would return to "the fold", being unaware that they had been initiated into Kriya Yoga themselves.

Guruji's comment on the matter was that no self-realised person would ever say such a thing.

'If man is reaching to God,' he said, 'he will never come back. He will never be an ordinary person again. It is impossible to realise God on one day and not another. Kriya Yoga is a not a religion, but a method through which to gain more perception. So you should still consider yourself a Christian. Christians celebrate Christmas and Easter according to social custom just as Hindus and Muslims celebrate their respective festivals.'

Guruji added that Kriya was about the development of soul. It was about finding the place where only equality existed. Soul was neither Christian, Hindu nor Muslim. God was not exclusive to any one particular religion. The differences and frictions were in people's minds. Jesus would certainly not have objected to his disciples practising for God-realisation and striving for the spiritual level that he himself attained.

SOME things are certain. The genuine spiritual master is beyond the pull of fame and riches. He tends to remain hidden. He has no need of publicity in order to call those who are ready for initiation. His great love is extended to everyone, regardless of religion, caste or background.

The master may sometimes appear to contradict himself in speech. Not even his own disciples will perceive him in the same way. Some people will be able to understand his teachings on a deep level, whilst others will miss what he is saying completely.

He will knowingly meet a person on their mental level, rather than swamping them with concepts beyond their comprehension. He cannot by any means explain everything which he understands himself. A scientist may exclaim that the theories in a child's textbook have been ridiculously simplified, but should nevertheless realise that the understanding of complex truths can only come with development and experience.

And it will always take more than a sharp pair of eyes to recognise a self-realised Yogi.

The Mahasamadhi of Tinkari Lahiri

"Physical death is not real death.
Real death is the death of the restlessness of the breath.
He who has attained this eternal Tranquillity
shall not have to die again." – LAHIRI MAHASAYA[7]

When Tinkari Lahiri became sick in 1926, Satya Charan took him to see Dr P. Nandi. The Yogi seemed to be in a critical condition and the doctor took care of his *Paramguru* twenty-four hours a day. Monitoring his well-being proved to be somewhat problematic since Tinkari kept going into *Samadhi*. Dr Nandi would frequently feel no pulse, respiration or heartbeat when he examined his patient. Then a few hours later the breathing would return to normal again, but only for a short while. The period that the Yogi spent in super-consciousness lengthened every time. It made the doctor nervous. Distress brought tears to his eyes at the thought that Tinkari might leave his body right there in his house.

The reason behind his perplexity was that an advanced Yogi could go into *Samadhi* for hours, days or even weeks. Without having left the body, there would be no external breathing. For *Samadhi* happens totally naturally – any prior announcement is out of the question. Since Tinkari had not given any specific warning, the doctor had no way of telling if the time had come to take him to the burning *ghat*, or whether he was planning to return to his body.

Satya Charan was also concerned, because his father was so silent in the brief periods when he was conscious. So the next time Tinkari opened his eyes, Satya Charan asked if the time for *Mahasamadhi* was near.

'We are worried,' he said. 'You are old and so is grandmother, and we are afraid who will go first.'

---

7 From *Lahiri Mahasaya's Commentaries on the Yoga Sutras of Patanjali*, part explanation of Sutra no.49.

Inherent in Satya Charan's question was an indirect hint that if his father really should choose to leave his body there and then, the ninety-year old Kashi Mani Devi would suffer a blow from which she might not recover. After a long silence, Tinkari replied,

'Don't worry. As long as my mother is alive, nothing will happen to me.'

Dr Nandi wept tears of relief and happiness, knowing that anything Tinkari said always came true. Soon afterwards, the Yogi made a complete recovery.

A MARRIAGE for Satya Charan Lahiri was arranged in 1931. Sadly, his wife Nalini Devi became sick with tuberculosis and died nine months after the wedding. For the short while that they were together Satya Charan gave his wife the best available treatment and looked after her with the utmost loving care. His parents-in-law were so impressed with him that they continued to treat him as a son even after their daughter's death.

Tinkari decided that Satya Charan should remarry, since Nalini Devi had not been able to bear him any children, whereupon he was betrothed for a second time to Renuka Devi from Bangladesh. They were to have three children together, a son and two daughters.

SATYA CHARAN and his father's disciple Beni Prasad knew of an immensely wealthy old man who used to pay regular visits to Tinkari Lahiri. They would watch him make *Pranam* and note how Tinkari dismissed him with a wave of the hand after the briefest of exchanges each time.

Satya Charan asked his father one day why he had so little time for this man, to which Tinkari replied that if people saw him coming they would start to gossip. No one knew that the man was interested in God and spirituality, and Tinkari did not want people to assume that he was in any way interested in him because of his money.

A few days before Tinkari Lahiri left his body, the rich man was again seen sitting at the feet of the Yogi. This time Satya Charan was curious to observe an expression of sheer joy on the man's face, but was not to discover what his father had told him until several weeks later.

FOUR YEARS after the passing of his mother in 1934, nobody suspected that Tinkari Lahiri was preparing for *Mahasamadhi*. He appeared to be physically fit at the age of seventy and was as serene as ever. But gradually Tinkari was spending more and more time in the state of *Samadhi*.

The day came when alarm bells began to ring. The other family members could not understand what was happening to him. Satya Charan called the family doctor who came immediately.

After the patient had been examined, the doctor packed his instruments away. His diagnosis was to the point. Tinkari was about to take *Mahasamadhi* and medicine was useless. All the Yogi required now was peace. Amar Nath Bandhopadhyaya offered a last *Pranam* and took his leave.

Nobody could believe it. There was some bodily weakness evident and Tinkari's metabolism had slowed, but there were no signs of death as such. The close family members came to the conclusion that the doctor must have been mistaken. So a short while later they summoned the homeopathic doctor, Kedar Nath Bhattacharya, who left a few packets of medicine to be given every fifteen minutes.

Tinkari Lahiri's face was shining. He was not breathing but there was no stiffness in the body either. Satya Charan discovered that it was impossible to give the medicine, as his father's tongue was in the position of *Khechari mudra*. Gradually, Satya Charan realised that his father really was leaving his body for the last time. He began to cry and shout and Tinkari opened his eyes, gesturing his son to be quiet.

There was no pain. All who were present observed what they would later refer to as a death of glory: a rare *Mahasamadhi*.

Many years later Satya Charan Lahiri recorded the actual moment when his father left his body in the introduction of *Purana Purusha*. The passage from the English translation reads as follows:

"What a unique death! He magnetised the entire *Prana*-air completely between the eyebrows, placed his mind there and departed. At this moment, the place between the eyebrows was quivering immensely which was indescribable. It seemed as though a marble was forcing its way out from within. Just at the moment of his death, father bore a placid countenance, a calm body and it seemed as though his whole body assumed the reddish hue of a fresh rose ... It was a wonderful sight, as though *Mahadeva* (*Siva*) Himself was lying there. While *Kutastha* was quivering, Bansidhar Kshettry, a disciple of my grandfather told me, "Look, Satya *baboo*, compare it with the eighth chapter of *Gita*, it only is the *Rama* door, it only is the permanent settlement of *Brahma*."[8] This state cannot be achieved with a few days' effort, to attain this permanence an entire life's yoga *sadhana* is required."

THE BODY was prepared and taken for cremation at Manikarnika Ghat. Because of the hue and suppleness of the body which seemed so untouched by death, Satya Charan expressed his concern to a doctor present that perhaps there was still life in his father's body. He received reassurance that this was not the case and that the funeral should go ahead. Even so, for a long time afterwards many family members felt rather confused and wondered whether they had done the right thing in burning the body at all.

THE TRADITIONAL thirteen days of funeral rites followed the cremation. Barely were they over, when one afternoon as Satya Charan Lahiri lay dropping off to sleep, he heard the unmistakable voice of his father in his ear, telling him to initiate Hari Shankar. It came so clearly that Satya Charan sat up.

Tinkari Lahiri had instructed Satya Charan that he was to initiate Kriya Yoga after his departure a long time previously. But now he felt perturbed for the simple reason that he did not know anyone named Hari Shankar. He hurried to tell Beni Prasad about it and learned that Hari Shankar was the affluent gentleman they had so often seen coming to visit Tinkari.

---

8 "*Rama's* door" is referred to in the Upanishads. Many people understand that dying at the door of a temple of *Rama* will result in no rebirth. This is the superficial meaning. However, as Mr Kshettry observed, the temple in question actually lies in the human body, and its door is reached when the Yogi draws up all the airs to the place of *Kutastha*. This is the place where the Indian god *Rama* really lives.

The "permanent settlement of *Brahma*" is another way of saying the same thing. It means the final attainment to the seventh *Chakra*, when the Yogi's soul dissolves in the Absolute forever.

The relevant verses in question from the *Bhagavad Gita* read as follows: "Having by the power of Yoga firmly held the life-breath in the space between the two eyebrows even at the time of death, and then contemplating on God with a steadfast mind, full of devotion, he reaches verily that supreme divine *Purusa* (God)." Also, "Having closed all the doors of the senses, and firmly holding the mind in the cavity of the heart, and then fixing the life-breath in the head, and thus remaining steadfast in Yogic concentration on God, he who leaves the body and departs uttering the one indestructible Brahma, OM, and dwelling on Me in My absolute aspect, reaches the supreme goal." (VIII:10, 12, 13 (Gita Press))

At first, Satya Charan Lahiri thought that it could not be right for him to initiate anyone so soon after his father's death. He went to a cousin and asked him to take over the task, but he refused, saying that he had not been given permission to initiate Kriya Yoga, unlike Satya Charan. The cousin advised that Beni Prasad should be sent to fetch Hari Shankar on an auspicious day for the initiation, and that Satya Charan should follow the order he had heard despite his father's recent *Mahasamadhi*.

At the time of initiation, Satya Charan was impressed by Hari Shankar's immense respect and dedication. It seemed that he could not control a flow of tears, and Satya Charan asked what was making him weep so much.

The wealthy man replied that he had asked for Kriya Yoga initiation many times. For a long time Tinkari Lahiri had not given him any answer. Then just a few weeks previously, he had been told that he would receive initiation when the time came. That day he had gone home overjoyed. But several days later he had been shocked to see Tinkari Lahiri's funeral procession passing beneath his balcony. It had thrown him into a state of depression, for an untruth had never been known to pass the lips of this true Guru. Yet it had led him to assume that the promise he had received would never be fulfilled.

But it was not so. The master's commitment had not been forgotten after all. He had actually sent his son to initiate him. For such a great blessing, Hari Shankar could not stem the tears of pure joy and gratitude.

AFTER the *Mahasamadhi* of Tinkari Lahiri, many people were surprised to see that Satya Charan did not have anything to show for his father's promise that he would receive "something more". However, the prediction did come true, albeit ten years later, when Satya Charan was given twenty thousand rupees from Professor Tarak Nath Sanyal, a disciple and nephew of Lahiri Mahasaya. This was a substantial sum of money in 1946 and enabled Satya Charan to purchase a large house and carry out the necessary repair work. In addition, Tarak Nath Sanyal purchased a forty-year bond in Satya Charan's name, worth a further eighteen thousand rupees, extracting a promise from Satya Charan that he would be sure to cash the bond when it matured in 1986, being the sole beneficiary.

LAHIRI MAHASAYA'S faithful disciple Bansidhar Khanna continued to work as a rent-collector for the Lahiri family even after Tinkari Lahiri took *Mahasamadhi*. His respect for Satya Charan Lahiri was equally great. But when he began to get old and Beni Prasad Khatri suggested that he should retire and move to Banaras, the faithful man replied,

'Guru *Maharaja*[9] has such grace on me, and I could never serve him properly. So I have devoted this physical body to his holy feet, to do his work. Everything depends upon his will: if he will throw my body in the jungle or put it at his holy feet, I have no worry of that.'

Even when Satya Charan gently suggested that Bansidhar should stop working and join his family, and that they would send money every month, he still rejected the offer. He replied that as long as he was able to hold a pen in his hand, he would not be in anyone's debt. He insisted that when he died, they should cast his body to the wild animals in the jungle rather than burdening themselves with the expense of taking him for cremation in Banaras. Above all, he desired to work for his Guru until his very last breath, by serving the Lahiri family.

This last heartfelt wish was granted. One day, whilst he was returning home with some rent he had just collected from a tenant, he fell unconscious on the path. When help arrived, the people could not understand why he was repeating over and over, 'four rupees, six ana'. They told Satya Charan Lahiri about this as soon as he arrived and Mr Khanna was taken to Banaras. Shortly afterwards, the old man passed away.

Bansidhar Khanna was accorded the last rights in the Hindu tradition through cremation on the banks of the Ganges. He had served the Lahiri family faithfully for no less than thirty-eight years, and there was no question of leaving his body to the animals of the forest.

A few weeks after the funeral, a tenant came to see Satya Charan Lahiri. He had paid his rent on the day Bansidhar fell unconscious and was concerned that the amount might not have been registered in the books.

---

[9] He was referring to his own Guru, Lahiri Mahasaya.

When Satya Charan asked him how much he had given and learned that it was four rupees and six ana, everything became clear. Bansidhar had wanted to note the payment in the accounts book but had been unable to. And due to his meticulous nature, he had been able to keep repeating the amount even in the state of unconsciousness.

❖ ❖ ❖ ❖ ❖ ❖ ❖ ❖ ❖

Andreas and I met in April 1996. The first time we were introduced, the sight of the tall, handsome man from Switzerland startled me. It was as if I recognised him from somewhere, although that was impossible. Yet there was something strangely familiar about him, and no denying the instant mutual attraction either.

Since Guruji had said just six months previously that there were four years to wait "for family side", which I was presuming meant the time that my husband would come along, a new boyfriend was out of the question. Besides, Andreas had come to England for three months to learn English and there were only a few short weeks left before he was due to return home.

My decision had already been made to return to India for one more year, and nothing could change my mind about that. I was also convinced that Andreas would be put off the idea of seeing me once I told him about my commitment to yoga meditation mornings and evenings. But to my surprise he was unmoved to hear this, and even expressed a vague interest of his own.

Despite endeavouring to remain aloof from the attraction, I found myself in the wraps of a fresh relationship just a few weeks before Guruji and his family were about to arrive for their first visit to England. They had barely finished unpacking before I asked Guruji's advice regarding the latest romantic developments, but he refused to say much. He said to wait and see, which did not sound like a definite no.

Within a few weeks of seeing each other on a daily basis, we were both independently thinking that the relationship could lead to marriage. Andreas wanted to leave his job and come with me to India. I tried to put him off at first, thinking that if he lacked his own reason to come except to be with me, he might not cope too well with the culture shock.

It turned out that Andreas, who trained as a joiner, had always suffered from a hereditary skin allergy which was now forcing him to look down new career avenues. He had been to at least fifteen different doctors and tried every medicine available from chemical to herbal to homeopathic. The last doctor had said that there was no permanent cure. When I told Andreas some more about yoga, he said that he thought it might be a last resort for his health problems. Rather than being an external solution like a cream which could be applied to the skin, it sounded like an internal remedy.

The fact that Andreas wanted to come to India for his own personal reason was a different matter entirely and made me feel at ease. We started to make plans to travel soon after that, although we were apart all summer. I was teaching English again, and Andreas was back in his job in Switzerland, having handed in his notice.

About a month before we were due to leave for India, Andreas came to England for a short holiday. One day we were sitting opposite each other in my room having a game of chess. I looked across at Andreas and he gazed into my eyes. At that very instant, I knew the origin of the feeling that we had met before. It was "the face" again: exactly the picture which had appeared that night in Thailand a year ago. And the same spontaneous thought, 'my husband', accompanied the *déjà vu*.

A few days later Andreas proposed to me. There were no doubts in my mind about accepting. A long-standing prayer had been answered, because I had always hoped to somehow recognise my husband and feel a certainty that he was "the one". It was somewhat ironic that after two years of world travel, destiny should have me find him in my home town.

It Began to happen that many of my subconscious desires were granted in a way which made me step back and take note. Some things came my way which I had fleetingly wished for, having dismissed the ideas as impossible or unrealistic at the time when they occurred. It was so uncanny that it made me think back to Guruji's words when he had said that in giving me Kriya Yoga, he was giving me everything.

When I questioned Guruji one day about the things which were happening, he said that it was a natural occurrence – one of the side-effects of Kriya practice. In India, there was a story about a magical cow[10] which came out of the ocean and could give unlimited amounts of milk at any time. It was symbolic of the way a perfect Yogi received everything he desired. The Christmas tree was a similar kind of symbol in the West, since it was hung about with garlands and toys which satisfied the wants of the children.

'We have this kind of tree inside of us,' Guruji said. 'When there is control on the mind, the things you want come automatically. Not just for the Yogi who has attained the state of *Samadhi*, but it can be possible beforehand, too. Sometimes because of the influence of the previous life.'

However, this was not to be misunderstood. There was a story in the Upanishads about a salt doll who decides that she wants to see how deep the ocean is. So she wades into the water and of course as she does so, her body becomes one with the sea.

It was a completely wrong concept to think that Kriya could be practised for the fulfilment of worldly desires. Any such motivation created an obstacle for progress, since the mind was distracted by an attachment to either material or spiritual gain. Even if the practitioner resolved before starting Kriya to have an especially good and long meditation, the likelihood was that practice would be a struggle. The mind should be free and empty, for in Kriya Yoga, the key to success was to have true devotion and no expectations or demands whatsoever. Only then did things come naturally and spontaneously.

It was a bizarre thought that a perfect Yogi could get everything he desired. But as Guruji illustrated with a short story from the Ramayan, the situation was somewhat different for the ego-less Yogi than the ordinary person might imagine:

The demon-king Ravana was a powerful magician. He was also very much in love with *Rama's* wife Sita and wanted more than anything to make the beautiful woman fall in love with him. So he abducted her one day in the forest, but despite his magic powers and great efforts to woo her, he was completely unsuccessful.

Feeling dismayed, Ravana went to a friend for advice, and was

---

[10] In Indian mythology, this cow is called *Kamdhenu*; *kam* means desire, and *dhenu* means full or complete.

told to assume the form of *Rama*.[11] Sita would thus be tricked into believing that he was actually her husband and would love him.

The demon-king thought that this was a wonderful idea. He was able to assume the form of anybody by meditating on the whole persona. However, in this case he was faced with an unforeseen problem. *Rama* was a god with a pure soul. Therefore, as soon as Ravana meditated on him, he lost all inclination to do anything immoral or evil to Sita.

WE WANTED to marry in England upon our return the following May, and then move to the Swiss Alps. Regrettably, a honeymoon was out of the question. We could not afford one for a start. But all things considered, we could hardly ask for more. As it was, we were going away for eight months of adventure together before the wedding.

The few weeks before departure were spent in Switzerland packing the contents of Andreas' flat into boxes. Then there were four days left in England before the actual flight to India, during which time we had to make as many wedding plans as possible including setting a date and organising the church. The rest had to be left to our parents to organise, since we had only just got engaged.

One of the things which had to be organised before we left was a wedding list. Andreas went with my father to a bridal fair to collect some catalogues. There was an entrance fee, so my father went in and told Andreas to wait outside. In the meantime a woman handed Andreas some slips of paper to fill in, which he completed with our names and addresses, quite oblivious to the fact that he was entering a competition.

My father thought it was a time-share offer with strings attached when he took a telephone call the next day. But it turned out to be a genuine call to say that we had won first prize at the bridal fair. Seven days in Majorca with flights, accommodation and car included.

The day before we flew to India we made the trip to the travel agent concerned to specify the date of our flight to Majorca and choose a villa. There was the honeymoon after all.

---

[11] Indian god; incarnation of Vishnu.

INDIA DREAMING (A Song)

I'm losing my senses
Deep in a pool of lotus and solitude
Waiting for sunrise, silently weaving
Patterns between the lines

There's oil in the lamp
To burn all night, till perfume fills the air
Watch the star till morning comes
I will meet you there

Keep going, and don't look back
Dark faces try to tempt you back
Don't believe in
India dreaming
Oh, I'm in India dreaming

Cascades and colours
Sweep through my heart and soothe away the care
Somewhere secret, nectar is flowing
Sweeter than honey

Rivers of joy
May swallow my tears, when heaven takes my tongue
The mountain is high, take rest in the shadows
Bathe in the moonshine

Keep going, and don't look back
Dark faces try to tempt you back
Don't believe in
India dreaming
Oh, I'm in India dreaming

But if you can't hear the truth
And if you can't see what I see
Start believing
in India dreaming
Oh, I'm in India dreaming

Part Three

Satya Charan Lahiri

Chapter Eight

THE ROOTS OF DESIRE

A Portrait

"If a man gets the ideal of non-injuring others,
before him even animals which are by their nature ferocious will become
peaceful. The tiger and the lamb will play together before that Yogi.
When you have come to that state, then alone will you understand that
you have become firmly established in non-injuring." –
SWAMI VIVEKANANDA[1]

A passer-by on the streets would not have recognised the clean shaven Satya Charan Lahiri as a saint, master or Yogi. He wore the simple *dhoti kurta* of the ordinary householder and went about his daily work in order to support the family.

Satya Charan Lahiri had been looking after the affairs of the family property since the age of twenty-two. He handled the responsibility so efficiently that his elder brothers never saw any reason to interfere. Satya Charan was always kind and fair towards the farmers who worked the land. It was his nature to help anyone in trouble or want. If a farmer was in financial difficulty because of a bad season, he would excuse the man from the rent that year. As a result of his diplomatic management the farmers were devoted to him and no disputes ended up in court, which was a frequent occurrence between other landlords and farmers.

Satya Charan Lahiri kept himself fit and healthy through regular exercise. He excelled in wrestling as a boy and was a strong swimmer. He taught swimming to several hundred children

---

[1] Explanation of Patanjali's Yoga Aphorism no. 35: "Non-killing being established, in his presence all enmities cease (in others)." (from *Raja Yoga*.)

"The wolf also shall dwell with the lamb, and the leopard shall lie down with the kid; and the calf and the young lion and the fatling together; and a little child shall lead them." Isiah 11:6

during his lifetime and used to swim daily to the opposite bank of the Ganges and back until he was fifty-seven. Thereafter he did so less frequently, but the last time was nevertheless at the age of seventy-two. He continued to bathe in the Ganges every morning until he was seventy-nine. And since he lived on the third storey of his house, he climbed up and down the staircases without assistance several times a day until he left his body.

One time when Satya Charan was swimming upstream through the flooded river as a young man, a terrific storm blew up. Thunder and lightning struck and several electric pylons with broken wires fell into the water near to him. When he emerged from the water alive and well, all observers hailed it as a miracle that the young swimmer had survived unharmed. Even Satya Charan could not understand why nothing had happened under the circumstances and attributed the miracle to his grandfather's protection.

His best friend was Shachindra Bandopadyaye, otherwise known as Shachi *baboo*. They had played together as children and remained close. Shachi *baboo* also received Kriya initiation from Tinkari Lahiri, and when he gradually began to realise that his best friend was an advanced Yogi, he felt great shame for the many times during their youth when he had treated Satya Charan as an equal. As a result, he gave his best friend the respect due to a beloved Guru throughout adulthood.

However, Satya Charan never ceased to treat Shachi *baboo* as anything but a friend. On one occasion when the Ganges flooded the main road in Varanasi, Satya Charan swam through the streets to Shachi *baboo*'s house. He had not been in contact with his friend for a week and wanted to see how he and the family were faring under the difficult circumstances, before returning home the way he had come.

SATYA CHARAN LAHIRI was known for his practicality. Anything he undertook in his daily life always came to fruition. When he first bought the family house, it was dark and dilapidated. Many other people had viewed it and were not interested in buying. But Satya Charan had many ideas for improvements to the building. He made it light and sturdy once more, much to the admiration of everyone who had seen the house before reconstruction work began.

In August 1953, his wife Renuka Devi became seriously ill and died just as the repairs were complete and the family was preparing to move into the new house. The children were aged fifteen, nine and four.

There was pressure on Satya Charan from both sides of the family to remarry because of the children, and his mother-in-law wanted him to marry Renuka Devi's younger sister. However, Satya Charan Lahiri was not interested in a third marriage and decided to bring up his children single-handedly.

Education was as important to him as it had been for his grandfather, and despite financial problems he took care of his children's physical and educational needs until they were all postgraduates. In addition, Satya Charan Lahiri gave scholarships to three other children whose parents could not afford to send them to school, from primary education right through to postgraduate certification. These three children eventually became professors, and two of them became famous not only in India but also abroad.[2] He was also a supporting member of three intermediate colleges.

Satya Charan fulfilled his duty as a parent by arranging good marriages for both his daughters. It was no easy feat for a single father to provide in the way he did, not only for his family but for others too, and the example sent a strong message to his disciples. Life's challenges were to be faced with a heart full of devotion for God and need not affect the practitioner's ability to stay on the Kriya path.

A STANZA in the *Bhagavad Gita*[3] states that it is a rare birth when someone is born into the family of a Yogi. During his lifetime, Lahiri Mahasaya emphasised that despite the truth of this stanza, nothing was possible in Kriya Yoga without practice. Merely being the blood relative of a spiritual master would never automatically elevate a person to the level of an advanced Yogi or Guru.

In the cases of Tinkari Lahiri and Satya Charan Lahiri there was clearly an influence of the previous life which meant that they could reach to the highest levels of yoga extraordinarily quickly:

---

[2] Professor Siddheshwar Bhattacharya (Banaras Hindu University), Professor Shivanarayan Goshal (Shanti Niketan, Bengal) and Professor Narayan Chand Goswami.

[3] "Or ... he is born in the family of enlightened Yogis; but such a birth in this world is very difficult to obtain." VI:42 (Gita Press)

and yet it was seen by their respective disciples that neither of them was spared long, dedicated practice. This was something which never ceased on any level. Even the Yogi who attained the Absolute in *Samadhi* was always in practice.

Whenever the subject of being born in the family of a Yogi arose amongst his own disciples, Satya Charan Lahiri was always clear in reiterating the words of his grandfather.

THE NIGHTS were always spent in meditation. In the morning after bathing and swimming in the river he did *puja* and read the *Bhagavad Gita*. For an hour in the afternoon, Satya Charan usually went to his room for a rest. After moving to the house in Chausetti Ghat, sometimes as many as two hundred devotees and disciples would come to the house to listen to his scriptural explanations between four and seven o'clock in the evening. At other times spiritual discussions led by other advanced disciples took place, followed by devotional singing for an hour. This was known as *Bhajan* and *Kirtan*.

Satya Charan Lahiri spoke Hindi, Bengali and English well. Although his general knowledge from books was limited to what he had learned in school, his internal knowledge was vast. Tinkari Lahiri's son earned the respect of many learned and famous academics[4] who came to listen to his yogic explanations of the Scriptures, for these were beyond the realms of personal opinion or what could be found in books. And as the name Lahiri Mahasaya became more and more widely known, people from every corner of the globe travelled to Varanasi to search out the spiritual master's grandson.

THERE was no inequality in the way Satya Charan Lahiri conferred his care and affection. Anyone who came to talk to the master was first questioned on the matter of their health and well-being. They received his undivided interest for all that they were doing and experiencing. They would feel how much their joys and troubles mattered to him, and went away convinced that they were a person of the greatest importance in his eyes.

Thus the disciples felt listened to, watched over and blessed.

---

[4] The famous academics included: *Pandit* Sitaram Omkarnath, Dr P. Nandi, Kaviraj Gopinath, Sri Surendra Nath, Tarak Nath Sanyal, Bhupendra Nath Sanyal and Shiv Narayan Goshal.

Whenever Satya Charan heard that someone was sick and therefore unable to come and see him, he would send a disciple to visit and bring news. The love he exuded was incomparable to that of any other human being they knew. It was completely unconditional. One close disciple likened it to the sunlight which encompasses everyone in its rays. Another said that he could never put into words the selfless love which he received from his Guru.

He had a jovial disposition and a wonderful sense of humour. Whenever he laughed, it was loud and hearty. At other times he could be rather serious and taciturn. But for the disciples, there was never any doubt about a single word which passed Satya Charan Lahiri's lips, for he only ever spoke the truth. He was always the first to be consulted in any matter of importance. Every blessing bestowed by him reached its destination without fail.

His disciples often invited him to eat in their homes, but only on rare occasions was he was able to accept. If it ever happened that some important matter prevented him from visiting a disciple who was expecting him, it was with deep regret that he would send someone to convey his apologies and explain why he was not able to come as planned. He always took his responsibilities and promises to heart.

Satya Charan ate little and was fully vegetarian. He ate neither meat, eggs nor fish, although most Bengalis, including many members of his own family, ate fish on a regular basis; nor would he touch alcohol, tobacco or any other intoxicating substance. He had no interest in these things.

❖ ❖ ❖ ❖ ❖ ❖ ❖ ❖

During our first few weeks together in Varanasi, Andreas and I stayed in a travellers' lodge whilst we hunted for a suitable flat to rent. The one we finally chose to be our temporary residence for five months had three rooms plus a kitchen, and smelled of fresh paint when we moved in. It was unfurnished, but we borrowed mattresses and blankets, and retrieved my cooking equipment from where it had been stored from my previous visit. Soon it felt like home.

Our landlords were kind, non-intrusive people. The next-door neighbours sold buffalo dung as cooking fuel, and the walls beneath our flat were permanently plastered with the small round cakes of excrement drying in the sun. We became accustomed to the view in time, and found it to be a relatively quiet and pleasant place to live.

By now I was fully accustomed to daily life in India and had plenty of confidence when it came to bartering for vegetables in the market and haggling with the rickshaw drivers. The multitude of different sights and sounds which had once either caused my head to turn, if not numbed or dismayed me, were now familiar and even comforting. Varanasi had become something of a second home. I loved the hustle and bustle of the markets; walking past silk shops bursting with colour in the cool shade of the narrow lanes and having to weave past the placid cows, and sleeping dogs warming themselves in fresh heaps of grey ash; the myriad smells, from light and sweet to heavy and rancid; sitting by Mother Ganges and imbibing the peace and magic of India's holy river; being jolted along in a rickshaw and marvelling at the ever-changing and refreshingly astonishing scenes which were a part of city life.

The concept of time was rather loose in India. A completely different mentality reigned. Work was not the "be-all and end-all". No one was in a hurry. People took time to chat, drink *chai*, rest and be with their families. At least, that was my observation in Varanasi, particularly amongst the shopkeepers in the old city.

The traveller began to notice the laid-back approach when a trip to the bank to change money took between three to four hours. She learned that buying a train ticket was best left to a travel agent if possible, for going to the station could mean spending half a day standing in a queue. Not the most pleasant of pastimes even if you actually remembered to take a gripping book along. Patience was required in enormous quantities each day. What you were promised by tomorrow was likely to take a week. Getting worked up about the pace of life gave you a red face and achieved absolutely nothing.

My fiancé was not used to any of this. And as was to be expected, it took him several months to adjust, during which time there were regular outbursts of anger and frustration. Understandably so, since the concept of punctuality considered such an essential quality of life and usually taken for granted by many brought up in a Western culture was suddenly non-existent. Haggling and bartering was something one had to accept and get accustomed to. The way of life and mental attitudes which accompanied it were vastly different. At first Andreas wanted nothing more than to go back home. I was reminded that my sentiments had not been much different during my first months in India two years earlier.

However, from the time we arrived in Varanasi, Andreas also started to take Hatha Yoga lessons with Guruji. He was given some meditation techniques too, and a couple of months after we arrived he received Kriya Yoga initiation. Within a short time the outbursts became less frequent. The tendency towards moodiness diminished. I was not sure if he was conscious of it himself or not, but the calming effect that a little daily yoga practice had on him was quite noticeable. And when it was time for us to leave, we were both equally reluctant to move on.

WHEN I was initiated in Kriya Yoga, Guruji made me promise never to drink alcohol or smoke. Being a teetotaller who had never taken a single puff on a cigarette, agreeing to this was not restricting in the slightest. As a church member, abstinence had previously been a matter of principle, but in truth I had never had to suppress the least desire for either alcohol or cigarettes. In fact, my lifelong aversion to both is such that it would not surprise me if I perhaps overdosed in a past life.

What bothered me when Andreas made his Kriya promises was that for some reason Guruji missed out that part about abstinence.

'Doesn't Andreas have to promise to give up beer?' I asked cheekily after his initiation, knowing my fiancé's weakness for a pint every now and again.

'No,' answered Guruji flatly. 'He can have it sometimes. Just not in excess.'

THE QUESTION of why the desire for meat and intoxicating substances decreased through Kriya practice came up for discussion again. I wanted to know why Guruji had told me not to drink, and yet specifically given Andreas freedom in that respect, whilst suspecting that I already knew the answer.

Guruji repeated what he had told me previously. There was little point in him ordering someone to give up meat, smoking or alcohol when they took Kriya initiation, since doing so could have the opposite effect. Artificially suppressed desires were sure to emerge again with yet more force later on. That was why he had told me it was fine to eat meat when I wanted to.

As far as meat was concerned, since that disappointing episode with the fast-food chicken, every now and again I had eaten meat in order to test whether my desire for it was genuinely diminishing. I wanted to be sure that it was not a figment of my imagination. But after some eighteen months of Kriya practice, there was no doubt that the mere thought of eating meat had become quite abhorrent. Not only had my taste buds ceased to derive any enjoyment from it any more, but my mind could not disassociate the idea of meat from the slaughtered animal.

When I told Guruji, he was not in the least surprised. He said that it was indeed the reason he had told Andreas to have a beer every now and again if he felt so inclined. There was no call to suppress any desires. If someone was practising Kriya conscientiously, it should happen gradually and automatically, as the cells in the body underwent a perfectly natural process of purification. When the mind took on the *sattvic* qualities of serenity and calmness, it tended to lose interest in meat, fish and intoxicating substances. Consumption of these after the desire had been lifted out from the root was likely to result in pain and sickness.

When I probed further if it was therefore morally wrong to eat meat, Guruji made it clear that there was no right or wrong about it.

'In Hinduism, we don't want to kill animals for business purposes,' he said. 'We want to follow the principle of *Ahimsa*, or non-violence. You will see that it is prohibited in many Hindu temples to wear a leather belt or take in a leather purse. Mostly in South India it is still that way, you have to leave these outside. But before the invention of plastic and rubber, people did wear leather in the temples.

'Earlier in the twentieth century everything was very different. Travel to Delhi used to take a month. Transportation facilities as we have today did not exist. In Kashmir, vegetables couldn't be grown in the snow. The people living there were entirely dependent on meat for their survival. Likewise, we cannot tell the Eskimos that they are wrong to eat meat and fish. In the snow and ice, there is no alternative. In such circumstances, man has to be grateful for whatever food he can get. For many people though, meat is a habit. A question of taste. Man is not born with the long canine teeth of meat-eating animals.

'We can say that if a human being has a choice, vegetarianism is good from the point of view of health. Man has a very long intestine and meat proteins are hard for the body to digest. There is a chemical reaction which can result in much gas and other troubles.

'For the practitioner, light food is definitely better, because the body's system should be clear before starting Kriya practice. Vegetables are fifty to sixty percent water and take only three hours to digest if cooked properly. Meat on the other hand takes about ten hours to digest competely, during which time the energy to make good practice is not there. The practitioner who wants to succeed in practice can understand and also observe the effect various foods have on the mind.'

I had read in the *Bhagavad Gita*[5] that foods fell into three categories: dynamic, active and static. Dynamic foods which promoted purity of mind were best for the practitioner, and these included milk, *ghee*, rice, *dhal*, pulses and most vegetables. Freshly prepared foods were also dynamic. Active foods which literally made the mind active were bitter, sour, spicy, or salty, for they gave the body a kind of shock. Static foods included meat, yoghurt, onion and garlic. They also included half cooked food, reheated leftovers and stale food. Apparently all of these made man lethargic, since they brought out the *Tamas* quality in mind.

When Guruji first mentioned that diet influences the mind, I was inclined to dismiss the idea, though admittedly it was something I had never given any consideration before. No one thought about such things in the West; or did they? Guruji pointed out that the continuing uproar over genetically modified foods showed that many Westerners were indeed also concerned about what they ate.

'You know that wild meat-eating animals have a restless and aggressive nature,' he continued. 'But yogis have no violence in

---

[5] Chapter XVII:7-11

them and do not eat meat. When there is violence in man's nature he will also fear danger. Yet it used to be quite common in India for holy saints to live unharmed in the forests, being surrounded by wild animals. I told you already about the tiger who went to Trailanga Swami for protection when it was being hunted by the King. Any animal can sense what is in man.

'Man, on the other hand, will argue that there is no violence in his nature although he eats meat. The same logic will claim a lack of ego, or freedom from jealousy and anger. But in reality these things cannot be conquered except through long practice.'

GURUJI also told me that his Guru Satya Charan Lahiri had been even more against alcohol, smoking and drugs than meat, because of their potential to harm man and cause addiction.

As far as the yoga practitioner is concerned, intoxicating substances can severely handicap a disciple's progress. They only dull, weaken and decay certain bodily organs which have to be in good health to enable success in *pranayama*. However, this is not to say that a deep-rooted habit cannot be eliminated completely through yoga.

Will-power alone is never sufficient to overcome such habits completely. Desires, the ego, anger, jealousy and ignorance are stubborn plants which break away in our hands above the ground, leaving the root preparing to send up a new shoot. But Kriya Yoga goes deep enough to dig up the root itself.

I HEARD about a woman who came to Guruji for lessons in Hatha Yoga. When she first arrived in Varanasi, she was smoking forty cigarettes a day. After a couple of weeks of daily yoga practice, she told Guruji that she knew such heavy smoking was detrimental to her health and wished she could cut down. He told her to carry on with the Hatha exercises. A week later, she reported an improvement. She was now smoking twenty a day, and felt some hope that the day would come when she could completely give up.

Before she left Varanasi, something extraordinary happened. Having just finished a meal in a restaurant with a friend, she reached for her packet of cigarettes as usual. She took one out and felt a sharp tap on her hand. An invisible tap, which made her drop the cigarette in shock. And as she told Guruji before she left

Varanasi, it was strange but she had not had the remotest desire to touch another cigarette since then.

WHEN Cord was initiated in Kriya Yoga, Guruji made him promise never to smoke again. Cord did not touch a cigarette for a year, until he and John went to a party in London on a stop-over to India. Everyone was smoking, and he saw no harm in accepting just one cigarette himself.

Shortly afterwards, Cord regretted having broken his promise to Guruji. He was plagued with an incessant cough which quickly turned into bronchitis and lasted for several months. A doctor who x-rayed his lungs asked Cord how much he smoked. He did not believe it when Cord said that he had only had one cigarette in the past year, for the diagnosis suggested that he was a chain smoker.

'THAT'S not the only story I can tell you about me and smoking,' Cord later told me on the telephone. 'It was soon after I first met Guruji and a group of us were taking lessons. I had a lung infection and was coughing constantly. At that time I used to sit by the river and smoke the occasional cigarette with a *sadhu* friend. Anyway, during one lesson, Guruji was telling us some story or other. It was nearly the end of the lesson and he suddenly changed the subject completely and told us about a woman who used to smoke casually and got a lung infection. Then he looked straight at me and laughed! It was really funny, actually. He had this look on his face which said, "That's why you've got that lung infection, Cord!" '

His Grandfather's Principles

"Therefore, do you perform your allotted duty;
for action is superior to inaction. Desisting from action,
you cannot even maintain your body." – BHAGAVAD GITA[6]

Although Satya Charan was born nine years after Lahiri Mahasaya took *Mahasamadhi*, he was faithful to his grandfather's example and principles in all things. He could not tolerate dishonesty or

---

[6] III:8 (Gita Press)

laziness and emphasised to his disciples the importance of making time for practice. He was always swift to disarm any disciple who claimed that it was too difficult to manage Kriya Yoga in addition to household and work responsibilities, whatever field they were in. It was no mere ideal, for his authority lay in the fact that he practised every word he preached. He brought up three children single-handedly after his wife's death, despite endless difficulties. He was a householder Yogi as his father and grandfather had been before him. Kriya Yoga *sadhana* was the daily spiritual responsibility which neither excluded the need for practicality, nor was it an excuse for avoiding worldly duties. When external work was executed in the spirit of devotion towards God, there need not be attachment to it.

Furthermore, he would not initiate everyone who requested Kriya Yoga by any means. When young people came wanting initiation, he was strict in telling them that education and finding employment were their first priorities. In this he made only a few exceptions where he saw particularly rare dedication.

The disciples were male and female, rich and poor, prominent and unknown citizens, holding jobs of high and low rank. Eligibility was always based on a person's inner qualities of love, truth and non-violence. There had to be determination, devotion and genuine spiritual yearning.

He was against any form of exhibitionism, including asceticism. As his grandfather and father had maintained before him, a change of dress could never alter an individual's inner constitution or make him detached. Since a person's desires were internal, they had to be conquered internally through Kriya Yoga, not superficially suppressed. There was no question of the truly detached Kriya practitioner wanting or needing to make any kind of external statement about his spirituality.

A young engineering graduate who received Kriya initiation from Satya Charan Lahiri was particularly zealous in his practice. His father had died when he was young, and it was thanks to his mother's struggle to keep him fed and educated over the years that he worked in government service. She had even supported his desire for initiation in Kriya Yoga.

Now he had a steady income and his mother was getting old. She was dependent on him. And yet the young man was considering how wonderful it would be to leave his job and spend his life in meditation as a *sadhu*.

Satya Charan explained to him on several occasions the reason why the practitioner should lead a domestic existence. He said that true detachment was an internal state best achieved in secret, for making oneself conspicuous was unnecessary, and shirking one's responsibilities inexcusable.

Despite these talks, one day this same disciple came to see Satya Charan Lahiri wearing the saffron robes of a *sadhu*. He smilingly announced to his Guru that he had left his job and would dedicate the remainder of his life to Kriya Yoga *sadhana*.

'And what is to become of your mother?' asked Satya Charan, taken aback.

'She can go and live with another relative,' was the reply.

The thoughtless attitude angered the spiritual master.

'Your mother has gone through so many difficulties to enable you to become an engineer. Will you not support her in her old age? Do you not feel any duty towards her?'

The young man did not reply. He just stood there, waiting. After a prolonged silence, Satya Charan said in a grave voice,

'Now go. Never come back to this house again.'

The young man left and never returned.

THE SHYAMA CHARAN SANGA in Bihar was a gathering of Kriya Yoga practitioners who met for discussions on spiritual matters and for scriptural explanations. Their president was Satya Charan Lahiri; he travelled from Varanasi from time to time to attend meetings at the request of members who were unable to visit him in the holy city themselves due to financial or other constraints.

A certain police officer from the group was once in a quandary. He encountered perpetual corruption at work and desperately wanted to leave his job. He felt that spiritual progress in Kriya Yoga was quite impossible in such a degenerate environment. His own guru had agreed and told him to become a *sadhu* instead.

The thing which troubled him about this instruction was that there would be nobody left in the family to support his mother, or his wife and three children. Neither of his two daughters were married yet either. However, his guru had assured him that God would take care of the family. If he were to trust these words, there seemed to be no alternative but to become a renunciant.

Still in doubt, and seeing that Satya Charan Lahiri was present at one of the committee meetings, the police officer decided to ask for his consent before making a final decision. After all, he was the most advanced Yogi. Everyone accorded Lahiri Mahasaya's grandson the profoundest respect, including his own guru.

Satya Charan Lahiri listened carefully as the man explained his situation before politely requesting a final permission and blessing on his way.

'If you have already decided and your guru has told you to do this, then there is no reason to take my consent and blessing now,' Satya Charan said.

A look of alarm spread across the police officer's face.

'Oh no, it is not definite!' he said hurriedly. 'You are higher than others, so without your permission and blessing I will not become a *sadhu*.'

'Then I will tell you to go home, take care of your family and do your work honestly. Do not look at the corruption if you cannot change it. Try to avoid it. It would be extremely unfair to leave your family.'

The police officer obeyed Satya Charan Lahiri's instruction. He continued in Kriya practice and worked to support his family.

WHEN a disciple once asked Satya Charan Lahiri if Kriya was lost when a person gave up practice for some reason, for example, through restlessness of mind which caused them to ask why they ever embarked on this spiritual path – the master replied that Kriya Yoga could never be considered lost or useless. If the disciple felt some dedication and willingness to practise even after many years had gone by, and did so properly, Kriya would never fail to give results.

There are two men, one blind and one lame, who want to traverse a mountain. So the blind man tells the lame man to sit on his shoulders. Thus the two men reach their destination together, using the blind man's legs and the lame man's eyes.[7]

In Indian philosophy, the blind man represents *Purusha*, meaning soul or consciousness, and the lame man represents *Prakiti*, or nature. Separate from each other they are forced to "play the game" of evolution. Yet they are also infinite and want to join together in order to return to their source. The implication of the fable is that self-realisation is only possible through the medium of both human body and consciousness.

In his explanations of Patanjali's Yoga Sutras, Swami Vivekananda also defines the concept of *Purusha* thus:

"Who is the seer? The Self of man, the Purusha. What is the seen? The whole of nature beginning with the mind, down to gross matter. All pleasure and pain arise from the junction between this Purusha and the mind. The Purusha, you must remember, according to this philosophy, is pure; when joined to nature, it appears to feel pleasure or pain by reflection."[8]

The Biblical story of creation tells of Adam and Eve in the garden of Eden. The man represents soul, the woman represents nature. For as long as the couple stay together, they are at one with their Maker. When they separate, the snake succeeds in tempting the woman to taste the fruit of the forbidden tree. She persuades her husband to take a bite too. But it is the fruit of good and evil, or of endless desire, and results in the couple's so-called fall from grace. Thenceforth they are banished from heaven and mankind finds itself in this earthly existence, caught in an eternally revolving wheel of evolution.

These two stories, well known to Hindus and Christians respectively, are similar analogies. And in both religious cultures, it is claimed that God is perfect. This may be true enough, but how can we be sure without experience?

Through accumulated knowledge and experience, man has invented the telephone, the fax machine and the computer. These things did not drop from the sky. They stemmed from an initial inspiration, not to mention the time and perseverance subsequently required to develop a scientific technique in order to get an end result.

---

[7] The complete story is told in the Sankarika, an ancient Indian book of philosophy.

[8] Explanation of Sutra no.17, "The cause of that which is to be avoided is the junction of the seer and the seen." (from *Raja Yoga*.)

Man cannot go to the moon without a rocket, nor can he reach Absolute Perfection without the help of a technique through which to find the spiritual world. Success is a matter of many lives of practice. It involves going beyond the brain and intellect. Yet in the Western world, there is no emphasis on practice. People are often told that He is beyond their reach. Though very few succeed in finding Him, the concept of perfection exists in the Holy Books because people have found the way to God in the past and will continue to know Him in the future.

Adam and Eve are banished from the garden of Eden, representing their fall from heaven or super-consciousness, which is our primate state. If it is the fruit of desire which keeps us separate from our Creator, where does this desire originate? The answer can be given in one word: respiration.

The advanced Yogi reaches a point when external respiration ceases to be important or necessary. He has controlled his breath through *pranayama* and experienced *Samadhi* or super-consciousness.[9] In this state alone, desire, anger, hate and ego are vanquished. So the Yogi realises that respiration, or unstable *Prana*, is the true cause of these negative traits.

Therefore, although it is easy for someone to say that they have no ego or desire, true detachment will only be found in the man who has attained *Samadhi*. He alone is the genuine *sadhu* or *sannyasi*.

FOR A MONTH before Christmas in 1996, I decided to do a Kriya Yoga retreat in our flat. By the end of it, practice was taking up to eight hours per day. The sheer effort involved could not be compared to that required in any money-earning job I had ever done in my life. It was incredibly tough on both mind and body to sit in inner concentration for such lengthy periods: soreness resulted from sitting for so long; it was a struggle to control the urge to fidget, and frequent leg-stretching was unavoidable. On the

---

[9] "Nothing is sweeter than the ambrosial cascade which flows from above; the head is quite heavy, remaining in *Kutastha* and executing *Pranayama* for a long period causes the causal water to flow down the Sahasrara; the *Omkara* sound which could be previously heard while practising *Dhyana* or *Pranayama* can now be constantly heard ... I am feeling ecstatic at this state and I realised that everything comprises the state of cessation of the inhalation-exhalation of that breath or else the still state dawns or in other words this is the actual state of renunciation. Prior to obtaining this state, this renunciation is futile." (extract from one of Lahiri Mahasaya's diaries, from *Purana Purusha* by Dr A. K. Chatterjee.)

other hand, I did learn that God truly gives ample reward for every small effort made to find Him, even by the beginner.

This time accentuated to me the extent to which Kriya Yoga could be likened to running for a prize, or entering the ring for a fight. Except here, you had to contend against your own ego and desire rather than against another individual. It was not a question of physical strength but of finding the power within. The challenge lay in the extent to which you could harness your own courage and discipline. It appeared to be the only field in life where everyone ultimately had an equal potential to succeed; and when the time came it was indeed his birthright to do so. No one was there to watch or judge the outcome from the sidelines except for God.

The "retreat" made me feel extremely sensitive to anger at close proximity. Any negative words or feelings from my fiancé made me want to withdraw as if into my shell like never before. For the first three weeks at least, I did not leave the flat once. When I did finally go outside with Andreas again, the noise sent shock-waves through my whole system. Guruji explained that this was to be expected after weeks of intense practice for the first time.

If it were only possible to adequately describe the overall experience and tell of the prize won from having sweated it out for a month, I would. But once again, what I "saw" and understood could never be put into words.

Regular daily practice was much easier immediately following the retreat, although that month did have the effect of quashing any previous romantic notions I may have had about renunciation. Being an ordinary, not-so-spiritually-advanced person, a retreat could be attempted from time to time. In the long term, however, it would be an achievement in itself to keep the commitment to practise Kriya on a twice-daily basis, through which significant spiritual progress was undoubtedly possible over time. So as far as ordinary people like myself were concerned, when the masters in Lahiri Mahasaya's lineage advised their disciples against becoming *sadhus*, they were probably just being realistic.

WE WERE due to be married in May 1997. But before Andreas and I left Varanasi to spend the last six weeks of our travels in Australia and New Zealand, Guruji gave us a marriage blessing ceremony. We put garlands over each other's heads, according to the Hindu tradition to symbolise the bride and groom's acceptance of each other.

Hindu weddings go on literally for days and the couple have to stay up all night for the initial ceremonies. Our blessing, on the other hand, lasted for about ten minutes, this conceivably being the shortest "marriage" which ever took place in India. But then Guruji was a Yogi, not a Brahmin priest.

Guruji's wedding speech to us was short, poignant and absolutely unforgettable. It went something like this:

'Actually, for marriage, there is no problem. The only thing which makes a problem is the ego.'

We had to laugh. That had to be perfectly true. Further elaboration was hardly necessary. But he added that most marriages, including his own, had one or two areas of sensitivity which set the sparks flying every time. One gradually discovered what these were and learned how to deal with them.

When we have the occasional marital dispute, Guruji's words often come back, reminding me to analyse the root of the anger directed at my husband. I have noticed many times that it is either a subtle or a blatant case of my own ego. The problem frequently stems from self-righteous thoughts such as, 'I know what is best' or 'I have been insulted and want an apology'. It is the kind of scenario deserving of Jesus Christ's rebuke: "Thou hypocrite, first cast out the beam out of thine own eye; and then shalt thou see clearly to cast out the mote out of thy brother's eye."[10]

When the cause of upset is seen through, the issue at the heart of the controversy ceases to be so personal. Backing down becomes easier if you are in the wrong, and humility is found if you are right. Surely, if it were only possible to quash personal sense or ego every time it appeared, there would be no anger, frustration or hurt to rock the boat of love.

---

[10] St. Matthew 7:5

To Give and to Receive

*"Divine Love always has met
and always will meet every human need."* – MARY BAKER EDDY

Satya Charan Lahiri was extremely generous. Beggars who came to the house never went away empty-handed. The master always dipped into his pockets for some loose change, and if he had only rupee coins he would give those. A family tradition instigated by Lahiri Mahasaya which Satya Charan upheld was an annual feast for the poor: on this occasion up to four hundred people were invited to the house and disciples would help to serve the meal.

He supported three charitable trusts on a regular basis. He also gave money to other institutions, but if any dishonesty in their dealings ever became apparent, he would immediately withdraw his support.

There was a temple in the grounds of the master's house where devotees came for worship and made offerings. The monetary donations were never kept for personal or family needs, but were given to charity. Satya Charan kept separate money bags and calculated precisely how much was to be saved in each. Their contents went towards education and scholarships, charities, or individuals in need to whom he wished to give financial help, including disciples. Every penny always reached its intended destination.

IT WAS not always easy, but the master managed to maintain a simple and adequate standard of living thanks to meticulous household management. The family was never in want, but on the other hand luxuries were not to be found in the household either. It was unheard of for him to be extravagant, for he lived by the maxim that man should know his limits. Whenever he bought anything, he compared prices beforehand and bartered in the market.

The family house was large and allowed for a few rooms to be let. The tenants were fortunate to have such a magnanimous landlord, for although some of them lived there for twenty-five years, Satya Charan never raised the rent.

Occasionally Satya Charan was obliged to borrow money for

repairs to the house, although he disliked debt immensely and considered it something to be avoided if at all possible, however small the amount.

Although many gurus make materialistic demands of their disciples, Satya Charan was only ever happy to accept gifts which were given from the heart. There was never any expectation. On the contrary: since he regarded his disciples as an extension of his own family, if someone was in financial need he would be the first to offer assistance.

When a disciple who was unemployed brought him sweets, Satya Charan reproached him.

'Why are you bringing sweets?' he would ask. 'What were you thinking! That you're rich or something?'

One day when a poor disciple wanted to give some money, Satya Charan refused to take it. He knew that it was being offered with great love and deep devotion, but the amount was somewhat beyond the disciple's means. The man started to weep and begged his Guru to accept it. He and his family had put the money aside especially for him. The thought of taking it back was unbearable. The master finally accepted it in silence.

A WESTERN man once came to the house asking for Kriya Yoga initiation. Satya Charan replied that he could not be given Kriya Yoga, for he did not understand the value of this practice. The man did not seem to be particularly perturbed and went away.

However, the next day he returned carrying a small packet, which he placed in front of Satya Charan. Several disciples were present at the time. The man asked him to open the packet and when the master did so, he found that it contained no less than ten thousand rupees.

'What is this money for?' he asked.

'It is for you,' replied the man. 'You were saying yesterday about the value of Kriya practice ...'

The Yogi laughed heartily.

'You cannot pay for Kriya Yoga!' he said. 'It is priceless. I did not mean for you to bring money. Things of a higher value are required to enter this spiritual world, such as dedication, devotion and faith. These are things you do not possess.'

IN THE 1960s, a certain Western organisation approached Satya Charan Lahiri and offered him the noble sum of four hundred dollars per month to become the president of a Kriya Yoga centre which they planned to open in Varanasi.

At that time, four hundred dollars was a substantial salary by any Indian standards, being approximately ten times the salary of a university professor. But, as Satya Charan told his close disciples, rather than involving any work in particular, the position appeared to be solely a matter of publicity.

Although Satya Charan was struggling to make ends meet for the children's education and repairs to the house, he was not tempted to accept the offer even for a minute. It was out of the question.

It was not just the fact that fame and publicity were of no interest to him. It was more his awareness that the establishment of Kriya societies was something his grandfather, the father of Kriya Yoga, had never endorsed. Lahiri Mahasaya had always made it clear that this secret practice should not be made into a separate religion or society, and taught his disciples to practise Kriya discreetly.

Satya Charan Lahiri was therefore not prepared to sell the family name. He explained to his disciples that organisations and the publicity they generated in the name of Kriya Yoga could easily put the continuation of the original method in jeopardy.

Some time later, close disciples of Satya Charan Lahiri also reported that their Guru received substantial offers from various Western Kriya Yoga societies wanting to purchase Lahiri Mahasaya's twenty-six handwritten diaries. However, this particular set of books constituted a spiritual treasure which he refused to sell under any circumstances.

FOR YEARS many of the disciples urged Satya Charan Lahiri to consider publishing his grandfather's life story. There were innumerable accounts which he had been told by family members including his grandmother Kashi Mani Devi, his father Tinkari Lahiri, his mother, his aunts,[11] not to mention many close disciples of his grandfather. Shortly before he left his body, Satya Charan agreed and gave his disciple Dr Ashoke Kumar Chatterjee

---

[11] Tinkari Lahiri's sisters.

permission to record the true story of Kriya Yoga's revival through Lahiri Mahasaya, including many extracts from the secret handwritten diaries of the great master himself, in his book *Purana Purusha*. Its publication resulted in Lahiri Mahasaya's name becoming increasingly well known in India.

Several disciples donated money for the book's publication. Satya Charan Lahiri gave the writer sole copyright and even insisted on paying for his copy, despite having provided all the information for it. His only interest and motivation in seeing *Purana Purusha* in print was to ensure that at least one reliable source regarding his grandfather's life story would be available.[12] For he was aware of a number of books beginning to appear in the East and West on the subject of Kriya Yoga, many of which were written by people claiming to have met Lahiri Mahasaya's Guru Babaji. Satya Charan Lahiri told his disciples that many of these books were teeming with exaggerations, attempts to sensationalise, or downright lies.

❖ ❖ ❖ ❖ ❖ ❖ ❖ ❖

Guruji never left the yoga studio without first turning to the picture of Lahiri Mahasaya which hung on the wall, bowing and making *Pranam*. His wife Vandana never left the house without touching Lahiri Mahasaya's feet on the picture which hung near the front door, and making *Pranam* either.

In many of the stories heard or read so far about the masters, I had gathered that Lahiri Mahasaya was frequently elevated to the same level as God. For example, Satya Charan Lahiri felt that his grandfather had saved him from electrocution when he was in the river during that thunderstorm. Why did he not say that it was his own Guru and father Tinkari who had blessed him, if he had to thank a Guru at all? Why was God not given the credit directly instead?

At times it seemed as if God and Lahiri Mahasaya were virtually one and the same for Guruji too. When people came to him for help, he would gaze at the picture of Lahiri Mahasaya, and tell

---

[12] *Purana Purusha* by Dr A. K. Chatterjee has been a prime source in establishing the true story about Lahiri Mahasaya's life and mission as the father of Kriya Yoga in this book. Available in English since January 2000.

disciples that everything would happen according to His will, just as much as he would promise to pray for God's blessing on their behalf.

The Indian concept of giving respect to a Guru was something I was gradually beginning to grasp, but surely not even a self-realised master should ever be referred to as a god. That was tinted with blasphemy for those brought up in a Christian tradition such as myself. It needed explaining at least.

The first part of Guruji's explanation began with the unfathomable question: 'What is God?'

'THE WAY we think about God often depends upon what we have been taught. To illustrate the point: if someone doesn't know your language, you could easily show them the sugar and tell them that it is salt. Ask them for the salt, and they will bring the sugar, according to the way they have been educated. And yet the substance of sugar and salt, despite the many words for them in different languages, remains the same. Likewise, the nature of the Creator does not change whether we worship Him as God, *Bhagavan* or Allah. These are also names invented by man.

'People learn how to worship through having observed others. Some pray to a deity and others to the Absolute. Everyone has a different concept. Primitive civilisations worshipped the sun as their God, since it was the source of life and light.

'But who or what is God? The word "God" is easy enough to pronounce, but what can we honestly say we know about His existence? Do we believe in a supernatural being above the clouds? If a million people were to repeat 'God! God! God!' at the same time and at the top of their voices, would He hear their call and come? Of course not. So why do we imagine that God is separate from us and therefore find the idea of man becoming God blasphemous?

'When asked where God "lives", most people will agree that He is within the inner consciousness. That heaven and hell are not physical places. So the question is, can the ordinary person attain the master's level of super-consciousness simply by thinking about Him? Because if thought alone could reach to God, there would be no need to make any effort for meditation practice. But it is not so. The only way to know God is to develop consciousness into super-consciousness. The senses can perceive the gross manifestations of nature, but the subtle manifestations which hold the key to all of creation will never be seen without practice. However much one may argue about what God is from a logical or intellectual standpoint, true knowledge will always be a question of experience. Lahiri Mahasaya used to say that God was not some being above the clouds. He would explain that God was the still state of *Prana*, and that this stillness was the original form of every living being.

'Jesus also said, "the kingdom of God is within you."[13] He was not excluding anyone when he made that statement. The masters have always tried to convey the idea that God exists in man. Lahiri Mahasaya sowed the lost seed of Kriya practice in the world once more to enable seekers to realise God for themselves through a scientific method. Without such a method, we can never know God as any of the masters knew Him.

'The masters taught that God is perfect. Which means that human beings have the potential to understand the nature of perfection. In the Gospels, Jesus states on several occasions that he is the son of his Heavenly Father.[14] Yet he also says, "I and my Father are one."[15] Apparently contradictory statements, but the first one was easier for the majority to understand. In spite of this, a Yogi would say that the second one was more accurate. For when man reaches to God, he himself becomes perfect. Self-realisation is actually the practice of worshipping God internally so as to become God, or attain union with Him.

'Just as God never dies, neither does the self-realised Yogi. He has conquered death, man's greatest fear, by going beyond the breath in *Samadhi* and is no longer bound by the laws of the body or of nature. He is as infinite as the ocean, having power beyond human comprehension. Lahiri Mahasaya said that as long as water is kept in a vessel it has no strength, but the moment it merges with the river it gains the capacity to do anything.[16]

---

[13] St. Luke 17:21

[14] St. John 8:28 and 14:13; St. Luke 10:22; St. Matthew 11:27

[15] St. John 10:30

[16] An extract from one of Lahiri Mahasaya's confidential diaries reads, "... the main gate opened, just as when tap water merges with the River Ganges it becomes the Ganges, similarly when the breath mingles with that pure void then it merges, this state is Brahma, this Primordial Brahma is true, then the self becomes God. From where does that breath come? I could understand that the breath is originating from within that infinite void." (from *Purana Purusha*.)

'So when we say that Lahiri Mahasaya was God, we mean that he was a perfect man in the eight *Siddhis*, which is also a definition of God.

'That is why a Yogi wants to live an ordinary, simple and natural existence in the world, so that no one can recognise him. Unlike others, he is untouched by ego. Through his oneness with God he is a creator, although there is no feeling of personal greatness or pride in his ability to perform miracles. Nor does he interfere with the course of nature.

'However, the ordinary person only sees the physical appearance and cannot appreciate the level upon which the Yogi operates, or the extent of that infinite power in *Samadhi*.[17] God is a separate entity for him. Someone who has ego cannot conceive of a person without any ego. If a master said, "I am God", and claimed to be a doer or creator, no one would understand him. They would imagine him to have a well-endowed ego rather than none at all. Hence a Yogi avoids such statements and hides his help, attributing the blessings he bestows on others to God.'[18]

THE SELF-REALISED master can only be known through perfection in the *Siddhis*. Swami Vivekananda explains these in *Raja Yoga*. He says,

"This means that the Yogi has attained the eight powers. He can make himself as minute as a particle, or as huge as a mountain, as heavy as the earth, or as light as the air; he can reach anything he likes, he can rule everything he wants, he can conquer everything he wants, and so on. A lion will sit at his feet like a lamb, and all his desires will be fulfilled at will."[19]

---

[17] Another extract from Lahiri Mahasaya's confidential diaries incontrovertibly records his experience of this state: "I am Krishna; I am Kisunji; I am Amorphous Brahma; I am the Soul-Sun, the entire universe is My creation; the total creation has manifested from My Form; I only am Brahma; I only am God, the Primordial Male Energy; I am the Soul-sun, Narayana, God, Controller of the universe and am Immanent; the Soul-sun is Krishna, I am the Soul-sun-Mahadeva." (from *Purana Purusha* by Dr A. K. Chatterjee.)

[18] "Raja Yoga does not ... deny the existence of facts which are hard to explain; on the other hand, it gently, yet in no uncertain terms, tells the superstitious that miracles and answers to prayers, and powers of faith, though true as facts, are not rendered comprehensible through the superstitious explanation of attributing them to the agency of a being, or beings, above the clouds. It declares that each man is only a conduit for the infinite ocean of knowledge and power that lies behind mankind." – Swami Vivekananda (from *Raja Yoga*.)

[19] Explanation of Patanjali's Yoga Sutra no. 50: "By making Samyama on the discrimination between the Sattva and the Purusha come omnipotence and omniscience." See also *Siddhis* in the Glossary.

'THE GREATEST lesson which Lahiri Mahasaya taught to his Kriya disciples was how to become a Yogi and live like an ordinary person,' Guruji told me. 'How to be soft and humble, simple and noble. These are important qualities. Many people like to tell sensational stories about how they met an enlightened saint and he was surrounded by a bright light or aura. Yet when I met Satya Charan Lahiri, I did not know what a Yogi or saint was, and there was nothing spectacular to be seen. If you can understand, this is the reality and the most profound example –'

'Why is that an example?' I interrupted. 'Can't you see auras?'

'Listen,' Guruji said. 'What I am telling you is that many writers sensationalise about their meetings with spiritual masters in this way – "I saw this person and a great white light was coming out of them," and so on. They want to thrill their readers, but it is a useless thing for us. It is nothing. Anyone can see an aura ...'

'I can't.'

'Certainly you can see auras if you want to. Every living thing is surrounded by an aura, and it is only a matter of concentrating the eyes. The easiest way is to gaze at someone's face for a long time when there is a solid cream or white background behind them. The aura of a person who is practising Kriya becomes more and more strong: it will be a creamy colour after some time. But a Yogi can hide his light from others completely at will, just as he can transform his body into pure light, in which case his physical form will become invisible. Spiritual vision goes deeper, it is very different.'

'So are you saying that you can see auras but it's not important – or when you see a person you see something more ...?'

'More.'

There was a lengthy pause whilst Guruji remembered what he was trying to tell me before the interruption on the subject of auras.

'Now, we were talking about why Satya Charan Lahiri gave respect and honour to his grandfather first and foremost. It is true that Lahiri Mahasaya, Tinkari Lahiri and Satya Charan Lahiri were equally great masters who left their bodies for a final time in *Mahasamadhi*. Guru is Guru. The point is that Satya Charan recognised Lahiri Mahasaya as being the source. He was the chosen one who returned Kriya Yoga to the world. Although his father Tinkari initiated him, in our Indian tradition we learn to give respect and regards to whoever is the senior person as a sign of humility. Without this quality, no one can walk the path to realisation.

'Although Satya Charan Lahiri would never admit anything and always thanked God and Lahiri Mahasaya, I sometimes understood it was his own miracle which had made the impossible come about. But he set the example that, as Kriya practitioners, we have to be grateful first to God, then to Lahiri Mahasaya and lastly to our Guru. We never say, "I did this", nor do we say to our own Guru, "you did that".

'In Kriya Yoga, "I" is a dangerous word. This is why Lahiri Mahasaya taught that practice should be secret. Disciples should avoid talking about experiences to others. For until the ego is conquered, which is not usually a question of a few years but of many lifetimes, it plays many tricks. Kriya practice shortens the route, but that means we must be more on our guard not to be fooled by illusion on the way. It is best to be grateful to God and think of ourselves as His children.'

THERE once lived a man who trusted in God to provide his every need. Although he and his wife were very poor and he could not find work, his faith remained as strong as ever that all would be well. But their financial situation worsened and his wife began to nag him constantly to leave home and find work elsewhere.

Finally he gave in to her demand, but not without reluctance and a heavy heart. Before leaving, he took a red pencil and boldly underlined his favourite stanza in the *Bhagavad Gita*. It read: "But those who worship me and my unity in all beings are the truly persevering, and to these I give what they do not have and increase what they have."[20]

A few days after he left, a man came to the door and delivered some money, saying that it was from her husband. The woman was overjoyed.

'He must have found a good job,' she thought to herself.

The same man regularly brought gold and riches to the house for years, and the woman built a magnificent house, gratified that they were accumulating so much wealth.

---

[20] IX:22 (Lal)

In the meantime her husband wandered far and wide looking for work without any success. He had to beg for his food. Sometimes people took pity on him and gave him rice and *dhal* to eat. His frame became skeletal and his skin turned coarse and leathery through exposure to the sun's merciless rays. His beard and hair straggled around his gaunt face, and he began to look aged.

Several years passed, and finally he decided to return home to confess to his wife that he had failed miserably. As he entered his home town, his old friends and neighbours clamoured around him, shocked at his appearance. He was barely recognisable.

'What has happened to you? Why are you in such a state when your wife is so rich?' they asked.

The poor man had no idea what they were talking about, until they led him to his wife's palatial residence.

'What happened to you?' cried the man's wife, horrified.

'I couldn't find a single job,' he answered. 'I have been begging for a living these past years because I was too ashamed to come home empty-handed.'

'Then who was the man who came to the house bringing money from you?' she asked.

'What do you mean, a man came bringing money? What did he look like?'

'He was an elderly man with a white beard,' she answered. And then she suddenly remembered something else. 'Oh, and there was one strange thing about him. There were red whiplash marks on his back.'

The man told his wife of how he had used a red pencil to underline the stanza about God's provision in his *Bhagavad Gita* the day before he had left to look for work. The couple then realised that the man's understanding of his favourite stanza had manifested as an elderly man delivering money. As a result of the miracle, they never doubted the Almighty again.

BORN TO DIE (A Song)

If I could speak a word
Untie a knot inside
If I could draw the breath
To start a hurricane
If I could lift the earth
Find a different moon
Watch the waves rise and fall
And take my life again

But the farewell tears are hard to find
Don't hesitate to think she is losing her mind
And you know there's a reason for everything
And no reason to be afraid
She'll come back some day
Because there's only one way

Too soon to say goodbye
Hasn't it just begun?
Too soon to kiss your face
And catch the rainbow
How will I tell the truth
Knowing we're born to die
How can I tear the wall down
Then try to hide?

Chapter Nine

THE NATURE OF KARMA

The Umbrella of Love

*"If you take shelter in me with true faith, then, I have to come to you.
How can I stay far away?"* – LAHIRI MAHASAYA[1]

Marriage in India has always been an expensive affair. For Harish Chand Singh, the financial implications seemed insurmountable when he had to organise a marriage for his niece on the pitiful income of an assistant engineer. He only had 25,000 rupees for the dowry, and no one would accept less than 100,000 rupees. After a year of searching in vain he began to lose hope completely.

Harish Chand Singh had never troubled his Guru with any personal problem before, but under the circumstances he did not know what else to do. So he explained the whole situation to Satya Charan Lahiri: that he had been the girl's guardian since her father's death and taken responsibility for her education; he would be able to organise a marriage for less with someone of a lower caste if she were his own daughter, but since she was his niece, doing so would subject him to severe criticism. Everyone would say that he was merely saving money because she was his brother's daughter, though this was far from being the case.

Satya Charan listened attentively, but gave no reply.

A fortnight later, a work colleague told Harish Chand Singh to visit a close friend of his who wanted to arrange a marriage for his son. Harish Chand thanked him but dismissed the idea, thinking that it would be useless in the light of his financial situation.

A few days passed and the same colleague asked Harish Chand if there had been any progress with the family he had suggested.

---

[1] From "Synopsis of Lahiri Mahasaya's Comments", in *Babaji* by Swami Satyeswarananda Giri.

Harish Chand was forced to admit that he had lacked the courage to go, since he had so little to offer. Upon hearing this, the colleague was quite insistent that he should nevertheless try, for the family in question would certainly not make any unreasonable demands of him. Harish Chand was no less sceptical than before, for whilst some families appeared to be modest in their expectations initially, it frequently happened that after the marriage had taken place and the dowry paid, endless demands were made for more money, or for gold and jewellery. Therefore he refused to go.

Several months later, all three parties met coincidentally and Harish Chand was introduced to his colleague's friend. The man was still looking for a suitable wife for his son. Harish Chand explained to him that he had not come to talk about his niece earlier, since his resources were so limited. But the man did not seem unduly concerned. He asked Harish Chand to visit his family with a photograph of his niece and her horoscope with the assurance that money need not pose any problem.

The marriage was arranged. There was no pressure from the groom's family, and Harish Chand was encouraged to make simple arrangements. It was nonetheless such a wonderful wedding that no one suspected it had cost a quarter of the amount normally required.

For Harish Chand Singh it was a miracle for which he felt immense gratitude. Surely such an unexpected turn of events would never have been possible without the grace of his Guru, Satya Charan Lahiri.

DISCIPLES often came to see Satya Charan Lahiri to discuss difficulties regarding marriage. Vidhyut Lal Dhar from Delhi once came for advice, because a family friend had a son who would be an excellent match for his youngest daughter Seema De, and he was keen to accept the offer. However, Indian tradition demanded that the eldest daughter be married first, so they had asked for a few months in which to find a suitable husband for the sister, Suleka De.

Mr Dhar and his wife had started searching for a husband for Suleka De several years previously without success, and despite doubling their efforts so that she might be married before her younger sister, no satisfactory match could be found. Now the

other family was threatening to pull out of the arrangement if the wedding for their son and Seema De was not promptly organised.

Satya Charan Lahiri told a confused and upset Mr Dhar that although it was against the dictates of custom, he should marry the youngest daughter first: if he did not, he would never find a partner for his eldest daughter. Once Seema De was married, a husband for Suleka De would also be found quickly.

The family was relieved to have an answer and had no doubt that events would turn out as Satya Charan had predicted. Indeed, just a few months after Seema De's wedding, a more than suitable husband was found for Suleka De. She married an upright young man from Delhi who worked in government service.

SATYA CHARAN'S childhood friend, Shachi *baboo* and his wife were both Kriya Yoga practitioners.

When Shachi *baboo's* wife became sick in 1945, she asked for Satya Charan Lahiri to come and bless her on her death bed. The doctors had given up hope and she was no longer able get up. Satya Charan Lahiri came and asked her if she had any last desire. Just before she died, the woman answered that she wished to be born as his son in her next life. Hearing this, Satya Charan became serious. He gave no reply.

A few years later, a son was born to Satya Charan Lahiri and his wife. The boy's face bore an unmistakable resemblance to the face of Shachi *baboo's* wife. Shachi *baboo* understood immediately that his wife's final petition had been granted, although Satya Charan said nothing about it. And although the baby was given much care and loving attention by both parents, it died quite suddenly when it was just one month old.

It was an unforgettable lesson to Shachi *baboo* on how to pray for "the grace of Guru". A desire which touched the heart of the *Mahayogi* was always granted. Every blessing reached its destination. However, he realised that his wife's request had been incomplete. Her wish to be born in the family of a Yogi had been fulfilled, but since she had not thought to be specific, the life-span given to her as Satya Charan's son was extremely brief.

Besides, when it was a matter of wishing to redefine the course of nature, perhaps the disciple should not burden the Guru with such requests in the first place.

❖ ❖ ❖ ❖ ❖ ❖ ❖ ❖

One day a poor fisherman is surprised to find a golden fish in his catch.

The fish can speak and promises the man, 'If you let me go, I will give you whatever you want every day.'

The man readily agrees and releases the fish back into the ocean. In the evening he relates the event to his wife. Naturally, she is overjoyed.

'Tell the fish that we want money!' she says.

So the next day he asks the golden fish for money, and when he gets home in the evening, he finds sacks of gold in his house. The couple go shopping for new clothes, furniture, and previously undreamed of luxuries to celebrate their good fortune.

'Our cottage is too small,' the wife tells her husband. 'Tomorrow you must ask for a fine new house.'

The following evening when the fisherman returns home from the sea, he sees a large modern house where their small ramshackle cottage had stood. His wife is ecstatic about their improved standard of living.

'Now I need plenty of servants to keep everything in order,' she says, and a day later the wish is granted. The woman becomes consumed with greed, imagining that there is nothing that she cannot wish for. So as soon as her material desires have been exhausted, she begins to dream about having God-like power.

'What a life it would be if I could control the elements,' she thinks to herself, whereupon she tells her husband,

'From tomorrow I wish to command the sunrise and the sunset.'

Her husband pleads with her not to make him request such a thing, but she remains stubborn and insistent.

'If you really love me, you will ask the fish for whatever I want,' she says.

When the fisherman repeats his wife's demand to the golden fish, it replies,

'If I grant your wife's request, the whole of creation will be turned upside down. It was a foolish thing to ask and because of it, everything I have given to you will be taken away.'

When the man reaches the shore that night he finds his wife weeping and lamenting in the old cottage. The noble house together with the money and possessions have all vanished without a trace.

ON THE morning of our wedding day in May 1997, I telephoned Guruji. He was laughing and happy, and it was balm for my nerves to hear him. I did not mention it during our conversation, but the one thing I desired more than anything on that day was his presence.

It turned out to be the most wonderful and unforgettable day of our lives. There was something indefinably special about the wedding and many guests said so. They still do. It was almost tangible in the atmosphere. For me it was a great blessing, because I felt Guruji there all day, so close by.

That same year, Andreas and I went to Varanasi for two weeks over the Christmas holidays. One evening as Guruji and I were talking, the subject of our wedding came up.

'Your wedding. Ahhh ...,' he said, as if he had been a guest and was blissfully remembering. 'You can say it was a very special day.'

Totally unselfconsciously, he talked about the people, the atmosphere and how happy everyone had been.

'So you were there after all,' I thought to myself.

'And it was strange how we won that honeymoon, wasn't it Guruji?' I said, half-hoping for some confirmation of another suspicion.

He smiled back so warmly. I understood exactly what the expression on his face meant. The self-realised Guru does not need to say anything explicitly if the disciple knows how to listen.

THERE was the time when Vandana shouted at Guruji that she would give up teaching, because in summer it was almost impossible to get a rickshaw home from her school and the scorching afternoon heat was unbearable. As usual, he remained perfectly calm and quiet whilst listening to her tirade.

The next day, to Vandana's surprise, a rickshaw was conveniently waiting right outside the gates after school. When she got home Guruji asked her, 'Did you get a rickshaw today?' And exactly the same thing happened for weeks afterwards, until school broke up for the summer holidays.

Every now and again she experienced certain difficulties at her school and would come home in tears. She always told Guruji everything, and even the worst troubles were always smoothed over as if nothing had happened. These were a few of the benefits of being married to a spiritual master, she told me with a happy laugh.

A Certain Kriya practitioner was walking along a road in Calcutta. He was concentrating in *Kutastha* and quite oblivious to the traffic. He did not see a bus headed straight at him, or hear the urgency with which the driver was honking the horn. There was no room to swerve and the bus driver had a split second to decide what to do. If he slammed on the brakes, the whole bus would skid, endangering the passengers. If he remained on course, the man in the road would be killed.

The Kriya practitioner saw the bus as it was almost upon him. The shock gave him no time to react. A fatal collision seemed inevitable, but in the instant his thought reached out to Lahiri Mahasaya, an invisible hand suddenly gave him an almighty push which sent him spinning to the side of the road.

One Of Guruji's disciples called Ganesh had a small son. The boy was about two years old at the time of this incident. He was an active child who especially loved to play with water. Whilst his mother was occupied in the kitchen, he toddled into the bathroom where the electric immersion heater was warming a bucket full of water.

The mother suddenly wondered where her son was and in the same instant remembered the immersion heater. She dashed to the bathroom and was stupefied to see him sitting with one hand in the bucket and playing with a frayed wire above the element with the other. The small boy could not possibly have survived the electric shock. By all accounts he had been saved by a power cut in the area which had occurred a split second beforehand.

It Was a cloudless summer's day in 1999, shortly after Andreas and I moved house. I was driving the car through the village and turned into a fairly steep and narrow lane, not realising that it was a cul-de-sac. The only space to turn was a small driveway down to the right, but in the process of backing down into it there was a crunch and a bump as the right rear wheel went right over a low wall which I had not seen. I got out of the car to examine the damage and was shocked and embarrassed at the sight of my lopsided car, straddled precariously across the wall. One wheel was hanging more than a metre above the ground and I stared at it, feeling at a complete loss as to what to do.

There was a painter's van parked a little way up the road, and hearing voices, I went to seek help. A couple of men came back with me to see what had happened. It did not look too good, they commented.

One of them had a look in an open garage just the other side of the wall. There were only a few things lying around, but they conveniently included three house bricks and two planks, one long and one short. My rescuers positioned the bricks in front of the wall using the short plank as a descending ramp, and discussed how they could use the long plank to lever the wheel from behind. They told me to get in the car and drive forwards slowly in first gear when they gave the word. I did so and moments later to my enormous relief, the car was over the wall. There did not appear to be any damage to the chassis. I thanked the men profusely.

Driving away again, I thanked God, Lahiri Mahasaya and Guruji. There were times when things happened and you knew it was His grace. The assistance seemed to have been pre-programmed to perfection. When my father looked under the car a couple of days later, he told me how narrowly I had escaped major damage. And although I have often walked up that road over the past few years, I have never seen those particular objects in that garage since.

GOD'S CARE and protection extends to everyone, wherever they are, and regardless of whether they have a spiritual Guru or not. The Almighty Creator is completely impartial. Qualities such as love, trust, faith and humility attract His mercy. Aid is always at hand when we wish to avail ourselves of it, and as Guruji often says, God is nearer to us than we realise.

If someone is practising Kriya Yoga conscientiously, the Guru is always close, ready to give instantaneous help. Even in life-and-death situations when there is no time to pray. However, certain things cannot be altered or prevented. Intervention is not always possible by any means. The course of nature must be allowed to flow uninterrupted.

Although the *Sadguru* can give help and fulfil certain desires, there should be no pressure, demand or expectation from the disciple. For the Guru cannot always give everything we ask of him.

Man has many desires but we need to trust that God provides for all our needs as He sees fit. Rather than praying for specific things or certain events to take place, it is always wisest to pray instead to God and Guru with complete surrender in acknowledging His authority:

'Oh Lord, you know what is best for me. Thy will be done.'

How a Spiritual Master Heals

"Then went the devils out of the man,
and entered into the swine;
and the herd ran violently down a steep place
into the lake, and were choked." – ST. LUKE[2]

Mr V. V. Sharma was a close disciple of Satya Charan Lahiri, and the entire family were devotees. So when his brother-in-law developed a serious eye condition which the doctors said would lead to blindness, Mr Sharma suggested a visit to his Guru Satya Charan Lahiri. It was the only remaining hope.

Satya Charan Lahiri told Mr Sharma's brother-in-law that there was nothing he could do except pray for him. He added,

'If it is God's will, it will happen. Let us see.'

Mr Sharma understood his Guru's words to be an assurance that a healing would follow and was overjoyed. Sure enough, his brother-in-law's eye condition rapidly improved until he was able to see normally again.

However, about a month later one of Satya Charan Lahiri's eyes became inflamed and he seemed to be in considerable pain. Many disciples heard about the problem and came to see if there was anything they could do. They suggested various medicines for him

[2] 8:33

to try. But Satya Charan insisted that the eye would heal by itself.

When the news reached Mr Sharma, he was extremely upset and rushed to see his Guru. The sight of Satya Charan's swollen eye reduced him to tears. He wailed that he was responsible for the suffering, which he knew his Guru had taken on his body as a result of having healed his brother-in-law.

Satya Charan Lahiri reassured his disciple, telling him that he was more in ecstasy than in pain.

'At this time I am not talking much. I am sitting comfortably with my eyes closed and seeing many things in *Kutastha*,' he said. 'I feel fine, there is no pain.'

Mr Sharma recalled the circumstances which had first led him to his Guru: it was 1969, and hope had been all but abandoned for the life of his bedridden ten-year old daughter. She had been suffering from a collagen disorder for four years which caused swelling in the joints. One of her knees was particularly affected. When Mr Sharma learned about Lahiri Mahasaya from a friend and heard that his grandson Satya Charan Lahiri was a *Mahayogi* living in Varanasi, he had rushed to find the master.

Satya Charan Lahiri had first asked his reason for coming, and Mr Sharma had poured out the story of his hospitalised daughter. Shachi *baboo*, sitting nearby, was amazed to hear Satya Charan promise to visit the girl in hospital the next day. That someone could come for the first time and receive his grace immediately was a rare event. The master always shrouded any help he gave in secrecy, so that people did not come to him for the wrong reasons. In this instance, Mr Sharma's great spiritual devotion was evident to the *Mahayogi* from the moment he entered the house.

The next day, Satya Charan Lahiri visited the girl in hospital as promised. She had heard that some saint was coming to visit her and begged him to make her well again.

'If it is within my power to cure you, I will have to take your problem on my own body. I will tell God and we will see,' he answered.

Returning home again with Mr Sharma, Satya Charan Lahiri explained that the situation was more complex than he had indicated in the hospital. The time was unfavourable since death was imminent. Transferring the energy which was causing the sickness could no longer save her.

Then he paused for a moment. 'There is only one thing which can save her life now,' he said, 'and that is if I give her initiation in Kriya Yoga. It is like a second life. But in her present condition I cannot initiate her. Within one week, perhaps it will be possible.'

The girl's condition had improved just enough by the following week so that she could be given Kriya Yoga. Thereafter she made a complete recovery, and although she had missed the first four years of school, she was able to catch up and achieve good grades. She later became a science graduate and was married into a wealthy family.

ONE OF Satya Charan Lahiri's disciples was beginning to feel despondent about his fruitless efforts to find work, despite being well qualified with a postgraduate degree in agriculture. His name was Shiva Narayan Lal and he paid daily visits to his Guru.

One morning, he was explaining his difficulties to the spiritual master. Whilst Mr Lal was talking, Satya Charan bent over to pick up some dry leaves from the ground by the stone staircase, and as he stood up again he hit his forehead on the sharp corner of a stair. He sat down and held his head to curb the bleeding whilst Mr Lal fetched a clean cloth to bandage the cut.

'I am happy to have this cut, if it brings something good for you,' Satya Charan Lahiri said mysteriously.

A few days later, Mr Lal met a friend who said an acquaintance of his owned a tea plantation in Assam. He offered to give Mr Lal a reference and assured him that it would be possible to find work there at any time. However, since Mr Lal did not want to leave the holy city and be so far from his Guru, he decided to continue searching in Varanasi.

Months passed and Mr Lal was still unemployed. He reluctantly decided to go to Assam and went to tell his Guru of the decision. But Satya Charan Lahiri told him that Assam was too far away, and that if he waited a few more days he would get the job he longed for in Varanasi.

'Sometimes we make a great effort and nothing happens. But if it is God's will, you wait and see how things can happen,' he said.

Mr Lal was walking down a street in Lucknow less than a week later when he heard someone shouting his name. A car stopped behind him and Mr Lal recognised the man calling him as the

Director of Agriculture for Uttar Pradesh. The executive told Mr Lal that he had been searching for him but had not been able to find his address. A post in the new agricultural office for Uttar Pradesh had become available and he was keen for Mr Lal to apply for the job. They needed a postgraduate in agriculture. Yet this was the office Mr Lal had applied to many times before without success.

Soon Mr Lal was working at the agricultural office, having been offered the position of district sales officer. The work involved some travelling. One day whilst riding his moped, Mr Lal saw four cyclists ahead who were fooling around and taking up most of the road. As he tried to pass them, one of the cyclists suddenly swerved and fell onto Mr Lal's moped, causing him to skid and fall onto the road. A car was travelling at high speed behind them, and although the driver slammed on the brakes as soon as he saw the accident ahead, a collision was inevitable. The car screeched to a halt and its bumper hit Mr Lal, cutting his forehead which started to bleed profusely.

A swarm of local villagers came running to the scene to offer their assistance. Incredibly, Mr Lal was conscious. The villagers exclaimed how lucky he was. They had witnessed how fast the car had been travelling, and said it was nothing short of a miracle that he was alive and the damage to his body was no more than a wound to the forehead. They asked what they could do for him and Mr Lal gave them his own details, the office telephone number to inform his company of the accident, and the address of his mechanic so that the moped could be sent for immediate repair. They promised to take care of everything and the car driver insisted on taking Mr Lal to hospital straight away.

At the government hospital Mr Lal was treated without delay. His eyes were bound with gauze, and his forehead was stitched. The doctor asked him if he wanted to report the accident to the police. Mr Lal answered that he did not, as the irresponsible cyclists were the ones who had really caused the accident. When the bandage was finally removed from his eyes, he was taken aback to see that the driver of the car which had hit him and the doctor who had treated him were the same person.

Mr Lal was soon back at work and the moped quickly repaired. The entire episode made him realise that his Guru had known about this accident for a long time. He had been spared life as a paralysed cripple with permanent brain or spinal damage. Spared from death itself. The comment which Satya Charan had made a long time ago upon cutting his forehead on the stairs had not been clear at the time. Now Mr Lal had stitches in exactly the same place and it did not appear to be a coincidence.

Of course Satya Charan Lahiri gave nothing away. He never did. At times his hints seemed purposely designed to confuse. And whenever a disciple came to report some impossible occurrence, evidently due to the bestowal of his grace, he would simply nod and say,

'A-ha. Good.'

❖ ❖ ❖ ❖ ❖ ❖ ❖ ❖

Sai Baba of Shirdi[3] was sitting around a fire with some of his disciples. All of a sudden, he flung his hands into the fire, severely burning them. One disciple bandaged his Guru's blistered hands, whilst another plucked up the courage to ask why he had voluntarily burned himself.

'One of my disciples was careless tonight,' he said. 'She was not watching her baby son and he fell into the fire. I pulled the boy out.'

It was later confirmed that in a village some distance away, a woman's toddler really had fallen into an open fire and been rescued by invisible hands. The boy had been saved but Sai Baba's hands took time to heal.

PHYSICS explains that energy can change form, but will never disappear. It cannot destroy itself, nor can it be destroyed. An apple may be chopped into a million pieces, but there remains a part which the knife can never split. It cannot divide the atom.

Imagine an old ink pen which spills onto a fresh page. You take blotting paper to absorb the surplus. It soaks up the bead of ink on the page and in the process becomes marked too.

Or you are cooking something and there is too much liquid in the pan. So you take off the lid and turn up the heat to make it evaporate. You achieve your aim, but the liquid has not

---

3 As previously mentioned, Sai Baba of Shirdi was a famous Yogi and disciple of Lahiri Mahasaya.

disappeared altogether just because it is no longer in the pan. The liquid has changed form and become steam. It has re-entered the atmosphere.

God is energy, the source of life. Egg and sperm develop to form an embryo which becomes a foetus in the mother's womb. Yet neither man nor woman is in control of the energy which gives the new baby its life. And where does that energy go at the time of death? Can it wholly disappear into nothingness?

'SO A SELF-REALISED Guru really has the power to help people by taking sickness onto their own body?' I was asking Guruji. 'Why would they do that?'

'For Love,' he answered, smiling. 'Here is another example. You are my disciple, and I am walking along the road with you. It is my duty to watch over you until you reach your destination, regardless of the number of lives and diversions you choose to take along the way.

'Imagine that I am carrying nothing, but you have a twenty-kilo backpack. A long journey lies ahead of you. It is a lonely place and there is no transportation available. The weight on your back is yours alone to carry. This is what we refer to as *Karma*. But one day you grow weak and it seems as though you are in danger of collapsing because of the heavy load and distance left to travel.

'At this point it is the Guru's duty to help. The challenges which you have to face in life are unavoidable. But to keep you from falling, he can lighten your burden by taking five kilos from you, should it become necessary. He will do so to help you on the journey if it means that you will continue to progress spiritually. However, when he does so, the load is transferred. It does not disappear. Your load is lighter, but he has to carry whatever he takes from you on his own body.'

I LEARNED that the spiritual master heals through his tremendous compassion for the sick and needy. When a disciple is in pain but totally surrendered and full of devotion, his suffering is also the Guru's suffering. He feels it and gives help. As soon as the disciple begins to recover, the advanced Yogi will often, but not always, start to manifest symptoms of a similar nature. Having broken the chain of *Karma* himself, there is no relief for him through conventional medicine or natural healing techniques as for the ordinary person, however hard this is for disciples to grasp.

When I tried to argue that the Bible mentions nothing about Jesus getting sick despite all the people he healed, Guruji told me that in recording the events and miracles of the lives of Lahiri Mahasaya, Tinkari Lahiri and Satya Charan Lahiri, the disciples frequently omitted to mention the times when the masters were ill. There was a reluctance to do so because of the seeming contradiction. Why should a perfect spiritual master who could heal others become sick himself? Why should the Yogi not make the remotest effort to heal himself? In his own diaries, Lahiri Mahasaya recorded numerous occasions when he became unwell himself for the sake of his disciples and devotees.

It reminded me of how they mockingly exhorted Jesus on the cross to save himself.[4] And despite his spiritual powers he made no attempt to avoid the most torturous moment of his career. He faced the pain, and as the Bible says, "gave himself for our sins, that he might deliver us from this present evil world, according to the will of God and our Father."[5]

IT DID NOT seem a particularly alien concept to my Indian friends who were also Guruji's disciples that a self-realised master could take someone's pain or sickness onto their own body in order to help them. But for two specific reasons, it was difficult for me to come to terms with the idea:

My first difficulty with the concept of a master's ability to transfer energy was due to the religious school of thought which had taught me that sickness was illusion. Was there no truth in that whatsoever?

Guruji laughed. 'Yes, that is true enough,' he said, 'but we tend to cling with the intellect to the superficial meaning. First of all we have to understand that energy cannot simply disappear, and then see where the concept that sickness is only illusion comes from.'

He went on to tell a story about an Indian mathematician from West Bengal:

Mr Ishwar Chand Vidyasagar needed an operation on his foot

---

[4] "And the rulers ... derided him, saying, He saved others; let him save himself, if he be Christ, the chosen of God." St. Luke 23:35
[5] Galatians 1:4

but refused to have an anaesthetic. Instead, he asked for a mathematical problem to solve during the operation. This was arranged, and having taken a brief look at it, Mr Vidyasagar said that it would take him about five minutes. The operation was going to take about the same amount of time, so on the word of Mr Vidyasagar to begin, they began to perform their respective tasks simultaneously.

When the operation was over and the mathematical problem solved, the doctor asked Mr Vidyasagar why he had not felt any pain. The mathematician said that the mind can only be in one place at a time. Through extraordinary mental self-control, he had succeeded for the duration of the operation to concentrate solely on the mathematics instead of his foot; therefore the operation had been quite tolerable.

THE NERVES send a message to the brain that we are hurt. A local anaesthetic puts those nerves to sleep so that the message can no longer travel to the brain. Similarly, if the mind can be completely disconnected from physical pain, all suffering is alleviated, even though the problem has not necessarily disappeared.

In the same way, physical discomfort is likely to be temporarily forgotten during a scintillating discussion. And in prayer, concentration is also diverted away from the body to thoughts of God. This is certainly beneficial. But because we notice that pain is lessened when the mind shifts away from the part of the body which is injured or sick, we may conclude that the mind is the central cause of suffering rather than the body.

The Buddha and several other spiritual masters have said that sickness is illusion, hence the belief has woven its way into several religious philosophies. But we have to understand the deeper meaning of what they were saying. For it is not mind alone which creates the pain, nor were the masters telling us to rely uniquely upon mind-power for healing. The aim is to get super-mind power or super-consciousness. The Buddha was telling his disciples that sickness was illusion when a person actually became one with the Absolute.

The mind is always wandering in our body. Without our being conscious of it, the body changes second by second through chemical action and reaction. The hair and nails grow, the skin flakes in the production of new layers, and the body requires the right amounts of oxygen, food and water for its development. As a biochemical energy structure, it functions entirely independently of a person's theological or philosophical belief.

According to Guruji, the idea of yoga was not to make the body perfect. There was no question of halting the ageing process, whether we prayed for good health or believed that sickness was illusion. And the person who had genuine respect for God and the five elements usually found it easier to adopt a balanced middle path in matters of prayer and healing.

To BRIEFLY DIGRESS from the subject of sickness and healing, Guruji revealed that there were two well-guarded and highly advanced esoteric yogic secrets of staying young. Yogis who were firmly established in yoga *sadhana* had been known to use these primarily in order to avoid the time-consuming process of rebirth, childhood and search for a spiritual Guru, though only in exceptional circumstances. The first was the technique of body rejuvenation *(Rasasiddhi)*, and the second was the method of changing the body in stopping the process of decay *(Kayakalpa)*.[6] It would be quite possible to conjecture that the youthful appearance of Lahiri Mahasaya's Guru Babaji was due to *Kayakalpa*. And it has been told of Trailanga Swami that he lived such an extraordinarily long life through having performed *Rasasiddhi*.

Lahiri Mahasaya recorded his personal knowledge of both techniques in his diary. It is said of the master that although his hair turned grey, he did not have any wrinkles on his body; however, it is known that he never used either technique to lengthen his own life-span.

Although Lahiri Mahasaya, Tinkari Lahiri and Satya Charan Lahiri regularly entered the state of *Samadhi*, their bodies also aged in a natural way. As spiritual masters in the highest stages of yoga, they all taught that there was no wisdom in eternal youth or holding onto the body. They were able to reach their final spiritual destination without the need for more time on earth, therefore none of them had any reason to digress from the ultimate aim of *Mahasamadhi*.

---

[6] *Rasasiddhi* is a complicated technique performed using mercury and other herbal medicines which keeps the body youthful; *Kayakalpa* is possible only after *Rasasiddhi* through an additional yogic method.

NEXT we talked about the cause of sickness and how a spiritual master was able to transfer it: Guruji explained that physical pain and suffering was caused by unstable air in the body, which in turn resulted in unsteadiness or blockage of the *Chakras*. Every organ in the body was controlled by one of the *Chakras*.

Put in simple terms, the self-realised master healed a disciple's sickness through his own storage of *pranayama* which had built up due to advanced and long practice. He lived in "a state of constant air", meaning that there was no instability in his own *Chakras*. He attuned the turbulence from the sick person's offending vibrating *Chakra* through his own control of *Prana* and had a method of steadying and dissolving it. A restructuring of atoms occurred through the transfer, but exactly how this was done could not be explained to the ordinary person having no experience or realisation, Guruji said.

The Yogi could give cod-liver oil to revive someone already at death's portal. He could prescribe the sticky yellow sweet, *jilibi*, to cure the cholera patient. But it would be erroneous to believe that the healings were solely due to these unconventional medicines or that they resulted entirely because of the disciples' faith.

When a Yogi entered the state of *Samadhi* or super-consciousness, his mind was completely disconnected from the body. He could transcend any amount of pain. The subconsciously functioning human system and mind were completely under his control. There were no external signs of life. He was free of physical chains and became Pure Soul. If someone cut, burned or hurt his body in some way whilst he was in that condition, he would feel nothing. Likewise, when a master took on a disciple's sickness, he was not suffering himself for the duration of time he spent in *Samadhi*. However, it was inevitable that when mind re-entered his body, he would feel and have to bear the physical pain.

And yet the Yogi could tolerate physical discomfort far better than the ordinary person. He could focus his concentration elsewhere, even when not in *Samadhi*. He was always on the higher planes of consciousness where thought was not tied to the body.

MY SECOND difficulty with the subject of healing through energy transfer was that Yogis were not alone in their ability to heal. No doubt the evidence suggested that their methods were beyond the scope of an ordinary person's imagination. But there were many spiritual workers who also healed through prayer, whilst being entirely unaware that they even had *Chakras*. If you told the healers in my church about these energy centres, they would probably be indifferent. And it would contradict their belief to the core to imagine that they could get sick themselves through helping others. So whether through prayer or some alternative healing method, what was spiritual healing about for the person who was not self-realised? Guruji began by telling another true story:

There was once a man who lived in the Himalayas. He had the gentlest and most truthful of dispositions and loved God with all his heart. But he did not know of any spiritual practice. Someone who was sick came by the place where the honest man lived, and the two men talked together for a while. The sick man asked for some water before he left. Having had a drink, he set off back to the village at the base of the mountain, and suddenly noticed that he had been cured. He told the people in the village to visit the man on the mountain if they were ever unwell, because he had healing water.

People began to visit the man every now and again, and although the man on the mountain never revealed his secret, whatever he gave them, whether it was a flower or a cup of water, they found themselves healed of their diseases.

Before long, word had spread like wildfire. A multitude of people came up the mountain to the honest man's hut. And they begged him to speak. To tell of his God-realisation. To share the technique which enabled him to heal everybody who came. And although nobody wanted to believe it, the man insisted that he was not doing anything. People were coming to his place and asking for water, and he was merely obliging. It was his pleasure that they were apparently healed through it. He had a firm belief in God but knew of neither *Mantra* nor meditation.

GURUJI explained that where there was stillness of mind, there was also peace and health. Many spiritual workers who prayed on behalf of others were successful in the healing field because they had their own mind under control to some extent. They had some spiritual qualities and purity of heart. They had not realised God, but with little effort, their sincere prayer reached its destination and blessed the receiver.

And yet most spiritual healers did not actually understand why or how a healing occurred, unlike the Yogi. Prayer was effective on one level, but the spiritual master did not need prayer to heal others. When Jesus healed people, was he praying to God? How was it possible that he could simply touch the diseased, or for them to touch him, for an instantaneous cure?[7] If someone was self-realised, there was no question of praying to anyone, Guruji told me. Nor was it possible. The operation occurred on a higher plane altogether.

Lahiri Mahasaya was initiated in Kriya Yoga at the age of forty. His way was prepared. With little practice he was able to reach the spiritual level he had known in his previous life. But how many people were like him? How many people were like the Buddha, or Christ Jesus?

Some books promised that a person could awaken the *Kundalini* within six months through a certain *pranayama* technique. When people practised for five years and still nothing happened, they wanted to know why. They did not understand that this could only be possible for someone who had reached an uncommonly high level in yoga in their previous life.

GURUJI added that healing was often a matter of belief. We prayed to God and when we were healed as a result of thinking about Him, we gave thanks that He listened and helped us. Without this belief, perhaps we would not pray to Him again.

Some people used objects such as copper bangles and stones, and were also healed through their belief. There was no reason to be rigid about the individual choice of a crutch when we were sick. Nor was there any right or wrong about it, since a person's need corresponded to their stage of learning. When we took medicine,

---

[7] "... he spat on the ground, and made clay of the spittle, and he anointed the eyes of the blind man with the clay, / And said unto him, Go, wash in the pool of Siloam ... He went his way therefore, and washed, and came seeing." St. John 9:6,7

"And he took the damsel by the hand, and said unto her, *Talitha cumi*; which is being interpreted, Damsel, I say unto thee, arise. / And straightway the damsel arose, and walked;... / And he charged them straitly that no man should know it ..." St. Mark 5:41-43

"And behold, a woman, which was diseased with an issue of blood twelve years, came behind him, and touched the hem of his garment: / For she said within herself, If I may but touch his garment, I shall be whole. / But Jesus turned about, and when he saw her, he said, Daughter, be of good comfort; thy faith hath made thee whole. And the woman was made whole from that hour." St. Matthew 9:20-22

the brain disconnected from the part of the body giving discomfort and we felt better. But for the ordinary person, whatever the method, cases of rapid or spontaneous healing without medicine were usually due to the surrendering of the ego.

One of India's most sacred treasures were the *Mantras* which could cure every disease known to man. Words came from the *Chakras*. Chanting the correct *Mantra* sent a vibration which stabilised the air causing the sickness. But whilst the healing would be certain, there was no self-realisation through it. It was the same with prayer and medicine. As soon as one problem was dealt with, the next appeared. It was not as if life's problems would suddenly cease. We could not avoid or separate ourselves from the endless chain of challenges which were a part of human existence.

Later I found the idea of balance which Guruji was trying to convey appealingly worded in one of Patanjali's *Yoga Sutras*. It was definitely something to work towards:

"In place of pleasure-and-pain, right–and-wrong, friendship, kindness, contentment and indifference (non-attachment) are to be developed. That is, in place of happiness, friendship; of pain, kindness; of righteousness, contentment; and of wrong, indifference (non-attachment).

These are to be cultivated with contemplative heart, holding onto the Self.

It usually provides satisfaction."[8]

MY MIND would previously have rejected most of these new ideas. However, now some of them were beginning to make sense. The pieces of the puzzle were gradually falling into place. At the same time, the new angle on healing had me somewhat confused about prayer. Was it some kind of self-delusion to think that prayer helped when one was sick? Why not rely on a copper bangle if it could heal just as well because of the belief attached to it? Or use a *Mantra* which had nothing to do with either prayer or medicine, for that matter? Not being a self-realised person in control of my *Chakras*, what was I supposed to do to help myself when I was sick in the future? How was I supposed to think?

'Don't let it become a matter for confusion,' Guruji told me. 'We

---

[8] Yoga Sutra no. 33 from *Lahiri Mahasaya's Commentaries on the Yoga Sutras of Patanjali.*

should be aware that petitioning God for healing is not constructive prayer. It is better to think that the trouble is temporary and try to engage the mind elsewhere. Lift thought to God by all means. Prayer is helpful, because it promotes dedication, trust and faith. When we are at peace and feel unified with nature and God's will, we can endure the trials of life more easily.

'At the same time, we have to understand that prayer is not self-realisation. In prayer there are two: God and devotee. There is no concept of how to become One. Certainly, there are many genuine spiritual healers in the world who are able to help people through the influence of their previous lives. But not everyone is able to heal, and not everyone will be healed. We have to go further than this. Why are we praying? Only for health? Never for wisdom?

'At the time of leaving his body, Sai Baba of Shirdi said that most people had come to him wanting their sicknesses cured and worldly problems solved. They had the attitude that since God was the cause of the world, he was also the cause of their afflictions. They felt that the desire to consign their problems back to Him was perfectly justified, being reluctant to accept the burden which was theirs to carry. Pitifully few had any real desire to become self-realised themselves.'

Guruji added that this was still true. As soon as people were aware that a self-realised person was in their midst, they clamoured for relief from their suffering and demanded help from everyday trials and tribulations. Whilst a few realised that their affliction had been transferred to the master and showed gratitude for his help, the majority remained primarily interested in relief from their pains and forgot to give thanks altogether.

Healing alone was not the point. It did not bring the individual closer to self-realisation or absolve him from breaking the chains of his own *Karma*, for which purpose Kriya Yoga was again given to the world through Lahiri Mahasaya.

The great spiritual masters were tempted by neither money nor fame. All they wanted was for their disciples to follow the spiritual path which they lighted to its ultimate goal. Secrecy was of prime importance, because otherwise people came for the wrong reasons. They shrouded their help even to the closest disciples, whilst inspiring the most devoted followers with yet greater faith and motivation through their examples.

Having the power to heal and save, the Yogi did not want the disciple to depend upon him every time. It was human nature to think of a Guru's help as the easy solution: he helped once and would help again. But this was not necessarily so. Hence Lahiri Mahasaya and the masters usually told their disciples to go to a doctor and take conventional medicine when they were sick. The emphasis had to stay on the disciple's own practice for self-realisation.

This could most truly be said of Guruji. Nothing pleased him more than when a disciple was practising hard. His eyes lit up with pure pleasure whenever you told him of something experienced on the practice-road. He made you feel as if you had just presented him with an exquisite platter of the most delicious foods the world had to offer.

ANDREAS and I went to Rajestan for two weeks in November 1996. During our absence from Varanasi, Guruji fractured his ankle. The doctor told him that it would take at least three months to heal.

I gathered that his wife Vandana was cross with him. He had 'done it again', as she put it. She told me that it had happened after dark when he had fallen into a sizable pothole whilst getting off his scooter. As he lay there, unable to move his leg, he had shouted for joy, giving loud thanks and repeating, '*Baba! Baba!*'

Which was not to say that he had been unaffected by pain at the time. He was rushed to hospital and the ankle put in plaster.

What Vandana also explained was that several times during the weeks prior to the accident, Guruji had spoken to a certain woman disciple who was pregnant for the second time. She had lost her first baby due to an accident. Guruji had been on the telephone to her at frequent intervals, telling her to take extra care wherever she went. He had been extremely upset about something which was apparently going to happen.

Having broken his ankle, he was happy. Something worse had been avoided. Vandana said she had understood that if it had not been for Guruji's accident, both baby and mother would have lost their lives this time. Of course it was good, she added, but she had mixed feelings about the way Guruji was always suffering on behalf of others.

THE ANKLE took a long time to heal. Even after the plaster was finally removed, for months Guruji had to walk with a stick. Observing him during these months following the accident was interesting: there was no sign of any pain when he was engrossed in conversation. And when he was sitting somewhere with closed eyes, he would look as serene as ever with bliss written all over his face.

But then he would get up as if the ankle had never been broken. It was enough to make my own face screw up to hear his agonised cry as excruciating pain shot through the fractured joint. The problem was that whenever he got up from sitting, he would routinely put his whole weight on the leg, having forgotten that a part of his body was still trying to recover from a fracture. Such detachment from the body was evidently something of a hindrance to the natural healing process.

When Death Knocks

"Sin brought death, and death will disappear
with the disappearance of sin." – MARY BAKER EDDY

Harish Chand Sibal was married with two young children. One day the youngest child swallowed a coin which lodged in his throat. The boy was rushed to hospital. An x-ray confirmed that it was too far down the respiratory tract to be dislodged by coughing. The doctors told Harish Chand that his son had no chance of survival without an operation, but the procedure involved a substantial risk. Since they were unsure about which course of action to take, they decided to wait. Meanwhile, breathing became increasingly difficult for the young boy and he was in considerable pain.

On the way to the hospital a few days after the incident, Mr Sibal decided to ask for his Guru's blessing. It was evening and he expected the devotional singing in the temple to be coming to a close, as was usual for the time of day. But to his surprise, the door was shut and the lights were out. Satya Charan Lahiri must have gone up to his room on the third floor exceptionally early. Harish Chand felt depressed and close to tears, having come too late.

When he arrived at the door of his son's ward, Harish Chand Sibal was stopped by a nurse. She told him that although the boy's condition had worsened, the doctors were still reluctant to operate. Whilst she was talking, his gaze wandered into the ward to where his son lay. His wife was sitting at the foot of the bed. Then he blinked several times, because he could not believe his eyes: standing at the head of the bed was his Guru, Satya Charan Lahiri. He was raising a hand to Harish Chand and seemed to be waving a reassurance.

'He must have closed the temple early to come and see my son in hospital,' thought Harish Chand to himself, feeling much more peaceful now.

The nurse left him and he walked over to his wife and son. In the meantime, Satya Charan Lahiri was nowhere to be seen.

'Where did Guruji go?' he asked his wife.

'Guruji? What do you mean, where did he go?' she replied in surprise.

'I saw him just a minute ago. He waved to me.'

A serious expression crossed her face. She had been sitting at the foot of her son's bed all day, and she certainly had not seen Satya Charan Lahiri.

Harish Chand was dumbstruck. He spent the night watching over his son in a semi-trance. His mind was fixed on the vision of his Guru standing at his son's bedside and waving to him. It had not been an illusion. But how he had vanished in the space of a few seconds was beyond comprehension.

The next morning, the boy sat up in bed, coughing.

'Father, the coin has come in my mouth,' he announced. A moment later the boy was holding the coin between his fingers and his breathing had returned to normal. Harish Chand was overjoyed and shouted to the doctors and nurses to come and see. Everyone hailed it as a miracle and said that such a thing was only possible through the grace of God.

The next day, the family went to Satya Charan Lahri's residence to give thanks.

'This happened because of your grace,' Harish Chand Sibal said, and laid some money at his feet.

Satya Charan Lahiri gave no indication that he knew what the family were talking about and returned the money. He told them that he had no need of it and that they should keep it. Especially now that there was a costly hospital bill to be paid. Harish Chand was close to tears at the refusal and begged his Guru to keep the money.

Satya Charan was silent for a while. Then he said,

'This time you have to take it back. When things have returned to normal, then you can decide what is best and do that thing.'

A while later, Harish Chand had an idea to replace the stone steps of the temple with marble ones. As soon as he was able to afford it, he carried out the plan as a gift for his Guru.

DR PREM SHANKAR MISHRA'S wife was heavily pregnant when a situation arose whereby she and her husband had to travel to Gorakhpur on Nepal's border without delay. Concerned about the approaching birth, the couple went to see their Guru Satya Charan Lahiri to tell him how important it was for them to go. Satya Charan did not say anything. He just gave his disciples a flower, which they accepted as his blessing for their journey.

They had to change trains twice. The second time there were only five minutes to make the connection, and so they quickly climbed into the last carriage. However, Dr Mishra suddenly felt extremely uncomfortable for no apparent reason. He insisted that they had to change compartments. Since it was not possible to walk through one carriage to the next, it meant that they would have to alight from the train and walk along the platform with their luggage, at the risk of the train leaving without them. His wife was tired and asked if it was really necessary. The other passengers told him that there was no time. The train was due to depart at any moment. But the doctor was adamant. Fortunately, the couple managed to get into the fourth carriage just a moment before the whistle blew.

At midnight, the train stopped. There was no signal ahead and the driver was waiting. Suddenly there was the most thunderous crash as another train crashed at full speed into the last carriage, ramming it and its own front carriage high into the air so that they were standing vertically against each other like a tree. The silence immediately following the impact was broken by wailing and screaming from the two end carriages which had collided. It was a tragic accident caused by signal failure in which a number of people were killed. Most of the passengers in the other carriages were shocked but unharmed.

Dr Prem Shankar Mishra told his fellow disciples later that Satya Charan Lahiri had saved him and his family from the jaws of death that night. The simple flower, silent blessing and intuitive message which he received were somehow all linked.

As usual, not before and not after the event did Satya Charan Lahiri ever allude to having helped, or to having known in advance about the accident.

VIDHYUT LAL DHAR once went to see Satya Charan Lahiri in a state of panic because of his sister-in-law. He told his Guru the story from the beginning:

Some time before, his brother's wife had received severe burns to her body in an accident, and although the hospital's treatment had appeared to be successful initially, the blisters began to weep and smart to such an extent that she had to be readmitted for an operation. This had resulted in some improvement, but the doctors had said that if the blistering reappeared, a second operation could have fatal consequences.

Yet the blisters had come back and given her more pain than ever. Although her husband would not allow the risk to be taken, she had desperately wanted a second operation. Therefore, in her husband's absence she had gone to see her brother-in-law to beg him to take her to the hospital and to sign the consent papers. She had wept pitifully and told him that she would rather die than endure the pain any longer. He had finally given in and authorised it.

Now her entire body was puffed up due to the operation and the doctors had said that there was nothing more they could do to save her life.

This was the reason why Vidhyut Lal Dhar had rushed to Varanasi. He had no idea what to do or how to justify his action to his brother. The responsibility lay on his shoulders.

Satya Charan Lahiri told his disciple to sit and be calm, whilst he did *puja*. When he finished, the *Mahayogi* plucked a flower from a garland and asked Vidhyut to give it to his relative, instructing that she should keep it close to her body.

Vidhyut Lal Dhar returned to Delhi immediately. His sister-in-law was literally on the brink of death when he arrived at the hospital, but he did what Satya Charan had asked him to do. Within a short time the woman made a miraculous recovery.

❖ ❖ ❖ ❖ ❖ ❖ ❖ ❖ ❖

There was once a community of mice which lived in constant fear of a cat. Not a day passed without one of their number coming to a tragic end between the jaws of the cunning feline.

One day, the Chief Mouse decided to call a meeting to discuss the seriousness of the situation, and the band of mice came along feeling full of anticipation.

'We must do something, and now is the time to do it,' he began, sounding self-important and militant.

After the Chief Mouse had finished his speech, they all sat in silence and thought as hard as they could. Suddenly one of the mice stood up.

'I have a plan!' he announced. 'Let us tie a bell around the cat's neck! We shall hear her coming and have plenty of time to run for cover.'

All of the mice agreed that the suggestion was brilliant. It prompted excited clapping and cheering. But as the shrill clamour began to subside, the oldest mouse at the back raised his hand, and soon an atmosphere of expectancy reigned in the cavern once more.

'I have a question,' he said in a soft voice, 'who is going to tie the bell around the cat's neck?'

SOMETIMES we are like the mice. We worry about death and wonder how to avoid potential problems instead of living in the present. There is certainly no need to invite challenges through foolishness, but we have to boldly face those which come our way in the natural course of events.

Once Lahiri Mahasaya and Krishna Ram were walking home from their daily bath at Ranamahal Ghat on the Ganges when the master told his disciple to tear a piece of cloth from his *lunghi*. Krishna Ram did not understand or react quickly enough, and the next moment a brick fell onto the path, cutting the master's foot.

'Master, if you knew what was going to happen, why didn't you step away to avoid it?' asked his disciple.

Lahiri Mahasaya replied that if he had avoided the pain, he would have to suffer more at a later date, because *Karma* was like a debt.

KARMA means action. It is the wheel which carries us from one life to the next. We are on a continuous journey which takes us through the transition of birth and death many times: not just once or twice but some eight to ten million times, according to the ancient yogis. We are not separate entities, for the whole of nature is one linked chain which moves in cycles – just as the water which rises from the ocean and forms rain and snow clouds over the land and mountains has to return to the ocean once more.

A human being cannot avoid *Karma*. The good we do comes back to us, and the harm we inflict on others returns also, whether in this life or another. Only the Yogi who has gained control over life and death is not affected by the *Karma* which the ordinary person has to face.

Since Lahiri Mahasaya was an advanced Yogi, it may seem illogical that he was injured by a brick as he walked with Krishna Ram. However, it was purely an example of the way he would steer certain events in his own life in order to give an example to his disciples. The lesson he wished to impart was that life's difficulties and challenges had to be faced. It was not in one's own interest to avoid them, for doing so would only cause more damage in the future.

Lahiri Mahasaya also taught that the individual could gain freedom from *Karma* through Kriya Yoga. Although *Karma* was generally thought of as human actions tied to cause and effect, such as sleeping, eating, talking and working, when the master spoke of freedom from *Karma*, he was actually talking about respiration.

From the moment of birth we inhale and exhale involuntarily. We may be able to hold our breath for a minute or so, but we cannot consciously stop this *Karma* forever through will-power. We are chained to our respiration.

Lahiri Mahasaya explained that the fetters of *Karma* could only be broken by the practitioner who controlled his respiration through *pranayama* in the higher stages of Kriya Yoga, when *Prana* passed through *Sushumna* and external breathing ceased. Then man could rise above the law of cause and effect.

'PEOPLE often have a false concept that if a spiritual master goes to a country of great political unrest, the situation will suddenly stabilise,' Guruji told me. 'Or that if a Yogi visits a place where plague is widespread, everyone will be healed of their disease. But a Yogi cannot help every time. No, it is not possible. However many Yogis there are in the world at any one time, disasters will continue to happen. We cannot avoid the serious accident any more than the minor mishap. Human existence is a cycle of birth and death.

'There is a reason why not everyone is born on the same day, nor does everyone die on the same day. One may wonder at the miracle of a small baby surviving when a bus swerves from the road and everyone else is killed. That in the aftermath of an earthquake, someone is recovered alive moments before the search is called off. That a parachutist somehow escapes death with a few broken bones, although both the main and emergency canopies failed to open.

'It is true that sometimes the Guru's love can be likened to a protective mantle. As many of the disciples' stories illustrate, the person who is actively working to free himself from *Karma* and rebirth is watched over when it comes to life-and-death situations.'

DISCIPLES have sometimes been given a second chance, or "second life" through Kriya Yoga initiation. Just as Satya Charan Lahiri was able to help Mr Sharma's young daughter when her life-span had run out, Lahiri Mahasaya did the same for his second son: when Dukari Lahiri became mentally sick, everyone asked the master why he was not helping him. But Dukari's time for death had come and the only way he could be saved was through Kriya initiation. Thereafter he became well.

In the ancient Hindu religious Scriptures there are plenty of other examples of this happening in the Vedic age. They say that when a *Mahayogi* or self-realised person gives *Brahmavidya* (Kriya Yoga), it is like a new birth.

But a Yogi will only go against nature in exceptional circumstances. Apparently, there are certain conditions. One is that the disciple has to possess the requisite inner qualities. Although

Kriya *pranayama* brings the life force under control, it would be erroneous to assume that anyone suffering from a fatal disease can simply receive initiation and be saved. This is something which only the self-realised Guru can determine.

WE MET Guruji's sixteen-year old nephew when he came to Varanasi for a few days. I learned later that he asked Guruji for Kriya initiation during the visit, but was told that his time had not yet come.

About a month later, we were shocked when Vandana told us that this same nephew had been kidnapped from his home in Lucknow. A couple of Pakistani terrorist groups targeting children were known to be operating in the city. One group was taking the children's organs to sell abroad and dumping the bodies, and the other apparently had military reasons for kidnapping.

Naturally the whole family was frantic, particularly his mother. According to Vandana, Guruji was spending hours pacing up and down the living room and had not slept since they had heard the news. The atmosphere in the household was braced with tension.

Three days later when we arrived at the yoga studio for our lesson, we were greeted with the good news that Guruji's nephew had somehow managed to escape his kidnappers and had telephoned. His father was on the way to collect him from a town in northern Kashmir.

In due course we heard how he had been bundled into a car as he was leaving for school and given an injection which knocked him unconscious. He had woken up at a time when his captors were out of the car, talking and smoking some distance away. He had slipped out of the car unnoticed and run for his life. He had not gathered the exact reason why he was kidnapped.

So all was well again. Guruji did not say anything, but the evidence pointed towards a case of divine intervention. Therefore, we were stunned by the news some two weeks later of his sudden death from appendicitis at home, shortly before he was due to have an operation. He had been in pain for a few days and had just returned from a visit to the doctor with his mother. He had asked her for something to eat, and when she came back from the kitchen he was dead.

Somehow I understood from the look on Guruji's face that his nephew's death had been unavoidable. There was no doubt in my mind that the boy had received a short extension of life, but intervention was not always possible if a person's time was up.

Guruji's sister was his first disciple. Even as an advanced Kriya practitioner she knew that the pain of losing her youngest son would not subside for a long time. Whilst it tore her apart, she told Guruji that she had been prepared for his death through an earlier vision – a result of Kriya practice. I even heard from Vandana that she was able to communicate with her son for a short while following his death.

That must have been a small consolation; the other, of course, was that he was allowed to die at home. His mother was at least spared the torture of never knowing his whereabouts or what had happened to him. That in itself was surely an act of grace.

LITTLE FISH (A Song)

Hey, little fish
As I'm dreaming
Swim as fast as you can to the ocean
For the way that you search for is chosen
And the power you need is behind you
Guiding you, and my dreaming

Leaving all to find your soul
You promised not to close your eyes
Till you see the light of pure white skies
And if I saw you in a net
Little fish, I hope I'd be
The one to set you free
'Cause I would be free of my dreaming
Knowing how I, knowing how I do

Hey, little fish
You have nothing
Least of all an idea of your journey
But the river is steady and flowing
And some voices are whispering, follow
Guiding you, and my dreaming

Hey, little fish
Keep on breathing
Find the source of your life before dying
Don't give up till you know why you're swimming
In the mysteries surrounding the waters
Guiding you, and my dreaming

Chapter Ten

RECOGNITION AND RESPECT

The Introduction of a Master

"For now we see through a glass, darkly;
but then face to face: now I know in part;
but then shall I know even as also I am known." – ST. PAUL[1]

To some, Satya Charan Lahiri was an enigma. To others, he was nothing more than an ordinary family man. This was because people only saw and knew as much about him as he wanted them to. The few who were allowed to understand him on a deeper level were close disciples. From time to time, he gave them what is termed in India as an "introduction". This meant that he revealed the truth about himself as an advanced spiritual master in some way, in order to strengthen a disciple's faith or increase their own determination to successfully proceed along the Kriya Yoga path.

For the most part, the disciples learned from experience that whenever they went to Satya Charan Lahiri in times of trouble, he would never openly show even to them that he was helping through yogic power. Instead, he would make *Pranam* and say that he would pray to God. In the case of physical problems, he would often conceal the result of his blessing by telling the person concerned to go to a doctor. But time and again, desires were fulfilled, predictions were seen to come true and the incurable were cured.

A GRIEVING woman came to see Satya Charan Lahiri. She cried uncontrollably to be in his presence, and Satya Charan also began to weep in deep sorrow. An observing disciple who had known his

---

[1] 1 Corinthians 13:12

Guru for over twenty years watched in astonishment and found himself questioning if Satya Charan really was a *Mahayogi* after all. Happiness and sadness were human emotions which did not touch the genuine Yogi. But then he realised that his Guru was showing his empathy externally. His tears had nothing to do with his inner state, but they certainly succeeded in giving the impression that he was an ordinary person.

There were times when Satya Charan Lahiri showed his anger, particularly when someone attempted to lie or hide some important matter from him. Yet likewise, these verbal outbursts had nothing to do with his spiritual realisation. Any emphatic reprimand was in the same spirit that a parent scolds a child: to teach the difference between right and wrong, or to prevent the loved one from repeating past mistakes, as necessity demanded.

SATYA CHARAN once told a disciple of the time he went to Badrinath in 1952 with a friend he had known for some forty years. They travelled by bus most of the way but had to complete the journey on foot. On the way to their destination, Satya Charan developed a high fever.

The friend persuaded Satya Charan to have a cup of *chai*, though this was one beverage the master never drank as a rule, and said that he would chant *Tantra Mantra* and blow cool air on his forehead to drive the soaring fever away. Satya Charan assured his friend that there was no need, but the method had never failed to be effective on a patient yet, so there was no stopping him.

However, no amount of *Tantra Mantra* or cool air was able to bring Satya Charan's temperature down that day, and his mystified friend eventually gave up.

'But Guruji, did your friend not know about you?' enquired Satya Charan's disciple upon hearing the story, incredulous that someone could have known his Guru for decades and yet remained ignorant that the grandson of Lahiri Mahasaya was also a *Mahayogi*. For no one could give help or healing to a Yogi.

But Satya Charan Lahiri did not answer the question. The corners of his mouth turned upwards in a soft smile, and he continued to tell his disciple what a fine holiday destination Badrinath was.

SATYA CHARAN LAHIRI could have made his life as a householder easier on many occasions due to his yogic powers. Yet he went about his work like everyone else, making no attempt to avoid any difficulties or setbacks.

There was the time when he had collect some papers from his daughter's university. When he arrived, they were not ready. The arduous journey by rickshaw in the scorching heat of high summer had been in vain. The disciple who accompanied him maintained that Satya Charan must have known from the outset that it would be a useless trip, even though he had not openly admitted it.

Then there was the trouble with the monkeys. They would jump up and down on the tin roof of Satya Charan Lahiri's house, right above the place where he used to take his afternoon rest each day.

When a couple of attentive disciples became aware of this daily disturbance, they first tried surrounding the roof with a barbed wire fence, but one monkey would hold the wires apart for the others to clamber through, and the creatures would continue to make a commotion. The problem was finally solved when it occurred to the disciples to fix barbed wire onto the roof itself.

These disciples were fully aware that Satya Charan could have stopped the monkeys himself, for it was a well-known fact that a self-realised saint had the ability to tame even the wildest creature through yogic power. But they also understood that Satya Charan Lahiri would never do this. He never gave anyone unnecessary cause for wonder, least of all the next-door neighbours.

WHEN Mr Lal's wife developed cervical spondylitis, she was told by some of the best doctors in Varanasi that there was no cure. The only temporary relief came in the form of pain-killers or when practising various Hatha Yoga exercises.

Eighteen months passed without any improvement. Mr and Mrs Lal went to see Satya Charan Lahiri about the problem, who advised them to see a homeopathic doctor. Mr Lal replied that they had already tried homeopathy, and it had not helped.

The *Mahayogi* sat in silence for a while with closed eyes. When he opened them again he said,

'Your friend is a homeopathic doctor. Go to him for medicine. It will also be cheaper than modern medicine. And she must take whatever he prescribes.'

One week after Mrs Lal started taking the homeopathic medicine which her husband obtained from his friend, she was completely and permanently free of the problem.

A FAMILY of disciples came to stay at Satya Charan Lahiri's house. Every afternoon they listened to their Guru's teachings in an upper-storey room, before joining the *Bhajan* and *Kirtan* downstairs in the temple.

Towards the end of their week's stay, Satya Charan suddenly told his disciple Suleka De to go and help her mother, who had already started down the stone staircase to the temple. Suleka De was surprised at the instruction, since her mother always went down the stairs by herself without any difficulty. But she obeyed without question.

The moment she caught up with her mother, the elderly woman lost her balance and slipped on the corner of a stair. Suleka De was just in time to catch her from falling, and realised immediately that Satya Charan had known in advance what would happen. He had saved her mother from a serious, if not fatal, accident.

IT IS TRADITIONAL in India for disciples to bring sweets or garlands for the guru, but Satya Charan Lahiri was renowned for his lack of expectation. He would never ask his disciples to bring anything. Hence Prem Shankar Mishra's surprise when he came to see his Guru after a long time, having written the last of his final exams in medical school, only to be reprimanded for coming empty-handed. However, Satya Charan was laughing and there was evidently some reason for his good humour.

'I will go immediately to buy some sweets, but is there some special reason?' Prem Shankar wanted to know.

'Congratulations! You have passed your exams. Go and see it for yourself!' Satya Charan told him, smiling broadly.

When Prem Shankar left, he first checked the newspaper and then went to visit a university friend, only to establish that the results had not yet been released.

He did not know what to think at first, but when they were published three weeks after his Guru had told him the result, he realised that Satya Charan had given him his "introduction".

Satya Charan Lahiri's daughter Bharati was extremely anxious after sitting her final university examinations. As the master explained to his disciple Mr Lal, she had switched courses during her years of study, and had doubled her efforts in the hope of achieving a good result.

Then Satya Charan unexpectedly said that he wanted to see her result. He sat in meditation for a short while, and thereafter told Mr Lal that Bharati would receive a First Class in mathematics with distinction. But he also told Mr Lal not to tell anyone, for Bharati had to wait. The results were released a few days later, and hers was exactly as her father had predicted.

When Mr Lal's marriage was being arranged, Satya Charan gave his disciple prior warning and advice pertaining to certain difficulties which would arise. He also gave his word that although these problems could not be prevented, everything would be resolved in time.

A troublesome time ensued as Mr Lal's family was forced to cancel the first arrangement due to deceit on the part of the girl's family. A second arrangement for marriage was promptly settled, but a week after the wedding Mr Lal became so sick with hepatitis that the doctors feared for his life. The entire family was in a state of panic. However, Mr Lal remained relaxed through the trouble and pain, resting on his Guru's reassurance to him a few months previously. Within a short time he made a complete recovery.

❖ ❖ ❖ ❖ ❖ ❖ ❖ ❖

When Guruji was staying with us that summer in 1996, he hurt his back through a fall whilst playing cricket. It gave him considerable pain for weeks. By then, I was beginning to be more on the alert whenever Guruji had an accident or was sick.

Soon after it happened, a fellow disciple and friend from Israel came for a week's visit to see Guruji. One afternoon we went to a local beauty spot together, and upon arrival Guruji lay down in the grass to rest his back. The disciple from Israel had a few years' experience as a Reiki practitioner and evidently enjoyed a high rate of success treating people through this healing technique. So he offered to give Guruji Reiki. Guruji smiled and did not refuse him.

My assistance was called for, since I had also learned the first step of Reiki in India. But I shook my head and apologised for not feeling able to help. To my mind, the idea of attempting to give Guruji a healing treatment did not bear contemplating even for a moment.

My friend said afterwards that whenever he gave someone Reiki, his hands always became either hot or cold as he held them above the part of the body undergoing treatment. With my minimal experience in this field of healing, I could relate to this. But after giving Guruji one hour of Reiki, he reported disappointedly that nothing had happened. He had not felt the energy flowing through his hands, nor was there any improvement in Guruji's back. I was sorry to hear it. But it hardly came as a surprise.

GURUJI rarely gives any clues about himself. You never know quite what to think. Sometimes he says things which he knows will confuse. He has a habit of purposely throwing a puzzling piece of advice your way with the challenge, 'Try to understand. If you do, it will be very nice.' You may work it out the same day, or it might only become clear several years later.

For example, Guruji gave me his "introduction" the very first day that I came to the yoga studio, when he told me that yoga was for life. His words perplexed me at the time, but later I found out that he had recognised me as a future disciple the moment I walked through the door.

VANDANA was aware that Guruji was continually helping people in trouble. She regularly overheard disciples telling Guruji their problems whilst she was in the kitchen making *chai*, and knew that at some point or other, every one of those same disciples would come back to give thanks. Sometimes it was a matter of a few days, and at other times it might take a month or even a year. They would tell how the impossible had come about and the irreversible turned around.

Guruji always showed his surprise when they came bringing their good news. The disciples would prostrate themselves before him and hold his feet, thanking him. But he would never admit to having done anything. It was perfectly true that he hid himself, unless he had reason to give someone his "introduction".

Most importantly, Vandana had noticed a common denominator amongst these disciples who received help. They were, without exception, dedicated practitioners of Kriya Yoga.

Well, almost without exception:

'A cousin of a friend of mine was helped a few years ago, and he was not a Kriya Yoga initiate,' she told me. 'He was in hospital for four months with a serious case of hepatitis. The medicines were not helping him and the doctors had given up hope. He was very thin and showed signs of slipping into a coma. His aunt came to Guruji in tears, and told him that her nephew was dying. Guruji listened and told her to pray to Lahiri Mahasaya. Before she left he gave her some ash to put on her nephew's head.

'His health steadily improved after that. The haemoglobin level increased so rapidly that the doctors discharged him temporarily from hospital, although the liver was still enlarged and they anticipated a relapse. He came to visit Guruji personally.

'When he saw Guruji's face, he seemed shocked. He made *Pranam* in front of Guruji and held his feet tightly. He said, "I am sure that he is the person who was there when I was sick."

'He had never met Guruji before, but afterwards he told us that when he was sick in hospital and on the verge of losing consciousness, he had seen him in a vision. Guruji had appeared in a sitting position and given him a sign of reassurance. Then the vision had disappeared and immediately afterwards he began to feel some energy returning. A few days later, exactly the same thing happened.

'He was a dedicated man, and had great faith,' Vandana added. 'Guruji gave him a *Mantra* to chant and told him that he was sure he would be perfectly healthy again soon. Within a few months his haemoglobin level was above average and the doctors pronounced him completely cured.'

IN DECEMBER 1998, one week before Andreas and I were due to fly to India for the Christmas break, one of our young cats, called Krishna, disappeared. We were worried about him because he had never left home for more than half a day at a time, and we put up posters in the area asking people to look out for him.

By the time we had to leave, he was still missing. We both had the feeling that he was gone for good.

As soon as we arrived in Varanasi, we told Guruji about Krishna. A part of me felt guilty for even mentioning it. I did not want it to sound as if we wanted to give Guruji any trouble or ask for his help. Krishna was 'just a cat', however much we loved him and felt upset about his disappearance.

But it was obvious that Guruji was genuinely concerned at the news. He seemed to be as worried and upset as we were, and the subject of Krishna came up every day. He reacted as though one of his own children had disappeared, rather than, 'just a cat', and the troubled tone in his voice when he talked about Krishna touched me deeply.

During that week, we talked in yoga lessons about how difficult it was to keep going in Kriya practice, and Guruji was trying to emphasise to Andreas and myself the importance of doing it regularly, however hard the work commitments were at home.

When we went for our lesson one evening, Guruji said in his most serious tone of voice that he had some news about Krishna. He kept us in suspense for what seemed like several minutes, saying nothing and having us fear the worst. Then suddenly his face broke into a beaming smile and he chuckled loudly. He said that Krishna had come home! My mother had telephoned earlier with the news. The neighbours had reported that our lost cat had turned up earlier that day. He was rather thin and had an insatiable appetite, but was otherwise well.

I tried to find out in a roundabout way what part Guruji had played, if any, in Krishna's reappearance. He refused to answer explicitly. What he did say, however, was that there was something which both Andreas and I had to understand. He wanted to give us a "hint". He mentioned that 'vibrations' came to him automatically when a disciple was practising Kriya, as if a radio were tuned into a certain frequency. Therefore he knew quite well if someone was practising on a daily basis or not. If they were, it was possible to help in times of trouble. If no vibrations were coming his way though, regardless of how much he might want to help in a particular circumstance, there was nothing that he could do. It was a humbling message.

The next day we were rejoicing at the dinner table about Krishna's reappearance and laughing together. Guruji was in a jolly mood. And quite spontaneously, as if he were totally unconscious of his words, he said,

'Krishna is a naughty cat. I told him that what he was doing was very dangerous. He knows now that he must stay close to home.'

When we arrived home in Switzerland, Krishna was in his basket by the window as usual, and appeared to be rather subdued. Whatever happened, and whatever Guruji said to him, he has not ventured far from home for long ever since.

A Question of Consent

"Trust in the Lord with all thine heart
and lean not unto thine own understanding." – PROVERBS[2]

There is a Hindu saying that *Saraswati*, goddess of wisdom, sits on the tongue of the self-realised saint or master. The implication is that a spiritual master always speaks the truth, and everything he predicts comes to fruition. Nothing is hidden from him about the past, present or future.

In explanation of Patanjali's 36th Yoga Sutra, Swami Vivekananda says:

"When this power of truth will be established with you, then even in dream you will never tell an untruth. You will be true in thought, word and deed. Whatever you say will be the truth. You may say to a man, "Be blessed," and that man will be blessed. If a man is diseased, and you say to him, "Be thou cured," he will be cured immediately."[3]

For this reason, when a disciple has some matter of importance to decide, it is usual in India to first ask the Guru for advice or consent.

The disciples of Satya Charan Lahiri learned through experience that whenever they trusted and accepted his advice, the outcome was without exception good.

WHEN an Indian marriage is to be arranged, the girl's parents send

---

[2] 3:5
[3] From *Raja Yoga*, the Sutra reads as follows: "By the establishment of truthfulness the Yogi gets the power of attaining for himself and others the fruits of work without the works."

out various details such as her education, hobbies, sports and cooking skills to prospective families. Sometimes her horoscope and photograph are also attached. The boy's parents respond similarly for their son, and when a good match is found the families will meet. It is customary for the arrangements to be finalised in the presence of an elder.

However, when Satya Charan Lahiri's eldest brother was arranging a marriage for his son, he wrote to the girl's father, asking him to go directly to his younger brother. On the condition that Satya Charan agreed to the union, he would be willing to start preparations for the wedding. The girl's father therefore came to Satya Charan with the letter in hand, and permission for the marriage to go ahead was granted.

Under normal circumstances, such a thing was unheard of. But all the brothers understood that Satya Charan was a self-realised master and gave the youngest member of the family the respect due to a Guru. They humbly asked his guidance on many occasions.

ONE OF Satya Charan Lahiri's disciples received Kriya Yoga at a fairly young age, as had his father before him. His name was Kailash and he was quiet and gentle by nature.

Kailash had an elder brother who was selfish and greedy. The family sold and manufactured hardware and kitchen utensils, and when Kailash came of age his brother refused to give him his share of the business. Since it was so difficult to support himself under the circumstances, Kailash went to ask his Guru for advice.

Satya Charan Lahiri told Kailash not to argue with his brother, but to make pots and pans and sell them himself. For the time being he only needed to meet his immediate living expenses. Kailash was obedient, and although the work was demanding, a year later he began to make a profit. There were always plenty of orders and he even had to take on a few employees.

During the course of that same year, the brother found himself in serious debt due to his extravagant lifestyle and laziness in managing the shop. Unable to cope with mounting pressure from the money-lenders and believing the situation to be irreversible, he offered his younger brother control of the shop, on the condition that he also accepted responsibility for the debts. Kailash agreed, but it did not occur to him to have a contract drawn up.

Kailash worked industriously to pay off the debts. By the end of the first year he had succeeded in doing so. But no sooner had the shop returned to profit once more, the brother decided to reclaim it as his own since no papers had been signed giving Kailash sole possession.

Many customers were outraged for Kailash, whom they favoured. An ombudsman was called in, who decreed that the shop had to be divided into two parts to be run independently. The brother was forced to accept the word of the ombudsman in order to return to the business at all.

Ownership of the front part of the shop seemed to be advantageous as it opened up onto the main road. Naturally, Kailash's brother said that this was the part he would take. The back part only had a small door opening onto a narrow lane, and this was the reason why Kailash once more sought Satya Charan Lahiri's advice.

'Accept the back part of the shop,' said his Guru straight away. And although Kailash tried to object, since everyone thought he should have his door opening onto the main road, Satya Charan would not be moved.

Kailash returned home feeling downcast, but there was no question of ignoring his Guru's advice. He obediently accepted the back of the shop, and this time a contract was drawn up.

For the next two years, Kailash's business prospered despite its disadvantageous location. And then there was an unexpected turn of events. A state of emergency[4] was declared in India, and by government order the main roads in Varanasi were to be widened. Subsequently, the brother's entire shop was swallowed up by the road widening scheme, leaving him with nothing, and Kailash's shop opened onto the main road.

MR SHARMA was employed as an executive engineer at the electricity board. In 1974 a notice arrived, transferring him to Lucknow. Asking for Satya Charan's direction was the first thing

[4] Prime Minister Indira Ghandi declared a national state of emergency in India in 1975. Accusations of government corruption were mounting, food riots were causing havoc and unemployment was on the increase. Her own parliamentary seat was also at stake following an election campaign, so she instigated drastic measures in an attempt to visibly improve the economic situation and lower the country's birth rate.

which occurred to him, and it was with dismay that he went to tell his Guru about the impending move. He and his wife were both Kriya Yoga practitioners and happy to live close to their Guru. They did not want to go.

To Mr Sharma's surprise, Satya Charan told him, 'You are not going to transfer.'

However, during the next few days Mr Sharma established that nothing had changed regarding his transfer. He went back to his Guru to report that he was expected in the Lucknow office within a fortnight.

'It has been cancelled,' Satya Charan repeated.

Then Mr Sharma's young daughter became sick and he had to take a month's vacation, during which time the official papers arrived for his transfer. Feeling dispirited, he informed Satya Charan that everything had been finalised and although he did not want to leave, there was no other option.

'I don't want it either. Let us wait and see what is God's will. Take another month's leave and stay here. Then we will see what is going to happen.'

So Mr Sharma stayed, although he was nervous about doing so. His employers in Lucknow telephoned him several times a week. They were angry that he was still in Varanasi and began to threaten legal action. Mr Sharma explained each time that he had no choice but to stay because of his sick daughter, and gave a definitive date for his arrival.

As the second month came to an end, Mr Sharma told Satya Charan that it was a hopeless situation.

'We will see,' said Satya Charan quietly.

But time really was up and Mr Sharma had to leave within the next couple of days. He went once more to see his Guru.

Satya Charan Lahri told him, 'Now you can go.'

Mr Sharma could not help but feel annoyed. Why had his Guru not told him that earlier? Now he was going to have to face unnecessary pressure and antagonism at work.

Upon arrival in the Lucknow office, Mr Sharma was sent to meet the director. He was told to return to Varanasi immediately and to continue his work there. The transfer order had been cancelled and the papers would be following in due course.

Mr Sharma could barely suppress his delight, although it

remained a complete mystery to him how such a momentous change could have come about in the course of a few days. He was nonetheless thankful that he had trusted Satya Charan's advice.

APPROXIMATELY nine years later, Mr Sharma was transferred to Lucknow for a second time. When he expressed his reluctance to leave again, Satya Charan reprimanded him for wanting to stay in the same place like a statue. He asked his disciple if he was really prepared to sacrifice the opportunity for promotion. Not wanting to understand, Mr Sharma did not reply. But this time there was evidently no choice in the matter, and when the papers came through he was obliged to leave.

In Lucknow, he was promoted from one job to the next, until he became head adviser to the chief minister of Uttar Pradesh.

Mr Sharma never forgot Satya Charan's words to him before he left Varanasi. He could never have imagined the success which he finally achieved in his career.

SOME disciples asked for their Guru's advice only to ignore it at times, imagining that they knew better.

Harish Chand Sibal was successful in his job and earned well but was keen to start his own business. When he consulted Satya Charan Lahiri, he was warned against doing so. Although Harish Chand repeated his desire many times over the course of six months, he always received a negative response. Since permission was not forthcoming, the disciple decided to stop asking. He handed in his notice at work and set up his own company.

After just one year, the engineer found himself in serious debt. His company in Varanasi had failed, but a loan enabled the family to move to Delhi where Mr Sibal made a second attempt at starting a business.

But before the second year was over, the family found itself in a pitiful situation. Harish Chand was forced to close his business and sell any extras the family possessed such as spare kitchen utensils, in order for them to survive.

They returned to Varanasi. Harish Chand begged Satya Charan Lahiri for a blessing to save him and his family from their predicament. Soon Harish Chand found employment, and gradually their situation improved once more.

A COUPLE of friends tried to persuade Mr Lal to buy a cow so that milk would be cheaper for his family of thirteen. He went to ask Satya Charan if he should do so, but his Guru reeled off a list of problems which would arise in the family if they owned one, so initially he decided to forget it.

However, the friends continued to use all their powers of persuasion. They finally managed to convince Mr Lal that he would be missing out on a number of financial benefits if he turned down the bargain they were offering. He told himself that it was a straightforward decision which could not possibly bring trouble. When he confessed to his Guru that he had bought a cow after all, Satya Charan smiled and said nothing.

It was not long before the cow became the sole responsibility of Mr Lal, although the other family members had also promised to look after the animal. And then, for one reason or another, they could not afford to keep the milk which the cow produced and had to sell it. A previously harmonious family atmosphere became strained, and the tension remained for as long as they had the cow. In retrospect, Mr Lal realised ruefully that the episode had confirmed every word of Satya Charan Lahiri's explicit warning.

ANOTHER time when Mr Lal was looking for accommodation, a friend whom he had known for more than ten years offered him a room in his house. When Mr Lal asked about rent, his friend said that he did not want any money from him. This disturbed Mr Lal somewhat, so he consulted his Guru. Satya Charan Lahiri told him that he should not move until the rent had been fixed.

Although Mr Lal tried to negotiate the rent, the friend would not hear of it. He said that it was something they could discuss in due course. Seeing no other option, Mr Lal moved in. Time passed and his friend still refused to discuss the question of rent.

When Mr Lal visited Satya Charan about the situation yet again, the previous advice was repeated. The rent had to be agreed upon, or problems would arise. Mr Lal insisted that there was no question of any disagreement, since he and the landlord were such close friends.

A month later, the landlord-friend told Mr Lal to pay an amount which he considered appropriate. He would be content with whatever was offered. Mr Lal felt uncomfortable about this proposal but as there seemed to be no alternative, he researched how much other tenants in the area were paying for their lodgings. Having done so, he gave his friend one hundred rupees for the first month, which was more than reasonable, especially given the lack of facilities in the house.

When he handed over the money, the so-called friendship evaporated in an instant. The landlord became angry and accused Mr Lal of insulting him. He had expected at least three hundred rupees. And from then on, he did his utmost to make his tenant's daily life a misery. Mr Lal found his scooter punctured at least twice a week on top of many other nuisances which his landlord instigated, until he managed to find alternative accommodation.

DESPITE these experiences, there were also many times when Mr Lal did follow Satya Charan Lahiri's counsel to his advantage. At one point he was earning particularly well, and felt that his wife could give up her job as a teacher. He could not understand why his Guru advised against it. Only when the couple had some financial difficulties a few years later, did it become clear why his wife's earnings were so important to them.

❖ ❖ ❖ ❖ ❖ ❖ ❖ ❖

Many of Guruji's Indian disciples come to discuss problems they are having with arranging marriages for their offspring, and to ask for his consent. He frequently helps people in that direction, so Vandana told me.

From personal experience too, I know that if you ask Guruji for his advice in some matter of importance, he will usually give it. However, if I stopped practising Kriya Yoga, my conscience would not allow me to ask any more.

One thing I have discovered as a result of regular practice is an indescribable feeling of closeness to Guruji. When you look his way, his eyes are directed right back at you. When you are in deep water, his hand is at the ready to catch hold of yours and keep you afloat.

What tends to happen, as Guruji once put it, when a disciple gives up Kriya practice, is that the disciple himself looks in the opposite direction. Despite this, the Guru is always watching. But if the disciple has no desire to avail himself of the Guru's assistance in times of trouble, having the attitude that he knows best and can manage by himself, the Guru is certainly not going to force his help upon him. He can learn the hard way if he so prefers, although all it would take is a knock at the door and a humble request.

When we moved to Switzerland after our honeymoon in 1997, my husband Andreas, who trained as a joiner, began to look for a new job. Guruji had advised him to find work other than in a joinery, because the fine sawdust produced by the machines would only aggravate his allergies again. Following his initiation into Kriya Yoga, Andreas had been overjoyed to watch his skin problems gradually disappear. Many dermatologists had told him that he would have to live with the allergy for the rest of his life, but according to Guruji, regular *pranayama* was a cure for many otherwise difficult-to-treat allergies and would keep his under control too.

Although Andreas was unable to find work for the first few months after our return, the opportunity for a place on a full-time business course presented itself which was state-funded and could help him back into the administrative side of his field of expertise. Being in doubt, he asked Guruji for his consent, and received it. It was a hard adjustment for my husband to go back to college for a year, but proved to be an important stepping stone which subsequently enabled him to find satisfying work in the office of a timber wholesaler.

We have asked for Guruji's advice as a couple many times and seen that whatever he says comes true, whether we are slow or quick to accept his counsel. For example, about our own relationship; difficulties regarding employment; whether or not to move house, and about starting a family. Experience has taught us what a priceless gift the Yogi's advice can be.

During my last visit to Varanasi in October 1999, I spoke to Guruji almost daily about a long-standing concern, hoping for some guidance. Andreas and I had been trying to start a family for some time without success, and we had reason to believe that my chances of becoming pregnant without medical intervention were fairly slim. It was time to start making some decisions.

Initially, Guruji said that we should seek medical help upon my return to Switzerland. There was no problem if we wanted to do that. I told him that we were equally prepared to wait longer, if there was any chance of a natural conception.

In the end, Guruji told me that in this case he could not simply tell me what to do or what was going to happen. It was time to learn some patience and not to lean on him for everything. He said not to worry about it, or better still, to stop thinking about it altogether. He promised to obtain some ayurvedic medicine for us. This was a comfort at least, and for the first time in ages I was able to push the entire issue out of my mind.

Vandana also told me not to worry. She knew a number of her husband's women disciples who had seemed unable to conceive. But having asked for Guruji's help, they were now all mothers several times over.

What was more, Guruji would often ask if they wanted a boy or a girl. The couple would give their preference, and according to Vandana, they got what they asked for without fail. She had seen this happen many times. Whenever Guruji made a prediction, it always came true; although admittedly she did usually refuse to believe his words until she saw solid proof, she added as an afterthought.

I confessed to Vandana that some six months or so previously, Guruji had asked during a telephone call whether we wanted a boy or a girl in the future. But the thought of being given a choice in the matter had taken me aback, and I had answered that he would have to choose for us.

Less than a month after my return from India, the pregnancy test was positive. Some of Guruji's words from the past came back to me with the realisation of how I had projected my own expectations onto them. He had once said that 'for family side' I would have to wait four years. And that had been in November 1995, precisely four years earlier.

EVEN at the time, I knew in my heart that Guruji was justified in telling me to be patient instead of categorically answering my questions: whether I could get pregnant and how much longer the wait would be. To all intents and purposes, I had been hoping that he would tell me the future.

The question of whether it was beneficial for the ordinary person to have knowledge of the future had cropped up in discussion during my first year in India. I had told Guruji about my visit to an astrologer, and Guruji had explained why he would never advise his disciples to have their palms read:

Astrology was an ancient science based on exact mathematical calculations which could be practised with total accuracy if followed correctly. The first astrologers were all yogis: they were followers of a spiritual master who recorded his realisation of how the stars and cosmos worked together with the *Atman*, or soul. There were still some genuine astrologers in India, but it was difficult to locate one nowadays, since astrology had become a popular and lucrative way to make money from tourists.

Just because someone practised Hatha Yoga every day, did not mean that they were a Yogi. A beginner could take up any science. Likewise, if an astrologer who was not a Yogi made a prediction, there was no guarantee that the forecast would be correct, whether they had consulted the ancient Scriptures or not.

Although many were curious about what the future held in store, it was rarely helpful or good if an ordinary person found out the truth. Problems in the future could not be avoided. Supposing you were told that you would have a serious accident in five years time, you would wake up upset and worried every morning. You would find it impossible to live life to the full. Rather than thinking about the future, it was best to live in the present moment and let things come as they may.

A Yogi did not need to examine someone's palm to know their past, present or future, because this knowledge came from inside in a natural way. There was no wish to tell others, especially not to satisfy curiosity. The spiritual master would only give a disciple advice pertaining to the future if there was a specific reason.

Guruji had told me in conclusion that if someone was practising Kriya Yoga and needed advice on which way to turn when an important decision had to be made, they could ask for consent. This did not involve knowing the future, but having the humility in times of uncertainty to put the Guru's wisdom above one's own.

FOR A FEW years, I assumed that Guruji was conscious of everything he said. But in time it became noticeable that this was not always the case. To give an example: one day I was telling Guruji my trouble with regular Kriya practice due to a physical problem which often made me feel tired and weak. Guruji said rather sternly that I could be excused to some extent, but that Andreas and I had got into the habit of missing practice at weekends which had more to do with mental laziness and allowing the body to feel relaxed than anything else. This was not so good. Since I did not have to work at weekends, there was plenty of time for practice then, however difficult it was during the week.

His words could not have been more true and proved once more that attempts to hide anything from Guruji were useless. How could he possibly have known about our weekend lie-ins? He evidently did not have to be there to know how much practice we were doing, or exactly when we tended to be lethargic.

I was too ashamed at the time to reply. But in the evening I brought up what he had said about our lack of practice at weekends again. Guruji looked at me blankly. He had no memory of thinking or saying anything about how my Kriya practice was at weekends.

This made other things much clearer. It illustrated the saying that *Saraswati* "sits on the tongue" of the self-realised, because there was never anything personal in the things Guruji said. Nor was there ever any sense of ego. You did not get the feeling that it was a question of mind-reading. Such omniscience was internal, and came from a place beyond the intellect. It was God in man expressed through the self-realised Guru.

The Indian Concept of the Guru

*"Humble yourselves in the sight of the Lord,
And he shall lift you up."* – ST. JOHN[5]

Although it is traditional in India to pay obeisance to elders, the disciples of his grandfather or father who came to Varanasi accorded Satya Charan Lahiri the same respect they had given to their Gurus, although he was their junior by many years. The fact that he was the grandson of Lahiri Mahasaya was entirely secondary: they recognised his spiritual realisation.

Professor Bupen Nath Sanyal was one disciple of Lahiri Mahasaya who came to know both his Guru's son and grandson. In his later years he used to go to Satya Charan Lahiri whenever he needed spiritual advice or consent on worldly matters. The professor became well known all over India, and was responsible for writing and publishing Lahiri Mahasaya's explanations of the *Bhagavad Gita*. He also established an *ashram* in Mandar and was known to many as an advanced Kriya practitioner.

Many other famous people visited Satya Charan Lahiri in order to show him their respect. One of them was the saint Anandmai Ma, who had *ashrams* worldwide and many followers herself. This spiritual woman felt deep reverence towards Lahiri Mahasaya and always made a point of seeing Satya Charan whenever she came to Varanasi.

Pandit Kaviraj Gopinath was a distinguished intellectual and the first president of the Sanskrit University in Banaras. He wrote several books, and prior to writing each one never failed to consult Satya Charan Lahiri.

The renowned lawyer Sri Surendra Nath Bandhopadyaya also came to meet Satya Charan Lahiri when he was representing a client in Varanasi. He became a disciple and decided to give up his career as a lawyer and thereby sacrifice greater fame and riches for a life of simplicity in Satya Charan's household.

THE DAY a marble statue of Lahiri Mahasaya was due to be positioned in front of the temple situated within Satya Charan's premises, many disciples were invited for the occasion. One of those present, Hari Narain, who was renowned for his wonderful voice, was asked to sing for everyone. However, he refused, saying that he could not possibly perform before a statue of Lahiri Mahasaya. When he was asked the reason for his reticence, he told about a particular time when he and his singing teacher, likewise a disciple, had visited the great master. They had talked about music, and in the middle of the conversation, their Guru had opened his mouth and produced the most beautiful sound Hari Narain had ever heard in his life. He could still hear it resonating in his ears. The memory was so fresh in his mind, that with all due respect he dared not sing in front of Lahiri Mahasaya.

Satya Charan Lahiri knew of two members of the family, both devoted disciples of his grandfather, who had experienced visions of Lahiri Mahasaya before their passing. He had also heard of a third such appearance.

When Kashi Mani Devi was preparing to leave her body at the age of ninety-four, she called for her youngest grandson, Satya Charan. She told him to lay a sitting mat on the floor for his grandfather Lahiri Mahasaya, saying that he would be arriving soon.

'Where is Grandfather now?' Satya Charan asked.

'He is in the dwelling of *Lord Vishwanath*,' she replied, with a trace of a smile.

'Does he come to see you every day?'

'Yes, he comes every day. He sits and talks about so many things with me. He will come today, so go and fetch the mat now.'

Satya Charan Lahiri went to find a mat and returned with it. A few days after this exchange with his grandmother, Kashi Mani Devi had prepared herself for death and left her body in a fully-conscious awakened state, having attained the higher planes of yoga practice.

More than twenty years later, Lahiri Mahasaya's eldest daughter Harimati Devi called her nephew to her bedside and told him that his grandfather had come to take her. She asked him to bring a mat. Satya Charan went and got the same mat he had brought for his grandmother those many years before. That night his aunt passed away, reciting verses from the *Bhagavad Gita*.

Ram Padarath used to visit the house where Lahiri Mahasaya had resided every day, long after his Guru had taken *Mahasamadhi*, in order to sit in the place where his Guru used to meditate. It was his unbroken routine, even when he became old and had to walk with a cane. One day he fell on the path and cut himself. Satya Charan Lahiri was passing and helped the elderly man to his feet. He asked Ram Padarath why he insisted on coming every day, when his eyes were dim and the visit cost him such physical effort. Ram Padarath smiled and said,

'Guru *Maharaja* has unfathomable grace on me. I am so small next to him and have never been able to do anything for him in my life. Therefore I am still coming every day to give him my attendance. One day if he takes mercy on me, I shall be saved.'

Eventually Ram Padarath became so weak that he could no

longer leave his own house. But shortly before he died he called his nephew and said,

'Guru *Maharaja* is standing up, please lay a sitting mat for him.' The old man was making *Pranam*.

'Where is your Guru *Maharaja*?' asked the nephew, seeing nobody else in the room.

'Can't you see him over there?' Ram Padarath asked. 'Now give him a sitting mat.'

The nephew obeyed, and shortly afterwards Ram Padarath passed away seeing his Guru before him.

❖ ❖ ❖ ❖ ❖ ❖ ❖ ❖

My appreciation and understanding of *Pranam* had steadily grown over the years. Watching how the Indian disciples touched Guruji's feet, bowed with hands clasped, or prostrated full-length on the ground before him seemed entirely natural now, although it had been hard to relate to such gestures of obeisance upon first arriving in India.

Something else I noticed was that when Guruji was sitting upstairs on the couch and Indian disciples came to see him, they always sat on the floor. Their respect was too profound to let them sit beside or on the same level as him.

Guruji explained to me that although this kind of veneration was an integral part of the culture and ingrained since early childhood, its significance should not be overlooked.

A guru can be a teacher of any discipline. In order for knowledge to be passed from teacher to pupil, or from guru to disciple, there has to be humility, surrender and respect on the part of the learner. If a disciple or student considers himself to know as much as his teacher due to an inflated ego, the exchange of knowledge possible will be minimal to zero. If Indian disciples are reluctant to sit on the same level as their Guru, it is in symbolic acknowledgement of this fact.

We are not surprised to read in the Bible that worshippers fell down before Jesus, their spiritual Guru. They also washed his feet in an act of reverence. His disciples acknowledged him to be their master, and did not consider him as friend or equal.

Surrendering to Jesus and accepting him into one's heart implies a letting go of personal will for the modern Christian. In the same spirit, Buddhists bow at their altars and statues of the Buddha, and practising Muslims worship Allah by prostrating themselves. There are symbols of devotion and surrender inherent in each movement of the prayer.

The word "guru" has been cheapened in the West – to a lesser extent also in India – and the real meaning, in the context of spiritual master, has become lost. Perhaps it is no wonder, since "gurus" are many, and genuine spiritual masters are few, especially if they have chosen to live unobtrusively in society.

But whether a spiritual master is famous or does not choose to reveal himself openly, nothing has changed over the centuries as far as the necessity for humility on the part of the disciple is concerned. Surrender is not about blind devotion or putting oneself down. It is a form of giving, and to give everything to the Guru in the true sense is to relinquish one's own ego.

If the ego is truly surrendered, which is only possible through faithfully practising the method which the spiritual master has passed on to the disciple, that person will learn from the Guru and perceive certain things about him which will remain forever hidden to others. Disciples who have the meekness to ask for help when in real need tend to receive it, just as those with a sincere desire often see their prayers answered.

On the other hand, if someone puts on a proud show of personal knowledge and intellect, the Guru is likely to nod and agree, and feign ignorance. People who think that they know everything will learn nothing from him, whereas those who really wish to understand and follow are blessed.

In India, the Guru-disciple relationship is unique, and as Swami Satyeswarananda Giri explains, it "transcends this earthly plane. Once the Guru commits himself to nurturing his disciple's spiritual advancement, that commitment is eternal."[6]

Since he is considered the omniscient parent who wants to see his offspring develop to their fullest potential, certain "rules" exist in Indian culture as to how the disciple should behave towards him:

The disciple has to accept the Guru's happiness or anger towards him. He should show childlike obedience. It is not fitting

---

[6] From *Babaji*, by Swami Satyeswarananda Giri.

to argue with the Guru. Nor is it right to show off or be ill-mannered towards him. It is particularly inadvisable to display any anger towards the Guru, whether internally or externally, as the effect of that negativity is directly returned to sender: it reflects off him like a mirror.

Trust is required that the Guru knows a disciple's needs. There should be no expectation, for the disciple is unable to judge the way in which the Guru may or may not give his help. To make demands for material gain or ask questions about the spiritual realm which bear no relevance to one's own practice would also amount to a lack of respect.

It is said in India that the disciple should be prepared to give his life, including body and mind, to the Guru. This does not imply any physical contact or hypnotic controlling, even though some false gurus have been known to twist the meaning for their own personal or sensual satisfaction.

On the contrary, the underlying meaning is that life is a precious gift. We do not know when death will come, but we do know that we will be taken from the world as empty-handed as we entered it. So life should be dedicated to the Creator of All. The human body should be recognised as the instrument through which self-realisation is attainable, via the method which the Guru has given to reach the spiritual goal. He has already realised the Absolute and is spending his time on earth to help disciples on their journey.

The more personal will is subdued, the easier and more rapid is spiritual progress. Laziness and other human weaknesses are hurdles to regular practice, so to give life and body to the Guru also implies harnessing the mind to overcome these through discipline.

I gathered that most of Guruji's Western disciples did not fully understand the significance of respect towards the Guru, and it was certainly true that regard for elders and teachers had steadily eroded in the West.

Hence Indian disciples often asked Guruji how Westerners could make any progress in Kriya Yoga, due to this lack of respect. For Indian disciples, it was natural that humility, devotion and surrender had to accompany growth on any spiritual path.

GURUJI said that if love came from deep inside, it was the most natural thing in the world to show respect. When we perceived nobleness in ourselves, we also saw it in others. If we insulted others, we would not be surprised if they insulted us. Respect grew in proportion to the extent an individual was in touch with the inner self or soul, because every aspect of creation, whether animate or inanimate, was an expression of the Absolute. The self-realised person made no distinction between king or beggar, gold or clay. He saw equality and unity in one linked creation.

Several months after I began to practise Kriya, the desire grew in my heart to make *Pranam* before Guruji like the Indian disciples, without there being any sense of obligation about it.

After a few years of watching Guruji make *Pranam* to the picture of Lahiri Mahasaya in the yoga studio, I also started to become conscious of a longing to be able to express my heartfelt devotion for the great master. We had an enlarged photograph of Lahiri Mahasaya by the front door at home in Switzerland, because in principle a feeling was there to touch his feet as a gesture of respect and remember God before leaving the house. But I usually forgot to do so or felt too self-conscious.

That was not all: for some time I had felt it would be a good discipline to raise the first mouthful of food to the point of *Kutastha* as Guruji did, in a conscious gesture of thanks for life-giving sustenance, since an uncomfortable awareness was growing in me of how much I took every meal for granted.

When I talked to Guruji about it, he said that if this kind of feeling truly came from the heart, it was important to listen to the message. There was no reason to be self-conscious solely because these things were not done in Western culture. 'And when you begin to give Him *Pranam* before going out,' he said mysteriously, 'you will feel something very different.'

Since that discussion, I began to make these things my habit. It was not long before I discovered that remembering God before eating or leaving the house began to permeate into other aspects of my life. For example, I would consciously surrender my work to Him prior to starting some challenging task, and afterwards be astonished at the ease with which it had been accomplished.

It was interesting to discover that it only felt right to raise wholesome food to *Kutastha* before eating it. Not being able to do so with chocolate, cookies, and ice cream indicated to me that these were usually consumed as indulgences rather than as necessary forms of sustenance. Guruji once pointed out not to raise foods such as eggs, meat and fish, in remembrance that the spiritual masters were fully vegetarian. The sight of eggs and fish on my plate now serves to remind me of the long road ahead to the spiritual planes of those masters.

There were other benefits to such gestures. They reminded me when I felt too lazy to practise, and made it twice as difficult for the ego-filled mind to block out the memory of what my aim was in life, and why Kriya Yoga was so important to me.

SINCE no disciples referred to Guruji as Mr Vyas, I gathered during the early days in India that it was disrespectful to address a Guru by his name. But it took a long time before it struck me that if this were so, perhaps it was also not entirely respectful to refer to the masters by their names, in particular to Lahiri Mahasaya, Tinkari Lahiri and Satya Charan Lahiri. When I sought confirmation from Guruji, he said that it was fine for the sake of writing their stories, but if someone wanted to remember and give respect from the heart, it was indeed more fitting to use the names given to them by their close disciples. These were as follows: *Barébaba* instead of Lahiri Mahasaya; *Choté Thakur*[7] instead of Tinkari Lahiri, and *Baba* instead of Satya Charan Lahiri.

---

[7] lit. Little God.

INSOLENCE (A Song)

My youth is steeped in insolence
But the shallow water calls me
To sail a deeper river
I try every road
Stumble through the crowds
I'm not participating
My mind is floating with the breeze

And I'll watch the tree grow
Blossom and fruit
Perfectly formed, every thought, every word
Till they fall – till they fall – till they fall
Eaten by the passing bird
And I'll watch the river flow
See my reflection
Transient, changing, waiting and listening
To the sound of the sounds, till the sounds
Melt into a single word

My heart is aching, won't let go
It hungers satisfaction
Inertia lurks in the shadows
I'm weary now
The conflicts of my mind
I'm not communicating
My soul is sailing in the breeze

And I'll watch the tree grow
Blossom and fruit
Perfectly formed, every thought, every word
Till they fall – till they fall – till they fall
Eaten by the passing bird
And I'll watch the river flow
See my reflection
Transient, changing, waiting and listening
To the sound of the sounds, till the sounds
Melt into a single word

Part Four

Guruji
(Prakash Shankar Vyas)

Chapter Eleven

TANTRA, MANTRA
AND THE GODS

Guruji Recalls how the Search Began

"What lies behind us and what lies before us are tiny matters compared to what lies within us." – OLIVER WENDELL HOLMES

'When I was about thirteen years old, something unusual happened. It was during my first swimming lesson in the Ganges. The trainer said to jump in, not expecting the beginners to do so. But I jumped right into the deep water and my shorts got hooked on what I suppose was an anchor. It was impossible to free myself but then finally I felt something underwater release me from the hook. I have no idea how long I was actually submerged, but by the time I was free and bobbed back up to the surface, the trainer was sure that I must have drowned. He had dived down several times to search for me without success. I was fine, apart from having swallowed some water.

'It was during my early teens that the life of a Yogi began to interest me. When one of my uncles came to visit, he told us about a Hatha Yogi who had been buried underground for a week or two in the premises of a Varanasi college, and was now due to be dug out, having told his devotees the date and exact time when this should be done. He asked me if I wanted to come along with him to watch.

'It was very interesting. First the devotees dug up the packed earth, and then they removed the boards which had acted as a roof above the Yogi, so that he could sit in a narrow hollow in the ground underneath. Then they lifted the old man out. He eyes were closed and he looked like a stone statue. They rubbed his hands and feet, and gave him honey and water. After some time, he opened his eyes and his body began to return to normal. He spoke a few words to the people who had come to see him, saying that the advanced practitioner could survive for a long time without oxygen through the power of Hatha Yoga.

'A few years later I used to go and watch another Yogi who regularly sat by the main Post Office in Varanasi. He did not wear any clothes, and most of the time he would lie on his enormous stomach. He acted like a small child and did not speak to anyone. Although people brought him food, he ate very little, and I would listen to them talk about him. Whenever I was there he used to gaze silently into my face. Many years later I heard that he was a spiritual person who performed some kinds of miracles, but at that time I had no real understanding of these things.

'At the age of fifteen, I met Swami Satyananda,[1] who founded the Bihar School of Yoga. An uncle took me to have Hatha Yoga lessons with him a couple of times. The field of yoga fascinated me so much that I purchased a book soon afterwards and started practising Hatha in my free time. The majority of the exercises in the book were very easy for me to do straight away. But even then, it felt as though something were missing. It was the physical form of yoga, but the spiritual aspect was not there.'

'AT BANARAS HINDU UNIVERSITY I was a student of Philosophy, English, Hindi, and Ancient Indian Culture, and graduated in 1978 with a Bachelor of Arts degree. There were brief times during university when I considered several career options ranging from acting to engineering. But the areas of self-study which I did keep up were homeopathy and herbal medicine. Electronics also became a serious hobby.

'At one point during my studies, I enrolled on a Government of India project and worked for a hospital doing research in primary health care for villagers. Much time was spent driving to small villages and teaching basic hygiene principles and Hatha Yoga.

'Once my education was complete, I moved to Patna in the state of Bihar. After working there for one year, my brother and I started up a business in the city. It was a shop selling and mending

[1] Swami Satyananda's Guru was Shivananda.

electrical and electronic appliances, and we were there for two more years. The shop quickly gained a good reputation for its repairs and fair prices. We employed an assistant technician but I did many of the repairs myself.

'Strange things began to happen to me for which there was no logical explanation. I didn't understand then that the way was being prepared for my future. Some mornings I would pick up a broken radio which a customer had brought in for repair the night before, only to find that it was working perfectly, or required one simple adjustment. No one could have touched it since the customer brought it in. It didn't happen just once, but many times. Whether it was a miracle or some sort of magic, the customers were always happy with their returned goods and paid their bills on time.

'Although I was hungry every lunch-time after returning home to my flat, there was no feeling to eat. No teacher had taught me how to meditate, but all I wanted was to sit quietly in the half-lotus position, to close my eyes and go deep inside of myself.

'As a result of the way the business was flourishing, soon there was a dispute with the landlord. When we moved in, the terms of the contract were that the rent could be raised by ten percent after nine months. But upon seeing our success, he doubled the rent after only six months and threatened to turn us out of the shop if he didn't get it. After that we had to get help from a lawyer who paid the correct rent to the landlord on our behalf.

'Soon afterwards he began to stir up more trouble. Twice during my quiet lunch-times I smelled the unmistakable rancid odour of burning flesh. Yet the burning *ghat* was at least ten kilometres from my flat. It seemed as if I was the recipient of some kind of *Tantra* malpractice.

'I told a friend about the problems with our landlord, because a colleague of his knew the landlord's family. A few days later my suspicions were confirmed. My friend found out that our landlord was paying regular visits to a famous tantric practitioner in Patna. However, we carried on with the shop.

'My parents arranged my marriage in 1983. Vandana and I were married in February 1984, but soon afterwards I became very sick. The interference by the landlord with our business increased and my health deteriorated. Despite visits to many doctors, none of

them could diagnose the problem. There were many times when I
felt depressed also.

'My father convinced me to return to Varanasi because of my ill
health, which we did in August 1984 after winding up the business.
Then my son Puneet was born in October of the same year, and my
father supported us until I was well again.

'A few years later I returned to my studies and completed a
Masters degree in Philosophy in 1990.'

❖ ❖ ❖ ❖ ❖ ❖ ❖ ❖

There were a few more things to be learned about Guruji's childhood
when I questioned his mother one afternoon up on the terrace:

She told me that soon after Guruji was born in 1956, his
grandmother went to see a practitioner of *Tantra* yoga who lived
nearby and was renowned for his good character and accurate
predictions. She took along the date and time of the birth, wanting
an assurance that her grandson would survive, and to know what
kind of person he would be in the future.

The man said to Grandmother that he was an exceptional boy,
and that there had never been anyone in the family like him, nor
would there ever be in the future. Grandmother was more than
delighted to hear this, since her husband had been famous in India
as a short-story writer.[2] He had written a great deal in a short time
and earned enough to make a comfortable living. He used to
prepare his *betel* with saffron, drink milk every day, and eat
cashews and raisins. Other intellectuals used to visit the house
regularly to see him.

Guruji's mother continued to tell me that the tantric's prediction
had certainly come true. All those years ago they had no way of
telling in which way her son was going to be special, but he was
indeed the first Yogi in the family.

She said that Guruji had been a quiet child. Then as a teenager
he had been to the Hatha yoga school with his uncle, and within a
short time he had perfected the most difficult exercises. But then he
had always been incredibly supple. Something else he was born
with was plenty of persistence: when he really wanted something,

---

[2] The work of *Pandit* Vinod Shankar Vyas is still being studied by Hindi literature students in universities
today.

he would never give up until he got it.

He had been interested in plants and gardening ever since he was a boy. Guruji's mother paused as if something had occurred to her and pointed to a beautiful jasmine pot plant on the terrace. There was a story about that one, she said.

Guruji had bought that jasmine whilst in his teens and the florist had promised him that it would bloom within two months. However, fifteen years passed and it did not show its colour once, despite being well fed and watered. Then one day, soon after Guruji had received Kriya Yoga, it suddenly started to flower prolifically. She had called him to come and see. And he had told her that he had talked to the plant in his mind a few weeks earlier, and had asked it why it refused to bloom year after year. It seemed as though the plant had answered him.

She confirmed that Guruji had told her of many strange things which happened to him in the period before he met Satya Charan Lahiri, and said that perhaps he would tell me about some of those himself. Since he had given his blessing for a book about the spiritual masters in Lahiri Mahasaya's lineage, she thought that he might be prepared to reveal a few of his own experiences.

WHEN I asked Guruji to tell me about *Tantra Mantra*, he told me that in its present form, it bore no relevance to Kriya Yoga.

In simple terms, *Tantra Mantra* was an Indian yogic science. The ancient tantrics were advanced yogis who only initiated as their followers devotees with the purity of vision to see their last seven lives. The practice involved *Mantras* or incantations: in other words the use of sacred syllables or numbers, or both. When perfected, these produced powerful energy vibrations which were as invisible as sound, light or microwave frequencies and reached their goal no less effectively.

The great master from whom *Tantra Mantra* stemmed was self-realised. And although the innumerable *Mantras* which he discovered were of inestimable benefit to mankind, the ultimate goal of *Tantra Mantra* was self-realisation.

However, as Guruji had explained before in the context of astrology, though a founder of a spiritual practice or religion may be self-realised, when his knowledge is passed down to followers who have not reached the same level of consciousness, changes and omissions are made with the passing of time. Thus various *Tantra Mantra* incantations have become useless, not unlike what is happening to Kriya Yoga itself in the present day. Some people are tempted by supernatural power and begin to misuse the practice for personal gain until eventually the principal aim becomes obsolete and corrupted.

Most people are familiar only with the superficial meaning of the five principal rites and rituals belonging to *Tantra*, these being alcohol, meat, fish, wealth and sexual intercourse. Practitioners often do not see beyond the superficial sense of these, although it is impossible for man to attain self-realisation through such material pleasures. I had to admit having associated *Tantra* only with eroticism until then. Having seen carvings on temples and illustrations in books, it appeared to involve some kind of "spiritual sex". *Tantra* was described as the "fusion of sexual energy into divine energy." That sounded interesting, but when I asked Guruji how "spiritual sex" was possible, and what I could write about it, his short answer was, 'Leave it. Sex is sex.'

Subsequently I discovered Lahiri Mahasaya's explanation to his disciples on the deeper meaning of *Tantra Mantra*. The Kriya practitioner can relate to these as being internal rites on the path to self-realisation:

ALCOHOL   To partake of alcohol meant to receive the intoxicating ambrosia, or holy nectar which dropped onto the practitioner's tongue when in *Khechari mudra*, making him feel ecstasy;

MEAT   The consumption of meat was the practice of inserting the tongue into the palatal cavity in *Khechari mudra*, which in conjunction with *pranayama* led to the cessation of desires;

FISH   The scriptural injunction that the practitioner must eat the two fish which swim together in the Ganges and Yamuna rivers was symbolic of the breath passing through the *Ida* and *Pingala* channels in the body – therefore consumption of fish meant to control external breathing through long *pranayama*;

WEALTH   To worship wealth referred to the ultimate attainment
                of the crown *Chakra* known as the thousand-petalled
                lotus, or to receive unsurpassable spiritual riches;

SEX   In the deep scriptural sense, reference to sexual
                intercourse bore no relation to the sensual physical act.
                It represented the various stages of practice leading to
                the ultimate state of union with Soul, where universal
                knowledge was to be found and human desires were
                overcome.

Lahiri Mahasaya would also say, "That which saves one from the
mind (restless breath), or *manasa*, is called *Mantra*; that which saves
one from the attachment of body is called *Tantra*."

IN PATNA, tantric power had been used as a weapon to harm
Guruji's business and health. That was before he had been initiated
in Kriya Yoga. So I was curious to know if he would still be
affected, were he targeted again. Guruji answered that a Yogi's
inner power acted as a protective shield. Evil was either
neutralised completely, or reflected off it like a mirror.

There was another famous story about Trailanga Swami which
illustrated the point. Some youths who wanted to test the Yogi put
a huge bucket of lime before him and told him that it was buffalo
milk. Trailanga Swami studied their faces carefully before drinking
the entire contents of the bucket. The onlookers were convinced he
would die, but after a while he simply stood up and urinated. The
youths, on the other hand, fell to the ground writhing in pain.
Whilst Trailanga Swami was able to neutralise the poison in his
own body with no ill effects, they suffered the fate they had tried
to inflict on the Yogi themselves. Begging for forgiveness, the
young men cried out to Trailanga Swami. The great Yogi healed
them, asking them if they did not realise that his life was not
separate from theirs.[3]

'And if someone is misusing the power which is in *Tantra Mantra*,
they cannot become self-realised either, can they?' I wanted to know.

---

[3] "And these signs shall follow them that believe; In my name shall they cast out devils;... They shall take
up serpents; and if they drink any deadly thing, it shall not hurt them; they shall lay hands on the sick,
and they shall recover." St. Mark 16:17,18

'Listen: there is one example,' Guruji said.

'One day, Basmasur asked *Siva* for a boon so that anything or anyone he touched on the head would turn to ashes. *Siva* fulfilled his desire, but soon observed that Basmasur was becoming obsessive and dangerous. *Siva* became concerned for the safety of the world as it seemed as though Basmasur might destroy everything.

'*Siva* was a god who could take on any form, so he turned himself into a beautiful dancing woman. As soon as Basmasur saw her, he thought that she was the most lovely woman he had ever seen and decided that he wanted to marry her. In his clever disguise, *Siva* answered Basmasur,

' "Very well, we will marry later. But first let us dance together and enjoy ourselves."

'Basmasur thought this was a wonderful idea and started to copy *Siva's* every dance move. He was soon so carried away by the music and so enraptured by the woman's beauty, that he quite forgot himself. Therefore, when *Siva* finally touched his hand to his own head at the end of the dance, Basmasur did likewise and was immediately turned to ashes.

'The story wants to tell that a person can get a boon as a result of much yoga practice,' Guruji explained. 'It may happen that after some years, a perfection comes – known as a *Siddhi*, or power. But despite this, the practitioner is not self-realised. There is a danger that the person may be tempted to misuse the power for materialistic gain. They forget their aim and then the spiritual journey stops. Instead of progressing, the downward spiral begins.

'As I have told you before, the ego has many subtle disguises, and until it is conquered completely, there are many temptations which come on the way. So this story is a warning to the practitioner not to stray from the spiritual goal.'

VANDANA told me another story which seemed to tie in with the whole concept of how a Yogi could offset negative influences and bad spirits without consciously doing anything.

Several years previously, Mr Lal had asked Guruji to accompany him on a visit to the house which his family owned in the countryside, because apparently an evil spirit lived in it. For many years the family had tried to carry out repairs on the dilapidated parts of the house and build an extension, but absolutely everyone who had ever been employed to work on it had died or been injured either through an accident or a snake bite, and now no one would go near the place. He wanted to know what Guruji thought about it all.

Guruji had told him that he did not know anything about evil spirits, but agreed to go and see. 'How nice,' he had said before going, 'if we would see a ghost.' But when the two men returned that day, Guruji had not seen anything special. Just an old ramshackle house. Apparently the local exorcist who had tried earlier to rid the house of the ghost had turned up whilst they were having a snack, and after staring at Guruji for a long time he had asked Mr Lal who he was. Mr Lal had introduced Guruji as his friend who had come to see the house and village.

But a few weeks afterwards, this exorcist told Mr Lal that without doubt, Guruji had done something on that day to finally rid the house of its ghost or bad spirit. Soon the family resumed repair work, and inexplicably, nothing adverse had happened since the day of Guruji's visit. Mr Lal asked Guruji numerous times afterwards if he really had not seen or done anything. And each time Guruji always shook his head in reply. The family had even been able to sell the house and land.

People say, as Vandana told me in conclusion, that if a spiritual practitioner or master ever comes into contact with any kind of bad spirit, the spirit is liberated and becomes free once more to take rebirth.

Mysterious Encounters

"The primary purpose of sacred images is not to give aesthetic enjoyment, but to serve as focusing points for the spirit. Born in meditation and inner visualisation, they should, and that is their ultimate intent, lead back to meditation and the comprehension of that transcendent reality from which they were born.
If they are beautiful, it is because they are true." – ALICE BONER

'It was during the year following our return to Varanasi that my spiritual journey began in earnest. It was as if something was lacking in my life which had to be found. I had little appetite and spent most of the time meditating behind closed doors, although still without any kind of method. I read about Swami Vivekananda's Guru, Ram Krishparamansa, who used to worship the goddess *Kali*, and began to focus my mind in meditation on the Mother myself.

'My father was acquainted with a woman who spent most of her time worshipping *Kali*. I met her once on the way to the temple, and she came along with me. She mystified me by saying that the something I was looking for would soon come. A while later, she came to our house especially to visit me. She asked to see my statue of *Kali*, and as she gazed at it, she seemed to go into a trance. Before she left, she said that the Mother was very happy with me, and that I should dress her and bring her fruits.

'I continued to worship *Kali* and doing so was satisfying on one level. When we do *puja* in India, we offer water to the statue; but every day instead of having to change the water, it was necessary to refill the pot completely. *Kali* seemed to be accepting whatever I put on the altar. There was an oil lamp there too. One time whilst putting a garland over the statue, I put my arm right into the flame, and was surprised that there was no burn. But then strange things were constantly happening.

'Especially during chanting, a feeling would come that I wanted to know the Mother. And soon afterwards, *Kali* began to appear to me in her physical form during every *puja*. Although I told both my wife and mother about these experiences, they didn't believe that God could appear in the form of a deity and dismissed it as a stupidity. They were convinced that I was doing more *puja* than was good for me. So I resolved to make them believe, by calling the holy Mother to come before them.

'As I prayed in front of the statue, *Kali* appeared to me as usual. My wife and mother were both in the kitchen. I asked the Mother to grant them a vision, since I also wanted them to believe and realise that her presence was everywhere.

'Having prayed in this way, I watched as her face became angry. Her expression said that it was not a matter of belief; and she turned her face towards the only light bulb in the room. It was suddenly clear what she was going to do and at that same instant the light bulb shattered. My wife and mother were stunned at the sight of hundreds of glass fragments all over the floor, and asked how it had happened. It seemed to me that the Mother must have been angry because I had wanted her to appear to others with my ego. It was a lesson never to show off in such a way again.

'Then I went through another period of darkness and depression. However, something further happened during that time which taught me how precious life was and gave a clear indication that there was some reason why God wanted me to live.

'Meanwhile, inexplicable events continued to be an everyday occurrence. Once I was lying in bed and there was a loud rumbling in my ear. The next moment I felt as though I'd been buried under the earth. The following day the news came on television that many people had been killed in an earthquake in Assam. From that time on, I would regularly see accidents before they happened. Aeroplane crashes, ships sinking and so on, only to see them reported on television or in the newspaper days or weeks afterwards. These experiences were vivid and upsetting, and the worst thing was that there was no one to talk to who would understand. It was no use even trying to explain to anyone. So the search intensified for a practice which would help me to make sense of these things. I continued to worship *Kali* in meditation as before, but couldn't dismiss the feeling that it was necessary to go further.

'I visited a number of so-called "self-realised" people, and each of them told me something different. One man told me to gaze at the sun, saying that this would give me great powers. Another had a strange theory about *Kundalini*, and how I could bring my already awakened *Kundalini* to the head. But not one of these people could answer my questions satisfactorily.

'During this time, I heard the name Lahiri Mahasaya mentioned twice. An astrologer from Calcutta who once came to our house could not help with any of my questions but said, "If Lahiri Mahasaya were here ..." and then drifted off in mid-sentence. Another time I approached a friend of the family. He was a lawyer who was practising some kind of yoga meditation.

' "How can I explain these things to you?" he said. "If only Lahiri Mahasaya were here, you could get your answers." '

'SOMETHING happened in February 1985, a few nights before our *Sivaratri* festival. It was about three or four o'clock in the morning.

Since returning to Varanasi, I could never sleep during those early hours, so I was lying awake in my bed. Then suddenly the bedroom started to fill with light, and it seemed as if something was coming through a tunnel from a far-away cave. I watched as the light took the solid shape of a man, maybe about fifty years old. Although he had a long black and white beard, he had the innocent face and smile of a small child. I was a little scared at first, but it seemed that he wanted to give a message, so I listened. He told me that I had to get salvation in this life. But he did not say how, nor did he reveal his name. He added that *Sivaratri* was coming, and on that day I was to fast and meditate. By the time he left, perhaps it was five minutes later, I felt so close to him, although I couldn't define the relationship between us. His body dissolved again, like scattered atoms separating themselves and changing, and he was gone.

'On the morning of *Sivaratri* my mother offered me sweets, and I took some, having forgotten what the man had said about fasting. Then I went to my room to sit in meditation, and searched for the old man with the young face very deep inside of myself for what must have been about half an hour. This time when he reappeared, I felt no fear. He was smiling in the same way as before. The first thing he asked was why I had eaten sweets and it came as a shock that he knew what I had eaten. Before he disappeared, he repeated his words to me: that I had to get salvation in this life. But that was all, and there was still no specific instruction of how to do so.

'I was sitting like a statue at the time of the vision, and remained in meditation even after he had gone. Later on I told my mother what had happened and she also thought that it was strange, but said that I should just sit and meditate, if that was what the man had told me to do.'

❖ ❖ ❖ ❖ ❖ ❖ ❖ ❖

Symbolically situated on the Trident of *Siva* and otherwise known as Banaras, *Kashi*, the City of Shiva and the sacred or holy city, Varanasi is the pilgrim destination to which every Hindu hopes to make the journey at least once during their lifetime in order to visit the city's temples and wash away sins through bathing in the holy waters of the River Ganges.[4]

There is a temple at every turn throughout the city, many of them ancient, at which devotees light incense sticks and offer sweets and garlands to the deities from dawn to dusk. They are places of worship which constantly call passers-by to remember God's omnipresence and give respect.

Many saints and masters have lived and passed through Banaras, Jesus reportedly amongst them. He was known here as Issu, or Yesu, and legends tell of how he was expelled from the city by the high priests for teaching people about God regardless of their caste, instead of exclusively to the Brahmins.[5]

I used to spend time in my friend Ganesh's jewellery and handicrafts shop in Golden Temple lane, drinking *chai* and trying to improve my Hindi. From my stool, I could watch the pilgrims carrying compact bundles on their heads as they passed by. They were mostly barefooted, since the lanes of Varanasi's old city are considered sacred. Apparently, if someone in the South of India hears that you are from Varanasi, they may touch your feet purely because they have trodden through those hallowed lanes.

Before making the descent to the Golden Temple, the pilgrims would stand for a moment, clasping their hands in *Pranam* with bowed heads. The sight of their countenances radiating genuine surrender and devotion could have stirred up a feeling of sanctity in almost anyone.

It shamed me to think of how superficially I had dismissed statue worship in Hinduism as some kind of pagan ritual before. Not just because of my ignorance at the time that Hinduism recognised one supreme God, *Brahma*, but because the depth of devotion expressed by these pilgrims made a silent statement containing the essence of unadulterated religion. I had never witnessed anything like it in the Western world. It had to be one of the reasons why Varanasi was crowned with such a magnetically vibrant spiritual atmosphere.

Dadaji was a grandfather who owned a general store in the old lanes and whenever I passed his shop, I usually stopped for a chat

---

[4] For a spiritual interpretation of bathing in the Ganges, please refer to *Kashi* in the Glossary.

[5] Although the fact of Jesus having lived in India is still denied by the traditional Christian church, Holger Kersten in his book *Jesus Lived in India* provides compelling evidence to the contrary. At the very least, as the author says in his introduction, it will be seen that, as "modern research into the life of Jesus stands, it is really not possible to *disprove* Jesus' stay in India."

and a cup of *chai*. Once he invited me to his house for an evening meal, and asked if I would like to see the family altar. It was adorned with antique bronze mini-statues of various gods and goddesses. In the middle of the table there was an old metal box, rimmed with fading purple velour. He told me that it contained the family god and its identity had to be kept secret. This special box was only ever opened in the presence of family members.

It was a lesson in itself to see Dadaji's respect for those ancient bronze forms on his altar. The faith and devotion which he expressed before them somehow transformed them into something entirely non-physical. This was no idolatry. It taught me that if the purpose of religion in the deepest sense is to destroy the ego and let go of personal self, then no particular way of worshipping can ever be considered superior to another. Surely God has no preference for the method and only sees what is in a man's heart.

OVER the years I learned that religion and culture are so intertwined in India that atheism is virtually non-existent. In Hinduism there is no proselytising, since it is only possible to be a Hindu if you are born one; and everyone is free to worship in their own way. Something which particularly impressed me was the sense of respect it brought into every aspect of daily life.

One day to Ganesh's dismay, I inadvertently placed a sheet of paper on my used clay tea cup. The counter was strewn with my first attempts to write in Hindi.

'*Saraswati! Saraswati!*' cried Ganesh, who whisked the paper off the cup, touched it to his forehead and put it elsewhere. I laughed nervously, not understanding until Ganesh explained that it had been a disrespectful thing to do. For *Saraswati* was the goddess of wisdom and knowledge, and one did not put paper on top of something dirty. Paper was made from trees, and it was important to acknowledge that God created all of nature. As a God-given tool of knowledge and learning, it should be treated with respect and kept in a clean place.

A few weeks later, after Guruji and I had been discussing a passage in the *Bhagavad Gita*, I put the book next to me on the floor. Guruji immediately picked it up and put it up on a shelf. He said that in India one cannot put any holy book, be it the *Bhagavad Gita*, the Holy Bible or the Koran, on the floor.

Understanding and wisdom come from a higher place in the body. If there were no books, man's education would be extremely limited. The point of real knowledge is *Kutastha* or the eyebrow centre. It should be natural, even in the West, that people know not to put their feet, the lowest part of their body which treads through dirt, on a holy book. But we also have to give respect to other books, he said, and told me how he disliked to see Westerners put books on top of shoes.

Although this baffled me at first, it began to make more sense when Guruji explained that it was about seeing God and his gifts in everything. Indian culture taught that man should never take for granted anything so essential to his existence and development as food and knowledge. Each and every thing was made from the five elements, and these were from God; they did not drop from the sky. Respect was about gratitude.

DURING a train journey from Delhi to Varanasi, I saw some Western travellers put a packet of biscuits in their boots, evidently thinking nothing of it. When the Indians in the compartment looked back and forth at each other in shock and dismay, I was not surprised. In their eyes, it had to be another form of disrespect towards God. Food was something sacred too. Just like books, food did not belong on the ground, or anywhere in the vicinity of dirty shoes. No doubt there was also the aspect of hygiene: after all, the streets in India were not generally as clean as some in the West.

IT WAS both fascinating and confusing to hear that the goddess *Kali* used to appear to Guruji. I knew that for Dadaji and Ganesh the Hindu deities were undeniably real and present. Yet now there appeared to be a contradiction, because once Guruji had explained that the deities were symbols which could be particularly well understood on the Kriya path. They represented different stages of meditation and were symbols of a Yogi's divine powers – an idea which had been somewhat easier for me to relate to.

Take, for example, the goddess *Durga*, who holds a different weapon in each of her hands and sits astride a tiger. The literal meaning of *Durga* is "fortress" or "the inaccessible". The physical body is the fort, since it is the place where *Durga* may be found, and the state of union with the ultimate Self which she represents is difficult to reach. The goddess is often depicted as having ten hands, which represent the five *Pranas* and five *sub-Pranas* in the body. The work that a man can do with two hands is limited, so *Durga's* many hands also symbolise the power of the Yogi who has brought these *Pranas* under control. The tiger is sexual energy which has been tamed to submission under the goddess' command. The beast is controlled rather than destroyed, for creation must to be allowed to follow its course.

Lord Krishna wears peacock feathers on his head, for the eye in the feather is a symbol of *Kutastha*; he plays a flute with seven holes representing the *Chakras*, because a flute-like sound can be heard in Kriya *pranayama*. The position in which he stands, with right leg crossed over the left, and with tilted head and waist, is significant in several ways: one of them being the yogic state whereby the obstructions of tongue and heart and root *Chakras* are lifted, illustrated by the three "bends" in his body.

So were they symbols or were they real? And why did Guruji stop worshipping *Kali* in the end?

'When I saw *Kali* at that time,' Guruji began, 'I was worshipping an image. Thus I expected to see God in that form. When we think about a god or a goddess, the mind reflects it back onto one's own body. This is a stage which has to dissolve in order for the spiritual journey to move forward.

'After I met my Guruji, Satya Charan Lahiri, and started to practise Kriya Yoga, I understood that our deities are symbols. As soon I started to experience that God was within, not separate or outside of myself, the image no longer existed for me. The other reason why I decided to stop worshipping *Kali* was that the Hindu system of *puja* is very complicated and difficult. Kriya Yoga can make the mind somewhat blank, and then it is easy to forget the order in which you have to worship, which is not so good.'

Guruji added that there was no need for confusion. A Christian who had no concept of *Krishna* or *Rama* would not gain any benefit in trying to think of their forms. Likewise, a Hindu was not able to relate to the Christian concept of angels. Angels were also messengers, but the source of the message came from *Prana* or Soul. Human projections and expectations were as malleable as clay and could be shaped into any form. Christians, Buddhists and

Hindus were bound to experience visions of totally different natures.[6]

The important thing to know was that in Kriya Yoga, there was no image of any kind. 'How can it be possible in a practice for the Absolute?' Guruji said. The deities existed in the universe but were also symbols. God was able to "change his dress" in the same way as we might wear jeans one day and something elegant the next. But His substance was unchangeable.

Whilst we were on the subject, Guruji remembered that there were a couple of pertinent stories from the life of Lahiri Mahasaya which he had as yet omitted to tell:

As A Result of long and dedicated scriptural study, the engineer Bhut Nath Sen came to the conclusion that the worship of gods and goddesses bore no relation to the Absolute One. He went to see many *sadhus* where he lived, wanting confirmation that man had to go beyond the worship of inanimate stone images. When he heard by chance that there was a "living *Siva*" by the name of Lahiri Mahasaya in Banaras, he was sure that he would find support in his conviction. Bhut Nath Sen made a long and deep *Pranam* before the master. After raising his eyes, Lahiri Mahasaya said to him,

'Now that you have come to Banaras, would you not like to take a holy bath in the Ganges and pay your respects at the *Vishwanath* temple?'

'I did not come to Banaras to see a stone carving of an inanimate *Vishwanath*,' replied the man. 'I came here to see a living *Siva*.'

'You do not have perfect knowledge in this matter. We have to give respect to these stones too. We should make *puja* and think of God according to our social custom until we attain true realisation. Take a holy dip and go to the *Vishwanath* temple. Then come back here.'

---

[6] "The Yogi teaches that the mind itself has a higher state of existence, beyond reason, a superconscious state, and when the mind gets to that higher state, then this knowledge, beyond reasoning, comes to man ... This state of going beyond reason, transcending ordinary human nature, may sometimes come by chance to a man who does not understand its science; he, as it were, stumbles upon it. When he stumbles upon it, he generally interprets it as coming from outside. So this explains why an inspiration, or transcendental knowledge, may be the same in different countries but in one country it will seem to come through an angel, and in another through a Deva, and in a third through God. What does it mean? It means that the mind brought the knowledge by its own nature, and that the finding of the knowledge was interpreted according to the belief and education of the person through which it came." (from *Raja Yoga* by Swami Vivekananda.)

Whilst Bhut Nath Sen was doing *puja* in the temple as he had been instructed, he was astonished to see a statue of Lahiri Mahasaya before his eyes in the place of the *Siva Lingam*, and realised that he was being taught a lesson.

The next day he returned to the master's house and made *Pranam*. Lahiri Mahasaya smiled a warm welcome, and began to tell Bhut Nath Sen various stories and examples to explain why no difference should be made between a stone statue and a living saint, since images and statues were also expressions of the One Absolute.

When he had finished talking, Bhut Nath Sen clasped his hands together and begged to say something.

'Master, I had so many questions to ask you today, and because I didn't want to forget any of them, I wrote a list,' he said, retrieving a folded piece of paper from his pocket. 'But you have answered every single question which I had. There is nothing more I wanted to ask.'

Before he returned to his home, Bhut Nath Sen received Kriya Yoga from Lahiri Mahasaya.

ANOTHER story is told of the time Lahiri Mahasaya was taking an evening stroll on Ranamahal Ghat with Krishna Ram. A stranger approached them clasping his hands in *Pranam*. A conversation ensued to this effect:

'I have heard much about you, Master, and this is the first time it has been my good fortune to meet you.'

Lahiri Mahasaya politely asked the man's name and where he came from, and having introduced himself, the man said,

'If you don't mind, may I ask you something?'

'Of course,' came the reply.

'With due respect, I have heard that you are meditating in your home. Please tell me, upon which god are you meditating?'

Lahiri Mahasaya smiled softly before answering, 'This I don't know.'

'Is it *Siva*? Or perhaps *Kali*, or *Krishna*? Surely it must be one of them,' objected the stranger.

'Yes, you are right. *Siva, Kali, Krishna*, and that which is in you, me and everyone is the subject of my meditation,' replied the master.

'I don't understand.'

'And I cannot explain this to you, for you will not understand.'

A FAMOUS renunciant called Swami Dayananda once convinced the *Kashi Maharaja* that the traditional practice of worshipping the deities in Banaras' temples should be stopped, since God, *Brahma* was pure consciousness, having no form. A conference was organised to discuss the matter, but since no one found a convincing counter-argument, Dayananda said that the next day his followers would break all the statues and have them thrown into the Ganges, unless his challenge was met.

Having heard from a disciple about the conference in the palace, Lahiri Mahasaya said that he would go and defend the practice of worshipping the deities. When he arrived the next day and began to speak, the followers of Dayananda began to mock so loudly that he could not make himself heard. Lahiri Mahasaya asked Dayananda to control his followers, but the Swami could not.

Therefore Lahiri Mahasaya began to contort his jaw and as he did so, the people making the disturbance suddenly found their own mouths twisting into the same strange position as the master's. They looked back and forth at each other in dismay, unable to speak. It was then that Lahiri Mahasaya answered Dayananda's challenge, saying:

'Although water is liquid, it becomes solid when it turns to ice. And although *Brahma* is pure formless Consciousness, it can also assume a form. Hence there is nothing wrong in worshipping the statues.'

It was a simple argument which had never occurred to Swami Dayananda. Then Lahiri Mahasaya asked Swami Dayananda to return his disciples mouths to normal, but the Swami was unable to do so. Both Dayananda and the King asked Lahiri Mahasaya to heal the people himself. The master said that water should be brought from the *Vishwanath* temple, and a few drops placed in everybody's mouth. This was arranged and the people who had been muted were cured. As a result of the episode, the statues remained in their temples.

SUCH events taught the disciples that Lahiri Mahasaya perceived the deities as results of yoga *sadhana*, or as a side-effect of focusing on the One Absolute. He would say, "One can see all the deities if one withdraws the restless mind and turns himself inward in *Kutastha*."

Although Lahiri Mahasaya was self-realised, he used to visit a temple every Sunday. A disciple once asked him why he went, since it was clear that he was in constant union with Soul. The master replied in a serious tone of voice, 'If I do not go, neither will you.'

His example showed that he also considered statue worship, when executed in the spirit of genuine devotion and faith, to be an important step on the external spiritual path. The Hindu should not claim that the god in the temple was merely made of stone and therefore cease to worship, any more than the Christian should begin to regard the church as an insignificant edifice.

The Kriya practitioner was only justified in proclaiming God's omnipresence when his conscious level had been elevated to the realisation of this truth through practice. For although there was no difference between devotee and god in so far as the image dissolved once the practitioner reached the state of Oneness, it was hypocrisy to talk on such matters before there was genuine inner perception.

Working for that perception did involve more than going to the temple or to a church, however. The practice for self-realisation was the most difficult of paths to tread. Man often lacked the respect and devotion required to walk it. This Kriya *sadhana* required no logic, but rather childlike simplicity of mind and plenty of faith.

Kriya Yoga Found

"We must not cease from exploration and the end of our exploring
will be to arrive where we began
and to know the place for the first time." – T. S. ELIOT

'After the appearance of that saint at the time of *Sivaratri*, I began to look even more actively for someone who could answer my questions. But still I had to wait. One man taught me how to practise *Mantras*. I bought a book on the subject, and within a short while found the *Mantras* becoming easy to perfect.

'Once I was sitting on the steps of the *ghat* when it started to rain. So I decided to use a *Mantra* to stop myself from getting wet. Whilst chanting, the rain fell heavily around me, but where I was sitting the ground remained completely dry. It was as if there were an invisible umbrella right above my head.

'This kind of thing happened often, and I sometimes experimented to see what kind of power I could have. But even at that time, I understood that controlling the rain was a useless thing.'

'A FRIEND told me that he knew a man who might be able to help me. We were introduced and that man seemed to take quite an interest in me and in my search. He told me that I could go to his temple in the afternoons to practise meditation. For a few days he stayed with me, but then he said that I didn't need him and should go there to meditate alone. He seemed like a guru, yet he always left flowers and sandalwood there for me. In that temple I had many transcendental experiences also.

'I used to go to that temple every day at four o'clock in the afternoon, after a lunch-time rest. Sometimes I felt lazy and would think about going later on, but as soon as the clock struck four, there would be a high-pitched girlish laughter in my ear and a voice telling me to get up. One time I tried to ignore it, but then it was like someone touched and prodded me. It gave me a shock and I left for the temple immediately.'

'DURING July 1985, my friend and I were searching for unusual temples in Varanasi which were quiet and little frequented. One day we heard about a sinister *Kali* temple. Apparently the statue was the most fearful-looking effigy of the Mother in the sacred city, and her mouth was lined with real human teeth. In old times, sacrifices were performed at the temple.

'We couldn't find it in the area where it was supposed to be, so we went into an antique shop to ask its whereabouts. The owner of the shop first wanted to know why two young men were looking for such a strange place, but we insisted on knowing if it really existed. He told us that it was the private property of a Bengali family and they only opened it in the morning when a priest went there to perform *puja*. It was a temple inhabited by bats and snakes, he said, and no private visitors went there any more. Nevertheless, my friend and I went to the temple the next morning. We didn't stay for long. Everything we had heard about the place was true.

'In India, it is customary to fast before going to a temple, and eat afterwards. So on our way home from the *Kali* temple we stopped at a sweet shop. There were pictures hanging on the wall of the shop, and as I bit into my *rusgula*, I was staring at one photograph in particular. It seemed to somehow come alive. Without even thinking, I asked who the man in the picture was.

' "Oh, he was a great spiritual master in India: a *Mahayogi* from Bengal." the shopkeeper replied.

' "What was his name?" I asked.

' "They called him Lahiri Mahasaya."

'This was the third time that I had heard his name, and now here was his picture. When I pressed the shopkeeper for more information, he said that his father had been a devotee of the great Yogi. We paid for our sweets and left, but a few seconds later the shopkeeper was calling us back again.

' "I know someone," he said, "and I think he is the grandson of that Yogi, or at least he is a member of that family. Perhaps you can try there." He gave us the address, so we thanked him and left.

'Full of anticipation, we went to look for the house. When we arrived, someone came out to ask us what we wanted, and we replied that we wished to see the *pandit* who lived there. But it was lunch-time and he was resting, so we were given a time when we could return. Another man was leaving the house at that moment, and he asked me who I was and what I was looking for. Having given a brief explanation, the man told me that I had come to the right place. I didn't reply, but noted the heartfelt way in which he said it. Later he introduced himself as Mr Lal.

'There were several hours to wait before we could go back. I told my friend to meet me later, and to come early. It was the longest wait of my life. I watched the minutes tick by. For some reason I felt extremely agitated waiting for that meeting.

'We arrived back at the house in the early evening and *puja* was going on in the temple. The *pandit* was sitting in the corner, a clean-shaven elderly man. We waited until the ceremony was over and watched disciples bringing him fruits and sweets. Finally we went forwards to make *Pranam*. The *pandit* asked our names and wanted to know why we had come. We told him, but he was getting ready to go upstairs. He said to us,

' "You can go now."

'It seemed like a peculiar thing to say, and it was a disappointment that we couldn't stay and talk with him. We left, but the next day I wanted to go again, and my friend agreed to meet me at the house. We arrived at the time of *puja* in the temple as before and were offered *prasad* – that is, fruits and sweets from the benediction. Afterwards, the *pandit* explained to us that the two statues in the temple premises were of his father, Tinkari Lahiri, and grandfather, Lahiri Mahasaya. Before he could tell us to go, I quickly said that there was something I wanted to ask. He gazed at my face and smiled warmly.

' "Okay. Come upstairs then," he said.'

'THE GURU'S name was Satya Charan Lahiri, as we had discovered by then, and he started to talk about the self-realised poet *Kabir Das*. It was fascinating. But then we were interrupted by a man who came into the room and began to discuss some matter with him in Bengali. I became impatient and wished that the man would leave. After half an hour my friend wanted to go, saying that it was a waste of time and that there was nothing special about this *pandit*. However, I insisted on waiting, having never heard such an interpretation of the work of the famous poet before. Eventually the visitor left, and Satya Charan Lahiri continued speaking for a while. Before we left, he told us that there was *puja* in the temple downstairs every day, and we were welcome to come whenever we wanted.

'It was clear that my friend did not share my interest, so I decided to go to the house alone the next day. I had made up my mind to question the grandson of Lahiri Mahasaya about my experiences in meditation.

'He allowed me to come upstairs with him again and I started to relate some of the things which had happened. When I told him about the saint who had appeared twice around the time of *Sivaratri*, and how he had instructed me to get salvation in this life, Satya Charan Lahiri seemed to be listening very carefully and with excitement. He was examining my face all the time.

' "I see. Did you not tell him to give you Kriya initiation?" he asked me with a wry smile.

I had no idea what he meant. It was the first time I had heard of Kriya Yoga. It was only much later that I understood why he asked this question in particular.

' "No, I don't know who he was or why he came," I told him. "All I want is to find answers to my questions." '

'THEN he said that he would initiate me in Kriya Yoga, but I would have to wait for fifteen days. In the meantime he asked me to read a book by one of his disciples called *Purana Purusha*, which would acquaint me with the life and principles of his grandfather, Lahiri Mahasaya. And he was insistent that I should ask my parents' permission. In procuring their blessing and good wishes, he said, my spiritual development in this field could proceed without hindrance.

'Fortunately, my parents had always been open-minded. My father went to visit Satya Charan Lahiri once and was happy for me. He gave his blessing wholeheartedly, saying that I had been on this path from an early age.

'Many years later my father read *Purana Purusha* himself with great interest. In time, my mother was also initiated into Kriya Yoga by a *Guru-brother*, as was my wife.'

'THE INITIATION was easy for me, and Satya Charan Lahiri[7] was happy. He told me that I had practised Kriya Yoga in my previous life. I went every day to check that I was practising properly, and to report the things I was experiencing.'

❖ ❖ ❖ ❖ ❖ ❖ ❖ ❖

A man went to see his Guru.

'Can you give me a *Mantra* so that I will be able to walk on water?' he asked.

'If that is what you really want,' replied the Guru, and gave him the *Mantra*.

---

[7] In speech, Guruji (Prakash Shankar Vyas) always refers to his Guru, Satya Charan Lahiri as "Guruji", because, as previously mentioned, it is not respectful to refer to one's Guru by name. But since I also refer to my own Guru (Prakash Shankar Vyas) as "Guruji" throughout the book, and it is he who is speaking here, I am using either the name Satya Charan Lahiri, or Satya Charanji (the suffix *ji* is a term of endearment and respect in India) in Guruji's own speech in order to avoid confusing the reader.

The man faithfully practised the *Mantra* for sixteen years until the day came when he visited his Guru with the proud announcement,

'I have mastered the *Mantra* you gave me, and can walk on the water surface.'

'Really?' asked his Guru, 'would you not care to show me?'

The disciple was more than willing to demonstrate, thinking how pleased his Guru would be with him. They went to the river and crossed over to the other side together.

'The time which you have spent for this is worth two *paisa*,' the Guru said.

'I don't understand what you mean,' replied the confused disciple.

'Listen. For two *paisa*, anyone can pay a boatman to row them across the river. You have wasted sixteen years of your life in the interest of showing off. Although you have gained a *Siddhi*, it is useless to you. Your ego is still there, and this is the greatest hurdle for God-realisation.'

A MANTRA could be a means to an end, but did not lead to self-realisation except in extremely rare cases, such as through the influence of the previous life, Guruji told me. At some point on the road to self-realisation, the *Mantra* became ineffective and obsolete without the support of *pranayama*. *Mantras* could not help the vast majority of people, and were useful primarily as a tool to develop concentration.

Apart from the *Mantras* to heal all kinds of disease, India held a vast treasure store of *Mantras* for many other things. For example, if you perfected one particular *Mantra* and chanted it whilst throwing a small amount of water from your hand on a raging forest fire, you could extinguish it instantaneously, though it would take the emergency helicopters several days to fight the fire from the air.

Trailanga Swami was renowned for making himself invisible. He would be sitting on the bank of the Ganges one minute and then suddenly disappear. There was a *Mantra* for this, so it was a power that man could have. It was not some form of magic. However, to perfect such a *Mantra* was extremely difficult. Nowadays there were few gurus who knew the real *Mantras*, and how to chant them properly. Depending on one's concentration and influence of the previous life, mastery of a single *Mantra* could take anything from a couple of months to many years.

Apparently, it was something of a problem in Lahiri Mahasaya's time that people would learn and master powerful *Mantras* only to misuse their ability afterwards.[8] Even nowadays, there were many people who took advantage of others' ignorance of these things. Some so-called self-realised gurus had developed various powers, relying on man's fascination for miracles to attract huge numbers of followers, although their own interest in self-realisation had been clouded by their own ego. It was not always easy to distinguish between miracles performed in a natural way for a spiritual purpose, and those practised in the cause of self-interest, for example to make money, through ego. Yet if a person's primary aim was to publicly perform miracles, they would not be able to guide others to the goal of Absolute Reality.

Therefore in theory, a man could spend many years perfecting a *Mantra* in order to gain a *Siddhi* which did not advance him spiritually in the slightest, so that followers would fall at his feet. If he chose to work towards self-realisation instead, it would mean rejection of that same power. So my next question was, did the self-realised saint or Yogi not possess all of the *Siddhis*, or yogic powers anyway?

Of course the self-realised Yogi could perform miracles too, Guruji confirmed. But when yogic power came in a natural way, it was another matter. The difference was that because the ego had been conquered, the Yogi possessed something much greater: the wisdom to know when to use those powers for spiritual advancement. The most famous masters came to fill a spiritual void at a particular time. The reason why they performed miracles openly was to give a wide-reaching example. But otherwise, the yogic master remained hidden, tempted neither to show off nor to interfere with the flow of nature. He would only perform a so-called miracle when absolutely necessary, and the disciple

---

[8] To quote from *Lahiri Mahasaya's Commentaries on the Yoga Sutras of Patanjali*: "... yogic powers, while undoubtedly useful on the practical plane of life, are nevertheless great impediments to the attainment of Samadhi, or attunement with the ultimate Self. / Hence, no sincere truth-seeker will ever exhibit such powers for material gain knowing (full) well that it would only obstruct or delay inner Realisation. / This ... makes crystal clear that Yoga is not a matter of working miracles, exhibiting yogic powers, but is strictly the instrument to realising the ultimate Self." (explanation of Sutra no. 38.)

concerned would not understand that he had been helped unless it was in the interest of his spiritual advancement.

When man experienced something as extraordinary as a miracle, it could affect him deeply and have the power to change the meaning and direction of his life. However, if miracles became a regular occurrence in a person's life, they would soon seem cheap and meaningless. That was yet another reason why the Yogi worked in secret and in silence. Those with sharp vision had to learn to recognise the smaller but no less significant signs.

FROM time to time I used to wonder about the kind of yogic powers Guruji had mastered himself, although instinct told me from the beginning that this was one subject he would never talk about, and that it would be disrespectful to ask. Guruji later acknowledged to me that being confronted directly with such questions, as he had been a few times, could be likened to an ordinary person being asked by a complete stranger to undress to full nakedness before them.

In time I also came to understand that, since entering the Kriya Yoga field, Guruji had not been tempted by *Siddhis,* or had any desire to do anything which the world would perceive as miraculous. In Kriya Yoga, the main aim and direct route to self-realisation involved the destruction of human ego. The side-effects which resulted from practice were secondary. Although these could be useful on some level, he said that they were the impediments towards God-realisation. Even as a beginner in yoga when he had successfully experimented with the power of *Mantra* on rainfall, he had seen how the ego liked to indulge in the thought of having supernatural power. And consequently, that there was no spirituality in practising such things.

'Some people are taught that levitation is the ultimate goal of their meditation practice. This is a serious misconception,' Guruji said.

'Others will categorically deny that man can go beyond the force of gravity; that levitation is a myth. It is correct that the ordinary person will never defy gravity, because it is impossible to do so without practice. However, it is true that an advanced Yogi may levitate. Everything is possible with practice. But who can understand this? Who will practise Kriya Yoga and see if it is possible to levitate? Who will practise Kriya Yoga with such a great love and desire to know God?'

Guruji added that there was no need for books or even for a belief in God in order for internal knowledge to be found and tapped into. If someone had the inclination, they were free to find out if this was correct for themselves. It was not a matter of belief or conversion.

Guruji told me that after Kriya initiation, one of the first questions he had asked Satya Charan Lahiri was whether it was possible for man to levitate and go against gravitational force.

'If you throw a stone into water, people will say that it cannot float, it will sink,' Satya Charan had answered. 'But it is true that it can float.'

DURING his first visit to England, Guruji and his family were invited to some friends of my parents for dinner. He told me afterwards of how the hostess had asked him to explain what a miracle was.

'Everyone was quiet and I was thinking how to answer her question,' he said. 'But a miracle is only Love; and Love is impossible to define. No one can ever define Love. So we sat in silence and I did not answer her. How could I? The woman was probably thinking what a foolish person she had invited. But mostly people imagine that a miracle is something akin to magic. What I feel about it is very different. This matter can never be put into words. Who will understand? When you write about yoga and the things we have been discussing, especially about healing and sickness, most people will read and try to understand with their intellect. It will not be clear to everyone. Remember that without practice, there is little to be said.'

ANGEL IN DISGUISE (A Song)

Taking a walk down the lane
And imagination
Follows close behind
A world of fascination
Taking pity and love
To the temple inside
She bows down her head and enters inside

The faded tones of the clothes she wears
Wrinkled cheeks and greying hair
Lost are cares in sacred memory
Hands are folded to the deity
Devotion has taken her there

There's something about her caring eyes
Mystical and black, and supremely wise
So you stop and stare in the stillness of her worship
Seems like an angel in disguise
An angel in disguise

Watching people passing by
In silent recreation
Lingering and lonely
Wanting God's consideration
She always does the best she can
Flowers and sweets held in her hands

Chapter Twelve

CONFIDENCE AND STRENGTH

Walking the Narrow Path

"Because strait is the gate and narrow is the way,
which leadeth unto life, and few there be that find it." – CHRIST JESUS[1]

'There was no limit to the amount I practised Kriya Yoga at the beginning, for it seemed from the outset as if it were my only purpose in life. At the time I wasn't working so my routine consisted of eating, sleeping and practice. The only time I would leave the house was to visit my Guru Satya Charan Lahiri to report how Kriya was going. He would explain about many aspects of practice and answer my questions. One week after the initiation, my tongue was in *Khechari mudra*, but he said it had to go further and gave me a date by which time this element of practice had to be complete. It reached there on the exact date he had said, in less than two weeks. He was happy.

'At first there were many things coming in *Kutastha*, but after a short time I stopped seeing things in the eyebrow centre during Kriya practice. I was upset, but Satya Charanji laughed when I told him. He said that it was a good sign, and there was no reason to imagine that anything was wrong.

'One day, I was telling Satya Charanji about some experiences in Kriya Yoga and asking him about levitation. He smiled very softly and told me about his first experience of *Samadhi*. He described how there was a pleasant smell, and then he felt as if his body were moving first in one direction and then the other – he was telling me indirectly that he levitated in that state – and after that the feeling in his body gradually left. It meant that he was not in the body any

---

[1] St. Matthew 7:14

more, his mind was fully absorbed in Self. When he came back to this level he could see his body in that state, and suddenly there was a feeling of suffocation. He got up and went to the open window to take deep breaths. Actually, it is a feeling like a gas balloon, when it is opened and the air comes out.

'Sometimes during a visit to Satya Charanji, I would massage him whilst he talked. Once I was massaging for a long time, and he became quiet; then I began to notice that there was no sign of life in his body. But I carried on, thinking to stop only when he asked me to. After about half an hour, he opened his eyes and said,

' "Oh, you are still massaging. You must be tired. Stop now." And then I knew that he had not been in his body at that time.

'For several months following my initiation, I searched for a job without success. Then finally I was offered a position in a company which had recently moved to Varanasi. I was reluctant to take it, but Satya Charanji said that it was important for the Kriya practitioner to have a job, according to the principles which his grandfather established. And especially since there was a family to take care of, he said that it was a question of giving an example. At the time I had no idea that he wanted me to be a Guru in the future after him.

'So the work began. My company manufactured pumps and fans and at the beginning I struggled under the workload. It was difficult to remember everything because of doing so much Kriya. During the first week I made a terrible mistake which could have cost both my senior overseer and myself our jobs.

'It was the end of season discount period and I made out an invoice in the book selling a customer fans amounting to 50,000 rupees. When my supervisor checked my work, he was shocked to see that the amount I should have charged was actually 150,000 rupees, since the fans which had been ordered were not of a colour included in the sale. The bill carried my signature and it was too late to reverse the situation by the time the mistake was noticed, so the responsibility for a loss of 100,000 rupees to the company lay on my shoulders. My supervisor said that we would both be fired. Of course I was upset and felt terrible for my supervisor who had worked at the company for more than twenty years. I prayed silently to Satya Charanji, not knowing what to do. It seemed unfair to be punished as a result of doing a spiritual practice.

'The next day when I went to work, the supervisor was looking through the invoice book again and said that he couldn't find the mistake. We looked together and found that the writing on that wrong order now showed the correct amount in both figures and words. Nothing was out of place or torn and it was still my handwriting, yet neither of us could understand how it could be. A change was not humanly possible. My supervisor was shocked; to my mind it was a miracle. So there was no problem when the customer came to pay the bill.

'After that, despite being under great pressure whilst working for that company, help always seemed to be at hand which took me through many difficulties. A few months passed and my boss offered me an executive position as head of one of the departments. It was my job to entertain prominent customers in my private office when they came, to present our products and answer queries about the company. But hardly any customers came, so sometimes I would see someone for five minutes and then no one else for the rest of the day. It seemed to be a tailor-made job for me and I could sit and meditate freely. Another person might have been bored. But it was a wonderful change after the stress of the first months.

'A security guard was posted outside my office and a runner appointed to fetch files whenever I needed them, who also brought me tea. Whenever they had a break they came and sat with me. They soon understood that I was doing some kind of yoga practice, and the security guard used to close the curtains of my office and tell me that he would warn me in time if someone was coming. They used to ask my advice with great faith and I would give it. Some things happened in their favour also.'

'SATYA CHARANJI gave me the authority to teach Kriya early on. But the first time I realised it was when some Bengali disciples came to visit him at the house whilst I was also there. They did not know me. And he said to them,

' "Do you know who this is? He will be the person for Kriya Yoga in Banaras after me." They stared at me, and I wondered why he had said such a thing. But shortly afterwards, another disciple who was a doctor came to see him, and again Satya Charanji introduced me as the person who would be initiating others in Varanasi. It was something that he repeated several times, and before he left his body, he instructed me again that he wanted me to initiate disciples into Kriya Yoga. There was no official declaration, so some disciples knew that he had given me this authority, whilst others were unaware.

'It was a surprise to many of Satya Charanji's disciples, especially to those who had been with him for many years, because I found him less than two years before he left his body. But he initiated me in all the stages of Kriya within ten months.

'Then, a few months after his *Mahasamadhi*, I started to teach yoga. One of my *Guru-brothers* reminded me that when Lahiri Mahasaya returned to Banaras after Babaji had given him Kriya, he did not make any publicity and the people still came to him. At the beginning, even though not everyone knew I had been given this authority, it began to happen. Since Satya Charanji's *Mahasamadhi*, people have been coming to this place for initiation in Kriya Yoga.'

❖ ❖ ❖ ❖ ❖ ❖ ❖ ❖

Vandana confessed to me how confused and upset she had been directly following Guruji's Kriya initiation. For the most part of a year, her husband had shut himself in a locked room. It used to make her feel jealous and she would imagine that he must be in the room with another woman. But he was meditating almost throughout day and night. He would hardly speak to anyone. No one could understand what had happened to him, and she had not been the only one who was worried at the time. She and her mother-in-law used to peep through the keyhole in an attempt to see what he was doing. There were times when the entire family thought that he must have gone mad.

At nights, she used to disturb Guruji by prodding and tickling him as he sat like a stone statue meditating on the bed. She had not been able to understand what he was doing. But soon she and her mother-in-law were both initiated in Kriya Yoga by a *Guru-brother* and since then, she had understood to let him be whilst he was practising.

Their married life returned to normal over time, and then Satya Charanji authorised Guruji to teach Kriya Yoga, for he was practising all the stages of Kriya correctly. In this he was a rare disciple.

It gradually became clear why Satya Charan Lahiri was not more open about authorising Guruji to teach after him: he was well aware of the temptation fame and publicity may present even to an advanced practitioner, and also knew that when it became public knowledge that a person had been authorised to initiate Kriya, large numbers of people would come asking for the method. Drawn by publicity rather than by a genuine spiritual yearning, such crowds generally consisted of people who were little more than curious. Yet at that time, it was very important for Guruji to be able to concentrate on his own Kriya practice without the kind of distraction which would have resulted had the news been published far and wide. So instead several trusted disciples were told and it was otherwise kept quiet.

'And he does not give Kriya initiation to everyone who asks,' Vandana told me. 'Some people have to wait and others never receive it. In the past ten years since Satya Charanji authorised him to teach Kriya Yoga, he has initiated less than eighty people. I know because he never initiates more than two people at a time, if they are husband and wife, and he writes all the names and addresses in a book. One Indian devotee has been coming here to ask for Kriya for the past six years. Guruji used to tell him, "When the time will come." Now he has called that man for initiation next month.'

I was reminded of the time I visited the house of one Indian so-called guru of Kriya Yoga on a day of spiritual significance. I was aware that he had achieved a measure of fame abroad, so it was astonishing to witness a show of transparent pride: full of his own greatness, he blessed the crowd who had come. My Hindi was not good enough to catch everything that he was saying, but the Indian friend who had accompanied me summed up the gist: he made wild claims about his latest miracles; told how he helped his sick and needy disciples and even called on the people present to come and touch his feet.

Later I came across a few of the written English lectures which this man had given abroad, and had noted that he was academically brilliant. However, his philosophy of Kriya Yoga was scattered with various ideas which were quite foreign to me. Several Kriya practitioners who knew him well, alleged that he had not mastered the first step in Kriya himself, namely *Khechari mudra*. Yet he was willing to initiate anyone who would fill in a form and pay a substantial fee in dollars. But for one reason or another, he did not seem to want questions: his speeches tended to over-emphasise that when the disciple had nothing to ask, it was a miracle and blessing indicative of the emptiness of mind.

What I observed at the yoga studio was quite a contrast. Admittedly, I did not know if Guruji was self-realised. How could I make any claims for him when he made none for himself? How was it possible to know all the things he did to help others when he kept these secret?

But that was exactly the point. He kept himself as hidden as his own Guru, Satya Charan Lahiri had done, and followed Lahiri Mahasaya's principles to the letter. Vandana told me that when Guruji's disciples came to the house on the annual Guru-festival known as *Gurupurnima*, he always told them to pay obeisance first to Babaji, then to Lahiri Mahasaya. He would tell them that they should not feel obliged to come and see him on that day. The only thing he wanted was for his disciples to carry on with their Kriya practice.

DURING my extended stays in India, I learned from Guruji that many Westerners who came to him for lessons were not practising the original method of Kriya Yoga as given by Lahiri Mahasaya. Guruji could not say who had changed the method, or why it had been changed.

'As far as the method is concerned,' Guruji said, 'a disciple initiated correctly and doing *Khechari mudra* properly can follow the path given by the masters with the correct scientific technique, yet these Westerners have been led to believe that self-realisation is possible through devotion alone. They have not learned the importance of *Khechari mudra*. Without doubt, I know that these people are immensely dedicated and have enormous faith in their gurus, and these are no doubt important qualities on the spiritual path. But do Westerners have the right to modify and simplify, as if indifferent to the original method? Man is man, wherever he comes from in the world.'

Guruji told me that when these people turned up at his yoga studio from time to time and showed him the method which they had been taught, he had seen that *Khechari mudra* was imagined rather than practised; *Nabhi Kriya* had almost been lost altogether;

Yoni mudra had been changed or omitted and the essential timing for *Kriya pranayama* and the other practices had become obsolete. They had not received the correct order for the stages of Kriya either. The method had been so unrecognisably altered that it could not be compared to Lahiri Mahasaya's Kriya Yoga.

When Guruji once told a devotee that the most important aspects given by Lahiri Mahasaya did not feature in her method, he received the reply that perhaps the guru at the head of her organisation did not consider such things necessary for Westerners. She had full faith that her guru and leader of the organisation knew the original Kriya practice, but thought that he must have some good reason for not passing it on.

If this were the case, Guruji said that it seemed as if the leaders wanted to make their members blind; they had established certain rules to dissuade people from questioning and searching. For whatever reason, they were not interested in seeing their disciples' progress. Moreover, it seemed that some organisations had turned Kriya Yoga into something resembling a church or sect, and hung monastic orders upon it.

'Apart from having changed the method,' Guruji said, 'they have strayed from the original source. They have forgotten who revived the lost practice, and they worship their guru only. Through publicity, the membership of these organisations is growing nonetheless, because people are not aware of the principles given by the Father of Kriya Yoga, Lahiri Mahasaya.

'My Guru Satya Charanji used to say that if someone was going to give lectures or teach the people, there should first be permanent soul-realisation,' Guruji added. 'He did not like the hypocrisy and deceit of people teaching without having proper experience in this yoga *sadhana*. He would say that although this kind of person may become rich in material benefits, they will never attain God-realisation in this manner.'

OVER the past half-century, interest in Kriya Yoga has increased enormously because of the publication of certain books.[2] Some

---

[2] The author of *Purana Purusha*, Dr A. K. Chatterjee, notes in the preface of his book that he wrote it under the guidance of Satya Charan Lahiri, who "repeatedly cautioned (him) to sequentially arrange true facts and essences, never to include any wrong facts or essences, or imaginary, baseless tales produced by the writer, which have been noticed in previous biographies."

imagine that they will reach the level of a Yogi and be able to perform miracles within a month. More and more gurus advertise their own expertise, taking full advantage of people's ignorance, and everyone receives a different Kriya Yoga.

There are gurus who offer a "short cut Kriya Yoga technique", claiming that five to fifteen minutes of practice per day is sufficient for self-realisation. Ironically, rather than the emphasis being on the main aim of Kriya, which is self-realisation achieved through the destruction of ego and worldly desires, they sell their alternative techniques by advertising health benefits; better sex; a more beautiful body; riches and every conceivable worldly desire fulfilled. They also maintain that everyone can practise. This may be true as far as their own method is concerned, but it should not be imagined that they are passing on Lahiri Mahasaya's Kriya Yoga.

Other false gurus publicise the myth that *Samadhi* can be attained with a single touch on the head. In India, this is known as the *Shakti* path. It is tempting for people to believe because it implies that no practice is necessary and sounds like an easy solution to a multitude of problems. But the idea that super-consciousness is possible in a moment usually gets propagated through blind faith. A group of people can easily get carried away by something they are supposed to experience but do not, by convincing themselves that they feel the same thing as their neighbour, perhaps for fear of being considered a lesser person.

Self-realisation in an instant is impossible, because this level of consciousness only comes once a person has worked to completely free themselves of ego, hatred, desire, and so on. Such deep-rooted negative human traits cannot disappear in a split second. More to the point, no one can control their breath through self-will alone. It takes practice.

There are exceptional instances: as when Babaji touched Lahiri Mahasaya on the head, making his disciple go into *Samadhi* and recall his past life in the cave. But this was only possible because Lahiri Mahasaya was already on that spiritual level due to the influence of his previous life.

RECENTLY I went to a lecture by an Indian evangelical Christian who told about his conversion to Christianity. During the first part of his discourse he won gasps of horror from his audience with tales of how the teachings of Hinduism had made him believe that he himself was God, not to mention how he had worshipped the cow, the River Ganges and his guru as gods. Then he went on to warn his audience about yoga and meditation, for he had ample experience of the dangers involved in such practices: on one hand there were the most spectacularly colourful astral journeys, and on the other, terrifying confrontations with demons and devils. He became so crazy and violent through "yoga" that he came close to killing someone, which prompted his conversion to Christianity. He had met innumerable gurus in his life, though evidently no genuine ones. Regrettably, his superficial understanding of Hinduism, plus the impact of many unfortunate experiences, had left an indelible mark which he evidently relished stamping on the minds of the several hundred present willing to hang onto his every word.

The mental damage which can be caused when a disciple is wrongly instructed in an esoteric method by a false guru is not to be underestimated. One undesirable effect can be unnatural dependency leading to an individual's inability to work or function socially in the world. At worst, the consequences of misplaced trust can be fatal, if side-effects such as confusion, physical pain or even derangement are not taken seriously. Any individual who experiences such symptoms as a result of a "yoga practice" they have been given should stop immediately. Yoga means "union with God" and no legitimate practice of yoga meditation produces false dependency, unbalance or suffering.

It can also be dangerous for a person to attempt the practice of advanced methods of yoga meditation from books alone. The genuine initiate is able to understand seeming contradictions in the various written texts and explanations of Kriya Yoga, for example in commentaries by Lahiri Mahasaya, which the non-initiate would misinterpret. Let me reiterate in this context that Kriya Yoga is based entirely on the Guru-disciple path, and the genuine Guru can only initiate when the disciple is ready. Otherwise, no progress is possible.

As far as devils and demons are concerned, Lahiri Mahasaya told his disciples, "The devil is perpetually present within the mind; you should be aware that the mind should not concentrate on anything else other than the soul." In the same vein he said, "Just as, if day exists night also has to exist; if happiness exists misery also has to exist; similarly if the propitious deity exists, the unpropitious deity also exists."[3] It would follow that as long as there are genuine self-realised spiritual masters in the world, there will also be false gurus.

A SIMPLE metaphor will illustrate what is happening in the Kriya Yoga field nowadays as far as teachers are concerned:

Suppose you wanted to take piano lessons. Would you be fooled into thinking that a certain teacher was an expert because he had inherited the house of a concert pianist who no longer lived there? Would you go to a teacher who did not master the keyboard himself? Surely not. A teacher's intellectual knowledge on the theory of music and his ability to lead you through a tune with one finger would never be enough if you wanted to make progress on the instrument.

And when it came to the method of teaching: would you take a teacher seriously if he told you that you may play fast or slow as you please, for rhythm was unimportant? Would you believe him if he took away certain keys on the piano, claiming that if there were less notes it would be easier for you to play? After all, he would say, you were only a beginner who was bound to play imperfectly at first, so the piano would have to be adapted to suit your incompetence.

Again, the answers would be 'no'. The piano keys should be in the right place from the outset and you would expect to be taught the correct rules of reading music. Mistakes have always been an inevitable part of the learning curve. Furthermore, you know that no one becomes a concert pianist within a week or two; years of practice, discipline and determination are required.

Alterations made to anything which has a scientific basis, including music and yoga, will never make a master of the beginner, however much time is dedicated to practice. Chapter Five on Kriya Yoga provides some helpful advice on how to recognise the original method, especially for those who have already been given Kriya Yoga or are seeking initiation.

---

[3] From *Purana Purusha* by Dr A. K. Chatterjee.

According to Guruji, if the correct method and principles handed down through these three generations of masters beginning with Lahiri Mahasaya is not followed, then there is no sense in practising Kriya Yoga. History repeats itself, hence permission was granted for this information to be published in the hope that the true Kriya Yoga might not be completely lost to the world yet again.

MANY Westerners are actively looking for spiritual guidance nowadays, Guruji once told me. And they will find the person they need at the appointed time according to their inner nature. If someone is looking for a famous guru who openly performs miraculous feats, that is precisely what they will find. If they are serious and committed in their desire for true spiritual development, they will be led to a different kind of teacher who can guide them. Those with a connection to a spiritual master will find one, whether they search for a Guru or not.

Not everyone is destined to find a spiritual Guru. But it is always helpful to believe that God is everywhere; to know that there is a supreme power and to think of oneself as a small river which has to find the ocean; to follow social law, and to be wary of the tricks played by the ego. Having not realised God, it is better to accept that there is something greater than oneself, rather than to deny Him altogether.

In the Hindu tradition, people have to go to the temple, find a guru and follow a spiritual path. Because of this social expectation, many found and accepted Satya Charan Lahiri as their guru. They sought his advice and listened to his teachings for many years, whilst never realising that he was a Yogi until after he took *Mahasamadhi*, when the close disciples began to talk more openly about their experiences with him.

Guruji and his friend met Satya Charan Lahiri on the same day, yet the friend was not drawn towards the master. Some time later he found a different guru and received *Mantra* initiation. This was what he wanted and was ready for at that point in his life.

Development has to come in a natural way and can never be forced. Pressure is one of the greatest hindrances to learning. Even when we have found the guru who is right for us, it is not always easy to stay on the path he or she has shown us.

GURUJI told a story to illustrate:

A man decided to take his calf to the next village in order to sell it. Three rogues watched him hoist the young animal onto his shoulders, and started to plot amongst themselves how they could steal it from him. They had soon devised a cunning plan.

A few miles along the road, the man was approached by a stranger who asked him,

'Why are you carrying a dog around your neck?'

'What a question!' he exclaimed. 'This is a calf, not a dog,' and after a heated argument the man continued on his journey, feeling somewhat annoyed by the strange encounter. He felt his forehead to see if he had a fever. It was decidedly cool.

'Perhaps I misunderstood,' he thought to himself. But a short while later he met a second man.

'Friend!' the stranger cried, at pains to suppress a devilish grin, 'where are you taking the old dog?'

'It is a calf,' replied the man with a trace of anger in his voice, 'and I shall be selling it at the market this afternoon.'

'My dear fellow, I don't blame you for wanting to get rid of the wretched thing, but nowadays if you want someone to take a dog from you, you're the one who will be parting with money!' He laughed heartily at his own joke.

As they passed, the man turned around and glanced dubiously at the animal on his shoulders.

'This is ridiculous!' he told himself. 'I left with a calf to sell at the market. This is a calf!' But he felt unsettled and his head was beginning to throb under the relentless glare of the midday sun. His four-legged load was weighing down on his neck and shoulders.

By the time the third rascal passed him and enquired if he always carried a dog on his shoulders, the man was utterly convinced that he had become mad or was not seeing properly any more. In distressed panic, he dropped the valuable calf, and ran home. The thieves rejoiced in the success of their cunning ruse.

'IT IS AN EXAMPLE of how nature is always playing games with us,' Guruji explained. 'It is hiding around every corner waiting to test our strength. With your experience in Kriya Yoga, you already know that it is not easy to control the mind and stay dedicated in practice. We start the journey by walking in the right direction, wanting to discover our spiritual nature, but soon attraction comes again for worldly things. It is easy to stop practice and forget the internal world. But if we succumb to this temptation, we lose the precious thing that we once held in our hands.'

The Eternal Existence of a Sadguru

"Be thou faithful unto death,
and I will give thee a crown of life." – ST. JOHN[4]

'One day in the summer of 1986, Satya Charan Lahiri said, "Now the time has come for my death." He was eighty-two years old by then. I told him not to talk like that because I didn't want to hear or believe that the time was approaching when he would go. But he was serious. He repeated that the signs of death were appearing in his body, and that he had to leave this world. He had already decided to take *Mahasamadhi* on *Gurupurnima* in July of that year.

'By the time of the festival, everyone had heard the news and the house was packed with disciples who had come to see Satya Charan Lahiri for the last time. Everyone was grieving, and calling him to change his mind and stay at least a few more years.

'Satya Charan was quiet and serious during the *puja* ceremonies of the morning, and came downstairs at about twelve noon. Everyone had already been given *prasad*, the benediction from the temple. He blessed his disciples and devotees and said how happy he was to see everyone. He looked close to tears and his voice was choked. Then he went to his grandfather's statue in the temple and lay down. We could hear him praying and weeping in there for about ten minutes. It seemed as if everyone gathered outside was in a state of shock, because nobody moved or said a word.

'To the surprise of everyone present, he suddenly got up and returned to his normal self. Addressing the crowd, he said, "Your desire has been fulfilled." And he went back up the stairs to rest in his room.

---

[4] Revelation 2:10

'So he didn't leave his body on the day he was supposed to after all. When I went to see him a few days later, he smiled and told me that he had been given a six-month extension. He hinted that whilst he was in the temple on *Gurupurnima*, someone reminded him that he was not yet free to leave the world. It was then that he remembered a promise made to Professor Tarak Nath Sanyal forty years ago, to cash the eighteen thousand rupee bond when it finally matured. This bond had been purchased for the temple in 1946 and the interest had covered the cost of *puja* and various charitable activities ever since. Satya Charan Lahiri was the only claimant to the bond, and without his signature, the money would have been seized by the bank. Not even close family members could have accessed it. A devotee who was a retired treasurer helped Satya Charanji through the formalities of what turned out to be a complex business matter, and the money was cleared a month after the bond matured, in October of the same year.

'After that, Satya Charan Lahiri did not declare the date of his departure or talk about leaving his body any more. So everyone began to hope that perhaps he would stay for a few more years. However, when his daughter-in-law became seriously ill and the doctors feared for her life, Satya Charanji reassured her by saying that she would stay in the world and he would go. And hearing about her illness, a devoted woman disciple from Bengal named Chandana came to look after the household and to take care of Satya Charanji.'

'THE DAY Satya Charan Lahiri chose to leave his body was on his birthday, 22nd January 1987. Just a few days previously he warned me once more that his time was coming, but didn't say the exact date. When it happened I was at work in the office, and later learned the events of that day from fellow disciples who were present in the household:

'In the morning, Satya Charanji asked a disciple to tell Chandana to bring a pot of Ganges water up to his room. The request was forgotten, so when the same disciple returned, Satya Charan asked for Ganges water to be brought again, and the disciple said he would bring the water himself. But Satya Charan remained insistent that Chandana should bring it. When Chandana received the message, she thought it unusual but obliged without question.

'It was a particularly cold and dark day, and in the early evening

Bhajan and Kirtan began as usual in the temple downstairs. Satya Charan sent all but one of the disciples who were in his room to go downstairs and listen. For some time, he was in *Shambhavi mudra*, then he lay down on the bed to relax.

'At six o'clock he sat up facing east and made *pranayama*, drawing a long breath up to the eyebrow centre. Then he lay back down on the bed. The one disciple remaining in the room became nervous. He didn't understand what was happening, and called a few of the others to come back upstairs.

'Satya Charan Lahiri's face was red and a swelling was appearing at the eyebrow centre. The scene fitted the description he had given of his own father Tinkari Lahiri's *Mahasamadhi*. It was as though a small, quivering ball was pushing that part of the forehead out from underneath. As soon as Chandana entered the room, she realised immediately that he was leaving his body, for otherwise he would not have been so insistent that she should be the one to bring Ganges water to his room.

'It is Hindu tradition for a Brahmin to put tulsi leaves or Ganges water into the mouth of someone who is dying, and to read from the *Bhagavad Gita*.[5] Chandana was a Brahmin herself, and understood that Satya Charan intended to uphold the religious traditions of Hindu society as an example to his disciples even in his last moment on earth. Although he was self-realised, he had always taught, like his grandfather, that such customs were not to be neglected despite Kriya practice. Satya Charan had chosen Chandana, and the faithful woman disciple knew what she had to do. Taking the pot of Ganges water from where she had placed it earlier in the day, she put a few drops into his mouth. Everyone present heard a long "ahhh" of satisfaction, as if he had received exactly what he had been waiting for. Then Chandana laid the *Bhagavad Gita* and a garland of tulsi leaves on the chest of Guruji's motionless body.

'So that was how my Guru, Satya Charan Lahiri, left his body. In retrospect, many of us understood why he did not make any announcement the second time, and why he sent the other disciples downstairs to listen to the devotional songs in the temple

---

[5] The tulsi leaf is a symbol of purification for the Hindu, and Holy Ganges water a symbol of freedom from further incarnation; therefore both of these are considered to give the soul peace in the last moments before death.

that evening. The final *Mahasamadhi* when *Pan* and *Apan* are raised together and kept at the eyebrow centre requires perfect concentration. It is the Yogi's final accomplishment to cease vibration in the *Chakras* completely and in so doing, to leave earthly existence forever. Satya Charanji had not wanted to be disturbed by weeping disciples begging him not to go.'

'AT THE EXACT time of his departure, I was about to leave my office when someone came in from the bike shop, offering me a calendar for the New Year. I opened it and there was a picture of *Krishna* standing and giving his blessing to Arjuna, with the stanza from the *Bhagavad Gita*: "Your duty is to work, not to reap the fruits of work."[6] It was a nice calendar and I took it home with me.

'The following day, my *Guru-brother* Mr Lal came to the office in the morning and told me that our Guru had taken *Mahasamadhi*. I excused myself from work to go to the house with him.

'His body was lying on ice and decorated with flower garlands. Everyone was standing around him and crying. The air was thick with incense and sandalwood. His children and other close relatives and disciples living in other cities had been informed and were on their way to see him.

'There were some doubts about whether he might come back to his body, so Satya Charanji was kept there for two days. His face was shining and everyone was shocked because it looked as though he were only sleeping. But on that first evening a doctor had come and confirmed that there was no sign of life. However, there was no swelling and despite the ice cubes, his body remained warm, even the feet. It is Indian tradition to change the clothes and to anoint the body of our Guru with *ghee* and sandalwood powder. This was unusually easy to do because he was so soft and supple. There was no stiffness and he did not smell like a deceased person.

'Later three or four disciples who were medical doctors re-examined him to check that it was alright to take him for cremation, but finally it was decided that these anomalies were all signs of a Yogi.[7]

---

[6] The second part of the stanza reads, "Do not seek rewards, but do not love laziness either." II:47 (Lal)

[7] Satya Charan Lahiri's body showed no signs of what is medically defined as rigor mortis, or the stiffening of the body after death. For the ordinary person, rigor mortis sets in about thirty minutes after the heart has stopped beating and only wears off between four and seven days later.

'During the few days prior to the last rites whilst we waited for the close family members to arrive, the atmosphere was bleak. The house was full of weeping and outside a thick blanket of fog hung over Varanasi. Finally, on the afternoon of 24th January, the sun penetrated through the fog and everyone felt some relief that at least the weather was better.

'It was Satya Charanji's will to be laid at his grandfather's feet in the temple for a few minutes before being taken for cremation, and this was done before we carried him to Manikarnika Ghat. His *Mahasamadhi* was announced in the newspaper and there was a long funeral procession of about five hundred disciples and devotees. The rites were performed according to our Hindu Scriptures, and after the cremation everyone remained in silence for a long time. There was a tangible feeling of great loss and emptiness in the crowd.

'In India, after going to the burning *ghat*, we have to take a bath in the Ganges. In winter the water is usually cold, but everyone noticed that the water was warm that day. Nobody felt cold during or after their bath. It was strange.

'Then we returned to the house for sweets, and according to social custom, everyone was invited to the feast which takes place thirteen days after the funeral.'

'IN THE DAYS which followed, I could not control my weeping. I was sure that I had seen my Guru for the last time. But the third night after the cremation, during a midnight attempt to practise Kriya in spite of my tears, Satya Charanji suddenly appeared. He was surrounded by a burning light, and his body was shining. He looked so strong and healthy. He was in a sitting position parallel to the eyebrow centre, and asked me why I was weeping.

' "I have lost you," was my reply.

' "No, the *Sadguru's* existence is forever. I am with you always in *Kutastha*. I have not gone anywhere. There is no need to weep for my physical appearance."

'His words made me realise that my tears were for his physical body. When the time comes, everyone has to go. Not even a Yogi stays in the earthly form for long. I had thought that he was confined to a body, because previously it was possible to see him at any time, but since that day I feel that he is everywhere.

'I never wept for him again. His energy is always present and it is as if his shadow shelters me at every step. This is my experience.'

❖ ❖ ❖ ❖ ❖ ❖ ❖ ❖

On the subject of perfected spiritual masters, there was one master whom we had not yet discussed: Lahiri Mahasaya's own Guru, known simply as "Babaji". A perusal of the yoga shelves in several bookshops back home indicated that various writers were claiming to have met, or lived with, this particular Babaji.

Several points have to be taken into account, Guruji said.

Westerners frequently do not realise that *Baba* is a way to address someone with respect, in recognition of their qualities such as nobleness and innocence. *Baba* can also mean "father" in both Bengali and Hindi, and "grandfather" in Hindi. The suffix *ji* can be added to any name to show endearment and give respect, as in "Guruji". In India, most *sadhus* are addressed as "Babaji". It is not a unique name in the slightest. Anyone can travel to the Himalayas and return with a report that they have met Babaji. And these days there are plenty of *sadhus* making money from foreigners by claiming to be Lahiri Mahasaya's Babaji.

People used to assert their right to take Kriya initiation from Satya Charan Lahiri, saying that Babaji had appeared to them in person. The master would ask them why they had not taken initiation directly from Babaji if that were the case, and send them away. In the Introduction of *Purana Purusha*, Satya Charan Lahiri suggests that individuals who allege such an encounter wish "to increase their dignity." Then he adds, "At present I know about four *Babajis*. Besides them, how many more *Babajis* exist, I cannot tell."

Satya Charan Lahiri also draws attention to the other stories about his grandfather which indicate how difficult it was for anyone to see Babaji:

For a start, when Lahiri Mahasaya called Babaji to appear to the unbelieving group of people shortly after his own initiation, Babaji told him sternly that he was not for show.

During his grandfather's lifetime, many people had an unrequited desire to see Babaji. Tarak Nath Sanyal was highly advanced in Kriya Yoga and once asked Lahiri Mahasaya to call

Babaji because he so wanted to see him. Lahiri Mahasaya replied that he did not think that Babaji would come, but that he would ask him. A few days later he told Tarak Nath Sanyal that Babaji did not wish to appear to him.

There was also the time when Babaji appeared to Satya Charan Lahiri's own father, Tinkari, and Lahiri Mahasaya forbade him ever to trouble Babaji again. He knew from personal experience that a *Sadguru* was bound to his promise. It was wrong to put a *Sadguru* under pressure because of personal will, just as a disciple should never make any demands of his own Guru.

These events indicated that in exceptional instances, Babaji might appear through a particularly strong desire if the person was on the higher planes of yoga, but by no means always. He certainly had no desire for members of the general public to see him.

Babaji did have other disciples in the Himalayas, but he told Lahiri Mahasaya that he was the only one whom he was authorising to teach Kriya Yoga. Otherwise he would have had no reason to wait forty years specifically for him. Babaji also gave an example when he sent a jealous disciple on his behalf to collect initiation money from Lahiri Mahasaya, so that he could see the master's great wisdom for himself and understand why Lahiri Mahasaya alone was chosen for the task of returning the lost practice to the world.

Since Babaji sent renunciants from his group to collect the initiation money from Lahiri Mahasaya rather than coming himself, it would appear unlikely that Babaji ever appeared in his human body to Lahiri Mahasaya after initiation. Nor did Lahiri Mahasaya travel to see his Guru. Yet Babaji promised to give his *Dharshan* whenever his disciple called. Lahiri Mahasaya's personal diaries spanning fourteen years indicate that Babaji came in his *astral body* during Kriya practice, and that regular contact was maintained between Guru and disciple on the spiritual planes.[8]

We understand from these diaries that Babaji was an incarnation

---

[8] In *Purana Purusha* by Dr A. K. Chatterjee, one of the relevant passages from Lahiri Mahasaya's confidential diaries including one written on 13th December, 1872 in Danapur is translated thus: "... while practising *sadhana* when the *Prana* air arose above the head, then I was united with Babaji. When I was united with Babaji, then I experienced the confidence of doing anything and everything or else tasks which could not be accomplished were now accomplished."

Another reads, "... *Sushumna* was awakened by the affection of the *Guru*, sometimes it is appearing, sometimes the effulgence can be experienced, I saw the *Sushumna* with naked eyes, in the states of awakening, dreaming and deep slumber, I held a conversation with *Gurudeva*." (Diary No.9, April 1872) of *Krishna*,[9] but Lahiri Mahasaya talked and wrote about his Guru simply as "Babaji". We do not know any other details about him such as his real name, his age, or where he came from. We do not know from whom he received Kriya Yoga, or exactly how he had Lahiri Mahasaya sent to Ranikhet for initiation. Nobody has ever taken a photograph of him.

Lahiri Mahasaya once made a very strange drawing of Babaji in his diary, writing that this was the shape of his Guru. The drawing makes it evident that he was seeing his Guru in *Kutastha*, but at the same time he intended to hide Babaji from the eyes of the curious.

'Such mystery gives people scope for imagination to write Babaji's life history. Next, they will say that they have met Babaji's guru,' Guruji said. 'Somebody actually told me a few weeks ago that Lahiri Mahasaya's Babaji called them on the telephone. If it is true, soon Babaji's e-mail address will also become available,' Guruji added with a chuckle.

'But to return to the many who are claiming to have met Babaji, or say that they have been given Kriya Yoga by him: Kriya initiation is never carried out by a saint appearing in a vision to someone. Some writers say that Lahiri Mahasaya appeared to them in a dream and authorised them to initiate Kriya Yoga. But this can never happen. Babaji could have come to Lahiri Mahasaya at any time and given him initiation and authorisation. However, when the time came, he called his disciple to Ranikhet with his yogic power and initiated Kriya in his physical body.

'The people alleging such events are also teaching a different Kriya Yoga. We cannot recognise it,' Guruji continued. 'They tell their disciples that they are advanced souls, so it is a mystery why they need Lahiri Mahasaya's diaries to teach things which the great master already explained in literal terms. They use his knowledge to compensate for their own lack of experience. If they do impress, it is because no other master in our age has given scriptural explanations as deep as those which Lahiri Mahasaya gave to the world.'

---

[9] Again from *Purana Purusha*, the translated handwritten note in Lahiri Mahasaya's diary (extract of 16th February 1873) reads, "... that Who is Krishna is the Revered Old Father or *Babaji Maharaja*." The author, Dr A. K. Chatterjee explains in another place that before Lahiri Mahasaya took birth as Shyama Charan Lahiri, he "notified His initial manifestation *Kutastha-Babaji* or Krishna-*Babaji* (*Kutastha* is Krishna) to remind this immortal yoga to (Shyama Charan) in due course; because it was obvious to (Him) that the moment He would mark His Advent as (Shyama Charan) He would remain oblivious about this immortal yoga. For this reason *Babaji* is Krishna ..."

I ASKED whether Satya Charan Lahiri used to communicate with Babaji, and Guruji nodded. But as with his father and grandfather before him, Babaji had only appeared to them in his spiritual form – in other words, in *Kutastha*. Satya Charan made it quite clear that there was no question of Babaji appearing to anyone in his physical form.

As for his own experiences around the time of *Sivaratri* in 1984 when a saint appeared, Guruji repeated that the man did not introduce himself with any name.

'How could I know who he was?' Guruji said. 'All I can say is that it seemed as if "Big Boss" was there. I described his appearance to Satya Charan Lahiri and told him the message which the saint had given. I didn't understand why Satya Charan wanted to know the man's name and why I hadn't asked for initiation.'

Guruji learned much later that he had been asked these questions because of people reading about Babaji and fabricating tales of their own meeting with him, in an attempt to convince Satya Charan Lahiri of their eligibility for Kriya Yoga initiation.

'You can write in your book that in the summer season of 1986, Satya Charan Lahiri told me that Babaji had left his physical body, and that he had been an incarnation,' Guruji said. 'He did not make public knowledge of this, for he knew what the reaction would be. Some people would criticise and others would start asking useless questions for the sake of curiosity. As usual, he preferred to keep silent.'

This was interesting news, since I had read that Babaji was supposed to be an immortal *Avatar*.

'People will believe what they want to believe,' Guruji answered. 'I can only pass on what Satya Charanji told me. It will be shocking news for many, because since then, no one can possibly have seen him in his physical form. As a *Sadguru*, he is everywhere. Just as Lahiri Mahasaya, Tinkari Lahiri and Satya Charan Lahiri are everywhere. When the sincere practitioner has a desire and great love and affection for them in the physical form, it is possible that they can assume that image, but shortly afterwards it also has to disappear.'

WHEN I asked whether or not a *Sadguru* could return to earth for a second coming, Guruji said that this was another misconception.

People had always believed that Jesus would return to earth, from the way he spoke about, "the Son of man coming in a cloud with power and great glory."[10] Guruji had even heard that some were spreading the news that Lahiri Mahasaya would be born again.

However, Lahiri Mahasaya never said that he would return to earth again and besides, this would be to misunderstand the significance of a *Mahasamadhi*. There was no rebirth when a Yogi left his body for the last time. It was the ultimate aim of Kriya Yoga, whereby the individual personality dissolved in the *Brahma-anu*.

Guruji added that the actual meaning of statements made by self-realised masters to the effect that they would come again was that we would see Him, or come face to face with God in *Kutastha* at the time of self-realisation, for every human being had *Kutastha* at their eyebrow centre. This was something which Lahiri Mahasaya himself explained.

'THIS way of communication and realisation is very different, and it is possible to be in touch with the *Sadguru* who is one's own Guru,' Guruji said. 'It cannot be told in words, but try to imagine something: you know that it is my habit to make *Pranam* and touch Lahiri Mahasaya's feet when I stand in front of a picture of him. The feeling comes automatically with that kind of respect. Now if I should see him in *Kutastha*, tell me how will I touch him with my hands or bow my head to him? How will I pray aloud to him when the tongue is in *Khechari mudra*? You have to think more deeply if you are going to understand.

'A number of Lahiri Mahasaya's disciples had to travel long distances to visit him, and he would frequently ask why they were so intent on seeing him. He would tell disciples that he would always be near the one who was practising Kriya.

'He wanted them to understand that he was already beyond the physical body, which would have to go when the time came; his shape and form could be found in *Kutastha*, so it was better for the disciple to keep their concentration on that point.'[11]

When I asked if another saint would take Babaji's place, Guruji

---

[10] St. Luke 21:27. Other references to the prophecy can be found in St. Matthew 16:28; St. Matthew 24:3,27,30,37,39 and St. Mark 13:26.

[11] As the master wrote in a letter to one of his disciples: "Why are you so anxious to see Me? What is the use of seeing My flesh and bones? Observe *Kutastha*, that is My Form, I am not flesh and bones or the word "I"." (from *Purana Purusha* by Dr A. K. Chatterjee.)

replied that this was not something he could explain. But he did imply that there was a certain system in this cosmos. When a practice for self-realisation like Kriya Yoga disappeared, God chose a particular person to revive it. So it was Babaji who appeared in the world to revive Kriya Yoga through Lahiri Mahasaya, and he waited for him until the time was ripe. But after some time his work on earth was finished.

My final question on this subject was how a *Sadguru* could appear in a form if he was everywhere, or whether such a vision existed only in the devotee's mind. Guruji answered that the pure mind could see a picture made up of atoms in a certain form, whether a Guru was in his physical form or not. It could come for a short while, in the same way that deities could be seen. The difference was that the Guru still living in his physical body could appear in his *astral* form, whereas this was no longer possible for the *Sadguru*.

Footsteps to Freedom

"Freedom is never to be reached by the weak. Throw away all weakness.
Tell your body that it is strong, tell your mind it is strong,
and have unbounded faith and hope in yourself." –
SWAMI VIVEKANANDA

'Perhaps as a concluding note for your book, let's review what we can learn from the lives of the spiritual masters and analyse some of the differing Eastern and Western religious viewpoints. We know that the stories which you are writing about Lahiri Mahasaya, Tinkari Lahiri and Satya Charan Lahiri are true events and not fairytales.

'The Christian may still feel some friction in his mind, if his church teaches that man either cannot or should not realise God; that everyone is a sinner.

'Therefore, here are my questions: the Christian believes that God sent Jesus to earth, or that he was God incarnate. Why has God's voice never resonated from the sky giving the message that He has decided to descend to earth? Why did God have to send a man to earth who was born as a small baby like the rest of mankind, who grew slowly day by day in a limited human body made up of the five elements and who also had to die when the time came? Since he was in the form of a human being, what is the reason that other human beings cannot realise the same thing as him?

'Jesus' life is an example which shows that something immortal exists in man. We know that he realised God, otherwise he would never have said, "As the Father knoweth me, even so know I the Father ..."[12] Jesus also directly commanded his disciples to take up the cross and follow him,[13] therefore it does not seem as if he wanted to deter his followers from walking the same path. If we think deeply about his example, to follow would be to understand what he understood. From their works after his ascension, and the symbolism contained in St. John's Book of Revelation, there is every reason to believe that he taught the secret way of practice to his close disciples even though he did not talk openly about it to the masses.

'Since Jesus Christ came in the form of a human being, his mission to show the pathway to God would have lacked credibility without the miracles he performed. The first thing he had to do was to awaken faith in his followers, otherwise no one would have believed the things he was saying. He commanded the waves, walked on water, healed the sick and raised the dead. So people saw that he was above the laws of nature and word travelled far and wide that God was appearing in Jesus Christ. Through his example, it is clear that he was self-realised.

'The idea that self-realisation is not possible originates from man's intellect. It is a wrong concept which has been propagated from one generation to another. Yet God-realisation is not a matter of belief but of practice.

'In terms of Indian philosophy, the definition of sin is to be far from God. We also have the idea of separation or dualism, because God and devotee are two, and without devotion we cannot realise God. Without a specific practice, it is sure that man is a "sinner" and will not be able to find God. But the moment he is in God and

---

[12] St. John 10:15
[13] "Whosoever will come after me, let him deny himself, and take up his cross, and follow me." St. Mark 8:34

realises Him, he is no longer a sinner.[14] He becomes as Jesus Christ was. Here in India we think that we first have to know what God is, before denying that man can reach the state of union with Him.

'Someone who is a fan of a particular rock or movie star may like to imitate that person's style or personality. But whenever we attempt to copy, however much we try to make another's idea our own, it never really becomes ours. Likewise, the idea that God is perfect would never have come to our human minds if the masters had not first realised Him and told us. Jesus was a perfect man, and he spoke about God's perfection. But how are we to know that God is perfect without realisation? We think that we know what this means, but are we not willing to understand the nature of perfection for ourselves?

'The thought that God is perfect can ease our worries if we believe that He can do anything for us. For the ordinary person, power belongs to a God who is outside of ourselves and cannot be realised. But we will never have direct experience of Him through reading or worshipping statues alone. In prayer, we try to fix our concentration on God. But in which direction do we have to think? Where is God? How should we pray? There is always separation in prayer. We say that God lives in our heart, but we are not literally talking about the organ which pumps blood around our body. People with a strong faith feel that there is some indescribable spiritual power acting in their lives, giving them love, strength and confidence. Yet few realise that the spiritual place where God lives in us is *Kutastha*, and that this is where He can be perceived with the inner eye.

'Our aim is to become One with God and this is the reason why there are numerous practices and methods in India. And there have been many saints and masters over the centuries here who became self-realised and spoke as Jesus did, each saying they were at one with their Heavenly Father. We cannot say that they were wrong.

'Supposing we see some ripe grapes above our head, but cannot reach them. We can either choose to say that they are not meant for us, or we can stand on a chair and reach up to them. In the same way, Kriya Yoga can bring man close to God. The more we are in touch with Soul, the more the mind becomes purified. Soul dwells

---

[14] Lahiri Mahasaya would also say that nobody was a sinner; it was the mind itself that became the sinner when it was not in *Kutastha*.

in every human being whilst not being attached to the body. It is unlimited and cannot sin.

'We tend to view the human body superficially. We only see its limitations and think that it is the cause of our sin. But we have to think more deeply about the whole of creation. To consider the five elements and the difference between earth, water, fire, air and ether. Each possesses a different quality: earth is solid; water is liquid and once frozen can melt again; air moves; fire gives warmth and ether has the quality of sound. The essence of the five elements are not only related to our five senses of smell, taste, sight, touch and hearing, but all of them can be found within the body: earth within the root *Chakra*; water in the sacral *Chakra*; fire in the solar plexus *Chakra*, air in the heart *Chakra* and ether in the throat *Chakra*. The essence of the brow and crown *Chakras* goes beyond these elements.[15] And the building block of every last piece of matter from the gross to the subtle is the atom. God is present in the atom, but we cannot see Him with our human eyes.

'Man has learned and calculated many things through the accumulation of knowledge in the sciences of biology, chemistry and physics. He knows that heat travels through the atoms in an iron rod from one end to the other. He knows that hearing is facilitated through the vibration of atoms. He knows that an intense light is dense with atoms, whereas they are sparse in a dim light. Similarly, many atoms in close proximity make an object heavy, whereas when they are scattered it will be light. A bar of iron will take much less space than cotton, for example, if their weights are to be equal.

'And yet someone will say, "I do not believe in God. I will only believe if you show Him to me." I will ask that person if he can see the atom with the naked eye. He will answer, "Of course not." But since God does not exist in a gross form, how can it be possible to show Him? The unbeliever can only see dust, one of the finest things on earth, in a stream of sunlight. And those minuscule particles are already in a form millions of times bigger than the

---

[15] Lahiri Mahasaya told his devotees, "Knowing these five elements within the body the external extensive five elements can be comprehended. But if attempts are made to learn about the external extensive five elements at first, it will not be possible, for then that person will lose himself. Thus by knowing all the five elements within the body, the internal and external all fuse into one. Duality is non-existent then. *Prana*-God prevalent in the five elements can then be realised and settlement in *Kutastha* occurs." (from *Purana Purusha* by Dr A. K. Chatterjee.)

God-atom, or *Brahma-anu*, as it is known in yoga. The atom known to man may be seen with the help of an electron microscope, but the *Brahma-anu* is so subtle that it will never be seen with any human instrument. It is only perceived in *Kutastha*. This is why it is impossible for man to comprehend that God is in this form without practice. Lahiri Mahasaya would also say that subtle objects are perceptible in the light but not in the dark.

'We know that ideas come when the mind is focused, whereas if the mind is scattered, nothing comes. For success in every field of life there has to be concentration. But true prayer involves practice: concentration not on the material but on the spiritual.

'First the meditation might be on some object, for example on a deity, but we have to go beyond this to understand who is the Creator of this world and the cause of the body. In the higher stages of yoga, realisation comes in *anu* form.[16] Through Kriya Yoga, the mind becomes so subtle and sharp that with much practice, it can focus on the finest dot called the *Brahma-anu* and stay in one place.

'This *Brahma-anu*, once it is attained, can be explained as a transcendental state of nothingness whereby the Yogi merges with the Absolute. It exists whilst being termed "indefinable", "immaculate", "subtlest of the subtle" and "beyond knowledge". Hence it is written that God or *Brahma* cannot be known in most religious Scriptures.

'In the Upanishads it is also written that the microscopic measurement of the *Brahma-anu* is equivalent to the size of the tip of one strand of hair divided into four thousand pieces.[17] Yet it can be visualised in *Kutastha*. The Yogi who can see the *Brahma-anu* is perfect, or what we call self-realised. He possesses the eight *Siddhis*, having supreme power over time and the elements, and will have practised for many lives to have reached that highest possible level of consciousness.

'The *anu* is everywhere. It is the cause of everything and the Creator of the earth, water, fire, air and ether particle; it holds every secret in the universe. It is in us, in the form of Soul or Self, even in the inanimate stone. This is God's form.

---

[16] In an extract from his diary dated 29th March (year unknown), Lahiri Mahasaya writes, "... I could see a white dot travelling within the triangular place of origin, it is known as the moon when it appears to be large and when small is termed to be a star. That is the perforation; entry must be made through this perforation." (from *Purana Purusha* by A. K. Chatterjee.)

[17] Brahmopanishad: Chapter 6.

'Our ancient yogis made very exact calculations: one hundred thousand *Brahma-anu* make up one atom of earth particle; ten thousand form one atom of water; one thousand form an atom of fire; one hundred form an atom of air and ten form an atom of ether. Each ascending element is more dynamic than the previous one.

'This is the other reason why in India, we acknowledge God in all the five elements. You have seen that in our culture respect has to be given to earth, water, fire and so on, for the people have faith that God is everywhere and in everything.

'The great spiritual masters from the world's major religions came to guide the people and to give man relief from his suffering and pain. Their aim was to connect the ordinary human being with God. Each of them was self-realised and had huge followings. Jesus Christ is to the Christian what the Buddha is for the Buddhist; Mohammed is to the Muslim what Mahabhir is to the Jain, and so on. Each religion will maintain that their Guru or master was sent by God, or was an incarnation.

'Lahiri Mahasaya was self-realised like these masters. If he had wanted to, he could have established a new, major religion in India, but instead he had a reason for telling his disciples to follow secrecy. He said that there was no need for publicity, since the desire to practise Kriya Yoga had to come in a natural way. Nevertheless, many people are practising. And his mission was unique, for he taught citizens living in society the direct way to inner perception. Until he came, the *Bhagavad Gita* was only understood on a superficial level. He was the first master to give its true explanation.

'There may be different ways to self-realisation, but the main aim and principle will always be to make the mind constant. Without this, there will be neither peace nor wisdom. If someone discovers a new way, it will be because they are already an advanced soul through the influence of their previous life, and through minimal effort they can have valid yogic experiences. But what is true for a handful of people in the world is not applicable to everyone; these people are the exception, and their way of realisation will not be possible for the majority. Hence Kriya Yoga is so valuable, being a scientific method.

'There should be no false concept that one life is sufficient for self-realisation, otherwise known as enlightenment or *Nirvana*. Man is still ignorant of the effort required, but at least the journey can begin once the mind becomes more constant and peaceful.'

❖ ❖ ❖ ❖ ❖ ❖ ❖ ❖

A saint was passing through a certain village. He met some people who warned him about one of the paths leading out of the village, because a black cobra lived there and attacked anyone who came by. The saint told them that he had already decided to go that way, and no amount of persuasion could change his mind.

He had hardly walked a mile along the path when a cobra slid out of its hole and began to hiss threateningly at him. The saint immediately reproached the snake.

'I have never done anything to harm you, so why are you hissing at me in this way? And why do you attack everyone who passes?'

'Because it is my nature to be angry,' answered the cobra.

The saint tried to make the creature analyse his attitude.

'Listen,' he said. 'You are injuring and killing people. But this is wrong, especially when they have not done anything to harm you. You should change your nature.'

'I suppose you are right,' conceded the snake. 'I will do my best to be less aggressive from now on.'

So the saint continued on his journey and the black cobra glided back into its hole having resolved to follow the saint's principle of non-violence.

The cobra had to leave its habitat every now and again to search for food, and gradually the villagers lost their fear of it when they noticed that it no longer attacked anyone. The children even began to laugh and throw stones at the poor creature, until it was covered in cuts and bruises.

When the saint passed through the village a few months later, he saw the black cobra lying almost lifelessly by the path. He stroked the snake and asked,

'What has happened to you?'

'You told me to forsake my anger and not to attack anybody,' the snake replied in a pitiful voice. 'But nobody is afraid of me any more and the children throw stones. I feel so weak that it is hard for me to find food nowadays.'

'Oh you poor snake!' exclaimed the saint. 'It is true that I told you not to bite anyone. But you can at least hiss in order to protect yourself. This is also your duty.'

IN OCTOBER 1999 I went to Varanasi for three weeks to gather the remaining material for this book. Even whilst doing so, I was consumed by self-doubt in my ability as an author. It was daunting enough that *Footsteps to Freedom* was to depict the lives of such awe-inspiring spiritual masters, and that in the course of writing, Guruji had revealed certain things to me which he had never told anyone else, in support of my idea to write a book which would reflect the true facts about Kriya Yoga and acknowledge Lahiri Mahasaya as the source, from the standpoint of a beginner.

I felt painfully conscious that the core of my subject-matter could never be put into words. Would my fumbling attempts to convey personal Kriya experiences be a waste of time, since no vocabulary on this planet existed to describe them adequately? Should I have explained somewhere that I knew Guruji more from the things he did not say, rather than from the things he did say?

Guruji told a reassuring story about the sculptor who was commissioned to carve the statue of Tinkari Lahiri. The artist was at the point of giving up. He could not get the expression on the master's face and had never experienced failure before. Satya Charan Lahiri told the man to forget that he was the one carving the statue.

'If He wants this work done, He will do it,' he said.

It is a question of surrender, Guruji told me. In every aspect of our daily work we should not think of ourselves as the creator, but as the instrument. Then everything would become very easy.

As I noted in my personal diary, before any visit to Guruji my mind was usually crammed with things I wanted to ask, or problems which were weighing me down. It was something of a phenomenon that whatever the dilemma, as soon as I told Guruji – even before I got the words out – it would suddenly seem hollow and without substance. Guruji would say,

'Why are you worried about such things?' as if to say, 'All is well. Have some trust.' Somehow in his presence, there was always peace; his love was so encompassing that fears of every kind had to flee the room and you were left wondering what the mental fuss was about in the first place.

A FEW DAYS before my return to Switzerland, we talked about the need to control anger. I was convinced that this was no problem for me, since I hardly ever shouted. However, being notoriously slow to react at the appropriate time, whenever I felt that some injustice had been done, my tendency was to bottle up the anger. Scenes of 'what I should have said' were played out in my mind days after the incident instead – admittedly, an unsatisfactory way of release. Guruji pointed out I had to be more alert, and that there was no difference between internal or external anger. Both needed to be controlled.

Anger was a test of ego, and it was up to me either to follow or ignore his advice, but Guruji said it was his duty to tell me something else. Now I had been practising Kriya for five years and because of practice, nature would be tossing more challenges my way. There would be more anger and more ego. If someone criticised me, I would be touchy and react over-sensitively. It was not something to worry about, but to be aware of.

This was already true: but his words made me conscious of it for the first time. 'So what am I supposed to do?' I asked.

'Remember Jesus' advice,' Guruji answered. 'If a man slaps you on your left cheek, offer him the right one. Or as we say in India, when someone criticises you, build him a hut in your premises. Anyone can praise you and you will be happy. Your real teachers are the difficult and hurtful challenges in life.

'Learn to forgive. Whatever other people say or do, think that it is their nature and don't let it affect you mentally because it can damage your system.[18] Learn to bury old hurts too, and don't dig up skeletons of the past. When anger comes, you have to analyse it. See it as a test of ego. Nature wants to see how you can balance. In Kriya practice, anger is controlled automatically. But if you do not control it, there will be more tests until you do learn. You need to become stronger. The story of the cobra and the saint teaches that to control your anger does not mean taking injustice in silence and letting others hurt you. It is also your duty to hiss sometimes!'

Guruji had a valid point there, I thought to myself. If only I could

[18] In explanation of Patanjali's Yoga Sutra no.33, Swami Vivekananda writes in *Raja Yoga*: "Every reaction in the form of hatred or evil is so much loss to the mind; and every evil thought or deed of hatred, or any thought of reaction, if it is controlled, will be laid in our favour ... Each time we suppress hatred, or a feeling of anger, it is so much good energy stored up in our favour; that piece of energy will be converted into the higher powers."

learn to hiss just a little at the appropriate time! But this would have to be learned gradually.

Guruji's advice was akin to some of the teachings I used to learn in church. He also reminded me of the promise made at initiation to read the *Bhagavad Gita* daily. The Scriptures were also essential for this path.

Lahiri Mahasaya insisted that his disciples did not forsake their religion, since scriptural knowledge and action, or practice, were two parts of a whole. We needed the Scriptures because they told us that a way existed whereby it was possible to reach heaven, or highest consciousness. But scriptural knowledge alone without practice was insufficient for self-realisation.

He said that the knowledge a person sought to impart to others whilst not having true experience of Soul would be of little benefit to others, however well-acquainted they were with the Scriptures. There was no doubt that the Hindu Scriptures were full of apparently contradictory rules and tenets, but it had to be remembered that deeper knowledge was needed to understand that the same precepts were not applicable to a multifarious body of individuals. They were all correct, but one lifetime of mere study would never be sufficient to grasp them in their unfathomable entirety.

Lahiri Mahasaya further explained that the word *sastra* (Scripture) could be divided into two syllables, *sa* meaning "breath" and *astra* meaning "weapon". In other words, mastery of *pranayama*, as the "breath-weapon" capable of destroying the ego and leading to salvation, was the key to scriptural knowledge.

We needed practice in order to attain salvation. And on this path the Scriptures guided and helped us to understand experiences in practice. For the Yogi, profound scriptural knowledge was possible through internal experience. Lahiri Mahasaya said that practice of Kriya was actual study of the Veda.

I had not read the *Bhagavad Gita* on a daily basis for a long time. So I resolved to get back into the habit. When I did, it once more became clear why reading it was so important for the Kriya practitioner. As Guruji said, it provided another source of answers about life's challenges as they presented themselves. It put you on the alert about maintaining a sense of balance and pointed out the pitfalls of ego and anger just when you needed some reminding. It also answered questions about Kriya Yoga itself.

ANOTHER time, just as Guruji had finished telling me the story of Tinkari Lahiri's *Mahasamadhi*, he suddenly stopped and looked me in the eyes.

'I have one question for you,' he said. 'Where will you be at the time of my death? Will you come here? You will have many responsibilities at that time. Can you get emergency time off? Will you still be in practice?'

I answered that I certainly hoped so. Guruji went on to talk about how easy it was to receive Kriya, as opposed to how difficult it was to stay in this field of yoga. Few managed to do so, he said. Very few. No one could say with certainty that they would be dedicated to their practice forever. There should be no pride in this matter.

The fact that Guruji was questioning how long I would practise Kriya brought tears to my eyes, although instinct told me that he did so to make me mentally strong; to make me feel all the more determined not to let him down. Not to let myself down, for that matter. And within a marital relationship, to stay focused on what I understood to be my own personal spiritual duty regardless of what my partner perceived his to be.

The long years of study at school and university had been necessary to gain financial independence. But as Guruji said, will we just spend our whole life accumulating money and possessions? Will we not take some small amount of time for our spiritual growth, to find Soul?

As Lahiri Mahasaya addressed his disciples:

"When you strive to become a yogi, why are you so weak-willed? No one has taken the tree's shelter and none will take river water away from you. Why are you so worried about transitory things? ... No one has achieved happiness through wealth and never will. It is the provocation of the mind which impels man to earn money. Why are you so anxious about the future? All behave like puppets and rave and rant for money. The world is a place for ordeals ... Now it is imperative to increase the mental strength ..."[19]

When I looked back, so much had changed during the first five years of Kriya practice. Although still a beginner, I had seen ample proof that knowledge of real significance came from the inner world alone. However, it was true that tremendous determination,

---

[19] From *Purana Purusha* by Dr A. K. Chatterjee.

love and dedication were needed to continue on this path. Sometimes it was hard not to turn Kriya Yoga into a "mechanical must". It was easy to forget what a privilege it was to have this spiritual and scientific method of the masters.

AT THE TIME of initiation, Guruji had said that it would be a good idea to keep a Kriya diary. To make a note of the sets practised each day, so that calculation of the number of *pranayamas* over the years would be possible. These were like pennies in the spiritual "piggy-bank" which would never be lost.

Looking back at this diary now gives a very accurate picture of the ups and downs in my practice. There have been times of greater and lesser regularity, of intensity and laziness. But the most interesting experiences have occurred in the longer periods of sincere, regular practice; things seen in *Kutastha* during actual practice, or events which have happened unexpectedly in daily life.

One morning last winter, without thinking anything of it, I told Andreas before he left for work to drive carefully. He told me later that he had taken note of my words quite consciously, because it was not something I ever said to him. And that day due to alertness he narrowly managed to avoid what could have been a serious road accident.

A while ago I was travelling in a car and suddenly had a flash vision about something which would happen to the young boy sitting next to me when he was older.

When I told Guruji about these and other experiences, he said that they were natural results of Kriya practice. Messages, flashes, knowledge about future events. They could come either consciously or subconsciously. The more you knew and were close to your soul, he said, the more this kind of thing occurred. It was intuition or light from that place of soul which was inside. A sign that consciousness was developing.

SO THOSE were some of the lessons from my last trip to India. I could not control my tears when the day came to return home. Guruji was telling me that there was no separation. No doubt it was true, since there was nothing theoretical about how close Guruji felt when you were doing regular practice; yet human nature still made you want to hang on to the physical appearance.

The Guru's blessing and infinite love is something indescribably precious. You may be a beginner on this spiritual path but he will walk next to you and watch over you with unceasing compassion for as many lifetimes as it takes you to reach the goal of life. Although there is no overnight magic or quick-fix to self-realisation, there is perhaps more wonder and reward on the spiritual journey walked one step at a time with discipline and patience. It is nevertheless the road to freedom.

No quantity of worldly riches will ever be sufficient to repay what the Guru gives to you. There is only one way in which you can show him your gratitude, and it is the only thing he wants of you. And that is your lifelong commitment to the promise you made to him at the time of initiation. Your daily practice of Kriya Yoga.

SPIRIT OF DHARMA (A Song)

Cool wind
Warm fire
Keeping alive
A mother's desire for You
To hold on to my new born babe
Carry me through

And the spirit of dharma
Sings a lullaby
Courage my child, no need to cry
Close your eyes
Can't you see, I am everywhere
Look in your heart
I will meet you there

Want to die for you
Want to go high for you
Want to fly with the wings of Love
Ishua Ishua Ishua

One Mind
One Soul
But demons would fight
To extinguish the light in you
Watch over my new born babe
Carry me through

And the spirit of dharma
Sings a lullaby
Courage my child, no need to cry
Close your eyes
Can't you see, I am everywhere
Look in your heart
I will meet you there

Want to die for you
Want to go high for you
Want to fly with the wings of Love
Ishua Ishua Ishua

GLOSSARY

Ahimsa lit. non-violence, or freedom from animosity.

Asana A Hatha Yoga posture; as the third step of yoga, *Asana* means the posture in which the body is kept perfectly still for long periods of time during meditation or *Dhyana*; it can also be the name for a meditation mat or seat.

ashram A hermitage or place of religious retreat; the four stages into which a man's life in the Vedic tradition is divided, namely *Brahmacharya, Grihastha, Banaprastha* and *Sanyas ashrams*, as explained in Chapter Four: Yogic Purification, Detachment.

astral body Every individual has an *astral body*, which is a non-physical counterpart of the human body and of identical appearance. Whereas the human body is composed of the five elements, the *astral body* is composed of fire, air (ether) and *Prana*. As a body of light, it may look solid but is actually an image.

The advanced Yogi has complete control over his *astral body* whereby in entering the state of *Samadhi*, he can appear anywhere and also speak to anyone he chooses in his ethereal form. The physical being is like the photographic negative and the *astral body* the positive which can be duplicated many times. An advanced Yogi is able to appear in as many as four different places simultaneously.

Atmasurya lit. Soul-sun.

Atman lit. Soul.

Aum The internal sound of cosmic vibration. In the Bible, *Aum* is "the Word" referred to in the first verse of St. John; it also appears throughout the Bible as "Amen".

From *Lahiri Mahasaya's Commentary on the Yoga Sutras of Patanjali*:

"27. "The inner Sound", or "OM (Aum), Amen, Amin," is the representative of the inner Consciousness of the Self."

28. "The seeker listens to the OM sound during the practice of *Yoni mudra*, or "Beatific Inner Revelation Kriya," in order to transcend the Same and to generate eternal Tranquillity, that is, highest Attainment.

"In the beginning was the Word, (Sound) and the Word (Sound) was with God, and the Word (Sound) was God." (St. John 1:1)"

Avatar lit. an incarnation of God.

ayurveda Ancient Hindu system of healing and medicine as conceived by Vedic physicians over 3000 years ago. The word *ayurveda* is of Sanskrit origin and can be translated as "the wisdom of life". The philosophy at its core is to treat the "whole" man, in promoting the harmony of body, spirit and soul. Its practices range through curative medicine and surgery to dietary health.

Baba A general term used to address a father, spiritual teacher or holy man to whom one wishes to pay respect.

baboo Baboo (also *babu*) is the nickname by which clerks are addressed in India; and when used more generally from one person to another, it is also a term of endearment.

Barébaba Baré means "great" or "the one who is eldest", and *Baba* is a term of respect to a person having qualities such as nobleness and innocence. *Baba* means "father" in both Hindi and Bengali, and in Hindi it may also be used as "grandfather".

betel The dictionary definition (Oxford 1990) is, "the leaf of a plant (the betel-vine or –pepper) which is wrapped around a few parings of the areca nut and a little shell lime and chewed by the natives of India and neighbouring countries as a masticatory." Sometimes tobacco and various spices are also added.

Interestingly, as far as the story of Matru is concerned, the *Penguin Dictionary of Symbols* says that *betel* is a symbol of love and conjugal fidelity.

Bhagavad Gita Of all Hindu Scriptures, the *Bhagavad Gita* or, "Song of the Lord" is regarded as the most significant, since it contains the fundamental essence of the Hindu faith, or the theory and practice of *yoga sadhana*. This Sanskrit poem is the sixth book of the Mahabharata epic and takes the form of a dialogue between *Krishna*, incarnate God, and the human hero Prince Arjuna.

The Scripture begins with Arjuna seated in a chariot on the holy field, Kurukshetra, and preparing for battle, realising with horror that he is expected to wage war against family and friends. *Krishna* tells him that he must do his duty: that he has no choice but to enter the battlefield and kill his enemies.

Krishna then directs Arjuna how to find God along the righteous path, instructing his disciple on the nature of immortal soul and relationship to *Brahma*, or the supreme Godhead; the system of rebirth, and the necessity of renouncing the fruits of one's actions along the way.

Lahiri Mahasaya's commentary on the *Bhagavad Gita* is unique in illumining its timeless spiritual significance, hence it is of particular importance to Kriya practitioners. (Refer to *The Bhagavad Gita Interpretations of Lahiri Mahasay In the Light of Kriya* for a verse by verse commentary.)

Put in very simple terms, the apparently monstrous battle which Arjuna has to engage in is an allegorical representation of the internal fight against the material senses and the ego. The ego is the Kriya practitioner's worst enemy or hindrance, which has to be overcome in the quest for God.

Bhagavan lit. God or The Almighty, in Hinduism: the omnipotent, omnipresent and omniscient Creator, Preserver and Destroyer, the Absolute Reality and Truth beyond form and gender, and beyond the senses and the intellect.

Bhajan and Kirtan Hindu devotional hymns and carols.

bhang lassi *Bhang* is a narcotic substance made from the leaves and flowers of Indian hemp. *Lassi* is a refreshing drink made with milk, curd and sugar.

Brahma *Brahma* is a Hindu deity, the first of the Triad responsible for Creation; *Brahma* also represents the pure and unchanging yogic state where there is no duality; Truth. An extract from one of Lahiri Mahasaya's secret diaries reads:

"While executing Pranayama in the morning, I envisioned with naked eyes the Soul-Moon; I further noticed that the Sun and Moon merged into one, when merging into one took place then duality being absent everything was empty or vacant, thus I visualised the Infinite Void. This Infinite Void is *Brahma*." (from *Purana Purusha* by Dr A. K. Chatterjee.)

Brahma-anu The "dot" which may be visualised in *Kutastha*; a transcendental state of nothingness whereby the Yogi merges with the Absolute. (see Chapter Twelve: Footsteps to Freedom.)

Brahmachari A young Brahmin who observed celibacy and lived in the house of his spiritual guru according to a strict code of conduct for the period of life preceding marriage. It was primarily a time for education and character development.

Such discipline aimed to keep the *Brahmachari* from becoming externally attached or drawn towards materialistic goals, and to promote an inward focus on the spiritual path in preparation for later life.

In spiritual terms, *Brahmachari* means "attunement with the Ultimate Self": *Brahma* means "God" or "Ultimate Self"; and *achari* means "he who lives in", or "is attuned to".

chai Indian tea, made by boiling milk and water together, then adding tea leaves and often sugar. Sometimes other spices contribute to this rather rich brew.

Chakra see Chapter Five: The Chakras and Kundalini.

chapati The flat, thin unleavened bread which accompanies a meal of rice, vegetables and *dhal* in India.

dhal A kind of stew made from a split pulse; an integral part of the Indian staple diet.

Dharma lit. religion. In the yogic sense, *Dharma* is to find union with God and all creation through the practice of *pranayama*. When *Prana* is controlled by the Yogi, it is *Dharma*, or the one "religion" common to and uniting every human being.

Dharshan A spiritual Guru's blessing sought by a disciple or devotee; when a devotee goes to see a spiritual or holy master; face to face perception. When a disciple or devotee asks his Guru for his *Dharshan* before death, he wants to be able to concentrate on the spiritual master's physical presence before taking the final breath.

dhobi Washerman or washerwoman.

dhoti kurta A length of white cotton cloth which is worn by Hindu men in India as a loincloth.

Durga Meaning "fortress" or "The Inaccessible". *Durga* is the ancient Indian goddess of supremacy. She is depicted as having four or more hands, which symbolise yogic power. Her mount is usually a lion or tiger, which in yogic terms symbolises perfect control over sexual energy.

ghat The stone steps leading down to the bathing place of a river, in this case to the Ganges. (The two burning *ghats* in Banaras are the city's principal places of cremation, likewise situated on the bank of the river.)

ghee Clarified butter.

gulab jamun Popular black-coloured Indian sweet made of white flour and dry concentrated milk, fried and dipped in a sugar solution.

Guru-brother A male person who has the same guru. (female equivalent: *guru-sister*)

Gurudeva The God-like Guru. (lit. Guru-god)

Gurupurnima Hindu festival originally dedicated to the spiritual Guru, although in the present day students, devotees and disciples also visit gurus of other disciplines in order to pay obeisance and bring an offering. This one-day festival traditionally takes place on an auspicious date (full moon) in July.

halwa An Indian sweet or dessert made of couscous or either gram or wheat flour, sugar, *ghee* and water.

Holi Otherwise known as *Holaka*. The Indian festival of *Holi* usually takes place in March. It is a two-fold celebration: first of all, it is a reminder of an Indian fable in which a people is liberated from the terrors of a cruel demon by Vishnu's envoy, Prahalad, and secondly, it is a celebration of the arrival of spring. People throw red powder and spray coloured water at friends and neighbours. The joyful festival activities symbolise fertility and literally celebrate the colour of life.

Kabir Das (1440?-1518) was a self-realised Indian poet and mystic. Some of Lahiri Mahasaya's disciples believed that the spiritual master was Kabir in a previous incarnation, since in explaining various aspects of Kriya Yoga *sadhana* he would often refer to the poet's couplets. Further evidence to support the theory was subsequently found in several of Lahiri Mahasaya's diary entries. Apparently, he also told his chief disciple, Panchanan Bhattacharya that he was Kabir Das in a previous incarnation.

Other diary entries indicate that the master was familiar with his past lives, since in one place he writes that his wife, Kashi Mani Devi, was his sister in the previous birth.

Kali Hindu goddess representing the Primordial Female Energy. Besides being black, the most prominent feature about her is a long protruding tongue, a symbol of the Yogi's *Khechari mudra*. She is frequently depicted with one leg on *Siva's* chest and the other on his thigh. The leg positions symbolise still and unsteady *Prana*, representing this duality in man and how the transition may occur from kinetic to still *Prana* and vice versa.

Kali also holds a falchion in the left hand and wears a rosary of one hundred and eight severed demon heads, symbolising the state when the Yogi attains soul-knowledge, omniscience and purity, thereby annihilating the one hundred and eight sins in man.

Karma The law of cause and effect. All actions, good and bad, have their consequences which we carry with us. However, *Karma* turns the wheel of life and rebirth only as long as *Prana* is in a state of vibration. The Yogi who attains the breathless state in *Samadhi* frees himself from the cycle. The concept of *Karma* is dealt with in more detail in Chapter Nine: The Nature of Karma.

Kashi The spiritual name for the city Banaras or Varanasi: *Kashi* means "luminous", therefore Banaras is also known as the City of Light. From a geographical stance, *Kashi* is situated on the *Shivas Trident*, or the place where the three rivers Ganges, Yamuna and Saraswati meet. From the yogic point of view, these rivers represent *Ida*, (left nerve) *Pingala* (right nerve) and *Sushumna* (central channel in the spinal centre) respectively. Therefore, *Kashi* is in the human body. The Hindu Scriptures teach that there is no rebirth for the person who dies in *Kashi*, for the spiritual meaning of going to *Kashi* is to reach the place of the eyebrow centre, or "spiritual eye". It is to achieve the still, breathless state of the Yogi, whereby salvation is truly won.

With great devotion, pilgrims flock to *Kashi* to take a holy dip in the Ganges. They believe that through the physical action, they will be purged of their sins and gain freedom from further incarnation.

Bathing is a symbol of purification, whereby earthly uncleanliness is washed away. Though important in its own right since external worship develops man's faith, the ancient yogic masters wanted to teach that the real Ganges is inside the body – and when the Yogi enters *Sushumna*, he becomes one with God. The breath is controlled and there is true perception. In this state of *Siva*, man is cleansed from all sin.

Kevala Kumbhaka *Kumbhaka* is the still state whereby external breathing ceases; *Kevala* indicates the spontaneous way in which this occurs for the Yogi who has practised yogic internal inhalation and exhalation (*puraka* and *rechaka*) for long periods of time.

Khechari mudra See Chapter Five: An Outline of the Original Method.

Kirtan lit. carols (see *Bhajan and Kirtan*)

Krishna lit. darkness, black. The son of Vasudeva and Devaki, *Krishna* is worshipped as God incarnate for his coming at the end of Dvaparayuga (3228BC). He had a wife and several consorts, the most prominent of these being Radha.

For the part he played in the legend of the Mahabharata, in advising Arjuna, see *Bhagavad Gita*.

In the yogic sense, *Krishna* may be understood less as a noun than as a verb, calling the practitioner to prepare the field of the body in order to conquer the kinetic mind and *Prana*, and attain the still state.

Kriyanwita A Kriya Yoga practitioner.

Kundalini See Chapter Five: The Chakras and Kundalini.

Kutastha See Chapter Five: Kutastha.

Lord Krishna See *Krishna*.

Lord Siva See *Siva*.

Lord Vishwanath Another name for *Lord Siva*.

lunghi A length of cotton which is principally worn as a loincloth.

maharaja lit. king.

Mahasamadhi A Yogi's final departure from earthly existence. See also Chapter Five: Samadhi.

Mahayogi lit. Great Yogi.

Mantra A phrase or formula made up of mystic syllables which is given from guru to disciple as a meditation practice. The spiritual purpose of a *Mantra* is to free the mind, and in Kriya Yoga *Mantra* is the state in which the mind becomes still through the practice of *pranayama*.

masala lit. mix; when spices such as cloves, cinnamon, cardamom, coriander, cumin and peppercorns are mixed in various combinations, it is termed in India as *masala*.

neem oil This oil comes from the East Indian margosa tree, whose bark, seeds and fruit contain medicinal properties effective in the treatment of many diseases, including leprosy.

Nirvana Buddhist term for self-realisation or *Samadhi*. The literal meaning is "to be extinguished"; in the yogic sense this can be understood as the cessation of breath, after which the cycle of birth and death is halted.

paisa Indian currency; 100 *paisa* is equal to one rupee.

palanquin A closed carriage or litter for one person which is carried by four men.

pandit A teacher or learned person; a Hindu having expertise in the areas of Sanskrit, religion, philosophy and jurisprudence of India.

paneer Indian fresh cheese.

Paramguru lit. Greater Guru; used only in the spiritual field, it is used to signify the Guru of one's own Guru.

Prana See Chapter Five: Respiration and Pranayama.

Pranakarma The action of practising Kriya Yoga.

Pranam Word and gesture of respect which shows devotion as explained in Chapter Two: Knowledge meets Wisdom, The Perfect Guru; to pay obeisance.

The action of bringing both the hands together at the heart is indicative of the feeling, "with all my heart". The action also carries the meaning, "I see God in you". In Hinduism, God is omnipresent. Since He is present in every human being, Indian culture teaches that everyone is deserving of such respect.

In India, the self-realised person is a symbol of Soul, since he is always in the Absolute. The disciple paying sincere obeisance by touching the feet of the spiritual Guru makes this gesture with the internal feeling that they are seeing God in front of them, and that it is His feet they are touching.

Since feet are for walking, and the leg of a person symbolises movement, the gesture may also serve to remind the person giving respect of how the soul travels from one body to another.

pranayama See Chapter Five: Respiration and Pranayama.

prasad Food becomes *prasad* after it has been offered to a deity in *puja* – in retrospect it is eaten by the worshipper, or distributed amongst devotees, as a benediction from that deity.

puja lit. worship. Understanding the external sense of the word, most Hindus worship the deities according to the rituals prescribed by their ancient Scriptures.

However, in the yogic sense, *puja* is the internal action of worshipping the one omnipresent God, resulting in true purification. For the Yogi, the body is the temple and outward symbolism is rendered obsolete.

puri Similar to a *chapati*, but deep-fried in oil.

Raja Yoga Another term for Kriya Yoga. Raja Yoga literally means the principal method whereby union with God, or the Absolute is attained. The *Bhagavad Gita* refers to Raja Yoga. *Patanjali's Yoga Sutras* is known as the book of Raja Yoga, even though Patanjali himself never uses this term.

Rama *Rama* was the incarnation of *Vishnu*. The ancient epic poem, the Ramayan, tells of his life and deeds, including how he rescues his wife *Sita* with the help of the monkey God, *Hanuman*, when she is abducted by the demon-king Ravana.

Rudraksa mala A *Rudraksa mala* is a rosary or necklace made of the dark berries of *Elaeocarpus Ganitrus*. There are one hundred and eight beads, one for each manifestation of the human ego which has to be destroyed. These are traditionally worn by followers of *Siva*.

rusgula A white-coloured Indian sweet made of *paneer*.

sacred thread The *sacred thread* is received by the boy born into the Brahmin family when he is between the ages of eight and twelve at a major spiritual ceremony performed by the family priest. The thread symbolises his qualification for spiritual life, and is looked upon as a new birth. The rites involve ancestral worship, and the boy commits himself to the spiritual path. Following the ceremony the boy is expected to do daily practice of *pranayama* together with a *Mantra*.

Sadguru Genuine spiritual master; the perfect and true Guru or teacher who is already established in the Absolute Reality. He is able to purify the disciple's heart and open the "spiritual eye". *Sad* means "truth", or "the soul", and *Guru* is the one who leads the way from ignorance to understanding. *Gu* means "darkness" and *ru* means "light": hence the spiritual Guru is one who banishes the darkness and leads to the light, or to the state of self-realisation (enlightenment or *Nirvana*).

In the yogic sense, the *Sadguru* is present in the body, for the transition from darkness to light occurs through the action of Kriya *pranayama*.

sadhana lit. practice. This word comes from Sanskrit and can refer to practice of any discipline; in the light of yoga it means the practice which leads to salvation, union with God or Soul-realisation.

sadhu An ascetic or holy man in India. The idea of renouncing the world and seeking self-realisation finds its origin in the Vedic tradition which divides a man's life into four stages or *ashrams*. The final stage in which a man becomes a *sadhu* is Sanyas ashram; further explanation is given in Chapter Four: Yogic Purification, Detachment.

Samadhi See Chapter Five: Samadhi.

sannyasi (Hindi & Urdu) The Sanskrit word, *samnyasin*, can be broken down as follows: *sam* – together; *ni* – down; *as* – throw; in other words, the laying aside of worldly attatchments. See *sadhu*.

Saraswati Indian goddess primarily associated with learning and the fine arts. She plays a *vina* (an instrument similar in appearance to a sitar) and her mount is usually a goose, symbolising knowledge and purity.

shakti lit. power.

Shambhavi mudra The state whereby the eyes are fixed internally in *Kutastha*, therefore they appear to be half-opened and unblinking; the tongue is in *Khechari mudra* and *Prana* is passing through the *Sushumna* channel which eliminates the need for external breathing.

Siddha lit. perfect person; one who has gained perfection in all of the *Siddhis*.

Siddhayogi See *Siddha*.

Siddhis Yogic powers. The eight *Siddhis* which make man perfect are as follows: the powers of becoming as small, as light or as large as the Yogi wills (*Anima* – subtelty; *Laghima* – lightness; *Mahima* – greatness); the power of attaining (*Prapti* – attainment); the power of satisfying desires (*Prakamya* – irresistible will); the power of controlling anything at will (*Basitwa* – self-control); the power of becoming Lord over everything (*Istiwa* – superiority) and the power to control passions (*Kamyabasayita*). (According to *Lahiri Mahasaya's Commentary on the Yoga Sutras of Patanjali*, originally published by Sri Panchanan Bhattacharya and translated from the Bengali by Satyeswarananda Giri)

Siva Hindu deity of mercy and destruction, associated with the powers of reproduction and dissolution. In the yogic sense, *Siva* is the state of consciousness when the practitioner attains the Absolute in the highest stages of *Samadhi*.

Siva Linga The *Siva Linga* is a phallic symbol in Hinduism: the *Linga* (male organ of reproduction) being a cylindrical stone or marble column emanating from the *Yoni* (female organ of reproduction). In terms of yoga, the union represents the energy of procreation in nature. *Linga* is the mind and *Yoni* a symbol of the triangular shaped *Kutastha*, or the place of origin or birth. *Brahma-anu*, being like a dot, and also known as the "seed of the universe" may be visualised in *Kutastha*.

When the mind attains stillness having entered *Kutastha*, the Yogi feels incomparable bliss and ecstasy. The spiritual *Yoni* or

Absolute place of origin is *Brahma*, being both Mother and Father, and when the Yogi reaches this state he becomes *Siva*.

Sivaratri The Hindu festival which takes place in February, dedicated to *Lord Siva*.

sub-Prana See Chapter Five: Respiration and Pranayama.

Sufi A Muslim ascetic or mystic; speaking of their spiritual state, Gai Eaton refers to two kinds of *Sufi* in his book *Islam and the Destiny of Man*: one group are "drunken" for they "are seized with ecstasy and care nothing for the conventions of ordinary life". The others are "sober", for they "contain their ecstasy within themselves, keeping it under strict control ... even when they reel inwardly under the divine touch, and maintaining discretion as to their spiritual state. The ideal, as it was expressed by a great *Sufi* Master of the present century, Ahmad al-Alawi, is to be 'inwardly drunken' and 'outwardly sober'."

Sushumna The fine nerve which runs through the spine between the *Ida* and *Pingala* channels, from the root *Chakra* to the crown *Chakra*, and through which the advanced Yogi directs internal respiration. (See also Chapter Five: Respiration and Pranayama.)

Tantra *Tan* means "body" and *tra* means "saving". *Tantra* is usually understood to be an esoteric discipline whereby sexual energy is overcome and channelled into spiritual energy, the aim being to reach the yogic state of pure Tranquillity.

An extract from one of Lahiri Mahasaya's confidential diaries reveals the meaning of *Tantra* in the light of Kriya Yoga:

"The present kinetic mind which is known to all as the mind, its state of release or the still state is termed as *Mantra* and the medium by which the body is nurtured is *Tantra*. Thus by the constant flow in each and every nerve, this body is being nurtured, therefore that flow of air is *Tantra*." (from *Purana Purusha* by Dr A. K. Chatterjee.)

Vishwanath Another name for *Siva*.

wallah Someone who is in charge of a specific thing, e.g. rickshaw *wallah*, the man who pulls a rickshaw.

yoga lit. union with God.

Yogiraja lit. King of Yogis.

BIBLIOGRAPHY

The Bhagavad Gita, Gita Press, Gorakhpur 1994

The Bhagavad Gita, transcreated from Sanskrit by P. Lal, Roli Books 1994

The Holy Bible, King James Version, Oxford

Chatterjee, A. K., *Purana Purusha, Yogiraj Sri Shama Churn Lahiree*, (Translated into English by J. Kapur), Yogiraj Publication 2000

Chattopadhya, S., (Bengali version, title may be translated as *Kriya Yoga and Kriya Yogi Sri Tinkari Lahiri*) S. Chattopadhya 1993

Chevalier, J., Gheerbrant, A., *Dictionary of Symbols*, Penguin 1996

Eaton, G., *Islam and the Destiny of Man*, The Islamic Texts Society 1994

Eck, Diana L., *Banaras City of Light*, Penguin Books India 1993

Eddy, M. B., *Science and Health with Key to the Scriptures*, The Christian Science Publishing Society, 1971

Kersten, H., *Jesus Lived in India*, Element 1988

Lal, S. N., *Yoga Evam Ek Grihasth Yogi*, (Hindi version, title may be translated as *Yoga and a Householder Yogi*) S. N. Lal (Yoga Sansthan Prakashan
S 25/221-6 Panchkoshi Marg, Orderly Bazaar, Varanasi, India) 1993

* Satyeswarananda Giri, *Babaji*, The Sanskrit Classics 1993

* Satyeswarananda Giri, *Lahiri Mahasaya's Commentary on the Yoga Sutras of Patanjali*, The Sanskrit Classics

* Satyeswarananda Giri, *The Bhagavad Gita, Interpretations of Lahiri*

Mahasaya, The Sanskrit Classics 1991

Srivastava, K. S., *Hindu Symbolism and Iconography*, Sangeeta Prakashan 1998

Thematic Dictionary of Quotations, ed. John Daintith, Bloomsbury 1997

Vivekananda, Swami, *Raja Yoga*, Advaita Ashrama 1998

Living at the Source: Yoga teachings of Vivekananda, Shambhala Publications, inc. Boston 1993

Yogananda, P., *Autobiography of a Yogi*, Rider 1994

* These commentaries and interpretations of Lahiri Mahasaya are just a few of those originally published in Bengali under the name of the master's chief disciple, Sri Panchanan Bhattacharya. They have been translated into English by Satyeswarananda Giri, and are available from: "The Sanskrit Classics", P.O. Box 5368, San Diego, CA 92165 USA.